Praise for Timothy G. McCarthy's
The Catholic Tradition Before and After Vatican II: 1878-1993, also published by Loyola Press

What is more intriguing than Catholicism? There is so much to love about it, so much to despair over, and so much to inspire hope and enthusiasm. To read Timothy McCarthy's *The Catholic Tradition* is to discover anew why all of this is so. . . . If you wonder what is going on Church-wise, you can't do better than to read this outstanding book.

—MITCH FINLEY, *St. Anthony Messenger*

As intellectually impressive and enlightening as it is, *The Catholic Tradition* offers nourishment not only to the mind but also to the heart. . . . Rather than just pointing the way out of our difficulties, it provides the reader with the tools to find one's own way, not in individualistic fashion but in faithful communion with the whole church. . . . One way to raise the morale of the Catholic community is to . . . put in historical perspective the unsettling events of the last few generations, to identify the cultural and theological roots of our divisions, and to work toward a shared vision of where the church should be moving at the end of this century. If one book can do all those things, it is Timothy McCarthy's thematic history of the 20th century Catholic Church.

—JAMES DIGIACOMO, S.J., *America*

McCarthy makes an original contribution: he provides information and analyses not found in theological works. Until now students interested in conflicts within the Catholic Church had to turn to reviews and journals to recover exactly what happened. Now they have a book that will be a liberating experience and one that helps the American Catholic Church to come to a more realistic and theologically appropriate self-understanding.

—GREGORY BAUM, McGill University, Montreal, Quebec

McCarthy begins with . . . the popes . . . [Leo XIII to John Paul II] and examines how the church dealt with the challenge of modernity. . . . He examines in considerable depth the issues that were central to . . . [Vatican II] including the Church in relation to its identity and mission, its authority, other religions, other Christians, eucharistic worship, social justice, sexual ethics, and Mary. He presents a comprehensive, soundly based analysis . . . that is both complete and readable.

—R. W. ROUSSEAU, *Choice*

In a distinct departure from academic tradition, [*The Catholic Tradition*] is a genuine pleasure to read. Excellent writing and editing. . . . The 30-page bibliography indicates the reason this volume will be an immediate reference for students of modern Catholic thought. There simply is no comparable overview of papal and conciliar teachings as well as theological reflections available. It may be appropriate to dispute interpretations and emphases, but the achievement cannot be denied.

—ANTHONY W. NOVITSKY, *Church History*

McCarthy is factual in his presentation, balanced in his judgments, and fair to opposing viewpoints. . . . The book's greatest strength is the clear and compelling manner in which it is written. McCarthy's prose is clean and uncluttered, much like a tidy, sun-filled room with nothing out of place. Would that all books on historical theology were so easy to read!

—RONALD EUGENE ISETTI, F.S.C., *Catholic Historical Review*

With one sentence, McCarthy establishes the theme of his book, namely that the "non-essential traditions" are expendable when they get in the way of the greater necessity of carrying on the ultimate Catholic "tradition" in which "the church is protected by the Spirit whereby it can not deviate fundamentally from the life of faith and from the truth of the gospel."

—Phyllis Tickle, *Publishers Weekly*

Christianity
and Humanism

Christianity
and Humanism

*From Their Biblical Foundations
into the Third Millennium*

Timothy G. McCarthy

Loyola Press
Chicago

Loyola Press
3441 North Ashland Avenue
Chicago, Illinois 60657

Cover photograph: Mosaic of the Resurrection (11th century); Jesus, the central figure, pulls Adam and Eve out of their grave (right), as prophesied by Kings David and Solomon (left). Monastery of Hosios Loukas, Phocis, Greece, from Loyola University Chicago Archives, Raymond V. Schoder, S.J., Slide Collection.

Interior design by Tammi Longsjo.
Photoshop work on cover art by Bob Masheris.

Library of Congress Cataloging-in-Publication Data
McCarthy, Timothy, 1929–
     Christianity and humanism: from their biblical foundations into the third millennium / Timothy G. McCarthy.
          p.   cm.
     Includes bibliographical references and indexes.
     ISBN 0-8294-0913-0
     1. Bible—History of Biblical events. 2. Bible—History of contemporary events. 3. Church history. 4. Man (Christian theology) 5. Catholic Church—Doctrines. 6. Christian ethics—Catholic authors. I. Title.
BS635.2.M35 1996
230—dc20   96-7998
                                                                                      CIP

Contents

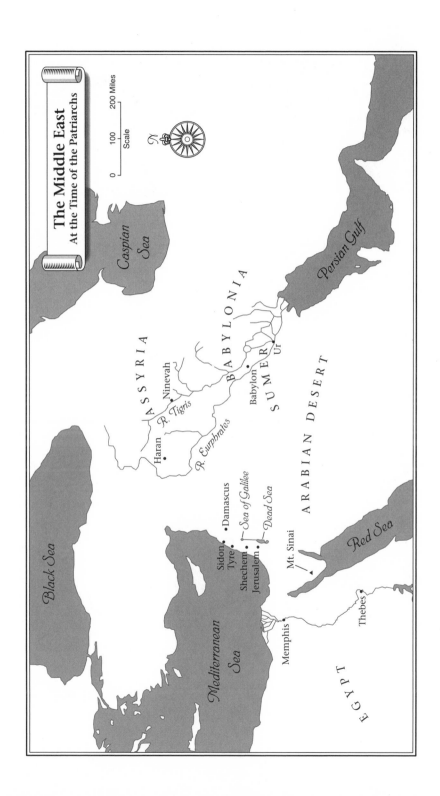

The Middle East
At the Time of the Patriarchs

0   100   200 Miles
Scale

Caspian Sea

Black Sea

Mediterranean Sea

ASSYRIA

Ninevah

R. Tigris

Haran

R. Eurphrates

BABYLONIA

Babylon

SUMER

Ur

Persian Gulf

ARABIAN DESERT

Sidon
Tyre
Shechem
Jerusalem

Damascus

Sea of Galilee

Dead Sea

Mt. Sinai

Red Sea

Memphis

Thebes

EGYPT

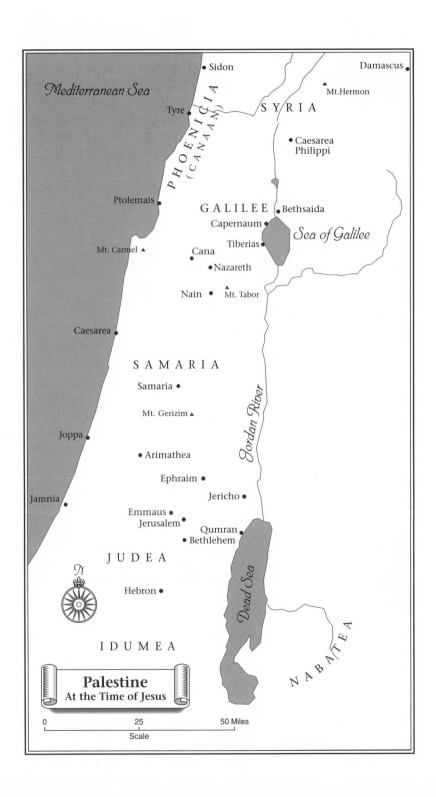

Mediterranean Sea

Sidon

Damascus

Mt.Hermon

SYRIA

PHOENICIA
(CANAAN)

Tyre

Caesarea
Philippi

Ptolemais

GALILEE

Bethsaida

Capernaum

Sea of Galilee

Mt. Carmel ▲

Tiberias

Cana

Nazareth

Nain • ▲ Mt. Tabor

Caesarea

SAMARIA

Samaria •

Jordan River

Mt. Gerizim ▲

Joppa

Arimathea

Ephraim •

Jamnia

Jericho •

Emmaus •
Jerusalem •

Qumran

Bethlehem

JUDEA

Dead Sea

N

Hebron •

NABATEA

IDUMEA

Palestine
At the Time of Jesus

0   25   50 Miles
Scale

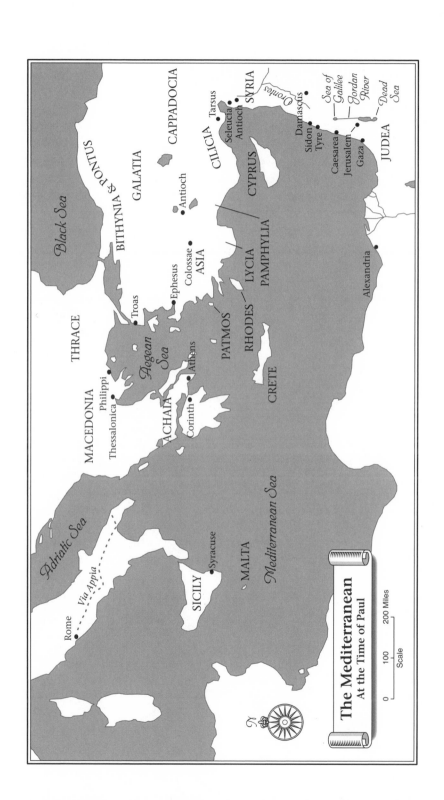

The Mediterranean
At the Time of Paul

Scale
0   100   200 Miles

Black Sea

THRACE

MACEDONIA
Thessalonica
Philippi

Aegean Sea

ACHAIA
Corinth
Athens

Adriatic Sea

Via Appia

Rome

SICILY

Syracuse

MALTA

Mediterranean Sea

CRETE

PATMOS

RHODES

Troas

Ephesus

Colossae
ASIA

BITHYNIA & PONTUS

GALATIA

Antioch

CAPPADOCIA

CILICIA
Tarsus

LYCIA
PAMPHYLIA

CYPRUS

SYRIA

Seleucia
Antioch

Orontes

Damascus

Sidon
Tyre

Caesarea
Jerusalem
Gaza

JUDEA

Sea of Galilee

Jordan River

Dead Sea

Alexandria

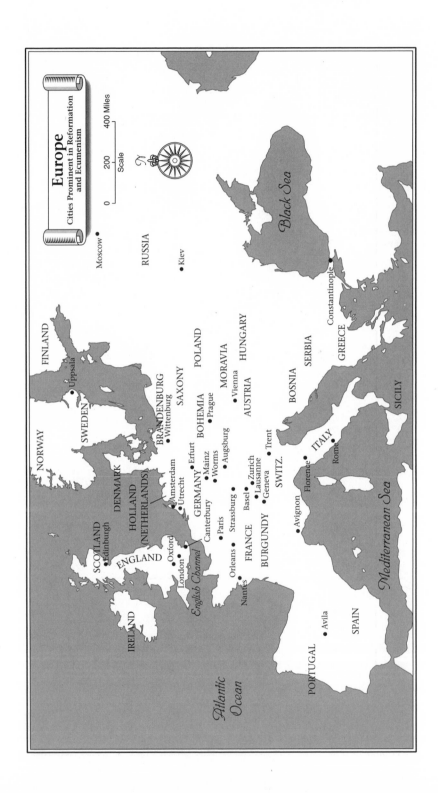

Europe
Cities Prominent in Reformation
and Ecumenism

Scale

0   200   400 Miles

South America
At the Time of CELAM I and II

COSTA RICA

PANAMA

Panama
Canal

Caracas

VENEZUELA

•Medellín

•Bogotá

COLOMBIA

Quito•

ECUADOR

PERU

Lima

BOLIVIA
La Paz

PARAGUAY

CHILE

Asunción

Santiago

Buenos Aires

ARGENTINA

Georgetown
Paramaribo
Cayenne

FRENCH
GUIANA

SURINAME

GUYANA

BRAZIL

Recife

Brasilia

Rio de Janeiro
Sao Paulo

URUGUAY

Montevideo

Pacific
Ocean

Atlantic Ocean

N

0   400   800 Miles
Scale

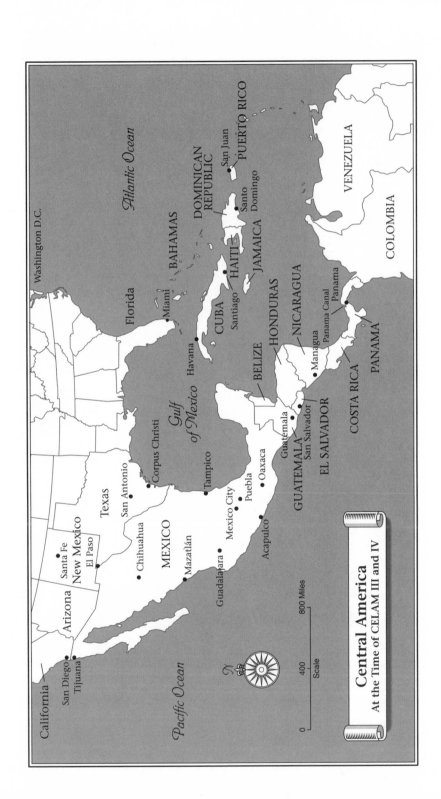

Central America
At the Time of CELAM III and IV

Preface

This book is for adults interested in learning about the biblical foundations of Christianity and Christian humanism. Although it is not a textbook, the book can be used in college classes and in discussion groups because it grew out of my experiences teaching a course to undergraduates at St. Mary's College of California, a Catholic college.

At the present time, most Catholic colleges and universities are quite pluralistic about religion. Many students are Catholic, but many belong to other Christian churches, other religions, and some profess no religious affiliation. Given this mix of students, one wonders how best to teach an introduction to Christianity. One approach I used consisted in a chronological study of some of the more important saintly and/or learned Christians: Peter, Mary Magdalene, Paul, Irenaeus of Lyons, Athanasius, Augustine, Monica, Martin Luther, and so forth. Another time I traced the origin, history, and distinctive features of influential denominations and sects. The history of such religious bodies as the Anglicans, Baptists, Congregationalists, Lutherans, Shakers, and Quakers is very interesting. However, I found that these two approaches have a built-in problem. Many students had difficulty judging the institutional, intellectual, and devotional contributions of either famous Christians or influential communities because they do not have a solid grounding in Christianity itself and especially the Bible. I next turned to the Bible since it is normative for Christians, is "the soul of theology," and contains the heart of Christianity, that is, what is sometimes called "the deposit of faith." Thus, this book of mine examines the inner core and outer limits of Christianity by probing the Bible.

Two points need to be brought to the reader's attention. First, I quote several documents from Vatican Council II (1962–65). I use the text edited in 1966 by Walter M. Abbott, a Jesuit scholar. His text is clear but it does not use inclusive language—hardly an issue in those days for most Americans. Nonetheless, I retain the Abbott text because it captures the ethos of that period. Second, some readers may be familiar with my first book, *The Catholic Tradition Before and After Vatican II, 1878–1993,* published by Loyola University Press in 1994. Some of the material on ecumenism, social justice, and sexual ethics from that book is repeated here. Now, however, these topics are related to Christian humanism and their scriptural foundations are given more detailed examination and analysis.

I am grateful to Loyola Press for accepting my book through Jeremy Langford, Managing/Acquiring Editor. I appreciate the careful editing of Dr. Ruth E. McGugan. In addition to their invaluable help, I received advice and encouragement from my students. Over the course of four semesters a total of 160 students studied the manuscript. Their questions and evaluations helped me to refine it, as many of them took great delight in finding typos and other errors. Significant insights, both organizational and theological, were provided by Jane Beretz of Alamo, California, Margaret Duffner of Marco Island, Florida, Odile and John Dwyer of Elka Park, New York, Mitch Finley of Spokane, Washington, and Thomas Rausch S.J. of Loyola Marymount University, Los Angeles.

The most help came from my wife, Virginia. She brought to the manuscript her writing skills (author of screenplays), her theological education (master's degree), and her teaching experience (seven years of religion teaching in a Catholic high school). This book is dedicated to Virginia. I could not have written it without her encouragement, advice, and steadfast love.

Introduction

The Christian religion has a distinct identity. Christianity is very different from Judaism, Buddhism, Islam, or any other religion. Vincent of Lérins a fifth-century theologian, wrote that the distinctive identity of Christianity is what has been believed by Christians "everywhere, always, and by all" (Pelikan 1971, 1:333).

Like other religions, the Christian faith must have an identifiable, coherent, and meaningful center. The epistle to the Ephesians refers to this center as "seven unities": "one body and one Spirit, as you were also called to the one hope of your call; one Lord, one faith, one baptism; one God and Father of all, who is over all and through all and in all" (4:4–6). In addition to a center, there is a need for boundaries or limits. A distinction is needed between faith and unfaith, between orthodoxy and heresy. Boundaries are needed because "a center without a circumference is just a dot, nothing more. Without boundaries a circle could not be a circle. If the circle of faith is seeking to identify its center, it cannot do so without identifying its margins and perimeters" (Oden 1995b, 396).

Several factors make determining the center and its boundaries difficult. First, we know that the Christian tradition has always been ambiguous, developmental, and pluralistic. For example, due to our historical perspective, we realize, in a way Vincent of Lérins never did, that "an honest look at the actual history of the first four or five centuries shows a great deal of variation, of localism, of uneven and uncertain development heavily influenced by imperial politics and the like" (Mudge 1995, 393). Today, even within denominations there are different perspectives. Self-styled "liberated Christians" dismiss more traditional believers as "fundamentalists." Liberated Christians suggest that they have the correct understanding of Christianity because they are "doctrinally imaginative, liturgically experimental, disciplinarily nonjudgmental, politically correct, multiculturally tolerant, morally broad-minded, ethically situationist, and above all sexually permissive" (Oden 1995a, 390).

Second, Christianity at the time of Vincent of Lérins was one church. Today, because the Christian religion is divided into thousands of churches, each with its own distinctive identity, authority structures, laws, disciplines, and theologies, it is difficult to specify what satisfies Vincent of Lérins' three criteria of universality, antiquity, and consensus.

Third, Christians have often distorted the Christian message. Parts of the Christian tradition "were and are oppressive and need to be corrected. The subjugation of women, connivance in slavery, collaboration with totalitarian regimes are parts of the tradition from which we are still trying to escape" (Mudge 1995, 393).

Fourth, while it is true that the first-century bishops were instructed "to hold fast to the true message as taught so that [you] will be able both to exhort with sound doctrine and to refute opponents" (Tit. 1:9), the Christian faith is not a closed system of beliefs handed on since the days of Peter, Paul, Mary Magdalene, Joanna, and Susanna (Lk. 8:2–3). Each generation discerns the gospel anew. The Holy Spirit bears fresh witness to Jesus Christ, whose identity and mission "yesterday, today, and forever" (Heb. 13:8) is repeatedly rediscovered and rearticulated by the community of disciples.

To get to the center of Christianity and its boundaries, this book focuses on the Bible, the normative book for Christians. Augustine, the saintly bishop of Hippo in Africa from 396 to 430, "declared that 'in the plain teaching of Scripture we find all that concerns our belief and moral conduct'; while a little later Vincent of Lérins took it as an axiom that the scriptural canon was 'sufficient, and more than sufficient, for all purposes'" (Kelly 1958, 43). However, even this biblical emphasis is not without problems. Not only are there several methods of interpretation of historical texts, but the Christian churches are also deeply divided over the correct interpretation of the Bible and who has the authority to validate any interpretation.

The scriptures tell us about God, but they also tell us about the origin, nature, and destiny of humankind. Christianity, like many other religions, offers its followers deep and abiding convictions about what it means to be human. We call this Christian vision Christian humanism. In our multicultural and religiously pluralistic society other humanisms compete with Christian humanism. Although the United States is called a Christian country, the Christian underpinnings have practically vanished. In many sections of the United States and in books, newspapers, and films, Christian humanism has been overshadowed by a secular humanism. This book explores the nature of Christian humanism as illumined by the scriptures and modern theology.

This work provides historical and theological background about the Bible and certain periods of church history, but its focus is on the scriptural foundations of Christianity, what constitutes its inner core and its outer limits. At the beginning of each section, there are scriptural references which should be read first, because this book presupposes a thorough familiarity with the scriptural texts. This book is an introduction to the distinctive center and boundaries of the Christian religion with an emphasis on Christian humanism as we prepare for the third millennium.

Chronology

Prehistoric Time

20 billion years	Creation of the universe.
4.5 billion	Creation of the earth.
3.5 billion	Creation of nonhuman life.
1.9 million	Creation of "Adam and Eve" (homo erectus).
600,000	Discovery of fire.
200,000	Evolution of our species (homo sapiens).
20,000	Invention of agriculture.

Historic Period before Christian Era

3100	History begins: invention of writing at Sumer.
2000	Amorites infiltrate Babylon.
1800	Babylonian myths *Enuma Elish, Gilgamesh* written.
1850	Abraham and Sarah: progenitors of the Israelites.
1350	Moses leads the Exodus from Egypt.
1000	David reigns.
960	First temple built by Solomon; Zadox is high priest.
950	Yahwist and Elohist sections of Pentateuch written.
868	Elijah's confrontations with Ahab and Jezebel.

750	Homer writes Greek epics.
750-45	Prophetic period: Amos (752), Hosea (750), First Isaiah (742).
722	Assyrians conquer ten northern tribes; Samaritans enter Palestine.
622	Josiah of Judea finds book of Deuteronomy.
587-538	Babylonian conquest and exile; destruction of temple; time of Jeremiah, Ezekiel, Second Isaiah.
550	Priestly account of Pentateuch written.
539-330	Persia conquers Palestine; King Cyrus permits Jews' return to Israel.
515	Second temple built.
400	Torah (Pentateuch) determined as Hebrew canon.
399	Socrates dies.
375	Plato flourishes.
350	Aristotle flourishes.
330-63	Greek conquest of Mediterranean world.
332	Alexander the Great (356-23) defeats Darius III of Persia (1 Mac. 1:1-9).
323	Alexander's kingdom divided between generals: Seleucid takes Syria and Galilee; Ptolemy takes Egypt and Samaria.
250	Torah translated into Greek; called Septuagint (LXX).
198	All Palestine under Seleucid rule (Antiochus III).
190	Romans defeat Greek naval forces.
175	Antiochus IV deposes high priest; desecrates temple (1 Mac. 1:29-35), enforces hellenization on Jews (1 Mac. 9:1-10). Mattathias and five sons resist (1 Mac. 1-2; 2 Mac. 9); Hasidim (pious ones) divide into Pharisees, Sadducees, and Essenes.

164	Seleucid ruler grants Jews some independence; Maccabees (Hasmoneans) restore the temple, usurp high priesthood (1 Mac. 7:9-16).
150	Essenes (Teachers of Righteousness) to Qumran; their writings found in 1947 A.D.
142	Seleucids grant Jews full independence. Hasmonean family reigns.
63	Roman conquest of Palestine under Pompey.
37	Herod the Great replaces Hasmoneans.
4	Death of Herod the Great; his sons Philip, Herod Antipas, Archelaus rule.

Historic period: Christian Era

c. 6 B.C.	Birth of Jesus of Nazareth and John the Baptist.
26-36 A.D.	Pontius Pilate procurator.
30/33	Crucifixion and resurrection of Jesus.
36	Stephen, the deacon, dies (Acts 6:1-14); Saul (Paul) of Tarsus converted on road to Damascus.
42	James, brother of John, son of Zebedee dies (Acts 12:2).
49	Council of Jerusalem (Acts 15).
62	James, brother of Jesus dies (Mt. 13:55-56).
67	Peter and Paul die in Rome during Nero's persecution.
66-70	Jewish rebellion under the Zealots.
70	Jerusalem and the temple destroyed.
73	Final battle at fortress of Masada.
68	Mark's gospel written in Rome.
c.80	Jewish Christians expelled from synagogues.
85	Matthew's gospel written in Antioch; Luke-Acts in Greece.
90	John's gospel written in Ephesus.

c.100	Jewish Christians formally excommunicated from synogogues.
135	Simon bar-Kochba's revolt; Jews driven from Jerusalem, without a homeland until 1948.
140	Marcion in Rome.
325	Council of Nicea condemns Arius, declares Christ is "one in essence with the Father."
330	Constantine founds Constantinople (formerly Byzantium).
381	First Council of Constantinople reaffirms Council of Nicea.
410	Rome destroyed by Goths.
430	Augustine of Hippo dies.
451	Council of Chalcedon affirms Christ is one person in two natures.
622	Muslim religion begins under prophet Muhammad.
1054	Mutual excommunications by Rome and Constantinople.
1274	Thomas Aquinas dies.
1375	Wycliffe calls for reform of church wealth, monasteries, papacy.
1378	Great Schism: two popes claim throne of Peter.
1415	Huss executed by Council of Constance.
1453	Constantinople captured by Ottoman Turks.
1517	Luther posts 95 theses at Wittenberg.
1536	Calvin writes *Institutes of the Christian Religion*.
1545-63	Council of Trent.
1738	Wesley's renewed understanding of Christianity leads to Methodism.
1869-70	First Vatican Council decrees papal infallibility.
1906	Pentecostalism inaugurated by William J. Seymour.
1910	World Missionary Conference at Edinburgh.

1919	Orthodox churches call for "league of churches"; Life and Work Commission organized.
1927	First meeting of Faith and Order Commission.
1943	*Divino afflante Spiritu,* Pius XII's encyclical encourages historical-critical method.
1945	Gnostic writings discovered at Nag Hammadi, Egypt.
1948	World Council of Churches founded at Amsterdam.
1962-65	Second Vatican Council: church retrieves its tradition.
1964	*Instruction on the Historical Truth of the Gospels* fosters historical-critical method.
1968	Martin Luther King, Jr. assassinated April 4; *Humanae vitae* reiterates church's ban on contraceptives; Gustavo Guttiérez proposes "liberation theology"; Latin American bishops meet at Medellín.
1979	Latin American bishops meet at Puebla, Mexico.
1980	Archbishop Oscar Romero, El Salvador, assassinated.
1982	Faith and Order Commission issues Lima Declaration/*Baptism, Eucharist and Ministry.*
1992	Latin American bishops meet at Santa Domingo.
1993	Pontifical Biblical Commission document on *The Interpretation of the Bible in the Church* fosters critical method/process of actualization.

The Hebrew Scriptures

Pentateuch

Genesis	Exodus	Leviticus
Numbers	Deuteronomy	

The Prophets

Joshua	Judges	1 Samuel
2 Samuel	1 Kings	2 Kings
Isaiah	Jeremiah	Ezekiel
Hosea	Joel	Amos
Obidiah	Jonah	Micah
Nahum	Habakkuk	Zephaniah
Haggai	Zechariah	Malachi

The Writings

Psalms	Proverbs	Job
Ruth	Song of Songs	Lamentations
Ecclesiastes	Esther	Daniel
Ezra	Nehemiah	1 Chronicles
2 Chronicles		

Apocrypha

Tobit	Judith	1 Maccabees
2 Maccabees	Wisdom	Sirach (Ecclesiasticus)
Baruch		

The Christian Scriptures

The Gospel Churches

Mark	Matthew	Luke
Acts of the Apostles	John	1 John
2 John	3 John	

Paul's Epistles

Romans	1 Corinthians	2 Corinthians
Galatians	Philippians	1 Thessalonians
Philemon		

Post Pauline Writings

2 Thessalonians	Ephesians	Colossians
1 Timothy	2 Timothy	Titus

Other Sacred Books

Hebrews	James	1 Peter
2 Peter	Jude	Revelation

Biblical Abbreviations

Acts	Acts of the Apostles	Jude	Jude
Amos	Amos	Judg.	Judges
Bar.	Baruch	1 Kgs.	1 Kings
1 Chron.	1 Chronicles	2 Kgs.	2 Kings
2 Chron.	2 Chronicles	Lev.	Leviticus
Col.	Colossians	Lk.	Luke
1 Cor.	1 Corinthians	1 Mac.	1 Maccabees
2 Cor.	2 Corinthians	2 Mac.	2 Maccabees
Dan.	Daniel	Mal.	Malachi
Deut.	Deuteronomy	Mk.	Mark
Eph.	Ephesians	Mt.	Matthew
Ex.	Exodus	Phil.	Philippians
Ezek.	Ezekiel	Phlm.	Philemon
Gal.	Galatians	Ps.	Psalms
Gen.	Genesis	1 Pt.	1 Peter
Heb.	Hebrews	2 Pt.	2 Peter
Hos.	Hosea	Rev.	Revelation
Isa.	Isaiah	Rom.	Romans
Jas.	James	1 Sam.	1 Samuel
Jer.	Jeremiah	2 Sam.	2 Samuel
Jn.	John	Sir.	Sirach
1 Jn.	1 John	1 Thes.	1 Thessalonians
2 Jn.	2 John	1 Tim.	1 Timothy
Job	Job	2 Tim.	2 Timothy
Joel	Joel	Tit.	Titus
Jon.	Jonah	Wis.	Wisdom
		Zech.	Zechariah

The Nicene or Nicene-Constantinopolitan Creed

We believe in one God, the Father, the Almighty, maker of heaven and earth, of all that is seen and unseen.

We believe in one Lord, Jesus Christ, the only Son of God, eternally begotten of the Father, God from God, Light from Light, true God from true God, begotten, not made, one in Being with the Father. Through him all things were made. For us and for our salvation he came down from heaven; by the power of the Holy Spirit he was born of the Virgin Mary, and became flesh.

For our sake he was crucified under Pontius Pilate; he suffered, died, and was buried. On the third day he rose again in fulfillment of the scriptures; he ascended into heaven and is seated at the right hand of the Father. He will come again in glory to judge the living and the dead, and his kingdom will have no end.

We believe in the Holy Spirit, the Lord, the giver of life, who proceeds from the Father and the Son. With the Father and the Son he is worshipped and glorified. He has spoken through the prophets.

We believe in one holy catholic and apostolic church.

We acknowledge one baptism for the forgiveness of sins.

We look for the resurrection of the dead, and the life of the world to come. Amen

1

Biblical Foundations

The Nature of Scripture
Luke 2:1–7; Matthew 1:18–2:1–15.

Human life is marked by many antitheses: order and chaos, wonder and terror, joy and sorrow, health and sickness, life and death, knowledge and ignorance, faith and doubt, hope and despair, love and indifference and/or hate. Religions illumine the ambiguities of life and express its ultimate meaning. Consequently, religions generate deep and abiding convictions about God, others, the world, and self, and they promote a special lifestyle, that is, a particular way of knowing, acting, and being. Often the teachings of a religion are found in its **scripture** (sacred writings).

Christians call their scripture the Bible. The word *Bible* comes from *biblia,* a Latin and Greek word which means *books.* The Bible, then, is not a single, unified book but a collection of books written over a period of more than a thousand years by many authors, most unknown.

The Jews recognize 39 books—all written in Hebrew—which were officially declared sacred and normative by Rabbi Johanan ben Zakkai and his colleagues at Jamnia near the Mediterranean coast around 90 A.D. (Neusner 1975, 85; Greenberg 1988, 286–90). These books were declared sacred and inspired because they were inspiring (able to arouse the faith of the people) and they provided guidance for the daily life of the community in its dealings with God, themselves, other peoples, and the created world. The technical term for designating which books are officially accepted into the Bible is **canon**—whose root meaning is "a rule of arrangement" or "measurement." The Jews have seven other books—all written in Greek between the years 200 B.C. and 100 A.D.—which they revere but do not include in their canon. These seven semisacred (or semicanonical or extracanonical) books are called **apocrypha**, a Greek term which means "hidden things." Apocrypha has two meanings. Literally, it indicates writings whose authenticity is questioned, often because they were kept secret by certain groups and were not accessible to the public. Technically, it denotes the books not incorporated into an official collection or canon.

Protestant Christians follow the lead of Martin Luther (1483– 1546), who accepted the Jewish canon and the 27 books written by Christians, a total of 66 books. Luther was so concerned that Christians immerse themselves in the sacred scriptures that he spent twelve years—1522 to 1534—translating the Bible into clear and polished German.

A Catholic Bible has 73 books: the 27 by Christian authors, the 39 in the Jewish canon, and the 7 apocryphal books. The latter are often referred to as the deuterocanonical or second canon. The Catholic canon of 73 books was officially declared authoritative at the **ecumenical** Council of Trent (1545–63). A council or church meeting can be either local or ecumenical (that is, universal or worldwide). Trent was assembled to respond to the teachings of Luther.

The Bible and Marcion of Pontus
In Christian history there was one major effort to deny the sacredness and value of the Hebrew scriptures. It came from Marcion of Pontus (c. 100–165), a teacher and missionary who was active in Rome around 140 A.D. In order to understand Marcion's anti-Semitism, it is necessary to recall that during the second and third centuries some Christians adopted some of the teaching of **Gnosticism**.

Gnosticism (from the Greek word for "knowledge") formed into various schools, but basically it accepted the Greek philosophical dualism of body and spirit. The Gnostics taught that the human body and the material world were inferior to the spirit and the spiritual world because they were created by a secondary, creator deity. Only the spirit and the spiritual had real and lasting value. Salvation consisted in freedom from the material world. Gnostics developed a hatred for the material world.

Those Christians who embraced Gnosticism described God as a God of light who was too spiritual to be involved with the created world. There is salvation from the material world, but only a favored few—a spiritual elite—learned the secret knowledge about God, human existence, and salvation. Salvation was not achieved by the life, death, and resurrection of Jesus. On the contrary, salvation was achieved by acquiring the secret knowledge that had been revealed through Jesus, a redeemer who descended from the world of light. Jesus' first disciples received and handed on this secret revelation to a spiritual elite.

Scholars were familiar with the Christian Gnostics mainly through refutation of their ideas in the writings of early church fathers, especially Irenaeus, bishop of Lyons (c. 130–200). But in 1945 in Egypt at Nag Hammadi, a major discovery was made. Thirteen fourth-century Gnostic manuscripts of some one-thousand pages were accidentally discovered in the sand in a large jar that was probably buried when all such writings were condemned and ordered destroyed. The manuscripts are in Coptic, the language of Egypt. One of them is titled *The Gospel of Thomas*. In this text, Jesus, the revealer of secret wisdom and saving truth, narrates many of the parables found in the canonical gospels. In *The Gospel of Philip,* Jesus is married to Mary Magdalene. These gospels also contain fanciful stories in which humans have preternatural powers. There is an imaginative story about the seven-year-old Jesus. One day Jesus was playing with other children of his own age. They were taking mud and molding it in the shape of donkeys, cows, and birds. Each child was boasting about how good his mud birds were. Suddenly, to everyone's amazement, the little clay figures flew out of Jesus' hand, circled overhead and then settled back on his hand.

In another very imaginative story, events special to Matthew (the flight into Egypt) and Luke (the so-called good thief) are harmonized and ingeniously developed. It seems that a band of robbers captured Mary and Joseph when they were fleeing from King Herod into Egypt. One of the robbers turned out to be none other than Dismas, the name the Gnostics gave to the unnamed "good thief" in Luke's gospel. When Dismas saw the baby Jesus, he realized that this was no ordinary child and said, "O most blessed of children, if ever there comes a time for having mercy on me, then remember me and forget not this hour." Then Dismas paid the ransom price for the family.

Influenced by Gnosticism, Marcion taught that there were two deities: the God of the Jews and the God of Jesus Christ. The God of the Jews was harsh, evil, and unforgiving; the God of Jesus Christ sent his Son to save humankind. The Jewish God was inferior to the supreme God revealed by Jesus. The Jewish God demanded strict justice, an eye for an eye and a tooth for a tooth; he destroyed cities like Sodom and Gomorrah with fire (Gen. 19:24); and he associated only with the righteous. He created Adam and Eve, thereby introducing evil into the world and making sexual intercourse the means of procreation. The Jewish God was a God of law, wholly capricious and cruel, who chose evil men like the adulterous and murderous David to enforce his will. The Christian God, on the other hand, is a God of love who sent his Son to save sinners and who insists on forgiveness and love of enemies. As a result of these teachings, Marcion rejected the Jewish scriptures and even purged Paul's letters and **Luke-Acts** from any favorable references to them. Since the same author wrote the gospel of Luke and the Acts of the Apostles (see Acts 1:1), these books can be referred to as Luke-Acts.

At an assembly of bishops in July 144, Pope Pius I (c. 142–152) condemned Marcion's gnosticism, his interpretation of the scriptures, and his very restricted canon (Kelly 1986, 10). The church held that the Jewish scriptures are in continuity with the Christian scriptures because both tell the story of the God who creates, covenants, loves, and saves. The God of Abraham, Moses, David, and the prophets is the God of Jesus. Jesus did not want to abolish the law and the prophets but to fulfill them (Mt. 5:17).

It is important to note that at this point in church history, the church had not officially listed the 27 books of the New Testament. Nonetheless, there is ample evidence that renowned church fathers like Justin of Palestine (d. 165) and Irenaeus of Lyons (d. 200) treated as scripture books that Marcion either eliminated or expurgated, because they proclaimed the glory of the Jewish God and his law (Kelly 1958, 57–58).

The actual development of the Christian canon is an exceedingly complicated story that falls outside the scope of this book. It is enough to state that acceptance of the official canon was a gradual process, with the broad outlines of the canon settled by the end of the second century. "The first official document which prescribes the twenty-seven books of our New Testament as alone canonical" is the Easter Letter in 367 by Athanasius, the saintly bishop of Alexandria who died in 373 (ibid., 16). When Jerome (331–420), the greatest Latin biblical scholar, was commissioned by Pope Damasus I (366–84) to translate the Bible into Latin, he automatically restricted his work to the twenty-seven books in Athanasius's canon.

The Word of God: Three Meanings

The Bible is a book about God. How do we write and talk about God since, as most Jews, Muslims, and Christians agree, God is totally unlike anything created, and his being and purpose are not fully known or disclosed? If the monotheistic religions insist that God is not a person (but is personal) and is not a thing (but is real), then all statements about God can only be weak analogies, often in the form of **metaphors**. Metaphors are comparisons that should not be taken literally. They say "is" and "is not" about the same thing at the same time, thus creating a tension in the reader or listener that demands thoughtful engagement. To say "Jeremy is a bull" does not mean he is an adult male bovine mammal, but is a large, strong, and aggressive man. The Bible has many metaphors for God. God is called rock (2 Kgs. 2:22), eagle (Jer. 49:22), and lion, panther, and bear (Hos. 13:7–8). Jesus directed his audiences and disciples to call God "Father." A father is a male who has sexual intercourse with a female to procreate another human person. Nothing in this description can be literally predicated of God who is not sexed, is not male, does not copulate, and does not produce little deities. But calling God father is not frivolous any more than calling God rock or eagle. These metaphors are intended to communicate something important and true about the relationship between God and humans (Schneiders 1993, 21).

The Bible is the word of God. But the Bible cannot literally be the word of God, that is, divine speech. God is pure spirit and does not have the physical apparatus that produces intelligible sound. However, God does reveal himself. He does not literally speak, but he does communicate. Since we use language to communicate our inmost selves, it is fitting that we attribute spoken words to God. It is those who have received a revelation—Abraham, Sarah, Moses, Miriam, Ruth, David, Jesus, and Mary Magdalene—who give expression to the divine revelation in their own words. This is what Jesus did when he said God is our Father. This is what the Christian authors did when they testified in writing to what they had experienced after Jesus' resurrection and in the historical events they shared with Jesus during his lifetime. In addition to being a book, the *word of God* is a metaphor for the whole process and reality of divine revelation. The Bible is called the word of God because this metaphor identifies the canonical books as mediators of the self-disclosure of God.

The word of God, written under the inspiration of the holy Spirit, is powerful. One inspired writer states: "Indeed, the word of God is living and effective, sharper than any two-edged sword, penetrating even between soul and spirit, joints and marrow, and able to discern reflections and thoughts of the heart" (Heb. 4:12). Another sacred author declares that "All scripture is inspired by God and useful for teaching, for refutation, for correction, and for training in righteousness, so that one who belongs to God may be competent, equipped for every good work" (1 Tim. 3:16–17).

The principal author of the Bible is God because he inspired it. Pope Leo XIII (1878–1903) described the **inspiration** of the biblical authors in his **encyclical** (a major papal statement of theology or policy) *Providentissimus Deus* on November 18, 1893: "God so moved the inspired writers by his supernatural operation that he incited them to write, and assisted them in their writing so that they correctly conceived, accurately wrote down and truthfully expressed all that he intended and only what he intended; and only thus can God be the author of the Bible" (n. 9).

Pope Leo's account of inspiration should not be interpreted as dictation. In dictation the writer is simply a stenographer or secretary who writes faithfully what is dictated. The pope should have added that each author had his own part in the composition of the books, a contribution conditioned by the author's social, educational, cultural, and religious context. Since Americans are brought up with the notion of "rugged individualism," they are inclined to think that God and they work together, side by side, like two persons rowing a boat together (Mahoney 1990, 247). Christian tradition teaches otherwise. God and humans operate on different planes. The sovereign and loving God is the principal agent. We are his free instruments with our own real but subordinate contribution. If we are sailboats, God is the wind that makes it possible for us to move. (Both in Hebrew and in Greek the same word can be used for *wind* and *spirit*.) The four authors of the gospels made their own contribution to our understanding of God's salvation in Jesus Christ and his holy Spirit, but due to divine inspiration and revelation, God is truly the principal author of the gospels and all the sacred books.

Muslims have two explanations of the origin and nature of their sacred *Qur'an,* which are similar to what is being explained here. According to the first, Muhammad, a poet-prophet, was inspired to compose a special book about Allah. He wrote the book of 114 chapters, verse by verse, over a period of twenty-three years. Like most creative acts, it was far from easy. Muhammad's early biographers "often show him listening intently to what we should perhaps call the unconscious, rather as a poet describes the process of 'listening' to a poem that is gradually surfacing from the hidden recesses of the mind, declaring itself with an authority and integrity that seem mysteriously separate from him" (Armstrong 1993, 139). The second explanation declares that the *Qur'an* is the literal dictation of the very speech and words of Allah by the angel

Gabriel to Muhammad. The book is said to have been "eternally pre-existent in heaven on 'a preserved tablet' (85.21–22)" (Cragg 1988, 16). According to this understanding, the Muslim scriptures are **inerrant** (free of error) and not subject to modification by translation or interpretation.

Christians are divided over inerrancy. Many believe that since God inspired the books they must be inerrant; many others hold that, since the scriptures are the word of God in the words of historically conditioned men and women, they are not perfect and do contain errors. For example, Luke 2:1–3 states that Mary and Joseph journeyed from Nazareth to Bethlehem where Jesus was born, because there was a universal census of the Roman world for taxation purposes. However, Matthew has no census nor do historians find evidence of one at that time. They do have evidence for universal registrations in 28 B. C., 8 B.C., and 14 A.D. Furthermore, Quirinus became governor of Syria in 6–7 A.D. There is a vague recollection of a local census only in Judea soon after Quirinus came into power (see Acts 5:37), but there is considerable evidence that Jesus was born towards the end of the reign of Herod the Great (37–4 B.C.).

Did Luke make a mistake or did he have a theological purpose in arranging these events the way he did? Luke-Acts clearly places Jesus and the church within the context of the Roman world. Perhaps Luke was indicating that this child is a far greater instrument of peace and salvation than the emperor Caesar Augustus, whose long reign (27 B.C.–14 A.D.) was marked by the **Pax Romana** (the so-called "peace of Rome"). Historians note that when Augustus took control of the empire he was able to bring a certain measure of peace and prosperity by stopping the civil wars that were tearing the empire apart. Nevertheless, Augustus was a despot whose Pax Romana was "enforced through rigid control, reprisals, and punishment through crucifixion" (Hill 1991, 159).

Not only does the Bible contain errors, it also contains some sinful ideas. In some places it is patently anti-Jewish (Jn. 8:39–59), condones slavery as a social institution (Eph. 6:5–8), and has God directing kings to wage ruthless wars against their neighbors (1 Sam. 15:1–3). The Psalmist (69:24–25,

28–29) petitions God to curse and inflict serious harm upon his enemies:

Let their eyes grow dim so that they cannot see,
    and keep their backs always feeble.
Pour out your wrath upon them. . . .

Heap guilt upon their guilt, and let them
    not attain to your reward.
May they be erased from the book of the living,
    and not be recorded with the just!

While many Christians acknowledge that the sacred and inspired scriptures contain some human errors and even sin, they believe scriptures are **inerrant** in the sense that they are without error when they address our eternal salvation from sin and death, and salvation for wholeness and life that God initiates and accomplishes. The Catholic Church reiterated this teaching at Vatican II in its 1965 document, the *Constitution on Divine Revelation:* the Bible "must be acknowledged as teaching firmly, faithfully, and without error that truth which God wanted put into the sacred writings for the sake of salvation" (n. 11).

Finally, in addition to being a book and a process, the term "Word of God" refers to the risen Jesus. "In the beginning was the Word, and the Word was with God. . . . And the Word became flesh and made his dwelling among us" (Jn. 1:1, 14). For Christians, Jesus is the Word [revelation] of the love, plan, and will of the one and only God. Jesus said, "Whoever has seen me has seen the Father" (Jn. 14:9). Jesus the Word is the pinnacle and paradigm of God's self-revelation and self-communication.

Interpretation of Scripture
Jonah 1–4; Psalms 22 and 69; Mark 15:21–41.

The preceding account of the authorship of the Bible indicates that the inspired scriptures are not easy to interpret. There are three approaches to interpretation.

The Precritical Method

The first is called the **precritical method**. This approach is based on three points. First, it maintains that since the books are God's inspired word, they record historical facts, contain no errors, and should be read and interpreted literally in all their details. Second, it does not apply modern critical methods to the text. It does not take into account the cultural and historical context, audience, and purpose of the text. It takes what is written at face value (literally) and does not differentiate the many different forms of literature (such as history, poetry, epistles, parables, myths, law, and prophecies) found in the biblical books. Third, it historicizes stories, myths, and parables which from the start never claimed to be historical.

Those who adhere to the precritical method are called **fundamentalists**. Most religions and churches have many who accept this method. For example, in 1910 the American Bible Conference, composed of Protestant laymen, met at Niagara, New York, to counteract liberal Protestant interpretations of the Bible. They insisted on the literal sense of the scripture and published a set of books, *The Fundamentals: A Testimony of the Truth*, that gave the name to the movement that had been developing through the nineteenth century.

Being interdenominational, the movement never developed a **creed** (an official profession of faith) but settled on this five-point statement of the fundamentals. They insisted on universal Christian acceptance of the inerrancy of scripture (no errors), the divinity of Christ, the virginal conception of Jesus, the substitutionary atonement of the death of Jesus, and his physical resurrection and bodily return to earth. Of these, the inerrancy of scripture, with its corollary, the literalist interpretation of the Bible, is the basic point.

The Historical-Critical Method

The second approach is called the **historical-critical method**. This method is the opposite of the precritical method. It carefully analyzes the scripture in order to judge its historical and literary components. First, it builds on the research of nineteenth-century scholars who showed that the Bible admitted of historical and literary explanations in quite the same way as did any other set of ancient and classical documents. These

scholars declared that the author's meaning can be reconstructed by deciphering the sense of the text within its own
historical circumstances. Second, the historical-critical method
investigates not only the different literary forms but also uses
all the tools of literary criticism: the ancient languages themselves, history, and archeology. Its goal is to get at the meaning literally intended by the biblical authors and editors. As a
result, it looks at the context of such passages as the time of
the birth of Jesus (Lk. 2:1–3) discussed above, to see its purpose and its relationship to other passages and to the whole
work in which it appears. The literary form and the historical
context affect the meaning. Marcion's interpretation of the
Hebrew scriptures was rejected because it was precritical.
Furthermore, interpretation is not individual or private but
corporate (2 Pt. 1:20). In the last analysis, it is the involvement
of the interpreter in a community of interpreters that makes
interpretation a meaningful activity.

Third, the historical-critical method does not historicize
myths, parables, and other imaginative stories that are forms
of symbolic communication. The word **symbol** means to draw
things together; the word **diabolic** means "to set at variance"
and, therefore, to tear things apart. A symbol is an object (a
sword or book), an aspect of nature (a tree or rain), an event
(a wedding or graduation), a person (Abraham or Moses), or
an expression or a word (mother or Eucharist) which points
to one thing *directly* (and makes it present) while pointing to
something *indirectly* (and takes its place). Symbols have the
ability to call forth reality and render it present. A symbol
makes an explicit call to a person to engage herself or himself
in its reality. For example, when Christopher Columbus
landed in the New World on October 12, 1492, he planted a
sword and a cross in the soil. The sword and cross represented Spain and the church. He was declaring that Spain and
the church were in the New World to stay.

Symbols are multivalent, that is, they have several meanings. They can convey a negative or a positive message. For
example, a wall can protect and unite people or it can separate them. When, on November 9, 1989, the German people
dismantled the Berlin Wall that separated the east and west,
they were saying quite clearly that they refused to be divided

any longer. When the Vietnam Memorial was dedicated on November 8, 1982, the people were saying that we cannot allow that war to continue to divide us.

Symbols are distinguished from signs. The chief function of signs is to provide facts or information. They point beyond themselves to something else, whereas symbols participate in the reality to which they point. Signs are straightforward and usually have one meaning, for example, stop, bus stop, room 120, library, restaurant, no smoking.

Symbols are either natural or cultural. Natural symbols such as the sun, a tree, a rock, rain, the ocean, and a river are common to all peoples. All peoples use these objects to express both positive and negative thoughts and meanings. Cultural symbols are special to a group. For example, special to the United States are the Statue of Liberty, the Golden Gate Bridge, and the Constitution.

Unfortunately, the word *symbol* has lost much of its positive meaning in our society. People often dismiss something important by saying, "It is only a symbol." We realize how important symbols are when they are defaced or degraded, for example, one's name, one's home, a flag, a religious statue, a tombstone, and a school's mascot.

Symbols should be revered because they are essential to human communication. We use them every day when we communicate with one another about ourselves, other persons, and things. Common symbols are a handshake, a smile, giving a present, sending a birthday card, and holding a loved one in one's arms. Symbols are even more necessary when we talk about God, the unseen, ineffable, and ultimate reality. It is only possible to communicate about God in any meaningful and extensive way in symbolic language or gestures.

A premise of the historical-critical method is that the Bible reports the profound religious experiences of such figures as Abraham, Moses, Ruth, Esther, Peter, Mary Magdalene, and Paul, experiences which profoundly changed them and human history through them. But their experiences are reported in symbolic language. The symbols should not be interpreted literally. To understand their experiences it is absolutely necessary to understand the cultural and conventional symbols employed by the sacred authors.

The Catholic church began, on September 30, 1943, to give its official blessing to the historical-critical method, with the encyclical *Divino afflante Spiritu* by Pius XII (1939–58). The pope encouraged scholars to explore the different literary forms found in the Bible. Because the scriptures contain such literary forms as myths, poetry, parables, infancy narratives and prophecies, the Bible cannot be read as a modern historical account of Israel, Jesus, or his church.

In 1964 the Pontifical Biblical Commission elaborated on the historical-critical method in its *Instruction on the Historical Truth of the Gospels.* This document states that the gospels are not biographies or lives of Jesus. It is impossible to harmonize the four of them and produce a life of Jesus. For example, in the gospel of John, Jesus' teaching ministry lasts more than three years whereas in the other gospels the ministry lasts a little more than a year. The gospels, then, do contain the words and deeds of Jesus—but as interpreted by the **evangelists** (editors of the gospels or heralds of good tidings, as in Isa. 52:7; 62:1–2). The evangelists edited, synthesized, and explained the apostolic tradition that had been handed on to them in oral and written form. The gospels are testimonies of faith in Jesus of Nazareth, the resurrected Son of God and the Christ. They are symbolic communication.

In November 1993 the Vatican's Pontifical Biblical Commission issued another document on the scriptures, *The Interpretation of the Bible in the Church.* The document accords the historical-critical method primacy of place among the different methods and approaches discussed. It calls this method "indispensable" and insists that the proper understanding of the scriptures "not only admits the use of this method but actually requires it" (p. 512). The document also contains a brisk attack on the precritical method, stating that its basic mistake is its neglect of the historical character of the scriptures. Because it treats the biblical text as though it had been dictated verse by verse by the Spirit, the precritical method suppresses the personality of the human authors. The document also declares that "What characterizes Catholic **exegesis** [the scientific explanation of a text] is that it deliberately places itself within the living tradition of the church, whose first concern is fidelity to the revelation attested by the Bible" (p. 513).

The presence within a church community of these two divergent methods of exegesis can cause serious conflicts and—unfortunately—even devastating divisions when both sides are deeply entrenched. For example, the Missouri Synod of the Lutheran Church, which had been founded in 1847 by German immigrants, was split in 1973 over the interpretation of the Bible and how it was being taught to the seminarians. Jacob Preus (1920–94), president of the denomination from 1969 to 1981, appointed a committee to investigate the way scripture was taught at Concordia Seminary in St. Louis. In 1973, as a result of the committee's report, the majority of the faculty was accused of false teaching. For instance, the committee found fault with their interpretation of the book of Jonah.

Written by an unknown author in the late sixth or early fifth century, this book tells the story of Jonah, an obscure eighth-century prophet (2 Kgs. 14:25) commissioned to convert the hated Assyrians. The Assyrians were despised by the Jews because in 721 B.C. they destroyed Samaria, deporting thousands of Israelites to the region of Persia (2 Kgs. 17:6). Jonah did not want to fulfill the divine command and attempted to flee by ship. Cast overboard by the sailors during a vicious storm, Jonah was swallowed by a great fish and later unceremoniously deposited near Nineveh, the capital of Assyria on the Tigris River. To the surprise of Jonah, the king and all his people heard his message of doom and repented immediately. When God did not punish the Assyrians, Jonah bitterly complained to God about the unexpected success of his mission. It was beyond Jonah's way of thinking that a nation as wicked as Assyria could escape God's wrath. Self-centered Jonah was more concerned for the life of his withered plant than for the well-being of the Ninevites. When the book of Jonah was written, Nineveh no longer existed, having been destroyed by a coalition of Medes, Babylonians, and Sythians in 612 B.C.

The seminary faculty at Concordia did not historicize Jonah the prophet. They taught that the book is a **parable**, which means "placing one thing beside another" for the purpose of comparison. C. H. Dodd (1961, 16) provided the classic definition of a parable: "A metaphor or simile drawn from nature or common life, arresting the hearer by its vividness or strangeness, and leaving the mind in sufficient doubt about its precise application to tease it into active thought." Parables are brief stories that go against people's expectations. Their authors use a familiar situation or action to illustrate an unfamiliar or previously unrecognized truth. In a religious context, parables often contrast an everyday, human experience with the mysterious ways of God.

The seminary faculty taught that the book of Jonah is symbolic communication to explain that there may be limitations and boundaries to prophetic zeal but not to God's mercy. Prophets perform interrelated functions: they confront and condemn those unfaithful to God's teachings; they offer God's mercy to the repentant. The book of Jonah teaches that God's mercy is greater than what Jonah thought. God's mercy and love are universal. The book reminds the Jews that their view of God is too small, that is, their special covenant with God is not a guarantee of privilege but a responsibility: to manifest that God's blessings and salvation reach out to all nations.

Jacob Preus was fearful that those who interpreted the Jonah story as parable would eventually dismiss fundamental Christian tenets like the resurrection of Jesus.

The controversy caused 100,000 members to withdraw from the Missouri Synod, a denomination with more than two million members. Among those who separated were 500 pastors as well as 400 students and 45 teachers from the Concordia Seminary. They eventually united with other Lutherans and formed the Association of Evangelical Lutheran Churches.

Over the years the historical-critical method has been supplemented by other forms of criticism, such as rhetorical, anthropological, literary and sociological criticism. Literary criticism investigates the literary dynamics of the text and sociological criticism attempts to reconstruct the social world of the original audiences addressed by the biblical authors. For example, it seems that the famine that devastated Palestine in the late 40s influenced the injunction of the Jerusalem assembly in 49 A.D. for gentile Christians to care for the poor (Gal. 2:10). Similarly, the harsh language Jesus uses in John's gospel to challenge "the Jews"—that they belong to their "father the devil" and they willingly carry out their "father's desires" (8:44)—cannot be the actual words of Jesus but must be understood in the context of the first-century interreligious conflict between Judaism and Christianity.

The Critical Method

The third approach to textual criticism is called the **critical method**. This method moves from the "then" meaning of the author to its pertinence for today, its "now" meaning for the reader. This method encourages the reader to bring a different horizon of cultural, religious, and socioeconomic meaning to the text. This new horizon makes it possible for the text to "say" something fresh.

This method is quite popular today, especially in Catholic circles, due to the convergence of two factors. First, this method employs the theories of such major figures in the development of contemporary interpretation of texts **(hermeneutics)** as Hans-Georg Gadamer (1975) and Paul Ricoeur (1976). These scholars showed that the historical-critical method, while it is an indispensable element in textual (biblical) research, is not enough. What must also be taken into consideration is the meaning of the text for today. Second, the Catholic church underscored the central role the scriptures (should) have in the life of the church at Vatican II on November 18, 1965, in the *Constitution on Divine Revelation.* The bishops wrote that "the force and power in the word of God is so great that it remains the support and energy of the Church, the strength of faith for her sons, the food of the soul, the pure and perennial source of spiritual life" (n. 21). Furthemore, the study of the Bible should be "the soul of theology" (n. 24).

In the critical method the primary task of the interpreter is understanding the truth-claims of the text. In this approach the reader reads the document for the meaning she or he finds in it for today's world. The historical-critical method asks what the text meant for the original audience; the critical method asks what the text means in light of contemporary experience. This method is based on the belief that "once one has written a work, the work lives on its own. The author becomes another reader—with some privileged knowledge of what she or he once meant, but with no hermeneutical privilege at all in interpreting what the text really says. For that latter task, for better or for worse, the work alone speaks" (Tracy 1990, 903).

The method of actualization is not an arbitrary process because the meaning is controlled by the text. For a person's interpretation to be valid, he or she must submit to that control. An interpretation that manipulates the text or projects novel opinions on it is to be rejected. A text is not whatever the reader makes of it. An interpretation which runs counter to the author's intent taken in its whole context cannot be considered valid. If the critical method is not rooted in the historical-critical method, it becomes meaningless and irrelevant. For example, Shakespeare's *Hamlet* and David McCullough's 1992 Pulitzer Prize biography *Truman* would be distorted if interpreted, respectively, as a comedy and a historical novel. The critical method actualizes the literal sense of the text because it builds on the properly ascertained literal sense, extending it to show how what was meant can have meaning today. Any critical reading of the Bible that is not in homogeneous connection with what was originally meant becomes the projection of an extraneous and subjective meaning on the text. For example, there have been times when people brought their ideologies to the scriptures whereby, contrary to the gospel message of justice and charity, they have interpreted the scriptures to justify anti-Semitism, slavery, sexism and racial segregation.

The critical method invites a plurality of valid meanings whether or not the author intended such meanings, because readers bring their own historical, educational, cultural, and religious background to the text. Today, for example, there are black, feminist, and liberationist interpretations of the scriptures. These have been encouraged in the Catholic church in the Pontifical Biblical Commission's 1993 document referred to earlier, *The Interpretation of the Bible in the Church*. The fourth section of this important document fosters the critical method, calling it a "**process of actualization**." This is the first time that an official document of the Catholic church has treated actualization. The commission declared that "Catholic exegetes must never forget that what they are interpreting is the Word of God. Their common task is not finished when they have simply determined sources, defined forms or explained literary procedures. They arrive at the true goal of their work only when they have explained the meaning of the biblical text as God's word for today" (p. 517).

The document explains that actualization is both possible and necessary (Fitzmyer 1993; Hebblethwaite 1994b; Williamson 1995). It "is possible because the richness of meaning contained in the biblical text gives it a value for all time and all cultures (cf. Isa. 40:8; 66:18–21; Mt. 28:19–20)" (p. 520). Actualization is necessary because it is vital for Christian faith to go beyond the historical and cultural conditioning of the texts. "To reveal their significance for men and women of today, it is necessary to apply their message to contemporary circumstances and to express it in language adapted to the present time" (p. 520). According to the Vatican document, actualization involves three steps: "1. to hear the word from within one's own concrete situation; 2. to identify the aspects of the present situation highlighted or put in question by the biblical text; 3. to draw from the fullness of meaning contained in the biblical text those elements capable of advancing the present situation in a way that is productive and consonant with the saving will of God in Christ" (p. 521).

The critical method or actualization is not totally new. One finds many instances of it within the Hebrew scriptures themselves. For example, God, the just one, is said to reward the good and punish the evil (see Ps. 1:1–6 and Ps. 112:1–10). But human experience shows us that the good often suffer and the evil prosper. There are passages that protest and question God's justice (see Ps. 44; Job 10:1–7; 13:3–28) and continue to examine the depths and nature of God's involvement in history (see Ps. 37; Job 38–42).

An example of the critical method or actualization in the Christian scriptures is in 1 Corinthians 15, one of the most significant Christian texts. This chapter is Paul's extended explanation of the nature and meaning of the resurrection of Jesus. The text states in verses 3 and 4 that "Christ died for our sins in accordance with the scriptures . . . that he was raised on the third day in accordance with the scriptures." One can look in vain through the Hebrew scriptures for the prediction in so many words of Jesus' death and resurrection. What the

Hebrew scriptures do describe, especially in the Psalms, is the story of the righteous sufferer, humiliated and abandoned by God, but later vindicated by him. Since the resurrected Jesus "fit into this pattern in a quite final way," the early Christians had no difficulty regarding Jesus as the fulfillment of this story (Fuller and Perkins 1983, 32). In Mark's account of the crucifixion (15:21–41), he uses details taken from Psalms 69 and 22 about the righteous sufferer and God's vindication of him. Jesus is offered wine mingled with myrrh (Ps. 69:22), has his garments divided by the soldiers (Ps. 22:18), and is mocked by the priests and others (Ps. 22:7). These narrative details are not reported in the same way in each gospel. John 19:23 says the soldiers "took his garments and made four parts, one for each soldier," but adds that the soldiers cast dice for Jesus' seamless tunic. Scholars think the evangelists include these details "because the crucifixion of Jesus is being interpreted as the death of a righteous sufferer whom God vindicated, and hence as the fulfillment of Psalms 22 and 69" (Perrin and Duling 1982, 59). In short, the early Christians applied the critical method to the Hebrew scriptures as they prayed and studied them in the light of Jesus' death and resurrection. The Psalms did not make sense of Jesus' death, but Jesus' death made sense of the Psalms.

Modern interpretations of the Constitution, its Amendments, and the Bill of Rights provide another example of how we can, on the basis of our own experience, discover new meanings in the historical texts. Justices in the United States Supreme court insist that one cannot find simple or automatic answers to constitutional questions in history or anywhere else. Oliver Wendell Holmes, a justice from 1902 to 1932, noted that "the provisions of the Constitution are not mathematical formulas having their essence in their form; they are organic, living institutions . . . Their significance is . . . to be gathered not simply by taking the words and a dictionary, but by considering their origin and the line of their growth." Felix Frankfurter, a justice from 1936 to 1962, speaking in 1955 of the 14th Amendment's clauses, said, "These provisions of the Constitution were not calculated to give permanent legal sanction merely to the social arrangements and beliefs of a particular epoch. Like all legal provisions without a fixed technical meaning, they are ambulant, adaptable to the changes of time" (see Lewis 1985).

It is fitting to include at this point a scriptural example of all three methods of interpretation. Genesis narrates the creation of all humankind from one couple **(monogenesis)** as opposed to the creation from many couples independently of one another **(polygenesis)**. A literal, precritical reading of Genesis raises many questions, some embarrassing. Adam and Eve had no daughters, only two sons, Cain and Abel. But after Cain the farmer killed Abel the shepherd (Gen. 4:8), he was banished from the family. Then the text states that Cain "had relations with his wife, and she conceived and bore Enoch" (Gen. 4:17). Where does Cain's wife come from? Are we talking incest?

The historical-critical method suggests that the Genesis story of monogenesis is the author's symbolic way of indicating that the whole human family is tainted by sin, that evil is contagious, and that all humankind needs salvation.

A critical interpretation of the text is not concerned with polygenism and monogenism or with where Cain's wife came from. Actualization seeks the religious interpretation of life and relationships found in the text. It asks whether that interpretation is true, and if so, what are the implications for the interpreter's own self-understanding. In Christian terms, reading the biblical stories critically invites us to put on the mind of Christ today. Christ regarded all people as children of his Father and, therefore, as sisters and brothers. After Cain killed Abel, God asked, "Where is your brother Abel?" Cain replied: "I do not know. Am I my brother's keeper?" (Gen. 4:9). An actualization of the Cain and Abel story reminds us that, since all humans have the same nature and form one family in our global village, then we are the guardians of our brothers and sisters. Our thoughts, words, and deeds—both moral and immoral—affect everyone in the global village. It is everyone's responsibility to build the human community of brotherhood and sisterhood. Christians are warned in 1 John 3:12 not to be unloving like Cain.

The rest of this chapter covers two topics from the Hebrew scriptures that were reinterpreted in the Christian scriptures:

the creation of the world and the creation of humankind. Each topic has four parts. There is an explanation of the scriptural passages, their context and theology. Then a historical-critical interpretation of the texts is contrasted with a precritical reading. Third, a Christian interpretation of each topic is outlined, especially as this interpretation has bearing on contemporary issues. Finally, the texts are interpreted by using the critical or actualization method.

Creation of the World
Genesis 1:1–31; 2:1–4a; 2:4b–14; Psalm 150.

The Bible abounds with praise for God the Creator. The Psalmist worships God the Creator who is "mightier than the thunder of many waters" (93:4). He says the trees "sing with joy before the Lord" (96:12) and "mountains melt like wax" before him (97:5). In Psalm 148 the sun and moon, the sea monsters, all cattle, and birds are told to praise God. The book ends with this stirring invocation: "Let everything that breathes praise the Lord! Alleluia" (150:6).

Most ancient peoples offered prayers to the Creator and composed myths about creation and other important subjects such as death, immortality, and what comprises good and bad conduct. For example, we have myths written around 1800 B.C. from ancient Babylon, a city that was situated sixty miles south of modern Baghdad. The myth *Enuma Elish* (its two opening words mean "When on high") tells the story of the creation of the deities, the universe, and humankind.

The *Enuma Elish* is sometimes called the Babylonian Genesis. It states that in the beginning there was a formless, watery waste—a substance that was itself divine. This sacred raw material had always existed. Three deities emerged from it: Apsu (identified with the river waters), Tiamat (the dragon of the salty seas), and Mummu (identified with the womb of chaos). These three were, so to speak, an early, inferior model which needed improvement. Consequently, a succession of other deities emerged from them in a process known as emanation. The new male and female deities emerged, one from the other, in pairs, with each pair becoming more powerful than its predecessors. Two of the deities were Anu (the heavens) and Ea (the earth). In order to survive, the new deities had to continue the struggle against chaos. They also rose up against their parents. Ea was able to overpower Apsu and Mummu but could not make much headway against Tiamat and her brood of monsters. Fortunately, Ea had a superb offspring, Marduk, the sun deity. He told the other deities that he would fight Tiamat on the condition that he become their ruler. After a fierce struggle, Marduk slew Tiamat and from her corpse created a new world. He split her immense body in two to form the arch of the sky and the world of men and women. He even established laws to keep everything in its appointed place.

Babylon, which means "Gate of the gods," was the sacred place, the center of the world and the home of the deities. A great temple had been built in honor of Marduk. Each year during the New Year Festival of eleven days, the creation epic was recited at an elaborate liturgy. The earthly temple was a symbol of the heavenly court. During the rituals the Babylonians renewed their contact with the powers of the divine world. Their creation epic reinforced their belief that the sacred power was the source of all being, power, and efficacy (Armstrong 1993, 8–9).

The *Epic of Gilgamesh* recounts the human search for immortality that ends in crushing disappointment because of the inevitability of death. After Gilgamesh's best friend dies prematurely, Gilgamesh sets out on a perilous journey in search of immortality. At one point he cuts down trees in the cedar forest of the deities. This act is forbidden and deserving of punishment and death. Gilgamesh is given a second chance: he is presented with a precious gift, a plant that causes continued rejuvenation. A serpent steals the plant and so Gilgamesh returns home fully mortal. This epic also tells the story of a flood. The deities were disturbed by the many sins of humankind and angrily decided to punish them by causing a flood. Their secret decision was revealed to a man by a compassionate deity. The man proceeded immediately to build an ark.

The biblical account of life, death, and sin bears some resemblance to these Babylonian myths. A **myth** for ancient peoples is a symbolic story, factual and/or imaginative, that demonstrates the inner meaning of the universe and human life. Myths often undergird the social order inasmuch they explain symbolically the origin and destiny of things and people. These imaginative stories convey the truth about God, self, others, and this world; vouch for the effectiveness of various rituals; and contain practical rules for the guidance of daily life.

Today the word *myth* in popular parlance denotes stories or statements that are false, totally imaginative, and/or not factual. This meaning is the very opposite of the ancient meaning in which myths convey the truth about human and divine life. This shift in meaning has taken place because the historical dimensions of a myth are often encased in highly imaginative details that modern readers have taken literally. The ancient myth-makers, on the other hand, composed stories to convey a meaning or a truth that is more important than "what actually happened." An example of the modern use of the word myth is demonstrated in the way the ability of girls and women to do well in science is perceived. In the educational world it is often erroneously stated that girls and women do not do well in mathematics and should avoid science classes in college. Not only will they not do well in these classes but they will never succeed in the world of science. Many scientific studies debunk this so-called myth.

Another example of the modern meaning of myth was its use in the 1994 debates over the Clinton administration's proposal to institute universal health care in the United States. Those opposed to the Clinton plan made comparisons with the Canadian health care system. The Canadian plan was denounced for three reasons: it involved waiting lines, there was no free choice of doctors, and the costs were out of control. Defenders of the Canadian plan label these three objections as myths. They insisted on the facts: Canadians get routine care within twenty-four hours, can choose their own doctors, and costs are $1,000 less per person per year than in the United States.

In both these examples, myth is synonymous with falsehood—the modern understanding of the word. However, the ancients understood myth as a symbolic story that told the truth about the deepest dimensions of human and divine life. The ancients were not troubled with the highly imaginative details of the story. Unfortunately, it is we who have misunderstood them.

Two Accounts in Genesis

Genesis contains two splendidly-crafted creation myths (Gen. 1:1–31, 2:1–4a and Gen. 2:4b–14). In Genesis 1, for example, a parallelism of two sets of three days is employed, with the second set of days populating the first: light and darkness (day one) are populated by the greater and lesser lights (four); firmament and waters (two) by birds and fish (five); earth and vegetation (three) by land animals and humans (six).

Scholars have provided evidence that the first five books of the Bible (the **Pentateuch**) were not written by Moses as had been traditionally thought. The Pentateuch is actually the work of many authors over many, many years. The books were given their final editing around 500 B.C. Scholars say there were many authors because the books show several distinct styles, are often repetitious, sometimes offer two accounts of the same event, and have some inconsistencies— characteristics not normally associated with a single author. The myth in Genesis 1 was written by a Priestly source around 550 B.C. This source prefers the generic name for God, **Elohim**. Elohim is a technical term. It was meant to signify all the special things about the nature and functions of the deities that should have ultimate meaning for human beings. The word is a plural form but why this is so is not clear, because the word is used only in a singular sense. By declaring God their Elohim, the Jews were affirming that he is "the only god who counted" (Armstrong 1993, 17). Genesis 2 was written by a Yahwist source around 950 B.C. **Yahweh** is the name for God given to Moses at the burning bush (Ex. 3:13–14). It is translated as *Lord*. In Genesis 2 God is called Lord God (Yahweh Elohim).

The crucial question in the Priestly account was **polytheism** (belief in many deities) versus **monotheism** (belief in one God). Every nation surrounding Israel, both great and small, was polytheistic. For ancient Jewish faith a divinized nature posed a fundamental religious problem. The prophets and priests had to constantly call the people from polytheism, idolatry, and syncretism because for most peoples in the ancient world the various regions of nature were divine. Sun, moon, and stars were deities. There were sky, earth, and water deities. There were deities of light and darkness, rivers and vegetation, animals and fertility. In addition, kings, heroes, and pharaohs were often regarded as sons of deities, or at least as special mediators between the divine and human spheres.

In the Priestly account idols are smashed on each day of creation. On the first day the deities of light and darkness are dismissed. On the second day, the deities of sky and sea. On the third day, earth deities and deities of vegetation. On the fourth day, sun, moon, and star deities. On the fifth and sixth day divinity is disassociated from the animal kingdom. "And finally human existence, too, is emptied of any intrinsic divinity—while at the same time *all* human beings, from the greatest to the least, and not just pharaohs, kings and heroes, are granted a divine likeness and mediation" (Hyers 1982, 826).

The myths in Genesis 1 and 2 present different versions of God's creative activity. In both symbolic accounts the one and only God makes everything: the heavens, planets, water, land, birds, sea creatures, and animals. In Genesis 1 the all-good, all-wise, and all-powerful God is totally **transcendent**. He is distinct from the created world and is absolutely different from all he has created. He is in no way controlled by the limitations of time and space. The transcendent God creates effortlessly—by his word. Creating by a simple word is a symbol pointing to the plan God had in mind in creating a harmonious cosmos. (The word *cosmos* means order whereas the word *chaos* means disorder.) God is so sovereign and so **holy** (different in being and in moral behavior) that all deities of all other nations were mere idols which can neither hurt nor help anyone.

The author of Genesis 2, on the other hand, uses many **anthropomorphisms** (attributions of human characteristics to things, animals, and deities). The Lord God is a potter who molds Adam from clay, a plastic surgeon who sculpts Eve from one of Adam's ribs, and a gardener who plants a lavish garden (oasis). The Yahwist myth is not concerned with the amount of time required for creation. On the other hand, the Priestly myth, says John Dominic Crossan, is "a very powerful message about the Sabbath. Even God creating the world had to get the divine work completed by Friday sunset. He couldn't begin on Wednesday and just go straight through" (see Gibeau 1994, 7; Ex. 20:11).

Modern Interpretations of the Creation Myths

The creation myths have often been interpreted in a precritical way. Those with this approach are called **creationists** or **scientific creationists**. They cite scientific data to support the premise of a divine creation. They claim that their views are different—but still scientific—interpretations of the fossils and other evidence on which the evolution theory is based. For creationists, the earth is relatively young (less than 10,000 years) and its geological formation was caused by a catastrophic worldwide flood that occurred between 7,000 to 5,000 years ago. They say the universe was formed in six days some 6,000 years ago. God created plants and animals according to their own original, separate, and distinct kind or species. The dinosaurs lived with Adam and Eve and drowned in the flood. Humans are not related to monkeys, chimpanzees or any other animals.

Advocates of the historical-critical method have three criticisms of creationism. First, they declare that creationists fail to understand that the Genesis narratives are myths, and not empirical science or recorded history. The myths are religious interpretations, divinely inspired in a prescientific age. They celebrate the creation of this marvelous world by the one true God. As such, they do not offer a particular cosmological picture that may then be placed in contention with existing or subsequent physical pictures of the cosmos. Second, they indicate that the creationists reject the massive scientific evidence about the lengthy evolution of the world. Many modern geologists, astronomers, and biologists report that the universe was created some 20 billion years ago, the earth some 4.5 billion years ago, and animals and plants some 3.5 billion years ago. The scientific creationists preclude any sort of evolutionary development of the earth, plants, and animals. For them, creation is an event at the beginning of time rather than a process over time. Modern geologists, on the other hand, view creation as a process because they "are convinced that 99 percent of all plant and animal species that have ever inhabited the earth are no longer present" (Peters 1995, 17). Third, advocates of the historical-critical method are disturbed because creationists assume that all evolutionists are necessarily atheists and secular humanists. Not all are—as will be explained below. But some are and they have significantly influenced the way many people understand the origin and nature of the created world. Their position is labeled **scientific naturalism** (Hyers 1985, 412). A prominent advocate of this methodology is Dr. Carl Sagan.

Dr. Sagan, a gifted professor of astronomy and space sciences at Cornell University, published *Cosmos* in 1980. It soon became a bestseller, and he became a celebrity when he explained his book for thirteen weeks on television. It is estimated that each weekly show was watched by more than ten million people. Sagan was so popular that his picture made the cover of *Time,* October 20, 1980, with the title "Showman of Science."

In his book Sagan explored the immensity, variety, and aliveness of the universe. But he denied that there is a Mind or Designer behind it. The opening sentence of his book states: "The Cosmos is all that there is or ever was or ever will be" (Sagan 1980, 4). The evolution of the universe was a great big accident: one day "quite by accident, a molecule arose that was able to make crude copies of itself" (ibid., 30). All of our "intelligent activities are reducible to the electro-chemical activity of the brain" (ibid., 276). With our brains we can recognize the laws and patterns of nature which are always and everywhere the same. Sagan acknowledges that there is a fascinating design in created things but he rejects the existence of a Designer. Things evolve through natural selection.

In chapter ten of his book, Sagan has a long explanation of the theory of curved space provided by Albert Einstein (1878–1955). This theory posited a fourth dimension to reality beyond the length, breadth, and depth we immediately experience. William O'Malley, a Jesuit religious educator, commented on Sagan's book and his failure to acknowledge the transcendent dimension of humankind (O'Malley 1981, 98; see also Frost 1982).

If he can conceive of a fourth dimension to our reality, can he not also allow the possibility of a fifth—where the laws of physics do not apply and where space and time have no meaning? It would be a dimension we are in now, thoroughly penetrated by it yet as unaware of it as we are of the neutrinos that are knifing through us every instant—as if we weren't even here. We get intimations of this fifth nonphysical dimension—in moments of ecstasy, awe, joy, prayer—when we are "taken out of ourselves," as Paul says (again inadequately) into "the Seventh Heaven." All trustworthy receivers need not be metallic to be trustworthy. They need not be restricted even to the two lobes of the brain. The receiver of messages from the transcendent dimension is that presence within us which we have always called the human spirit. Science cannot dissect that receiver because it is not itself subject to space and time. It is the infection of God in us.

In addition to scientific creationism and scientific naturalism, there is a third interpretation of the creation myths: **theological evolutionism**. The advocates of this theory propose that evolution is God's method of creation. They hold that God created a world in which the development of plants and animals was the result of natural selection, a process in which random mutation in the offspring of the species enabled some to adapt themselves to their environments more readily than others, thereby surviving in greater numbers and passing on to their offspring their invaluable assets. Charles Darwin (1809–82), English naturalist and author of *Origin of Species* in 1859, popularized these evolutionary theories. Until the discoveries of Darwin, people regarded the plant and animal worlds as one large happy family crafted by God during the six days of creation. In contrast to this vision of a peaceable kingdom of flawless specimens, Darwin's evolutionary view pitted the species against each other, each competing furiously for the limited resources available, either becoming extinct when they failed to adapt or overpopulating when they adapted all too well. Darwin did not publish his findings in order to debunk the Bible. On the contrary, he was a

Christian who was deemed worthy of burial in Westminster Abbey, a national shrine (Phipps 1983).

In the United States the debate between the creationists and evolutionists has gone on for years, actually reaching the Supreme Court in 1968 and several times after that. In 1987 some school districts in Louisiana demanded that where the theory of evolution is taught, creation science must also be taught and given "equal time." The Supreme Court declared by a 7–2 vote on June 19, 1987, that this position was unconstitutional because it required the teaching of a religious belief, not a scientific theory (Kamen 1987). That decision of the Supreme Court has not ended the debate. It is reported that there is ample evidence that the agenda of the creationists is an increasingly important factor in all levels of public education. It is said that "an era of suppression [of empirical investigation into the history of geology and life] has entered into public education in this country" (Peters 1995).

Jesus Christ and Creation

The Christian scriptures make frequent references to God the Creator. However, they put the creation within a Christian perspective, that is, they declare that creation took place through and for the Word of God. In both Genesis myths humans are the crown of creation and the other creatures are made for them. Christianity proclaims that humans—and all creation—are created in anticipation of Jesus Christ. If creation takes place in relation to Jesus Christ, then we have to ask about the preexistence of the Word of God. The theology of Jesus' preexistence takes several forms in the scriptures.

First, there are passages where Jesus was present in Jewish history. John's gospel reports that Abraham rejoiced to see Jesus' day (Jn. 8:39–59) and Paul said Christ was with the Israelites in the desert with Moses (1 Cor. 10:1–5). Second, Jesus is identified as the Word spoken by God before the act of creation. John's gospel (1:2–3) states that the Word of God "was in the beginning with God. All things came to be through him, and without him nothing came to be." Third, there are many passages which declare that Jesus is the one through whom all things were created. Paul taught that there is "one Lord, Jesus Christ, through whom all things are and through whom we exist" (1 Cor. 8:6). He later added that "The Spirit itself bears witness with our spirit that we are children of God, and if children, then heirs, heirs of God and joint heirs with Christ" (Rom. 8:16–17). The author of Hebrews states that God spoke to us through his Son whom "he made heir of all things and through whom he created the universe" (1:2). The author of Colossians declares that all things were created through and for the Son: "He is before all things, and in him all things hold together" (1:17). Ephesians 1:3–4 proclaims that the Father of Jesus Christ "blessed us in Christ with every spiritual blessing in the heavenly places, even as he chose us in him before the foundation of the world, that we should be holy and blameless before him."

None of the above texts declare precisely that the Son existed from all eternity with God the Father. That theology was not officially expressed until the Council of Nicea in 325 and the Nicene Creed, which was given its final form at the Council of Constantinople in 381. This creed states that the Son is "eternally begotten of the Father, God from God, Light from Light, true God from true God." Nevertheless, many Christians interpret the preexistence of the Son to mean that Jesus of Nazareth, the Jewish craftsman and prophet whose mother and father were Mary and Joseph, existed eternally in heaven with God and waited patiently for history to take its course until it was his time to enter human history. Part of the reason for this interpretation is that the gospel of John clearly points in this direction. It explicitly speaks of the preexistence of Jesus at creation. It declares that Jesus had glory with his Father before the world began. He came down from heaven to reveal to people what he had seen and heard when he was with the Father (see Jn. 7:29; 8:14–18; 10:15; 14:9, 20; 16:27; 17:5). But scripture scholars using the historical-critical method insist that these texts must be understood as they were understood by the Johannine church. The authors made these statements while taking it for granted that Jesus was fully human. If Jesus of Nazareth is fully human and like us in all things except sin (Heb. 4:15), then his humanity had no existence until he came forth from his mother's womb. What these passages are referring to is the "pre-existent divinity of

Jesus" (Brown 1984, 112). The sacred writers underscore the preexistence of Jesus because they were in heated debate with "the Jews" (Jn. 16:8–9) and others who denied the divinity of Jesus. The sacred writers were underlining the divine wisdom, power, and being of Jesus that the first Christians experienced at the resurrection. The resurrected Jesus is the Word of God who is co-eternal with the Father. At Vatican II the Catholic bishops reiterated this theology in the *Constitution on the Church in the Modern World:* "Before he became flesh in order to save all things and to sum them up in himself, 'He was in the world' already as 'the true light that enlightens every man' (Jn. 1:9–10)" (n. 57).

Human Care of the World

Over the course of Christian history there have been negative and positive interpretations of the creation of the world that have influenced the understanding of Christian humanism.

A refrain in Genesis 1 is that everything God created was good (see 1:10, 12, 17, 21, 25, 31). In the early church it was the Gnostics who maintained that the created world was evil. Their theories were rooted in their interpretation of Plato (427–347 B.C.), one of the major philosophers in human history. Plato made a sharp distinction between the eternal world and this physical world. The former is eternal, unchangeable, and knowable; the latter is temporal, changing, and known only imperfectly and tentatively since it is a mere copy of the eternal world. This material, physical world is the creation of some inferior deity and not of the supreme God, the God of light and goodness.

The Gnostics hated the material world but they were not simplistic. They envisaged themselves as characters deeply involved in a cosmic drama that went beyond the physical world of appearances. They believed that proper knowledge of ultimate reality would enable them to escape this material world of deceit and apparent reality, and return to the eternal and really real sphere from which they had originally come.

The church condemned the Gnostics for several reasons: they were polytheistic, declared the material world evil, denied the incarnation of the Word of God, devalued human history—the story of the interactions between God and humans—and attributed salvation to secret knowledge rather than to the death and resurrection of Jesus Christ. At the ecumenical Council of Constantinople in 381, the church approved the final form of the Nicene Creed. It opens with this sentence: "We believe in one God the Father all-sovereign, maker of heaven and earth, and of all things visible and invisible."

Over the course of Christian history, God's creation and material things have been acknowledged and celebrated as great blessings. Perhaps the most famous teacher of the goodness and beauty of creation is the saintly Francis of Assisi (1181–1226), whom Pope John Paul II designated the patron of ecology. Francis composed a *Canticle of the Sun* in which he declared that the sun and moon, earth and air, fire and water, all animals and plants, his own body, and even death itself to be his brothers and sisters. There is a famous legend that Francis preached to birds and wolves, reminding them that all created things are united as God's creatures in the depths of their being. In other words, all things and persons are finite creatures who never asked for existence but were given it by a gracious and loving God. All of creation is dependent on the gracious will of God. Indeed, "he is not far from any one of us. For 'In him we live and move and have our being'" (Acts 17:27–28).

The most famous twentieth-century advocate of the goodness, beauty, and unity of the world all around us and within us is Pierre Teilhard de Chardin (1881–1955). Teilhard was a Jesuit priest, author, and world-famous **paleontologist** (the science of ancient life forms, based upon the study of fossils and their evolutionary development). He was born in France into a wholesome family of eleven children on May 1, 1881, and died of a heart seizure on Easter Sunday, April 10, 1955, in his Jesuit community in New York City, where he had resided since 1951. During his very active and productive life, he studied in England and Paris, was ordained a priest on August 24, 1911, served for several years as a stretcher bearer during World War I, taught physics and chemistry in a high school in Cairo, Egypt, and did scientific research in Burma and China. In China he was part of the famous discovery in 1928 of the Peking Man, a fossil some 1.5 million years old. This discovery was an important contribution to the search for the time and place of human origins.

Catholic spirituality during the time of Teilhard emphasized a series of dualisms: this world and the next, spirit and matter, science and religion, and God and humans. Teilhard rejected these dualisms. He advocated an **evolutionary humanism** in which the whole universe is not only moving toward systems of greater complexity and higher levels of consciousness but is also coextensive with the body of the risen Christ. He insisted that theologians should give serious consideration to the physical relation between the material world and Christ who took on a cosmic existence at his resurrection. Teilhard underscored that we encounter God primarily through the created world and not through mystical prayer. He took this position partly as a result of his attempt to integrate Christian theology with the theory of the evolution of human life and the cosmos. He wrote that God shines through the universe, that since the Word of God became human the created world was now part of God, and that the risen Christ, the beginning and end of the evolutionary process, is the activating energy of the entire cosmos. Furthermore, the eucharistic presence of Christ is the symbol and concrete sign that the Word of God's assumption of matter is extended throughout the universe and, as such, constitutes the promise of its eventual complete transfiguration.

The official Catholic church found Teilhard's radical writings, such as *The Phenomenon of Man* and *The Divine Milieu,* too ambiguous. It was said that his mystical vision of Christ immersed in the world as the beginning and the end of the evolutionary process was a form of **pantheism** (the identification of God and the material world). As a result Teilhard was silenced and forbidden to publish. After his death his Jesuit friends published his scientific and spiritual writings, especially his classic on the spiritual life, *The Divine Milieu.* His writings were translated into sixteen languages and read with such great enthusiasm in the 1960s that he became something of a folk hero.

On the eve of the twenty-first century, Teilhard's vision of the inevitability of progress and the unity of all creation in Christ seems naive and too optimistic because our planet is seriously endangered by the deterioration of the environment. We are facing an ecological crisis. There are daily reports of how animals, sea creatures, soil, forests, air, and water are wantonly abused, polluted, or destroyed. For example, it was reported in 1994 that the world population of 5.7 billion people was experiencing a water shortage. What will happen by the year 2025 when the world's population is projected to grow to 8.5 billion? Those living in developed countries do not experience the shortage because they simply turn on a tap to get fresh and inexpensive water. Nonetheless, in 1994, 1.2 billion people lacked potable water. Many complicated reasons account for the shortage, but the consequences are of serious concern because they are staggering: 80 percent of all diseases in the developing countries are related to tainted water.[1]

The nations of the world have been concerned for years about the pollution and depletion of the earth's resources. The United Nations sponsored a series of international conferences on population and development. The first was in 1974 at Bucharest, Romania (136 nations attended); the second in 1984 in Mexico City, Mexico (147 nations attended); and the third in 1994 in Cairo, Egypt (170 nations attended). The 1994 conference from September 5 through 13 had as its theme "Choices and Responsibilities." The "choices" concerned issues related to the projected population growth from 5.7 billion to 8.5 billion. According to one source, 1 billion people already struggle to survive on a dollar a day, and 3 million children die each year from malnutrition (Cowell 1994). There is a disproportionate consumption of natural resources and contribution to pollution. "The richest fifth of the world controls four-fifths of its wealth, while the poorest three-fifths live on a single-digit fraction of the world's life-giving products" (Maguire 1994, 917).

The intention of the 1994 conference was to draw up a twenty-year global plan which would include steps to slow the pace of population growth, lest it outstrip the world's ability to feed and shelter all its inhabitants; to foster economic development; to promote women's equality and rights; and to increase global spending on population control and related health services.

Religious leaders are also deeply concerned about the ecological problems. For many it has become increasingly clear that ecological destruction is deeply linked with the struggle to create a just and peaceful social order. Rosemary Radford Ruether (1978, 1132) wrote: "When human beings break their covenant with society by exploiting the labor of the worker and refusing to do anything about the social costs of production—i.e., poisoned air and water—the covenant of creation is violated. Poverty, social oppression, war and violence in society, and the polluted, barren, hostile face of nature—both express this violation of the covenant."

From August 29 to September 5, 1993, the Parliament of the World's Religions assembled in Chicago. It drew 6,000 delegates and representatives of 120 religions. Present were not only representatives of the major religions, but also self-styled "neo-pagans" and goddess worshipers. The delegates agreed that unless humans are guided by an overarching global ethic, the future of the planet and the human race would be bleak (Stammer 1993). Approximately 250 religious leaders signed *Towards a Global Ethic: An Initial Declaration,* a statement which had as its principal author Hans Küng, a Swiss Catholic priest-theologian (see Küng and Kuschel, 1994). This document of five thousand words does not pretend to offer a comprehensive ethic but does offer principles to which all religions could hold themselves and others accountable.

This important document opens with these sentences:

The world is in agony. The agony is so pervasive and urgent that we are compelled to name its manifestations so that the depth of this pain may be clear. Peace eludes us . . . the planet is being destroyed . . . neighbors live in fear . . . women and men are estranged from each other . . . children die! This is abhorrent!

The document ends with this paragraph:

In conclusion, we appeal to all the inhabitants of this planet. Earth cannot be changed for the better unless the consciousness of individuals is changed. We pledge to work for such transformation in individual and collective consciousness, for the awakening of our spiritual powers through reflection, meditation, prayer or positive thinking, for a conversion of the heart. Together we can move mountains! Without a willingness to take risks and a readiness to sacrifice there can be no fundamental change in our situation! Therefore, we commit ourselves to a common global ethic, to better mutual understanding, as well as to socially beneficial, peace-fostering and Earth-friendly ways of life.

A critical or actualization interpretation of the Genesis creation myths yields two important truths about human life and our relationship to the created world. First, we are inextricably intertwined with the created world. All too often humans are so centered on themselves **(anthropocentrism)** that we tend to see ourselves as separate from nature. This perspective could be the result of a distorted interpretation of the injunction to Adam and Eve to "fill the earth and subdue it" (Gen. 1:28). But we are not separate from the material world; we are part of it, created "out of the clay of the ground" (Gen. 2:7). We are not outside nature but within it. Consequently, neither humanity nor nature is rightly seen in isolation. We cannot live without air, water, and food, which comes from the plant and animal worlds. "To consider human culture apart from the nonhuman is to invite the impoverishment of the first and the devastation of the second" (Himes and Himes 1990, 43).

On May 10, 1994, Nelson Mandela became the first black president of South Africa. With the commanding dignity that carried him through more than a half century of struggle for civil, political, and economic rights, he poetically reminded his fellow citizens in his inaugural address of the connection between humans and nature. He declared:

> To my compatriots, I have no hesitation in saying that each one of us is as intimately attached to the soil of this beautiful country as are the famous jacaranda trees of Pretoria and the mimosa trees of the bushveld. Each time one of us touches the soil of this land, we feel a sense of personal renewal. The national mood changes as the seasons change. We are moved by a sense of joy and exhilaration when the grass turns green and the flowers bloom. . . . Let freedom reign. God bless Africa![2]

Teilhard wrote about our interconnection with creation:

> The masters of the spiritual life continue to repeat that God wants only souls. To give these words their true value, we must not forget that the human soul, however independently created our philosophy imagines it to be, is inseparable, in its birth and its growth, from the universe into which it is born. In each soul, God loves and partly saves the whole world which that soul sums up in an incommunicable and particular way (Teilhard de Chardin 1960, 29).

A second critical interpretation informs us that all humans have a part in God's continuing creation. For Christians this entails two projects: using the natural resources within a just economy and bringing Christ and his mission to fulfillment. The first project will be developed in chapter 6; Teilhard de Chardin explained the second:

> We may, perhaps, imagine that the creation was finished long ago. But that would be quite wrong. It continues still more magnificently, and in the highest zones of the world. . . . And we serve to complete it, even by the humblest work of our hands. That is, ultimately, the meaning and value of our acts. Owing to the inter-relation between matter, soul and Christ, we lead part of the being which he desires back to God *in whatever we do*. With each one of our *works,* we labor—atomically, but no less really—to build the Pleroma; that is to say, we bring to Christ a little fulfillment (Teilhard de Chardin 1960, 31).

Creation of Humankind: The Adam and Eve Myth

Genesis 1:26–31; 2:1–9, 15–25; 3:1–24;
Romans 5:12–21; 1 Corinthians 15:20–28, 42–49.

In the *Enuma Elish,* after Marduk created the sky, earth, and the laws which govern all things, he created a man—but almost as an afterthought. He seized Kingu (the slow-witted and deformed companion of Tiamat), slew him, and shaped the first man by mixing the divine blood with the dust. The other deities watched in astonishment and admiration.

This symbolic account of the creation of human beings seems to have served two purposes. First, it emphasized that since the first human being had been created from the substance of a deity, humankind shared the divine nature, in however limited a way. Second, the Babylonians, realistically comprehending their human weaknesses and limitations, did not take their divine pedigree that seriously. There is some humor in the fact that humans derived from "one of the most stupid and ineffectual of the gods" (Armstrong 1993, 9).

The two biblical creation myths—Genesis 1:26–31, 2:1–3 and 2:7–8, 15–25—offer different accounts of the creation of human beings. In both of these stories, humankind is not an afterthought but the purpose and pinnacle of creation.

In Genesis 1, Adam and Eve are created at the same time and in the image of God. Created on the sixth day, they are the crown of creation. In Genesis 2, humans are again the purpose of creation. Adam is created before the rest of God's creatures. When it is clear that the animals are not fitting partners for Adam, Eve is created from Adam. They are bone of bone, flesh of flesh, female and her man (the Hebrew is *ishshah* and *ish,* respectively). In the two accounts the manner and time of the creation are different but the result is the same: men and women are equal, called to live and work together side by side. In a later chapter women are described as subordinate to men because sin has entered the picture (Gen. 3:17). The reason offered as the justification for the subordination of women is that it is the consequence of the disordering of the created world.

The first myth states the most important characteristic of humans: they are made in the image of God. What does this description mean? Some say it refers to the holiness and righteousness of God given to Adam and Eve; others say it refers to human consciousness, the ability to reason and make decisions, attributes that animals do not possess. But the Bible does not attempt to describe God in his inner being, that is, "God considered apart from the creating God" (Himes and Himes 1990, 43). The Bible never depicts God in solitude, apart from humankind and the world. God is always described in some relationship: he creates, loves, saves, and **covenants**, that is, he forms a contract or a treaty or an alliance or, in the metaphor of the Jewish scholar, Irving Greenberg, "a partnership" with humankind (Greenberg 1988, 74).

There is some truth to the notion that Adam and Eve's likeness to God is their ability to exercise rational dominion or power over the rest of creation. This dominion over the animal, vegetable, and mineral world does not (and should not) mean the subjugation of these creatures. We have already seen that humankind should not be separated from nature. We are related to it, despite the modern exaltation of the individual to the detriment of both human community and humane relationships with the nonhuman world. But, humans are also related to each other by their bodily differences, by being male and female. The differentiation of male and female does not mean the sacred authors attribute gender to God. It is another one of their ways of symbolizing that God is essentially relational. "Humanity is sexed in order that human beings may be driven into relationships with each other" (Himes and Himes 1990, 43).

For the Jews, God is essentially relational. Genesis 2 continues the theme that humans are relational beings like God. Adam is so connected to the animals—his companions—that he can name them. However, God realizes that Adam needs more companionship than the animals can provide. Since animals are not human, Adam is really alone. God said, "It is not good for man to be alone. I will make a suitable partner for him" (2:18). In Genesis 2 companionship and partnership (covenant love) are the reasons for the creation of the two sexes.

The biblical account of creation is myth. These symbolic stories are divinely inspired, religious interpretations that originated in a prescientific age. Modern science holds that humans were not created in the form in which we exist today. Humans did not come from one couple but evolved independently from many couples in Africa, Asia, and Europe. In his revolutionary book *Descent of Man* (1871), Charles Darwin applied his theory of natural selection to the human race. He argued that humans had a close kinship with other primates such as chimpanzees and apes and had perhaps evolved from some other forms of life.

Modern anthropologists and paleontologists maintain that **homo erectus** (humans in an upright posture) appeared about 1.9 million years ago. These creatures were hunter-gatherers who made stone tools and had human characteristics, that is, they had consciousness, emotions, morality, humor and spoken language. Nevertheless, all the earlier species gave way to our species, **homo sapiens** (thinking man), some 200,000 years ago. Some 20,000 years ago humans learned to farm, a skill which made them less nomadic and set up the conditions for the formation of villages, towns, cities, and nations.

The findings of modern science about the evolution of humankind are controversial. The most famous instance of the controversy is the Scopes "Monkey Trial." This trial, held in Tennessee in the summer of 1925, attracted worldwide attention. John Scopes, a biology teacher in a public school, violated a Tennessee law that forbade the teaching of evolution. Teachers were required to teach that humans developed from Adam and Eve, who were created by God. The trial was really between creationists and evolutionists. The creationists hoped for a major defeat of modernism; the evolutionists hoped to show the ignorance and irrationality of the creationists. Scopes was found guilty and fined $100. Two years later the Tennessee Supreme Court cleared Scopes on a technicality— but upheld the anti-evolution law. This law was repealed in 1967. In 1968 the United States Supreme Court declared unconstitutional all laws that required teaching religious doctrines in public schools.

The Yahwist's idyllic picture of Adam and Eve in a garden at peace with God, the nonhuman world, and themselves was soon shattered by the disobedience of Adam and Eve. Their disobedience is technically called **sin**, a word which points to the deliberate violation of a relationship, especially with God. The root meaning of the word in both Hebrew and Greek is "to miss the mark." Sin can be passive (the omission of a good deed) or active (a thought, word, or action which disrupts relations with God, others, the nonhuman world and self).

The sin of our first parents is referred to as the original sin. Actually, the Hebrew scriptures do not have a formal concept of original sin. The story of the fall of Adam and Eve is simply the first of many stories in Genesis 4 to 11 which describe how sin picked up momentum, spread everywhere, and caused terrible suffering, destruction, and death. The rest of the Hebrew scriptures relate the history of God with his people and the whole human community, and his unending attempts to help humans turn from sin and the death it brings.

Interpretations of Original and Personal Sin

The Christian scriptures continue the history of God's involvement in human affairs, especially those of his chosen people. But now the history is focused on Jesus of Nazareth and his church, "the Israel of God" (Gal. 6:16). The inspired authors reflect on the place of Jesus Christ in the whole history of sin and salvation. Many references are made to Adam. Luke's genealogy of Jesus' ancestors traces Jesus back to Adam. Jesus is a true member of the entire human race and has universal significance.

Paul, especially in Romans 5:12–21 and 1 Corinthians 15:20–28, 42–49, contrasts Christ with Adam. We bear the image of Adam, a man of dust, and shall also bear the image of the man of heaven, Jesus. Jesus is "the last Adam" (1 Cor. 15:45), the one who initiates a new creation with his resurrection. The first Adam brought sin and death into the world when he tried to achieve God-like status (Gen. 3:5); the last Adam brought wholeness (justification) and life to himself and the whole human race through his obedience even unto death on a cross (Phil. 2:8).

Paul never explains *how* we are affected by the sin of Adam and Eve without any personal decision. He simply states *that* it is so, based on the fact that death is universal. Because we all die, we are implicated in sin, since death is the effect of sin. By his death and resurrection, Jesus triumphed over sin and inaugurated a new creation (2 Cor. 5:17). The sign of the first covenant is male circumcision (Acts 7:8); the sign of the second covenant is baptism (Mk. 1:8), which is administered the same way to persons of both genders. Baptism, especially when the ceremony involves immersion of the whole person in the water, is a symbol of entrance into the death and resurrection of Jesus (Rom. 6:3) and dying to a life of sin. Baptism is an initiation rite. It is a sign of a person's commitment to Christ and an instrument of becoming one with him and his Holy Spirit. Baptism does not "take away" or "wash away" original sin. Would that it did! **Original sin** is the alienation from God experienced by all human beings. We can be alienated from God because we are alienated from ourselves. Original sin denotes our "loss of a center, diffuseness of personality, lack of a sense of self leading one to drift or to take direction unthinkingly from others" (E. Johnson 1992, 102). Like the apostle Paul, the Christian says: "For I do not do the good I want, but I do the evil I do not want. Now if [I] do what I do not want, it is no longer I who do it, but sin that dwells in me. So, then, I discover the principle that when I want to do right, evil is at hand. For I take delight in the law of God, in my inner self, but I see in my members another principle at war with the law of my mind, taking me captive to the law of sin that dwells in my members" (Rom. 7:19–22). During life Christians constantly struggle to maintain their commitment to Christ as they face choices between good and evil deeds. Baptism reminds Christians that they can achieve the final victory through Christ and his holy Spirit (Rom. 8:1–17).

Because sin is so pervasive, it is often said that "To sin is human." Some take this literally. "In one way or another, the various schools of Gnosticism depicted man as the victim and slave of forces over which he had no control, and therefore they diagnosed sin as inevitable" (Pelikan 1971, 1:283). Today those who connect sin with human nature probably mean that, since humans are weak and have strong desires for material, sensual, or psychological satisfaction, they cannot always hit the mark. However, to take the sentence literally creates some serious problems about both the nature of God and humankind. If the sentence means that sin is natural, is part of human nature, then God is the cause of sin, and humans are not completely responsible for the evil they do to themselves and others.

It is more accurate to say that humans are free to act in a human or a subhuman way. An action is human when it is moral and good (for example, telling the truth, assisting the sick and needy, caring for children, teaching the truth). An action is subhuman when it fails to respond properly to a relationship. To cheat, lie, steal, or kill is to deny or destroy the rights, dignity, and life of another human. To use God's name with disrespect or not to pray are failures to give honor and glory to the sovereign God. To abuse nature or animals is to fail at our stewardship role. Subhuman actions are immoral and sinful. To sin is to steal and/or withhold life from God, another person, a nonhuman creature, or oneself. Only humans can sin. Animals never sin. But the fact that humans do sin does not make sin an essential part of being human or even a human act. Sin is a technical term that denotes *subhuman* conduct. The more we sin the less human we become. Jesus is the perfect human precisely because he never sinned (Heb. 4:15).

The Christian churches are deeply divided over their interpretation of human sinfulness. Catholics teach that all humans are basically good and never lose their identity as creatures made in the image of God. The original sin was not inevitable. All descendants of Adam and Eve are damaged and bruised by original sin and their own enactments of subhuman actions. Our minds and wills are limited, not because of sin, but primarily because of our creaturehood. As finite creatures, humans always need God's grace to think and to decide properly. Because of sin, we do not need grace more, but *for more*. Now we need the forgiveness, healing, and strength that can only come from God. Humans are like apples that fall to the ground and get bruised. Bruised apples are still edible.

Martin Luther (1483–1546), the originator of Protestantism, taught that humans are basically corrupt. Jaroslav Pelikan (1971, 1:279) called Luther "one of the most eloquent interpreters of the inevitability of sin." Christians may get baptized, Luther said, but this ritual simply indicates that God has declared them to be just. In actuality, they remain sinners. Influenced by Augustine of Hippo, Luther maintained that the Fall had so compromised human nature that sinfulness is a condition which holds the human reason and will in bondage. Because of our sinful condition, the mind can only produce false conceptions of God and our relationship to him. When we use our reason alone (that is, without faith) to understand God, reason, said Luther, acts as "the devil's whore." Humans need divine revelation. Also, due to our sinfulness, we can only will evil. We cannot even will to do good. No human act is truly good. That is why good works are ineffective in trying to get sinners right with God. Luther quoted the words of Jesus, "Without me you can do nothing" (Jn. 15:5), to prove that free will in relation to God was a delusion (Pelikan 1989, 5:43). According to Luther, humans are like an apple that falls to the ground: cut off from its source of life, it not only gets bruised but becomes rotten to the core. Rotten apples are not food.

The teachings of John Calvin (1509–64) about human sinfulness are even more radical. Calvin was born a Catholic in Noyon, France. His father was a lawyer and a secretary to the bishop. Calvin studied for a career in law, earning his degree in 1532. In 1533 he had a major religious experience of the glory and sovereignty of God and the sinfulness of humankind. He imagined an infinite gulf between the all-holy Creator and his totally sinful creatures. This theme pervades his theology. For example, Luther did not want to destroy church statues and paintings but merely to forbid worship of them. Calvin, on the other hand, did not dismiss images and ceremonies as harmless externals but saw them as blatant evidence of crass superstition that was a consequence of our lack of knowledge of the true God. Hence, he felt compelled to reject all images and likenesses of God.

As a result of his religious experience in 1533, Calvin felt called by God to restore the church to its original purity and holiness. He taught that a true Christian life consisted in knowledge of the sovereign will of God and obedient submission to it by fulfilling the divine commandments.

In 1534 he withdrew from Catholicism and turned to Protestantism. He preached reform in France but his efforts were soon cut short when he and other reformers were persecuted. He was forced to flee to Switzerland in 1535. There in 1536, he wrote the first edition of the *Institutes of the Christian Religion*. This book brought Protestant theology to a very large group of people. By 1559 Calvin had expanded the *Institutes* into a four-volume work that remains one of the great systematic theologies in Christian history. Calvin became the most influential figure in shaping the character of the Reformed tradition in Switzerland, France, Holland, Scotland, England, and the American colonies.

Calvin became pastor of the Protestant church in Strasbourg, France, from 1539 to 1541. In 1541 he moved to

Geneva where he lived until his death in 1564. In Geneva the people had pledged "to live according to the law of the gospel and the Word of God and to abolish all papal abuses."

Calvin's theology has many distinctive traits, but one that is central is his teaching on the total depravity of humans. He believed that because of the fall of Adam and Eve, humans are totally bound to sin. The divine image, which consisted in holiness and righteousness, was lost at that time (Pelikan 1989, 5:204). As a result humans can only perform sinful acts. God's irresistible grace is the only source of good deeds.

Today the theologies of Luther and Calvin may not be so strongly drawn as they were in the sixteenth century. But some of the consequences of their theologies remain. For example, Catholics underscore that all things and persons are gifts from God and can be **sacraments** (signs and instruments) of his love, presence, or judgment. Catholics enjoy such things as wine, dancing, and gambling. Proper use is good; abuse is wrong. Many Protestant groups, on the other hand, prohibit alcohol, dancing, and gambling because they can lead to sin. For example, Baylor University, founded in 1845 as the first college in Texas and presently the largest Baptist university in the world, lifted its ban on dancing in early 1996. The ruling by the president came after years of surveys and votes, and months of preparation by a thirty-member commit-tee of students, professors, and alumni. Many students favored the lifting of the dancing ban, but one Baptist pastor declared that the university "has been on the slippery slope for some time, and this is just one more slip. Wherever modern dancing is, there is alcohol and promiscuousness" (Meyerson 1996).

Kinds of Humanism

If the Christian churches are divided about how close to God humans are, they are united against those who exalt humanity to the point where there is not room for God, and, as a conse-quence, say religion is an illusion based on wishful thinking for an afterlife that gets in the way of achieving a fulfilling life now.

The name for the philosophy or system of thought that takes human development seriously is **humanism**. Since the Greek philosopher Protagoras (490–421 B.C.) taught that "Man is the measure of all things," there have been humanistic movements. Most humanist movements have been religious. For example, the Stoics, founded by Zeno around 300 B.C., taught that, while all reality is material, it has been shaped by God. They maintained that there exists an eternal and unchangeable moral natural law whose author and interpreter is God. This law issues from within reality itself. Its purpose is to direct humans and other creatures to their true end. If humans would live harmoniously with nature and thus achieve freedom, they must put aside indulgence in pleasure, passion, and unjust thoughts.

The Renaissance was based on the principles found in the classical humanism of the Greco-Roman culture. Scholars like Petrarch (1304-74), Erasmus (1466-1536), and the saintly Thomas More (1478-1535) advocated a curriculum of studies that stressed rhetoric, history, poetry, the arts, and ethics as a reaction to the heady metaphysical refinements of medieval scholasticism. The ideal of the Renaissance was for humans to control the natural world and to create a perfect society of free and educated humans.

The humanism of the eighteenth-century Enlightenment built on the gains of the Renaissance. For example, the English poet and satirist Alexander Pope (1688–1744) became rich through his popular translations of Homer's *Iliad* and *Odyssey*. He wrote that humans should not presume to know God because "The proper study of mankind is man." The Enlightenment is considered one of history's great moments of human progress and liberation. Underscoring human autonomy and freedom, it asserted that human reason must be emancipated from past views of philosophy, authority, science and tradition. The faith of the Enlightenment was a faith that believed it had transcended the need for faith. Many Enlightenment thinkers were decidedly anti-Christian.

The anti-religious and anti-Christian humanism that has been carried over into the twentieth century is often labelled **secular humanism**. It has been given concrete, public expression in the United States on several occasions. In 1933 Roy Wood Sellars, professor of philosophy at the University of Michigan, issued *A Humanist Manifesto*. His statement was endorsed by thirty-four American intellectuals and educators, of whom the educator and philosopher John Dewey (1859–1952) was by far the most famous. The document's fifteen short articles were variations on the proposition that the established religions should be replaced by a humanism that regards "the universe as self-existing and not created." Secular humanists regard human life as noble and precious in itself. Nonetheless, it ends irrevocably with death.

In 1973, a *Humanist Manifesto II* updated the 1933 document and secured one hundred twenty signers, most of them philosophers, scientists, and social scientists. This document was drafted by Paul Kurtz, professor of philosophy at the State University of New York at Buffalo. The manifesto touched upon more topics than the earlier declaration but had the same unifying theme: "No deity will save us, we must save ourselves."

In 1980, Paul Kurtz drafted another document, *A Secular Humanist Declaration*. Among the fifty-eight signees were the prolific author Isaac Asimov (1920–92), the Noble Prize-winning biologist Francis Crick (1916—), and the Harvard University psychiatrist and leading exponent of behaviorism B. F. Skinner (1904–90). Most Americans would probably subscribe to most of the ten statements listed in this declaration. The humanists declared that they favored free inquiry, moral education, respect for reason, separation of church and state, political freedom, the use of intelligence to make ethical judgments, and the cultivation of science and technology. Religious groups objected to three of their principles. First, "Secular humanism places trust in human intelligence rather than in divine guidance." Second, "The scientific method, though imperfect, is still the most reliable way of understanding the world." Third, they advocated an ethic or way of life based solely on human experience and imbued with compassion for one's fellow human beings that calls for commitment to the betterment of humanity through the methods of science, reason, and democracy. For followers of Christ, on the contrary, morality is primarily a free response to the invitation of a loving and saving God to be, think, and act like Jesus Christ.

At Vatican II the Catholic church addressed secular humanism—or what the bishops called a "new humanism" (n. 7)—in the *Constitution on the Church in the Modern World,* a document written "to all men in order to illuminate the mystery of man and to cooperate in finding the solution to the outstanding problems of our time" (n. 10).

The bishops observed that the new humanism has a positive dimension. Around the whole world "an ever-increasing number of men and women are conscious that they themselves are . the artisans and the authors of the culture of their community" (n. 55). The result is that today the term "new humanism" denotes everyone's responsibility for the well-being of every person and for giving a positive direction to history. On the negative side, the bishops noted that this new humanism "is merely earth-bound, and even contrary to religion itself" (n. 56). The result is that today "many look forward to a genuine and total emancipation of humanity wrought solely by human effort" (n. 10). Today, "Unlike in former days, the denial of God or of religion, or the abandonment of them, are no longer unusual and individual occurrences. For today it is not rare for such decisions to be presented as requirements of scientific progress or of a certain new humanism. . . . As a consequence, many people are shaken" (n. 7).

There is a **Christian humanism**. It is grounded in God's creation, the incarnation of the Word of God in the person of Jesus of Nazareth, the redemption of the human family through the death and resurrection of Jesus Christ, and the abiding presence of the Spirit. Christian humanism maintains that everything human has value and should be developed, though subordinated to God. Christians maintain that every person must be treated with dignity because everyone is created in the image of God's Son and has the gift of the Spirit. Jesus taught that God's care for his creatures is such that sparrows do not escape the notice of his Father. As for humans, "Even the hairs of your head have all been counted. Do not be afraid. You are worth more than many sparrows" (Lk. 12:7).

The biblical accounts of the creation of humans can be read in a precritical way. Read literally, there was no evolution and no polygenism. The historical-critical reading of the creation myths highlights the dignity of humans (made in God's image) and their destiny (to be in partnership with God and one another). A critical reading directs readers to interpret their own self-understanding. In a world marked by both order and chaos, we often ask if our lives are ultimately immersed in order or chaos. The creation myth informs us that ultimately there is order and not chaos. Before God created the universe there was chaos: "the earth was a formless wasteland, and darkness covered the abyss, while a mighty wind swept over the waters" (Gen. 1:2). God created the cosmos (order) out of chaos. It is sin that recreates chaos. To counteract sin, God is faithfully active in history, enabling and requiring humans to live an orderly, human life. Jesus said his ministry was not to the just but to sinners (Mt. 9:13), and he is pictured so frequently at meals with the so-called sinners of his times that he was denounced as "a glutton and a drunkard, a friend of tax collectors and sinners" (Mt. 11:19). Jesus directs all sinners to his loving Father, who forgives all sins. The gospel of Matthew, however, contains two disturbing statements. The first text says all sins will be forgiven except "the blasphemy against the Spirit" (12:31). Some modern biblical commentaries say this very puzzling phrase consists in attributing to a demonic spirit what is the work of the Holy Spirit. Some theologians suggest that the sole unforgivable sin could be a narcissism so imbedded in the human heart that it refused to admit that one had committed evil deeds. This kind of insensitivity to evil might be impregnable to the Spirit's movement (O'Malley 1994, 9). Many commentators favor the interpretation of Augustine: the unforgivable sin is that hardness of heart which refuses forgiveness to the end (Mahoney 1990, 3). The second text indicates that the Father's forgiveness will not extend to the one who does not forgive "his brother from his heart" (18:35). Perhaps these two texts are a variation on the theme of forgiveness found in Matthew's Our Father: "and forgive us our debts as we forgive our debtors" (9:12). The gospels make clear that Jesus offered forgiveness aplenty and "the *only* requisite—in the moral practice of Jesus—was admitting one's need of forgiveness" (O'Malley 1994, 9).

Christian humanists affirm the secular humanists' noble goals of order and human development, but transfigure these goals in two important ways. First, Christians insist they are incapable of achieving order and development without the Holy Spirit. Paul taught the Galatians (5:22–23, 25–26) that the virtues we need to live with one another in a human way are gifts from the Spirit. The fruit of the Spirit, he taught, "is love, joy, peace, patience, kindness, generosity, faithfulness, gentleness, self-control . . . If we live in the Spirit, let us also follow the Spirit. Let us not be conceited, provoking one another, envious of one another." Second, Christians believe that human development in freedom and dignity will reach a gracious fulfillment. Secular humanists, however, continue the ever-painful death and rebirth experience of personality but without hope. They strive to transcend their present limitations to become more fully what they are capable of being, but hold that the whole process is ultimately defeated by death. When all is said and done, there is actually no purpose to their efforts at personal growth and enrichment.

For secular humanists life is but a brief period of time between two oblivions. For Christians, on the contrary, death is not absurd. It is the door to eternal life, when God brings everything to fulfillment. Christians continue, firmly and steadfastly, the ever-painful death and rebirth experience, remaining "fully devoted to the work of the Lord, knowing that in the Lord [their] labor is not in vain" (1 Cor. 15:58).

2

The Story of Israel

Abraham and Sarah: Progenitors of Israel

Genesis 11:27–32; 12, 13, 15, 17, 22; Hebrews 11:17–22, 12:1–13.

The history of Judaism begins with Abraham and Sarah. Their story is found in Genesis 11 to 25. Abram, or Abraham (which means "my divine father is exalted"), and Sarai, or Sarah (which means "princess"), lived around 1850 B.C. They were selected by God to be the parents of a nation he had chosen for a special task in his providential plan. Abraham was born in Ur, a Sumerian city. Sumer consisted of a dozen small cities united by language, custom, and religion. Sumer is considered the cradle of civilization because it is here that cities, art, and written history emerged around 3100 B.C. The human race is indebted to the Sumerians "not only for the inventions of the wheel, the potter's wheel, the chariot and the oldest system of calculation (for temple finances and the establishment of a divine order in the cosmic system), but above all for the invention of writing" (Küng 1992, 4).

At the historical level the Genesis chapters narrate the story of the nomadic life of Abraham and Sarah in search of safe and rich grazing lands for their livestock, mostly goats. They moved from Ur to Haran, to Canaan, then to Egypt, and back to Canaan. They purchased land at Hebron where they finally settled. Here they died and were buried. Today their burial place in the city of Hebron is called the Cave of the Patriarchs and is sacred to both Jews and Muslims.

At the theological level these symbolic stories tell of the birth of a people to whom God made promises. The stories describe their successes and failures in relating to God's everlasting covenant (Gen. 17:7).

Judaism is a monotheistic religion. How monotheistic Abraham was is not certain. "There is evidence that his tribe also venerated ancestral images" (Smart 1984, 285). He was probably a **henotheist,** "someone who presupposes the existence of a number of gods but who accepted only the one God, his God, as the supreme and binding authority" (Küng 1992, 9). The experts believe that earlier accounts of Abraham's faith may have been edited and reshaped to demonstrate that monotheism went back to the earliest times. But the biblical account of the Jews makes clear that monotheism was achieved after years of controversy and struggle. Moses and the classical prophets argued against polytheism. Once in Canaan the Jews shared many of the polytheistic beliefs of their neighbors. At any rate, according to the edited Genesis account, Abraham had many **theophanies** (manifestations of God). Because of these profound religious experiences, he became convinced that God the Most High (Gen. 14:19; the Hebrew is *El-Elyon*) is the one and only God. He converted from polytheism to monotheism, from deities immersed in all things, especially the stars, to a God who is transcendent, that is, totally free from the limitations of space and time. He became convinced that the Most High God is the one true God and "is not a tribal god . . . is not the divinization of a ruler or some natural force (like the sun), but a God who *invites to an encounter in history"* (Hebblethwaite 1994a, 16). Abraham bound himself to follow the way of God, that is, to practice justice and righteousness (Gen. 18:19). Genesis contains stories of Abraham's generosity (13:8–11), his hospitality to strangers (18:1–5), and sense of justice (18:23–33).

The generic name for God among the **Semites** (the people of the eastern Mediterranean area) was *El.* This name was frequently used in various combinations by the first Israelites. In addition to El Elyon, God is called *El Olam* (God Everlasting), and *El-Shaddai* (God of the Mountain or God the Almighty)

(Gen. 17:1; 35:11; Ex. 6:3). God the Almighty, the God of Abraham and Sarah, promised three things: Sarah would bear a son and from this child would develop a great nation; all the communities of the earth would be blessed through their nation (Gen. 12:3) that would equal in number the countless stars (Gen. 15:5); and they should leave their country for a new homeland that would be shown them (Gen. 17:1–8). The sign of the covenant was the circumcision of males on the eighth day after birth (17:11–12).

God's promise of a son was at once confusing, awesome, and even humorous. Abraham laughed and wanted to know how he and Sarah could have a child since they had reached an age when that was physically impossible: he was 100 and she was 90 (Gen. 17:17). Nevertheless, they had faith in God and when the child was born they named him Isaac, which means "laughter." When Isaac was a young boy, they had another test: God commanded that the boy be sacrificed. In faith Abraham set out to obey, but God intervened, providing a ram in place of Isaac (Gen. 22:13).

The Abraham and Sarah story is often read in a precritical way. Proponents of the historical-critical method reject this approach for several reasons. For one thing, scholars judge that by the time of the Yahwist source around 950 B.C., the many traditions of early tribal heroes and cult legends had been "fairly well harmonized into the story of a single family bound together by the relation of father and son: Abraham, Isaac, Jacob, Joseph. The Yahwist, however, was primarily responsible for giving to the patriarchal period a unity that did not exactly exist at that time" (Anderson 1975, 219). Moreover, the symbolic stories have a theological purpose. The miraculous birth of Isaac underscores the extraordinary means God took to fulfill his promise that they would have a great progeny when the promise seemed incredible. The sacrifice of Isaac represents the belief of the Jews that God accepts animal sacrifice but rejects human sacrifice. The Ammonites and Phoenicians worshipped their deity Moloch (or Molech) by sacrificing children by burning (Lev. 18:21; 1 Kgs 11:7; Acts 7: 42–43). Above all, the Abraham stories teach that the most fitting response to God and his covenant is faith.

Abraham in the Christian Scriptures

Abraham is mentioned more than 70 times in the Christian scriptures. In Matthew's genealogy of Jesus' ancestors, he traces Jesus back to Abraham (Mt. 1:1) to symbolically communicate that Jesus is both a member of the Jewish people and the fulfillment of God's promises to Abraham. During his ministry, Jesus challenged his listeners who boasted that they were descendants of Abraham to "do what Abraham did" (Jn. 8:39), that is, to believe. Throughout his gospel the Johannine author highlights Jesus' divinity. Jesus said, "Your father Abraham rejoiced that he was to see my day. He saw it and was glad" (Jn. 8:56). When the audience balked, Jesus said, "Amen, Amen, I say to you, before Abraham came to be I AM" (Jn. 8:58). I AM is the majestic designation of divinity.

The early Christians replaced circumcision with baptism, in part because circumcision is an ethnic symbol, whereas cleansing in water is a universal symbol. Furthermore, Jesus was baptized in all four gospels and even performed baptisms (Jn. 3:22). Paul argued that true circumcision is not in the flesh but in the heart. "Rather . . . circumcision is of the heart, in the spirit, not the letter" (Rom. 2:29). Nevertheless, Paul underscores Abraham's faith, a faith that "was reckoned to him as righteousness" (Rom. 4:3, 9; Gen. 15:6). Paul meant that faith is the "right" response we should have to the all-holy God. Paul also stated that Abraham, "the man of faith" (Gal. 3:9), is "the father of us all" (Gal. 3:7; Rom. 4:16) because of his faith in God's promises.

The unknown author of the letter to the Hebrews goes far beyond Paul. In chapter 11, after describing at length those who had run the race of faith, the author declares that Jesus is "the leader and perfecter of faith" (12:2). As a son of Adam, Abraham, and David, Jesus lived a life of faith. He, too, had to reach out to a God more hidden than revealed, especially when "he endured such opposition from sinners" (12:3) and when "he endured the cross, despising its shame" (12:2). For Christians, Jesus is the supreme example of a life of faith.

Faith is an essential **virtue** in human life. Everyone has faith in someone or something. "A virtue is a personal disposition which enables one to realize his destiny as a person" (Johann 1968, 152). A virtue is "the faculty, disposition, or attitude that moves one to accomplish moral good and to do it joyfully and perserveringly even against obstacles and at the cost of sacrifice" (McBrien 1994, 1,254).

When a man decides to marry, he decides to devote himself totally to one woman. He makes a commitment to love her faithfully until death. He will sacrifice for her. If his parents or friends question his decision, he says he loves her and he definitely knows what he is doing. He has been in her company often and enjoys her gentleness, intelligence, beauty, goals, common sense, and sense of humor. He has been in situations and in conversations which have convinced him that he can rely on her. She is to be trusted with his life.

Another case. A young woman decides to join the Marines and serve her country. She is willing to commit herself to twenty years of service, knowing full well she could be placed in harm's way and be killed. However, she not only knows what the Marines stand for, she also knows some Marines and judges that she compares well with them in strength, intelligence, and devotion. She is sure she can rely on the Marines to train her well and to help her develop as a mature and honest woman.

In both of these scenarios there are three interrelated factors or components: commitment, conviction, and confidence (or trust). These three elements constitute faith, whether it is faith in another person, one's country, a cause, a value, oneself, or God. What distinguishes religious faith from other types of faith is that the commitment is to God. Faith, then, is a commitment supported by conviction and confidence.

Commitment involves love; confidence involves hope; and conviction involves knowledge. Not complete knowledge, otherwise it would not be faith. But there is sufficient knowledge to make the commitment desirable and reasonable. The knowledge is incomplete because the commitment is a process that takes place over time, and the future is always unknown. Faith is an act of courage by which a person pins the meaning of her or his life on something not seen or provable. Faith is symbolized by a star. From our perspective on earth, a star is a dot of light in a sea of darkness. When a person decides on marriage or a career, there may be about 60 percent knowledge, but there is also 40 percent darkness.

Religious faith might be a mere 10 percent light and 90 percent darkness, because God is more concealed than revealed. "No man has ever seen or can see" the one who "dwells in unapproachable light" (2 Tim. 6:16). Furthermore, God's presence is made known to us only through symbols, that is, he is always mediated through people, nature, or events. These symbols are ambiguous, susceptible to multiple interpretations. For example, some regard the thousands of homeless persons who roam the nation's cities as other Christs; others regard them as lazy degenerates who live off welfare.

Implications of the Abraham and Sarah Story

A critical or actualization reading of the Abraham and Sarah stories yields many implications for the interpreter's own self-understanding.

First, many people make reference to "blind faith." A common answer to a difficult religious or theological question is that "there is no explanation, only faith." The scriptures seem to encourage this view when they declare: "Faith is the realization of what is hoped for and evidence of things not seen" (Heb. 11:1). Faith certainly entails a leap in the dark. The response of Abraham and Sarah to their two tests surely seems like "blind faith." How can a very old couple even think of procreating a child? How can an all-wise God first promise Abraham and Sarah that their offspring will be as numerous as the stars in the sky and then ask Abraham to sacrifice the boy?

Some read these stories in a precritical way. When read literally, the faith of Abraham and Sarah certainly seems blind. However, the historical-critical method suggests that these highly imaginative stories are filled with exaggerations for a theological purpose: trust God even when the situation seems impossible and incredible. Such faith is not blind because God can be relied on. Christians know that God is reliable from personal experience, from the biblical stories of Abraham and others, and especially from Jesus' resurrection, which followed his terrible crucifixion—that dark time when he seemed forsaken by his loving Father (Mk. 15:34). Actually, "blind faith" is irrational and has no place in any human relationship. Remember, the blind do not see any light, whereas faith always involves some light, some knowledge. This light may be a mere ten percent, but even that is enough to support a free commitment. A love commitment always involves some knowledge.

Second, there are two stories of Abraham and Sarah acting against their faith. The first tells of the time they entered Egypt to escape a famine. Sarah, at Abraham's insistence, passed herself off as his sister and, as such, was invited to join the pharaoh's harem (Gen. 12:10–20). This deception brought prosperity to Abraham. Later God struck the pharaoh and his family with severe plagues. In the second story of infidelity, Abraham, at Sarah's insistence, had a son, Ishmael, by Sarah's maid, Hagar the Egyptian (Gen. 16). Since Sarah was barren, she believed Abraham could have sons only through Hagar.

Read in a critical way, these stories remind us that doubt is an aspect of faith. Since faith involves a large degree of darkness, it is always provisional. Doubt is always possible. The opposite of faith is not doubt but faithlessness or unfaithfulness. Sometimes doubt and/or weakness lead people to be unfaithful. Such rare and isolated failures do not destroy faith. Because of his deep-rooted faith, Abraham is called "the father of us all" (Rom. 4:16).

Third, faith and belief(s), although inseparable, are quite distinct. Belief belongs primarily to the intellectual order. A belief is an explanation of a faith commitment that is strongly held. It is a tenet or doctrine accepted as true. With the arrival of new knowledge, a belief can (and should) change. Several examples drawn from the previous pages will illustrate this point. Christians have faith that the scriptures are the word of God, but the belief of some people is that they should be interpreted in a precritical way and of others that they should be interpreted in an historical-critical way. Christians have faith in an omnipotent Creator. The belief of some is that creation took place in a week, and others believe that it took place through an evolutionary process that encompasses billions of years and still continues today. Christians have faith that God created humans. The belief of Catholics is that humans are basically good whereas the belief of Luther and Calvin was that people are basically sinful. Jews have faith they are God's chosen people and were promised a land. (Most Christians affirm the right of the state of Israel to exist and to prosper.) Some respect the belief of those Jews who think Israel must retain the land by force, even if it is excessive at times. Others, like Alfred E. Block, disagree. In 1982, after Israel's blockade and bombardment of Beirut resulted in the indiscriminate maiming and killing of innocent victims, Block wrote:

> Israel is not a Jewish state. Israel is not a homeland for Jews. It was meant to be such a home. And more, it was to be the home of the permanent consciousness of the greatness of a humanity made in the image of God. But Israel has become a tragic parody of such a homeland. Artillery fire is not a hearth. A gun is not an instrument of the spirit. A flag is not a symbol of a culture. And the Star of David has been besmirched till the end of time. . . . After 60 years of being a Jew, I have been stripped naked. I have been humiliated, brought down to my knees, and must beg not only God, but you, to forgive me—because Beirut is also my sin (1982, 24).

Fourth, faith is a response to God's providence: his creating, covenanting, and saving love. For the Jews the greatest sin is **idolatry**—putting complete faith in a thing or a person instead of God. Only God can claim our total faith. The Nazis in Hitler's Germany knew the Jews stood for the absoluteness of God and his unique role in salvation. The faith of the Jews was a challenge to the absolutes proposed by the Nazis and this led them "to try to kill every single Jew whether the Jew 'believed' or not" (Greenberg 1988, 71). The absoluteness of God—that God should be loved with one's whole heart, mind, and soul—was carried over into the Christian covenant. Christian faith also rules out idolatry. Nothing—neither a person nor a thing—should occupy the place in the heart reserved for God alone.

Fifth, the covenant with Abraham and Sarah and their offspring convinced the Jews to have faith in Abraham and themselves as God's chosen people. Later they would have faith in Moses. At Sinai the Lord said to Moses: "I am coming to you in a dense cloud, so that when the people hear me speaking with you, they may always have faith in you also"

(Ex. 19:9). Jewish faith has a communal dimension. Similarly, Christians have *faith in the church,* the new people of God. Faith has an **ecclesial** (church) dimension. Ecclesial faith is not the same as *faith in the triune God.* Only God can claim total faith. However, Christians have faith in the church community because its source is Christ, its ground the Holy Spirit, and its goal the reign of God. Because the risen Christ and his Spirit are always present to the church community, the church is the body of Christ, the house of God, and the sacrament of Christ. Because the church is the body of Christ and his Spirit, it must have an **infallible** hold (free of error) on the gospel, the message of salvation.

The Catholic Church has always fostered the infallibility of the church, that is, it teaches that Christ delivered the truth about his Father to the church. When the church collectively discerns this truth, it is infallibly protected. This teaching was addressed at Vatican II in the *Constitution on the Church:* "The body of the faithful as a whole, anointed as they are by the Holy One (cf. 1 Jn. 2:20, 27), cannot err in matters of belief" (n. 12). "Belief" here means faith. Edward Norman, an Anglican priest and historian, stated that it is the Catholic understanding of the infallibility of the church itself "which is the major difference between Catholics and Protestants" (1991, 459).

Catholics claim that in addition to infallibility residing in the church community as a whole, it becomes tangible when the pope and bishops solemnly interpret the Christian faith. The Catholic Church teaches that the Spirit does not speak through the scriptures in such a way that individual readers can indiscriminately challenge the teachings of the pope and bishops.

For Protestants, the pope and bishops, neither individually nor collectively, serve as the representatives of the infallibility of the church. For Luther and Calvin, the Spirit speaks primarily through the scriptures in the church. The Orthodox churches also reject the individual authority of the pope. They believe the church protects the gospel through ecumenical councils: meetings of all the bishops of the world.

This overview of the ecclesial dimension of the faith shows that the churches have a long way to go before they can solve the intellectual, institutional, and devotional issues that divide them. Meanwhile, individual Christians can manifest their ecclesial faith by working for the unity of all Christians, by participating in the liturgical and devotional life of their church, and by supporting it morally and financially.

Moses the Prophet
Exodus 2–3, 19–20; Romans 11:25–36; Hebrews 11:23–29.

The person most honored in the history of Israel is Moses. He dominates every book of the Pentateuch except Genesis. Considered Israel's greatest prophet (Deut. 34:10), he reinforced the monotheism of Abraham, persuading the Israelites to adopt whole-heartedly their ancient belief that there is but one God who is ever-present with them in their history and daily lives.

Moses (whose name is Egyptian and means "is born") was a priest (Ps. 99:6), born about 1390 B.C. of the tribe of Levi (Ex. 2:1). It is not easy to determine his biography because in Jewish culture there is no sculpture, no representation of the human form, and no biography as a branch of literature. Personality is a Greek notion and not a Hebrew idea. Also, the narratives of Moses' leadership were not written until some 400 to 600 years after his death. Furthermore, the Pentateuch is not a historical account similar to our modern understanding of a work of history. The Pentateuch is theologically interpreted history. As symbolic communication, its focus is not Moses' personality but "the God who prepares and summons him to be the agent in the accomplishment of the divine purpose." (Anderson 1975, 49).

The tradition of Exodus 2 that Moses was brought up and educated in Egyptian circles is probably authentic, especially since his name is Egyptian. What also appears authentic is that, despite his Egyptian upbringing, he continued to have a strong sense of identity as an Israelite. This seems to be the point behind the story (Ex. 2:11–15) in which Moses, moved by ungovernable rage, killed an Egyptian who was beating an Israelite slave. When Moses found out the next day that his crime had become common knowledge, he fled eastward beyond the Red Sea to the land of Midian. Here he married and had two sons.

One day while tending the flock of his father-in-law, he had a major religious experience, a theophany. God appeared to him in a burning bush and gave him the mission to free the Israelites from their slavery in Egypt. Moses was reluctant to take up this awesome mission for several reasons: he had a speech impediment (Ex. 4:10); he doubted the pharaoh would acknowledge the power and authority of God; and he wondered if the Israelites would know who the God of their fathers is. Moses asked God for his name so he could tell it to the Israelites when they asked for it. God said, "I am who I am" (Ex. 3:14). The Hebrew word is *Yahweh,* translated as *Lord.* Yahweh said three times that he is the same God who was known to Abraham, Isaac, and Jacob (Ex. 3:6, 15, 16). In Egypt Moses should say, "Yahweh . . . has sent me to you" (Ex. 3:15).

Books have been written about the mysterious name Yahweh. Some read the burning-bush story in a precritical way, that is, the name Yahweh was uttered for the first time by God himself. The historical-critical method takes a different approach. There is some evidence that Moses found the name in use among other religious groups. While it is true that scholars honestly do not know for sure the specific desert tribe from whom Moses learned the name Yahweh, nevertheless, there is evidence that it was "in use in the pre-Mosaic period, perhaps among the Amorites or in patriarchal clans" (Anderson 1975, 57). Furthermore, according to contemporary theology, the all-holy and omnipotent God reveals himself, but not in spoken words. It is humans inspired by the Spirit who give expression in their own words to the divine revelation they receive (Brown 1981, 13). The Bible contains symbolic stories of covenants and name-giving because the words *covenant* and *Yahweh* captured God's active power among the Israelites and his irrevocable commitment to his people. Covenant and Yahweh are human-made words employed to communicate Moses' religious experiences. The message is the message *of* God but the words are the words of Moses. In summary, the Bible contains the words of God because God communicates himself "to the extraordinary extent that one can say that there is something 'of God' in the words" (ibid., 18).

Yahweh can be variously translated: "I am the one who is"; "I am that causes to be"; "I will be what I want to be"; or

"I will be there as the one who will be there." Obviously, the name hardly gives out much information. It could be that Moses chose it because it underscores the transcendence of God. For the Jews, to name something or someone was to have a certain control over it—as when Adam named the animals. Furthermore, for many ancient peoples the use of a power-laden name could heal the sick, or bring rain, or strike someone dead if used in a curse. The mysterious name Yahweh kept the Israelites at a respectful distance from God, the holy Lord of creation and history. Nonetheless, it was not easy for the Jews to understand and commit themselves to a transcendent God because they were surrounded by people who imagined that the deities were tied into the rhythms of nature, the cycles of life and death, and the power of blood and fertility. Much of their worship involved fertility rites for themselves, the vegetation, and their livestock. For example, they would sacrifice a lamb to maintain the fertility of the rest of their flock. Their deities were not transcosmic. "The cosmos is so massive a presence to early peoples that they find it almost impossible to live by a transcosmic reference" (Carmody and Carmody 1987, 108). This inability to comprehend the transcosmic explains how easily the Israelites turned to the worship of a golden calf in the desert (Ex. 32:1–29), why the Psalmist poked fun at idols which have eyes, ears, and mouths but never see, hear, or talk (Ps. 135:15–17), and why over the years the prophets had to warn the people about idolatry (Jer. 35:15; Bar. 6:3–64; Ezek. 20:32).

The name Yahweh is also significant because "it was filled with new meaning at the time of the Exodus" (Anderson 1975, 58). The Israelites discovered that the meaning of God's name can only be known in the actual unfolding of Israel's story in the process of history. When God's name was invoked, it evoked the saving and loving (Ex. 20:2–5) intervention of God at the Exodus. Yahweh had heard the cry of the oppressed slaves and graciously intervened on their behalf, leading them toward a future full of promise. Yahweh is the one who guides, strengthens, and liberates his people. The Exodus is the central event in the history of the Jews. This is proclaimed in Deuteronomy 4:32–35:

Ask now of the days of old, before your time, ever since God created man upon the earth; ask from one end of the sky to the other: Did anything so great ever happen before? Was it ever heard of? Did a people ever hear the voice of God speaking from the midst of fire, as you did, and live? Or did any god venture to go and take a nation for himself from the midst of another nation, by testing, by signs and wonders, by war, with his strong hand and outstretched arm, and by great terrors, all of which the Lord [Yahweh], our God, did for you in Egypt before your very eyes? All this you were allowed to see that you might know the Lord is God and there is no other.

The Exodus—or Passover—is the major annual holy day of the Jews. They celebrate their freedom from slavery and death and their creation as a covenanted community with special teachings, laws, and worship. All the important events in the Hebrew scriptures lead up to the Exodus and out from it. A modern Jewish scholar explains that the Exodus experience—from slavery to freedom—is "to be felt in one's bones, tasted in one's mouth. That is why much of Jewish religion consists in reliving the Exodus" (Greenberg 1988, 38).

Moses hurried to Egypt to confront the pharaoh with the threatening words of Yahweh: "Israel is my son, my first-born. Hence I tell you: Let my son go, that he may serve me. If you refuse to let him go, I warn you, I will kill your son, your first-born" (Ex. 4:22).

This confrontation took place probably in the year 1350 B.C. It should be noted that most books on the exodus date it to around 1250 B.C., during the time of Rameses II who ruled from 1290 to 1224 (Anderson 1975, 42). Today, however, Egyptologists believe that Rameses II ruled from 1304 to 1237, which means that it was actually a relatively obscure pharaoh in 1350 who was the wicked king that the Israelites recall at Passover.[1]

When the wicked pharaoh balked at Moses' demands, he and his people were afflicted with ten terrible plagues. The last—"the passover"—was the worst. An angel of death slaughtered the first-born of each Egyptian household but "passed over" the houses of the Israelites whose doorposts were marked with the blood of the sacrificial lamb. Consequently, with the aid of Aaron, who was his brother and also a priest, Moses persuaded the pharaoh to relent and to accept Yahweh's demands. The Exodus took place. The Israelites passed from slavery to freedom.

The Israelites reached Mount Sinai after journeying for two months. It is here that Yahweh manifested himself in another theophany, delivering to Moses the ten commandments (Ex. 20:1–17; Deut. 5:6–21). These commandments or "ten words" **(Decalogue)** were not unknown to the Israelites (or even other peoples) until they were promulgated at Sinai. Similar laws are found in the world-famous code of laws of Hammurabi, king of Babylon from 1792 to 1750 B.C. The commandments comprise God's sacred teachings **(Torah)** about their proper relationship with God and one another. They represent the people's participation in the covenant. They communicate symbolically the ways the people should live as an authentic religious community at peace with God and one another and without sin.

The Pentateuch ("the book of the five scrolls") has more laws than ten commandments. It has 613. There are decrees on almost every phase of the Israelite's daily and religious life, especially their prayer, sacrifices, diet, and treatment of animals and one another. This explains in part why the seventy-two Hebrew scholars who translated the Hebrew scriptures into Greek in 250 B.C. in Alexandria translated Torah as *nomos,* meaning "law." Torah, then, has three meanings: the ten commandments, the Pentateuch and its 613 laws, and all of the Hebrew scriptures. Torah is the foundation stone of the Jewish religion. The Jews' history and theological divisions result from various interpretations of Torah. In modern times, for example, Jews are divided into Conservative, Reform, and Orthodox branches. Conservative Judaism declares that the Torah is binding but subject to evolution. Reform Judaism regards the Torah as nonbinding and adaptable to contemporary attitudes and conditions. Orthodox Judaism considers the Torah to be divinely authorized in all its specifics.

The Israelites wandered in the desert for a generation. Moses never delivered them to the Promised Land. It is reported that God told Moses to strike a rock with his staff to secure water for the desert-bound Israelites. This he did (Ex. 17:6). But in Numbers 20:12 it is reported that Moses struck the rock twice, perhaps a sign he had insufficient faith the miracle could be worked with a single blow. "Because you were not faithful to me in showing forth my sanctity before the Israelites, you shall not lead this community into the land I will give them." It was left to Joshua to lead them across the Jordan and to successfully conquer the land. Moses died and was buried in an unmarked ravine in the land of Moab (Deut. 34:1–8). According to the text he was 120 years old, "yet his eyes were undimmed and his vigor unabated."

Moses in the Christian Scriptures

The vigor and faith of Moses carry over into the Christian scriptures, where he is mentioned 80 times—more times than any other person in the Hebrew scriptures.

Paul's seven letters contain a mere eight references to Moses, but many, many references to the law. Both the Hebrew scriptures and the gospels indicate that the Pentateuch's 613 laws can be reduced to two: love of God and love of neighbor (Deut. 6:5, Lev. 19:18; see Mk. 12:28–31). Paul summarized the law in one commandment: "Owe no one anything, except to love one another, for he who loves his neighbor has fulfilled the law" (Rom. 13:8; see also Gal. 5:14, 6:2).

Moses has a prominent place in the gospel of Matthew. This gospel was probably written in Antioch around 85 by a Greek-speaking Jewish Christian and a former **scribe** (a class of scholars who were certified to make systematic studies and expositions of the law). Most modern scholars agree that all four gospels at first circulated anonymously. In the second century there was great concern that the gospels have an apostolic origin because this would bring them closer to the eye-witnesses of the Jesus of history and give them more authority. The four gospels were named after Mark and Luke, disciples of Peter and Paul, and Matthew and John, disciples of Jesus.

It is generally agreed, also, that the communities of Matthew and Luke knew Mark's gospel but eventually found it inadequate for the signs and needs of their times. The gospel of Matthew, for instance, has as one of its major themes that the church is the true Israel. Matthew wrote in this vein because the Jewish Christians had suffered a dramatic break with their roots in Judaism. The Jewish Christians were excommunicated from the synagogues. The Jews even composed a prayer—one that reflects ideas in Ps. 69:27–28: "May the Nazarenes and heretics be suddenly destroyed and removed from the book of life." Not only were the Jewish Christians excommunicated from Jewish society, but there was no place for them with God. The chasm between the synagogue and the church was so wide and deep that it emptied into hell.

In order to bring comfort to the displaced Christians, Matthew underscored that the church was the true Israel and that the Jewish Christians had not in fact been cut off from their Jewish roots. This purpose of comfort explains in part why "Matthew presents Jesus first and foremost as a Moseslike figure" (Fuller and Perkins 1983, 84). Therefore, not all the stories should be read in a precritical way as historical facts. For example, the stories of Jesus' birth recapitulate the stories surrounding Moses' birth. Herod sought to slay the children of Bethlehem (Mt. 2:16), just as the pharaoh tried to kill the Hebrew children (Ex. 1:15–16). After Jesus' birth, Mary and Joseph take the child to Egypt so that, like Moses and Israel, Jesus could come out of Egypt into the holy land (Mt. 2:19–23). Moses and Elijah are at the transfiguration of Jesus (17:1–18), but it is Jesus who is the Father's beloved Son. Jesus' Sermon on the Mount (Mt. 5–7) parallels the lawgiving at Sinai. Jesus is a "new Moses giving a new Torah" (Perrin and Duling 1982, 272). Jesus had no desire "to abolish the law or the prophets" but "to fulfill" them (5:17). He taught that all should seek first the reign of God (6:33) and "be perfect, just as your heavenly Father is perfect" (5:48). Consequently, Jesus taught a radical interpretation of the law (8:18–27; 9:1–17). The Torah permits divorce and swearing before God; Jesus denounced divorce and swearing. The Torah condemns killing, adultery, and hatred of enemies. Jesus calls for a radical observance of Torah. He condemns not only killing but also anger and insults, not only adultery but also lustful thoughts and desires, and not only hatred of enemies but violence of any kind.

The epistle to the Hebrews was written by an unknown author to a Christian community in Rome (Heb. 13:23–24) sometime between 75 and 90. Scholars think the community included some Jewish Christians who wanted "to preserve the pre-eminence of Moses and to retain the cultic heritage that was associated with the Mosaic tradition" (Cwiekowski 1988, 167). It must be remembered that the first Christians were Jerusalem Jews who viewed themselves as a community renewed by Jesus the Messiah. They viewed themselves as a special community within Judaism. Jesus fulfilled the covenant promises and inaugurated the **end-time**. In Jewish theology the end-time is the final day in human history which would be followed by a new age when God would fully establish wholeness and life. The Jewish Christians in Rome favored this theology because "the church in Rome was likely founded by missionaries from the Jerusalem church" in the 40s (ibid., 177).

The author of Hebrews wants the Roman church to temper its devotion to Moses. He insists that God's definitive word has been communicated in Jesus (1:1) and that his word has priority over any communication made through angels (2:2–5) or Moses (9:15–28). While it is true that Moses was a faithful servant (3:5; 11:23–28), Jesus is the faithful son (3:6).

The author also wants to dissuade the Jewish Christians from their attachment to forms of worship that come from the Mosaic tradition. "The law and priesthood have been changed" (7:12). Jesus is the eternal high priest whose sacrifice on the cross has atoned for sin once and for all (10:10). Jesus established a new covenant between God and humankind. The first covenant and the Mosaic way of worshiping God have been abolished by Christ's sacrifice: "He takes away the first to establish the second" (10:9). The second covenant has made the first one obsolete (8:13).

The gospel of John also makes frequent references to Moses. This gospel was probably written about 90 in Ephesus by an unknown evangelist. Matthew depicts Jesus as a new Moses; John, like the author of Hebrews, consistently presents Jesus as superior to Moses (3:4) because a major Johannine theme is that the church community has replaced Israel. Jesus is the sole source of divine revelation and divine life. There is a choice: either Moses or Jesus. John's choice is Jesus, the *only one* who has seen God (1:18). The law was given through Moses, but Jesus brought the graciousness and truth of the covenant (1:17). During the exodus the Israelites ate the bread from heaven, but Jesus is the true bread from heaven, the bread of life (6:32–35). Jesus, the Word of God, provides divine life through his death. "As Moses lifted up the serpent in the wilderness, so must the Son of man be lifted up, that whoever believes in him may have eternal life" (3:14). Moses lifted up a serpent; in John it is Jesus who is lifted up on the cross.

Despite these sharp contrasts between Moses and Jesus, the Johannine community did not discount Moses. After all, Moses prepared for Jesus (1:45; Deut. 18:15). To reject Jesus is to reject Moses. Jesus declared: "For if you had believed Moses, you would have believed me, because he wrote about me" (5:46).

If the passages from Hebrews and John are interpreted in a precritical way, it seems that the Jewish covenant is abolished. It must be remembered that the authors of Hebrews and John are making theological points that apply to their respective churches. The Roman church of Hebrews was engaged in the late 70s in theological refinements about the relationship of Moses to Jesus; in the early 90s the Johannine church was struggling with Judaism about the divinity of Jesus. Paul's theology is quite different. In the late 50s he told the Roman church that God's covenant with the Jews continues because "they are beloved because of the patriarchs. For the gifts and the call of God are irrevocable" (Rom. 11:28–29). The Catholic Church at Vatican II publicly made its own the Pauline view of the mystery of Israel's eternal election in its *Declaration on the Relationship of the Church to the Non-Christian Religions*. The bishops wrote that the Jews "still remain most dear to God because of their fathers, for he does not repent of the gifts he makes nor of the calls he issues" and that the church should not forget "that she draws sustenance from the root of that good olive tree onto which have been grafted the wild olive branches of the Gentiles (cf. Rom. 11:17–24)" (n. 4).

Implications of Moses for Today

A critical or actualization reading of the Sinai event offers insights into law and Christian discipleship. **Law** is defined as a regulation of reason for the common good. Laws are essential for order, justice, and community. Laws, while not perfect, are necessary. They are both instructive of our ignorance and corrective of our weaknesses and inconstancy. For example, at some point in Christian history some Catholics wanted to know just how often they should assemble for community worship. The church promulgated the law of Sunday worship. The church said a true believer should join the community at least once a week. Now that the law is in place, it acts as a prod on those occasions when people might absent themselves from community worship because of laziness, inconvenience, leisure activities, or just plain apathy.

God's intervention at Sinai was an act of love (Ex. 20:2–5). Christian discipleship is a life of love. But the scriptures are filled with commandments. Can love be commanded? Why are the scriptures loaded down with commandments? The reason is that our relationship or partnership with God is expressed through the metaphor "covenant," a legal word. A covenant is a solemn agreement to act together. It is a contract that is legally binding on both parties. God's commandments, then, should not be conceived as an external imposition. The covenant should be accepted in one's heart. Moses instructed the Israelites to find the law in their hearts. God's law is not mysterious or remote. You do not have to send someone across the sea to find it. "No, it is something very near to you, already in your mouths and in your hearts; you have only to carry it out" (Deut. 30:14). Centuries later the prophet Jeremiah (c. 650–c. 585) underscored internalizing the law in these engaging sentences:

> The days are coming, says the Lord, when I will make a new covenant with the house of Israel and the house of Judah. It will not be like the covenant I made with their fathers the day I took them by the hand to lead them forth from the land of Egypt; for they broke my covenant and I had to show myself their master, says the Lord. But this is the covenant I will make with the house of Israel after those days, says the Lord. I will place my law within them, and write it upon their hearts; I will be their God, and they will be my people (Jer. 31:31–33).

King David

1 Samuel 16:1–13; 2 Samuel 5:1–12, 7:1–17, 11:1–27, 12:1–25.

David was the son of Jesse of Bethlehem, the youngest of eight sons (1 Sam. 16:1–13), who became king about 1000 B.C. It is not necessary to review the personal, socioeconomic, political, and religious factors that contributed to David's succession to the throne and reign for forty years. He succeeded Saul, a charismatic and popular leader whom the people chose as Israel's first king. Saul's reign of eight years was troubled and came to a tragic end when, after being seriously wounded in a losing battle with the Philistines, he committed suicide (1 Sam. 31:1–6).

David was a skilled warrior, a brilliant military commander, and a charismatic leader. "One of his most brilliant maneuvers" was the capture of Jerusalem on Zion from the Jebusites (Anderson 1975, 181). He made the city his capital because it was situated between the northern and southern tribes. It became known as "the city of David" (1 Sam. 5:9). Here he would reign for thirty-three years.

For the Israelites, Yahweh is the true king (see Ps. 24:7–19; 93, 96, 97, 99). The human king, adopted as a son of God at his enthronement, is God's representative. David, the inspired author of many Psalms, was a man of deep religious feeling who linked his authority to the Mosaic traditions. He brought the Ark of the Covenant (the symbol of God's presence) to Jerusalem, making the city of David also the city of God. Jerusalem became the holy city in the holy land.

Once David was established in Jerusalem he wanted to build a temple in which to house the Ark. He asked the prophet Nathan to seek divine approval. Nathan reported that Yahweh refused David's request. However, God promised David an unending dynasty, that is, Yahweh's covenant love would never be withdrawn from the Davidic dynasty (2 Sam. 7:15–17). It is from this promise of perpetual covenant (2 Sam. 23:5) that royal **messianism** developed. The Hebrew word *messiah* means "to anoint" or "the anointed one" (see I Sam. 16:3, 6, 12–13). Messiah in Greek translation is *christos.*

The successful reign of David, God's anointed, took tragic directions once his lust for Bathsheba got out of control. David had an affair with Bathsheba, the wife of Uriah the

Hittite, one of his soldiers. To cover up Bathsheba's pregnancy, David recalled her husband from the front where he was fighting in a holy war. But Uriah, a religious man, would not go home to his wife because this would break the rules of purity that forbade a soldier to have sexual intercourse with his wife during a holy war (2 Sam. 11:11). David then had his general Joab send Uriah into an extremely dangerous battle, knowing Uriah would be killed. God's anointed committed adultery and murder. After the death of Uriah, David married Bathseba and she bore their son, who died seven days after his birth and therefore without circumcision (2 Sam. 11:1–27).

One of Israel's greatest prophets was Isaiah, who received his call in the temple in 742 B.C. (Isaiah 6). He exposed the moral breakdown of Judea and its capital, Jerusalem. Nevertheless, he offered his fellow Jews a sign of hope from God: "[T]he virgin shall be with child, and bear a son, and shall call him Immanuel" (7:14). The authority of this son shall be "vast and forever peaceful, from David's throne, and over his kingdom which he confirms and sustains" (9:6). When the Davidic tree has been cut down so that only a stump remains, hope should continue because "a shoot shall sprout from the stump of Jesse, and from his roots a bud shall blossom. The spirit of the Lord will rest upon him" (11:1–2). Faithful Jews today cherish these prophecies about their future and find hope in them.

At the time of Jesus, David was recalled as the one who brought in a unique era of unity (he was able to unite the twelve tribes) and prosperity. "Never before or after the time of David did Israel exceed his zenith of political power" (Anderson 1975, 180). Also remembered was God's unique, permanent covenant with David, the founder of Jerusalem, their holy city, and, therefore, many were expecting God to establish a kingdom like David's. Despite his personal failures, David was extolled as the ideal king. He was revered as "Yahweh's servant" and as a king who judged and administered justice to all his people (2 Sam. 8:15). We will see later that the expected messiah took three forms: an anointed king like David (Jer. 23:5–6); an anointed priest like Aaron (Zech. 4:14); and an anointed prophet like Moses (Deut. 18:15).

David in the Christian Scriptures

David has an important part in the Christian scriptures because Jesus Christ is proclaimed as the son of David and the Messiah who "will rule over the house of Jacob forever, and of his kingdom there will be no end" (Lk. 1:33).

The gospel of Matthew devotes considerable attention to David. On the one hand, Matthew emphasizes that the church is the true Israel, that is, the church is in continuity with and is the fulfillment of the covenants with Abraham, Moses, and David. On the other hand, he insists that Judaism and Christianity are quite distinct because the church proclaims that Jesus, the son of David (1:1), is truly the transcendent Son of God (3:17).

In Matthew, Mary and Joseph live in Bethlehem and here Jesus is born. According to the prophet Micah (5:2) the messianic-king would be born in Bethlehem. That Jesus was actually born in Bethlehem is problematic. Matthew and Luke say he was born there, but no other inspired author does. Mark indicates that Nazareth was Jesus' hometown and Galilee his native region (see Mk. 6:1), but he never mentions that Jesus had an auspicious beginning by being born in the Davidic city of Bethlehem. In fact, the people in Nazareth were astonished that Jesus has become a famous religious figure, "precisely because such fame was not presaged by anything extraordinary in his previous family situation in Nazareth" (Brown 1977, 515). John's gospel (1:46) explicitly disassociates Jesus from the Michan prophecy, "asserting that Jesus' place of origin is Nazareth" (Kee 1970, 220). Matthew has the parents of Jesus settle in Nazareth after their stay in Egypt. Do Matthew and Luke place the birth in Bethlehem in order to associate Jesus' messiahship with David's birthplace? It is hard to say. Nonetheless, the evangelists insist that Jesus is a son of David (Mk. 12:35; Lk. 1:32) and the messianic king. The genealogies of Jesus in Matthew and Luke "coincide specifically over David, but in other respects diverge widely and cannot be harmonized" (Küng 1992, 75). These textual points explain why many scholars do not think that Jesus was of direct royal lineage. On the other hand, "there is no insuperable difficulty in positing that Joseph belonged to one of the non-aristocratic lateral branches of the house of David" (Brown 1977, 511). Jesus was a son of David because Joseph accepted Jesus as his son.

The major titles for Jesus in Matthew are Lord and Son of God. The title "son of David," although used ten times by Matthew, is not a major title because it was associated too much with narrow nationalistic hopes (Meier 1979, 72), and because it did not really capture the mystery of Jesus' divine identity. After the resurrection, the disciples understood that all power in heaven and earth has been given to Jesus (Mt. 28:18). Moreover, Matthew stresses that "this king is not a political or military leader, but a peaceable, humble healer, who nevertheless can speak an authoritative word" (ibid., 146). Matthew uses the title "son of David" in stories which contrast the leaders of the Jews with the so-called outcasts of society: Gentiles and Jews who were lame or blind. The blind and the lame were excluded from temple worship because of their illnesses. The Pharisees reject Jesus' messiahship, whereas some Gentiles and some sick persons acknowledge it. For example, Jesus cures a Canaanite woman's daughter who is possessed because she invokes him as son of David (15:21–28). When Jesus cures a blind and dumb demoniac, the people ask if Jesus is the son of David. The Pharisees respond that Jesus casts out demons only through his association with the prince of demons (12:22–32). Just before Jesus' entry into Jerusalem, two blind men request a cure from the son of David (20:29–34). Jesus eventually challenged the Pharisees and their understanding of the Davidic messiah. Jesus reminded the Pharisees that David, the inspired author of some of the Psalms, addressed the messiah as his Lord in Psalm 110: 1–3:

> The Lord said to my Lord: "Sit at my right hand
>   till I make your enemies your footstool."
> The scepter of your power the Lord will stretch forth
>   from Zion:
>   "Rule in the midst of your enemies.
> Yours is princely power in the day of your birth,
>   in holy splendor;
>   before the daystar, like the dew, I have begotten you."

If David used such a title of respect, how can the messiah simply be David's son? The Pharisees had no answer. Jesus showed that the so-called experts on the subject of the messiah did not really know who the messiah is (Meier 1979, 159). Matthew's community knows that Jesus is the Davidic messiah because he is the Son of God.

Implications of the Davidic Covenant

A critical reading of the Davidic covenant points to the virtue of hope, a virtue essential to Christian humanism and discipleship. Unfortunately, this virtue is little understood, in part because the word is used so loosely. The noted philosopher Robert O. Johann (1968, 148–153) explained two erroneous meanings of the word. First, the word points to a natural optimism. We tell others not to worry because everything will be all right. When we hear that someone is sick, has lost a job, or been hurt in an accident, our natural response is that we "hope" everything will get better. But "this blind optimism is more a matter of temperament than virtue." Our hope really is a "wish." Second, what we sometimes call hope is really "shrewd realism." It is "simply a matter of everyday desires plus a reasoned calculation of their chances of fulfillment." In other words, we can often see something coming. For example, a woman hopes that because she has been on a job for a year and has been praised often, she will get a raise. A student judges his quiz scores to be excellent and hopes for an "A" grade. These are not the virtue of hope. They are particular desires that are the result of reasoned calculation.

To hope is to rely on another. It is to trust in another's goodness and his or her concern and love for me—for my growth or happiness or freedom as a person. To hope is to count on another's reliability now and for the future. This explains why the symbol for hope is an anchor. We experience great pain when someone turns out to be untrustworthy, leaving us adrift.

A person can grow in virtue because the virtue comes *from us*. We have a disposition (or attitude or propensity) built into us which enables us to naturally rely on others. In order to develop as persons, we need to be in communion with others. Our vocation to communion is the reason why we have the general disposition of hope "that is identical with our very constitution as persons." Hope, according to Johann, "is that cast of mind and heart which a person must bring to life as a whole for the simple reason that *he is a person and is called to fulfill himself in a relation of love with other persons."* The Jewish and Christian religions maintain that we are always in a relationship with God. In him we live and move and have our being. Hope, declares Johann, "is simply the ratification of this original relationship and calling." For example, Isaiah had trust in God and expressed this by predicting the birth of a child who would be the messiah.

Hope also comes *to us*. It can be triggered by any reality. We have hope-renewal experiences. These experiences are overwhelming, penetrating the whole person and providing a new sense of purpose. Isaiah's sign provided the Jews with hope. It pointed to the purposefulness of their history, which was not a series of unconnected events. Isaiah linked his contemporaries to their great, cosmic story. He reminded them that hope is the fundamental response they owe God. God can be relied on. In the past he raised up Abraham, Moses, and David. He would raise up another leader in their future. Jesus proclaimed a similar message of hope. He told his contemporaries not to be anxious about such things as clothes or food because the Father, who watches over lilies and birds, will certainly support and save them (Mt. 6:25–34).

The loss of all hope is called despair. The Bible rules out despair by presenting stories of a God who is faithful to his covenants and who is oriented towards the future. Too often this future dimension has been unduly separated from God's transcendence. Thoughtful Christians advise us that God's transcendence has a temporal dimension. "God revealed himself to Moses more as the power of the future rather than a being dwelling beyond all history and experience. God is not 'above us' but 'before us'" (Metz 1969, 88). This orientation toward the future is also fundamental to the Christian message. The proclamation of the death and resurrection of Jesus "is essentially a proclamation of promise which initiates the Christian mission. This mission achieves its future insofar as the Christian alters and innovates the world toward the future of God which is definitely promised to us in the resurrection of Jesus Christ" (ibid., 89).

King Solomon

1 Kings 8:1–21; Mark 11:15–19; John 2:13–25.

After the death of the son of David and Bathsheba, they had another child, Solomon, the man of wisdom.

It was Solomon (961–922) who succeeded David and who built the temple, "a dwelling for the Mighty One of Jacob" (Ps. 132:5), that David had been so anxious to build. After seven years of construction, the building was completed around 950 B.C. and became, with the Torah, a pillar of Jewish identity. The building "was modest in size (about 90 x 30 x 45 feet), but for its time it was a great architectural achievement" (Anderson 1975, 191). It was the holy place in the holy city in the holy land. Faithful Jews made Psalm 122 one of their favorites:

> I rejoiced because they said to me,
>   "We will go up to the house of the Lord."
> And now we have set foot within your gates,
>   O Jerusalem. . . .
>
> Pray for the peace of Jerusalem!
>
> Because of the house of the Lord, our God,
>   I will pray for your good (1–2, 6, 9).

Even Jonah prayed while in the belly of the fish that he might once "again look upon your holy temple" (2:5).

The priests who served in the temple were in three categories. **Levites** were from the tribe of Levi. They were subordinate functionaries (1 Chron. 24:20) who could not enter the court of the priests but did serve as musicians, servers, and doorkeepers. **Aaronites** (1 Chron. 24:1), named after Moses' brother, could enter the court of the priests to serve at the altar of burnt offerings. The father of John the Baptist was such a priest (Lk. 1:5). **Zadokites**, named after Zadox, or Sadox, high priest during the time of David and Solomon, served as the high priest. Which priest presided at worship in the temple was crucial to the Jews. The Zadokites were the only priests who could "come near to minister to the Lord" (Ezek. 40:46).

Jerusalem and the holy temple were destroyed by the Babylonians in 587 B.C. Around 400 B.C., the author of the two books of Chronicles interpreted destruction of the temple and the city as God's punishment for despising the warnings of prophets such as Jeremiah (7:1–15) about destruction of the temple, for adding "infidelity to infidelity," and "for practicing all the abominations of the nations and polluting the Lord's temple" (2 Chron. 36:14–21). The Jews mourned the loss of the temple during their years of captivity—the so-called **Babylonian Captivity.** In Psalm 137:1–4 they recall that while in Babylon as slaves they could not sing happy songs because these were out of harmony with their remembrance of what had happened to their holy place in the holy city in their holy land:

By the streams of Babylon we sat and wept
    when we remembered Zion.
On the aspens of that land we hung up our harps,
Though there our captors asked of us the lyrics of
    our songs,
And our despoilers urged us to be joyous:
"Sing for us the songs of Zion!"
How could we sing a song of the Lord in a foreign land?

After their return to the holy city around 538, the Jews erected another holy place under the leadership of Zerubbabel around 515. This second temple did not compare in splendor to the first. Nevertheless, it served as the center and support of Israel's life in the post-exilic period. Faithful Jews prayed about the temple, as in Ps. 84:2–5, 11:

How lovely is your dwelling place, O Lord of hosts!
My soul yearns and pines for the courts of the Lord.
My heart and my flesh cry out for the living God.
Even the sparrow finds a home, and the swallow a nest
    in which she puts her young—
Your altars, O Lord of hosts, my king and my God!
Happy they who dwell in your house! continually they
    praise you. . . .

I had rather one day in your courts than a thousand
    elsewhere.

The temple played a significant role in the life of Jesus. He was presented there as a newborn infant and he visited it as a boy with his parents. He prayed, taught, and conversed there with people as an adult. All four gospels recount his "cleansing" of the temple. In the first three gospels the event takes place the day after Jesus' triumphal entry into Jerusalem. This is the last week of his life and ministry. In John the cleansing takes place during a visit to Jerusalem in the first year of his three-year ministry. John's timing fits into "a Johannine theological pattern of having a fundamental controversy with Judaism and its authorities run through the gospel" (Brown 1994, 1:81).

Jewish worship entailed the sacrifice of animals. Jesus judged that the buying and selling was marked by greed and cheating. Merchants were more interested in making money than being of service by providing animals for sacrifice. Because the temple had a marketplace atmosphere rather than one of proper ritual, prayer, and devotion, Jesus angrily drove out the merchants. Using the words of Jeremiah, he declared that his Father's house should be a house of prayer and not "a den of thieves" (Jer. 7:11; Mt. 21:12–13). Since the priests were responsible for the temple, Jesus' disapproval of their administration angered them and seems to have played a part in their plans to eliminate him.

In 66 A.D. the Jews in Jerusalem revolted against Roman occupation, a conquest dating back one hundred and twenty years to 63 B.C. After a long siege, Jerusalem and the temple were destroyed in the year 70 A.D. The earliest Christians, following the lead of Jesus, interpreted the destruction of the city and temple as God's punishment for handing over the innocent Son of God to the Romans for crucifixion (Mt. 23:35–36, 27:25; Lk. 13:35, 19:44, 23:28–31) (Brown 1994, 1:396).

To this day the Jews have no temple, priesthood, or animal sacrifice. In Israel today there are ultraorthodox Jews who want to build a third temple where the other two had stood. But on that site stands a special Muslim shrine built in 691 A.D., the Mosque of Omar (the Dome of the Rock). Any attempts to remove that sacred building would probably result in untold bloodshed.

The Prophets

Isaiah 6:1–13; Jeremiah 1:1–19, 20:7–18; Mark 6:1–6.

The meaning of the word **prophet** is so stretched today that it covers "reformers" and even "statesmen." Strictly speaking, the word denotes a person specially called to be a spokesperson for God. Israel's prophets were charismatic men—and women like Miriam (Ex. 15:20–21) and Deborah (Judg. 4:4). They had a deep experience of God, who called them to speak his word in trusting faith. Some report a vision of the heavenly court (Isa. 6:1–13; Jer. 1:4–19; 1 Kgs. 22:19–22). These inspired poets, preachers, and teachers were not microphones. Even though they prefaced their message with expressions such as "The word of the Lord is," they brought to God's message their own personal, historical, and social images and terminology. They were masters of the art of symbolic communication. Their views, like ours, were affected by the conditions and limitations of their time and by the sources of knowledge to which they had access. As we have already seen, humans are God's instruments, with their own real but subordinate contribution to make to the work and plan of God.

The Jews were blessed with many prophets, such as Abraham, Moses and his sister Miriam, Samuel, and Nathan. However, the word *prophet* usually denotes those charismatic poets who lived between 750 and 450 B.C. and who are associated with fifteen prophetic books. Isaiah, Jeremiah, and Ezekiel are called major because their poetic writings are extensive, occupying one scroll each. Twelve are called minor, not because their theological insights and influence were less than that of the major prophets, but because all twelve of these inspired books are written on a single scroll. No religion has had writing prophets of the same quality and quantity as the classical prophets of the Jews.

The symbolic stories of the call of the prophets make interesting reading. Some, like Isaiah (6:8), gladly accepted their invitation and mission; others, like Jeremiah, were quite reluctant to take on the responsibilities and dangers (1:6, 20:7–18). Tradition says that all of the prophets were murdered. The reason for this tragedy is that the prophets confronted kings, priests, and other people about their faithfulness to the covenant and Torah. Prophets dramatically symbolized God's active involvement in the day-to-day history of the people of God. Through the prophets God destroys and overthrows what is evil (Jer. 1:10). The prophets reiterated that Judaism is an **ethical monotheism**, that is, the sign of one's devotion to God is faithful execution of God's will by obedience to the Torah. For the Israelites the most significant link between God and themselves is the commandments. Eugene Borowitz, a Jewish scholar, has written (1980, 127–28): "Jews testify to the reality of God by being faithful to the commandments as they face the challenges of the everyday. From this perspective, to soften the ethical demand or qualify it in any way is to demean God's sovereignty and to lessen our reflection of God's image. To be sure, Torah is wisdom and prophecy as well as commandment. While Judaism is far more than pious doing, acts are its unqualified primary interest as its basic response to the sovereignty of God."

In addition to confrontations and reinforcement of the Mosaic tradition, prophets also offered words and signs of consolation, comfort, and hope. They announced the good things their faithful God would do for them. For example, Isaiah prophesied about a royal messiah and Jeremiah was told to use his powerful words not only to destroy but also "to build up and to plant" (1:10).

When the prophets offered hope, they often spoke of the future. Their prophecies of future events should not be read in a precritical way. To predict future events would be an extraordinary feat. Can it be done? Does anyone know the future? It does not seem so. The best we can do is anticipate and plan for the future. Due to accident, chance, the intrusion of others into our plans, or our freedom to change our minds, specific and detailed plans often get changed. We have very little control over the future.

A search through the Bible will not reveal any instance of future events being accurately predicted and coming to completion. Prophets project ideas based on God's past deeds and faithfulness, but without knowing the actual future. Prophets do not pinpoint future events. They correctly diagnose the signs and needs of their times and thus prepare symbolically for the future. For example, when Peter and the other disciples left the upper room in Jerusalem on Pentecost to address the people about Jesus crucified yet "exalted at the right hand of God" (Acts 2:33), Peter declared that they spoke in the Spirit, as prophesied by the prophet Joel (see Joel 3:1–5). The book of Joel was composed about 400 B.C., so there is no way Joel could pinpoint what would happen in Jerusalem 400 years later on the feast of Pentecost. In fact, the apocalyptic imagery in Joel 3 suggests the end of the world when the sun will be turned to darkness and the moon to blood, rather than with a whole new stage of God's involvement in human history. Similarly, Nathan predicted that David's dynasty would last forever and Micah said the Messiah would come from Bethlehem. But David's dynasty was destroyed in 587 and faithful Jews still await a messiah. If the prophets are read in a precritical way, they can easily be judged as deluded dreamers who spun illusions. However, since prophecies are symbolic communication, they take unexpected and unforeseen turns. For example, Christians interpret Isaiah and Micah in terms of Jesus. He is the messiah born in Bethlehem and in him the Davidic dynasty continues. Jesus was not a political king or even desirous of being one. His spiritual kingship and his triumph over sin and death exceed the imagination of any prophet or the accomplishment of any king in human history.

Hellenization of the Mediterranean World

In Greek mythology Hellen and his three sons were the progenitors of the principal Greek nations. Greek culture—its language, art, architecture and philosophy—was in existence for centuries before the rise of Alexander of Macedonia (356–323 B.C.), the military genius who conquered the western world. The biblical judgment of Alexander the Great is harsh: "He advanced to the ends of the earth, gathering plunder from many nations; the earth fell silent before him, and his heart became proud and arrogant" (1 Mac. 1:3). Alexander's conquests and career came to a sudden halt when he died in Babylon at the age of thirty-three. It is reported that, after contracting malaria, he tried to cure himself by drinking at one sitting four quarts of wine.

Alexander, the son of Philip II of Macedonia (359–336), was tutored by Aristotle (384–322), one of the world's great philosophers. He succeeded his assassinated father at the age of twenty, hoping to carry out his father's plan to invade the Persian Empire, then in a period of political and economic instability. Alexander wanted to establish one empire, based on universalism rather than nationalism. His vision of a united world transcended national boundaries. Citizenship was available in self-governing cities and it did not depend on nationality. He encouraged his soldiers to marry the local women. Those who did were given land on which to settle their families. This spread of Greek culture is called **hellenization**.

Alexander fostered hellenization in three ways. First, he founded city-states like Alexandria, the greatest and richest of all the hellenistic cities. In these cities, Greek ideas and values flourished. Here he introduced Greek architecture. Modern engineers claim that men and women build cities, but the cities build their sons and daughters. Alexander put this axiom into practice by constructing gymnasiums for schooling and sports. Here young men received their training in military skills and the duties of citizenship. He also constructed baths, aqueducts, fountains and theatres. It was quite difficult for non-Greeks to resist philosophers like Plato and Aristotle, poets like Homer and Pindar, and playwrights like Aristophanes and Euripides.

Second, he fostered education. Alexandria with its vast library was the greatest learning center of the ancient world. It became more influential than Athens. Alexander also encouraged the people to form into social and political clubs and professional guilds—each with its own protective deity.

Third, he made world trade possible by protecting the seas and lands from pirates. The Greek language became the common language for commerce, education, and government. After the Babylonian Captivity, Jews migrated to other countries for socioeconomic and religious reasons. This dispersion of the Jews is called the **Diaspora**. During the hellenization period Jews once again left Israel, induced by the possibilities of economic advancement. By the time Paul started his missionary journeys around the Mediterranean basin, there were large, well-established Jewish communities in the major cities of the empire: Rome, Athens, Corinth, Antioch, and Philippi.

As a group the Jews were deeply influenced by hellenization. Palestine was not a hermetically sealed compartment shut off from the hellenistic environment of the Mediterranean. Hellenization was unavoidable, not only because Alexander conquered Syria and Palestine in 333 B.C., but also because, when people of one culture come in contact with those of another culture, aspects of the cultures rub off on one another. This is called **acculturation**, as opposed to **enculturation**, the adoption of one's own culture through language, education, stories, and so forth. Hellenism soon affected the internal life of the Jews. To many of them their own traditions began to look old-fashioned compared to the new art, literature, and sports of the Greeks. For example, it is reported that some Jewish men who visited the baths were so embarrassed by their circumcision that they sought surgery to cover it up (1 Mac. 1:15). "The brightest and the best, the richest and the most powerful were increasingly attracted" to hellenism and, consequently, abandoned the holy covenant (Greenberg 1988, 259). Acculturation to the Greek culture was so pervasive in Alexandria that in the year 250 B.C. a group of seventy-two scholars had to translate the Hebrew scriptures into Greek **(Septuagint)**. Some of the Greek words persist even today. The first five biblical books are called the Pentateuch. Yahweh became Lord *(kyrios)* and Torah was translated as Law *(nomos)*. The place of assembly for worship is still called a synagogue. Jews adapted Greek names like Andrew, Philip, Stephen, and Timothy.

The Maccabean Revolt

1 Maccabees 1:1–15, 41–63; 2:1–48; 2 Maccabees 9:1–10.

After Alexander died in 323, some generals agreed to divide his kingdom. Ptolemy and Seleucid, two of his generals, claimed independent kingdoms for themselves. Ptolemy founded a dynasty in Egypt which lasted until the death of Cleopatra in 30 B.C. This Cleopatra has been made famous through literature. She was actually Cleopatra VII, the wife of Ptolemy XII.

Seleucid assumed control of Syria, Mesopotamia, and Persia. He established his capital on the Orontes River, naming the city Antioch. The Jews found themselves positioned between two great, antagonistic powers. For more than a century they were under Ptolemaic rule, but in 199 B.C., Antiochus III of Syria (223–187) took over Palestine.

The Jews did not protest their new ruler or his successor Seleucus IV (187–175) because both kings allowed them to live according to their religious laws and traditions. However, things changed dramatically when Antiochus IV Epiphanes (175–164) took control of the land. With the support of some of the Jewish aristocracy who favored Greek ways, Antiochus began to aggressively enforce the adoption of Greek culture. He adopted this policy less from a desire to eradicate the Jewish religion than from a desire for cultural uniformity as a means of consolidating his political power (1 Mac. 1:41). Later, however, he was determined to abolish the Jewish culture and religion. He took several drastic steps. He burned copies of the Torah, forbade the Jews to observe the Sabbath and their other religious feasts, and outlawed circumcision and the dietary laws. Schools for boys were organized where they were indoctrinated into hellenistic ways. Antiochus sold the office of high priest, granting it to the highest bidder. Even the temple was looted and desecrated. "Sacred prostitution" was introduced. A statue of Zeus was placed in the most sacred part of the temple (the **Holy of Holies**) and sacrifice was offered there on the twenty-fifth of each month. For the Jews this placement was the "horrible abomination upon the altar of holocausts" (1 Mac. 1:54; see also Dan. 11:31). Antiochus even required that he be worshiped as Zeus (2 Mac. 6:2). He had adopted the title "Epiphanes" (it means "manifest") to suggest that Zeus was manifested in him. Finally, after sacrificing pigs, animals considered "unclean" by the Jews, he poured the blood on the altar and forced the priests to eat the meat.

There were Jews who, in their desire to stay completely loyal to their traditions and the Torah, firmly resisted the normal hellenization process. These were called **Hasidim**, meaning "pious" or "loyal ones." These **pietists** feared hellenization because they realized that like flood waters out of control it could reach into every area of Jewish life, enticing many to abandon their religious and cultural traditions in order to gain

social, intellectual, and economic advantages. When the soldiers of Antiochus came to Modein, a village twenty miles
northwest of Jerusalem, to enforce the king's life-or-death
decrees, an elderly priest named Mattathias, surrounded by his
five sons, refused to obey the command to sacrifice unclean
animals upon an altar. However, when a collaborator came
forward to sacrifice, Mattathias slew him and the king's messenger. Mattathias and his sons fled into the wilderness. The
Hasidim rallied behind these brave loyalists who quickly mus-
tered troops for an offensive against Antiochus and his army.
They vowed unremitting warfare, even on the Sabbath, in
defense of their religion and traditions. Until the rebellion of
Mattathias, there was no armed resistance to the enforced hellenization of Antiochus, because the Jews believed that as long
as they were faithful to God they would enjoy divine protection. They also believed that it was sinful to revolt against any
king God had placed over them. Mathathias was soon convinced, however, that any king who commanded the violation
of the Torah could not rule Jews by divine right. "In effect,
Mattathias was operating out of a covenantal model in which
humans could not 'leave it all to God' but had to initiate some
action to save the Torah and the Jews" (Greenberg 1988, 263).

Within a year of these events and shortly before his death,
Mattathias made his second son, Simon, the leader of the
Hasidim, and his third son, Judas "the **Maccabee**," the commander of the army. The word Maccabee probably means
"hammer." The term was applied to the whole family because
they inflicted hammerlike blows upon the enemy.

The Maccabees continued their successful guerrilla warfare
until early in 164 when Antiochus died a horrible death (2
Mac. 9:1–10). The Jews were able to negotiate peace with his
successor. The priests removed from the temple all signs of its
desecration. In December 164, an eight-day festival was held,
celebrating the rededication of the temple. Faithful Jews still
celebrate this event each December as Hanukkah, or the Feast
of Lights (1 Mac. 4:42–58; 2 Mac. 10:1–8). Each night they light
eight candles to symbolize God's gifts of light, life, and faith.

Divisions among the Hasidim

The Hasidim gradually divided into three groups—Sadducees, Pharisees, and Essenes—based on their interpretation of the two pillars of Judaism: Torah and temple.

Sadducees

The Sadducees were priests and aristocratic landowners who were dependent for their own livelihood on the preservation of the temple and the nation. As a result they tended to accept the hellenistic culture and to maintain cordial relations with the Roman authorities. Their cooperation with Roman authorities at the time of Jesus may be due to the considerable authority the Romans allowed them to exercise through the **Sanhedrin**, the ruling religious court of seventy men under the presidency of the high priest. When Herod the Great was in power, he suppressed this governing body and assumed responsibility for all administration himself.

The meaning of the name Sadducee is not clear. Some think it means "doing right," while others suggest that it derives from Sadok, the high priest mentioned earlier. They may have formed their own group in opposition to Jonathan (160–143), one of Mattathias's sons, who, as king, also assumed the high priesthood in 152. Although the Maccabees were from a priestly family, they were not of the family of Sadok.

The conservative political stance of the Sadducees was paralleled by their conservative religious stance. They underscored the holiness of God, holding that God was set apart from ordinary life and could be approached mainly through temple rituals and sacrifices. They accepted only the Pentateuch as the authoritative word of God. For them, the Mosaic covenant was in place and had been given its final form. Reinterpretation and development were severely restricted. Any interpretation of the Pentateuch was the exclusive prerogative of the priests. Consequently, they rejected as binding the oral traditions that had built up over the years. They denied the ontological existence of angels and demons, the immortality of the soul, and the resurrection of the dead to either punishment or heavenly reward.

The views of the wealthy Sadducees were quite different from Jesus'. They were not concerned about the poor; they denied the bodily resurrection and therefore God's eternal love; they overemphasized the importance of temple sacrifice to the detriment of mercy and kindness in everyday life; and they restricted the Torah to what was written centuries before without consideration of present needs and problems.

The chief priests and Sadducees were the primary opponents of earliest Christianity because some Christians, like Stephen, not only promoted the ancient prophetic argument that "the Most High does not dwell in houses made by human hands" (Acts 7:47; see Isa. 66:1–2), but they also claimed that Jesus would destroy the temple (Acts 7:14).

Pharisees

This group was composed of shopkeepers, businessmen, craftsmen, artists, and lawyers (scribes). The origin of their name is not clear. It probably means "separate" or "set apart" by their piety. Did the term define their separation from hellenization and/or the Maccabean priest-kings and/or anyone unfaithful to the Torah, especially its rules concerning the sabbath, ritual purity, and tithing? The Pharisees were very strict about any association with sinners (Gentiles, tax collectors, prostitutes, thieves and so forth) and those unclean (the lame, blind, insane, and lepers) because "uncleanliness" was associated with sin.

We have seen that the entire life of the Jewish nation was subordinate to the Torah. The Pharisees demanded strict observance of the Torah. They taught that the Torah comprised the written books as well as the oral traditions that developed as the Torah was applied to new situations and new needs (for example, rules for fasting, tithing, and almsgiving). The oral law, linked with the scriptures, was equally the will of God. The Mosaic covenant was still open and could be further skillfully interpreted, developed, and applied. The Pharisees regarded the rabbis (the teachers) as having religious authority not much different from the authority of the priests. They believed in the ontological existence of angels and demons and the resurrection of the dead.

Since the Pharisees were not priests, they were not as attached to the temple as the priests. The temple was not the exclusive place for the people to encounter God. They believed the whole world was God's temple. They urged all Israelites to consider themselves "a kingdom of priests, a holy nation" (Ex. 19:6). As such, they should be as holy in daily life as the priests were required to be when they served in the temple. They extended the realm of the sacred from its close association with the temple to the synagogues. Since the temple was located in Jerusalem, they regarded the synagogue communities where most Jews gathered for prayer and study as sacred institutions alongside the temple.

Like the Pharisees, Jesus taught that each person was called to a deep intimacy with God and the whole world was God's temple. Jesus differed from the Pharisees on other issues. Jesus proclaimed a nonlegalistic relation to God as opposed to the view that law was the way to God. He did not try to build "a 'hedge round the law' with rules for behavior, a protection to guarantee that the commandments were observed" (Küng 1992, 328). Jesus accepted the oral tradition but did not place it on the same level with the heart of the Torah. Finally, Jesus' ministry was among the very people the Pharisees shunned: the poor, sick, oppressed, and the so-called sinners.

The sect most mentioned in the gospels is the Pharisees. The Sadducees as a group are mentioned six times in Matthew, once in Luke, but never in John. The priests are mentioned often in the gospels because they had a major role in the death of Jesus. The reason for the few references to the Sadducees is that they declined as a significant force after the destruction of Jerusalem in 70. Nevertheless, the Sadducees made several attempts to rebuild the temple. Their last great effort occurred in 132 A.D., when they supported the messiahship of Simon Bar Kochba (his name means "son of the star"). His revolt was provoked by the decision of the emperor Hadrian (127–138) to build a temple to Jupiter in Jerusalem on the temple mount. This revolt—often called the Second Jewish Revolt—ended in disaster because the Roman forces were too strong. Simon's troops "were destroyed and the remaining population of Judea was deported. With this defeat, immediate hopes for the restoration of the temple were set back indefinitely" (Greenberg 1988, 286).

The Pharisees are mentioned often in the gospels because, as we will see later, the gospels reflect not only Jesus' encounters with them but also the conflicts between the Pharisees and the first Christian communities. The revitalization of Judaism after 70 A.D. is attributed to Rabbi Johanan ben Zakkai, a Pharisee. He escaped from Jerusalem during the Roman war and fled to Jamnia. Here he re-established Judaism. Modern Judaism has its roots in the reforms he initiated: the institution of a common calendar, clear guidelines for worship in the synagogues now that there were no more temple sacrifices, and a call for extensive study of the Torah. Such study would insure "an extraordinary increase and application of covenantal principles to every aspect of life" (ibid., 288).

Essenes

Their name means "pious or loyal ones." They are not mentioned in the gospels for two reasons: they were not involved with the early church community and they had ceased to exist by the time the gospels were written.

Scholars had known of their existence for years but there was little primary-source material about them available until 1947. At that time a shepherd boy in search of his goats wandered into caves around Qumran near the Dead Sea and discovered the sect's manuscripts. The scrolls, written in Hebrew and Aramaic (the language Jews spoke in Jesus' day), were probably placed in the caves during the war with the Romans, 66–70 A.D.

The scrolls are an important historical and religious discovery for several reasons. First, they supplied "many details hitherto unknown about the Palestinian Jewish world in which John the Baptist and Jesus lived and about the Palestinian Jewish matrix from which early Christianity emerged" (Fitzmyer 1986, 68). Second, they contain not only parts of every book of the Hebrew canon except the book of Esther, but also documents that detail the history, theology, and lifestyle of the Essenes. For example, scholars knew that Mark 1:3 is a combination of verses from Isaiah 40:4 and Malachi 3:1. They wondered if this technique was special to Mark. But they found many instances of this technique in the Qumran scrolls. The technique, therefore, is not peculiar to the gospel writers. What is special to the gospels is that Mark was able to combine these prophecies because his community has experienced their fulfillment in Jesus. Third, the scrolls helped scholars get a better handle on the Aramaic language.

Scholars had biblical texts in Aramaic dating to several centuries before and after Jesus but not from the time of Jesus. Since living languages change and develop new words and new meanings, it was very difficult to construct the actual vocabulary of Jesus' times. It would be like trying to construct Shakespeare (1564–1616) from the writings of Geoffrey Chaucer (1340–1400) and today's newspaper.

The founder of the Essenes was called the Teacher of Righteousness—meaning "uprightness" or "wholeness." The Essenes never use their leader's name, only his title. He was probably a Zadokite priest who was replaced by Jonathan in 152 B.C. He led his community into the desert at Qumran at the northwest corner of the Dead Sea around 150. Not all Essenes lived at Qumran. There were communities in many Jewish towns and in various desert settlements or camps in Palestine, Syria, and Egypt. Qumran was the chief center where some 200 lived. Their leader was later executed by a "wicked priest." Some scholars identify Jonathan as the wicked priest, a man accused of cultic impurity and illegal seizure of wealth (J. Collins 1989, 162).

The Essenes moved into the desert because they considered the temple worship to be defiled once the high priesthood was in Maccabean hands. According to tradition, only a Zadokite could serve as high priest. One of their documents, *The Temple Scroll,* states that the Essenes considered their community to be a spiritual temple and they looked to the end-time when God would create the temple anew and establish it for all time.

The writings about their own community indicate that, because they had great devotion to Moses, they observed the laws of the Torah scrupulously, especially the Sabbath laws. They considered themselves to be the sons of light, the true Israel. They believed they were living in the penultimate phase of human history and predicted that they would win the forty-years war with the sons of darkness. Like other messianic groups they had baptism, although theirs seems to have also served as a daily cleansing and refreshment in the midst of the desert heat and dust. They had ritual meals, which consisted in sharing bread and wine. Their superiors—twelve men, who symbolized the twelve tribes—were given unconditional obedience. Their teachings were held in secret and the members shared their goods with the community. They anticipated two messiahs, a king and a priest, based on Zechariah 4:11–14.

Jesus would never have joined the Essenes, because he rejected legalism, exclusiveness, and violence. His understanding of God as Father leaves no place for these three misplaced emphases.

Sometimes when Christians first hear that many of the Essene practices parallel Christianity, they wonder about the originality of Jesus and his church. We have maintained and reiterated that people often do not transcend their historical and cultural situation. The Jewish Christians naturally brought some of the symbols, theology, and disciplines of their times into the church. While it is true that Christians also have bread and wine rituals, baptism, and are called sons of light (1 Thes. 5:5; Lk. 16:8; Jn. 12:36), these symbols were placed within their rich and unique relationship with Jesus, their resurrected Lord.

The theme of this section is that hellenization pervaded Judaism since the time of Alexander. All forms of Jewish culture were hellenized, although in varying ways and degrees. Opposition to hellenization created the Hasidim. This opposition was so strong that Martin Hengel, a Catholic priest-theologian, ended his two-volume study (1974) on the relation of Judaism to hellenism with this sentence: "The zeal for the law aroused at that time [175 B.C.] made impossible all attempts at an internal reform of the Jewish religion undertaken in a prophetic spirit, as soon as the nerve center, the law was attacked."

The struggle to preserve the Jewish nation and religion against the forces of hellenization helps explain in part why Jesus' contemporaries had trouble with Jesus' prophetic reforms and why the Christian movement was rejected by post-temple Judaism as a dangerous hellenization of the tradition (see Acts 6–8). Surprisingly, the fear of hellenization continues to this day. For example, in 1979 the mayor of Jerusalem acceded to the prime minister's request to suspend construction of a controversial $100 million sports stadium for at least two months. The mayor's concession called on the Israeli government to propose an alternate site and reimburse the city administration for the considerable sum of money already spent on the project in the northeast outskirts of Jerusalem. The concession was considered a victory for one of the ultraorthodox sects, which bitterly opposed the idea of a "hellenistic, idolatrous" sports center in the holy city in general and in that district in particular. The site is near the quarter occupied by the sect's members, whose Sabbath would presumably be disturbed by soccer games.[2] Only someone familiar with the hellenization of Judaism can understand the significance of the adjectives used to describe a sports center in 1979 as "hellenistic, idolatrous."

John the Baptist
Mark 1:1–11; Matthew 3:1–17; Luke 3:1–22; John 1:1–34.

John the Baptist is an important person in the gospels and in the history of Christianity. It is believed that communities of his disciples lasted until the early part of the second century. A dozen of his followers were baptized in the name of Jesus by Paul at Ephesus around 55 (Acts 19:1–7).

John was the only child of Zechariah and Elizabeth. According to Luke 1:8–13, the boy was a gift in their advanced age and they were told to name the boy John, which means "God is gracious."

John went into the desert near the Jordan, where he lived ascetically, probably because he felt called to be a voice crying out in the wilderness to prepare the way of the Lord and to make straight in the wilderness a highway for God (Isa. 40:3). Here he probably had contact with the Essenes, with whom he shared a high regard for baptism. John probably borrowed his baptismal ritual from Qumran and combined it with the prophetic idea of some type of cleansing before the coming of the reign of God. For example, the sixth-century prophet Ezekiel wrote that God will show the nations his power when he brings the diaspora Jews back to their own land. At that time, "I will sprinkle clean water upon you to cleanse you from your impurities, and from all your idols I will cleanse you" (Ezek. 36:25). It is doubtful that John had been a member of the Essene community before beginning his own teaching ministry because he was the son of a loyal temple priest. Since the Essenes vigorously opposed the worship conducted in the temple, John's family background would not have been a recommendation for membership (Brown 1977, 376).

John baptized to prepare a messianic people for the coming, fearful judgment of God. He denounced all sin, even the adulterous marriage of King Herod Antipas with Herodias, wife of his own brother. Many people went into the desert to hear John and be baptized. The king had him arrested and executed by beheading because he feared John's preaching might cause a revolt.

John the Baptist had considerable influence on Jesus, who was so impressed by John, his mentor, that he praised him as the greatest person born of women and as a man of character, not a flimsy reed shaken by any passing wind (Mt. 11:7–11). Nonetheless, the historical Baptist is not easy to sketch because the gospels portray him in different ways, mainly for theological reasons. In Mark's gospel, John prepares the way for Jesus. The basis for his ministry is explained by the combination of two prophetic passages: Isaiah 40:3 and Malachi 3:1 (see Mk. 1:2–3). John preached "a baptism of repentance for the forgiveness of sins"—although Mark mentions few of his actual words. His baptism is with water; Jesus baptizes with the Holy Spirit. When Jesus is baptized by John, a heavenly voice tells Jesus he is "beloved son" and the Spirit comes to Jesus to help him with his mission. Jesus begins his ministry *after* John is arrested. This sequence is followed in the **synoptics**. Mark, Matthew, and Luke are called synoptics (it means "presenting a common view") because they have the same outline of Jesus' teaching ministry and death. In the gospel of John, Jesus begins his ministry *while* John is still active. Both teach and baptize at the same time (Jn. 3:24).

There are theological and historical problems with Mark's presentation of the activities and teaching of John the Baptist. Did John know he was preparing for Jesus or was he simply preparing for God's coming judgment? Did the early Christians give the Baptist's words a christological meaning because they believed that God's judgment had been manifested in the person of Jesus? How can John know of the Holy Spirit, since the **trinity** (that the one God is tri-personal) is a post-resurrection revelation? Why these questions are asked will become clearer as we look at the other gospels.

Matthew has reworked Mark's presentation of the mission of John. Since Matthew was concerned with the fulfillment of the prophetic tradition, he begins with John's own announcement of who he is and then Matthew identifies the Baptist as the one Isaiah had foretold (Isa. 40:3). Matthew gives us some of John's prophetic words—which are specifically addressed to the Pharisees and Sadducees—by adding verses not found in Mark (see Mt. 1:7–10, 12). The Baptist's message about the imminent reign of God is the same as Jesus' (3:2, 4:17, 12:34). When Jesus is baptized by John, he receives the Spirit and is proclaimed God's beloved Son. But Matthew's account differs from Mark's explanation of the event. Initially, John protests that he should not baptize Jesus, his superior (3:13–15). At the baptism, the heavenly voice proclaims to all present that Jesus is "my beloved son." Matthew explains that Jesus was baptized, not because he needed to repent of sin, but rather his baptism was an act of righteousness. Jesus said, "Allow it now, for thus it is fitting for us to fulfill all righteousness" (3:15). Joseph Fitzmyer, a renowned Jesuit scripture scholar, believes that, since righteousness is a theme of Matthew's gospel (see 3:15; 5:6, 20; 6:1; 21:32), then by submitting to John's baptism, Jesus "acknowledges the Baptist's role and the heavenly origin of the salvific way of righteousness which his preaching announced among his contemporaries" (1982, 42). It could also be that, since Jesus taught that he came to call sinners to salvation, his baptism helps identify him with sinners. In hindsight, it would seem that the baptism of Jesus by John was later embarrassing to the Christians for several reasons: the Son of God does not need a baptism of repentance, the greater instrument of God submitted to the lesser, and it seems that for a short time at least Jesus was a disciple of John.

In Luke's gospel, the Baptist is filled with the Spirit even while in his mother's womb (1:15). The stories of the birth of John and Jesus are parallel in structure. But John— a prophet—is subordinate to Jesus, the Son of the Most High (1:32). In the desert, John directs his prophetic words to all the people and some of these sayings are not found in the other gospels (see 3:10–15). In Luke, John is more successful than in Mark and Matthew because he is able to attract tax collectors and soldiers to repentance.

There is another major difference between Luke and the other synoptics. The Baptist prepares for Jesus' ministry and, as such, is not part of the Christian era. John is relegated to the end of the first covenant as the last of Israel's prophets (16:16). In fact, John does not baptize Jesus in Luke's gospel because he had been arrested before Jesus was baptized (3:20–21). Jesus' ministry begins the time of salvation as promised by the prophets. The reason why Luke reports this sequence is that he divides the entire history of salvation into three parts: from creation to the Baptist, the time of Jesus, and the time of the church. Jesus, the center of salvation history, preaches the good news to the poor, prisoners, and the blind (4:16–21; see Isa. 58:6; 61:1–2).

John's gospel echoes a synoptic theme: John baptizes with water whereas Jesus baptizes with the Spirit. Otherwise, John's gospel contains statements both about and by John not found in the synoptics. John, who is never called the Baptist in this gospel, clearly states twice that he is not the messiah (1:20, 3:28). Scholars think that the Johannine community was opposed by the disciples of John the Baptist, who rejected Jesus, claiming that, if the Baptist was not the messiah, he was "at least the envoy of God" (Brown 1979, 29).

But the Johannine community did not take a negative view of John. Not only was his ministry in continuity with Jesus' ministry, but the Baptist was sent by God (1:6); he did baptize Jesus (1:23); two of his disciples became the first of Jesus' disciples (1:35–40); and everything John taught about Jesus was true and accurate (10:41). In fact, the Baptist serves as a spokesman for Johannine theology. He does not proclaim the message of repentance as in the synoptics, but is primarily a witness to Jesus' true identity: Jesus is the light of the world, the Lamb of God who takes away the sin of the world, the preexistent Son of God, and the source of the Spirit (1:8, 29, 30, 34). The polemic against the Baptist's disciples is not severe because "they had not preferred darkness to light but had simply mistaken a lamp for the light of the world" (Brown 1979, 71).

The Catholic Church has an intriguing way of symbolizing the relation between the Baptist and Jesus. It celebrates the birth of the Baptist on June 24, a few days after the summer solstice, and the birth of Jesus on December 25, shortly after the winter solstice. Jesus' birthday coincides with the first miniscule triumph of sunlight over darkness as the day lengthens; John's natal day corresponds with the first shortening of the day after the longest day of the year. The Baptist said, "He must increase; I must decrease" (Jn. 3:30).

Finally, it should be noted that the four gospel accounts of John the Baptist indicate once again the difference between a precritical and a historical-critical reading of the scriptures. For instance, the message of the Baptist in John's gospel in the 90s could not have been his actual message in the 30s. If it were, it is inconceivable that in the 90s, the Baptist's disciples would be in conflict with Jesus' disciples. After all, the Baptist and the evangelists have the same understanding of Jesus' messianic and divine identity.

Although the evangelists edit the words and deeds of the Baptist for symbolic and theological purposes, it is clear that Jesus and his disciples celebrated the baptismal ritual and there was never a time in the life of the church when there was no baptism. Nevertheless, the "New Testament evidence for the development of baptism is quite thin" (Cwiekowski 1988, 76). The first baptisms were performed in the name of Jesus (Acts 2:28, 8:16, 10:48, 19:5). Paul reminded his Corinthians that baptism bound them together as church. "[I]n one Spirit we were all baptized into one body, whether Jews or Greeks, slaves or free persons" (1 Cor. 12:13). He later reminded the Romans that their baptism in Christ was a baptism into his death. "We were indeed buried with him through baptism into death, so that, just as Christ was raised from the dead by the glory of the Father, we too might live in the newness of life" (6:4).

The Lima Declaration and Baptism

Baptism is one of the "seven unities" of Ephesians 4:4–6. Nonetheless, over the years some controversial interpretations of the sacrament developed. For example, some communities refused to baptize infants, administering the sacrament only to those old enough to make a personal profession of the faith. This ritual they called **believer's baptism**. Other communities rebaptized persons. To bring some order and to set some boundaries around the ritual and meaning of baptism, Christian organizations have held numerous meetings to discuss this important sacrament. Chapter 5 of this book is devoted to the efforts of the Christian churches to heal their divisions and be reunited, especially through the World Council of Churches (WCC). One arm of the WCC is the Faith and Order Commission, a body that consists of some 120 theologians and church leaders from all parts of the world and from a variety of churches, Protestant, Orthodox, and Catholic. Its most famous meeting was held in Lima, Peru, from January 3 to 15, 1982 (Dulles 1982, 126–29). On that occasion the members accepted by a unanimous vote a major document that had been in the making since the 1960s, namely, *Baptism, Eucharist and Ministry*. This text was sent to the more than 300 churches that form the WCC, asking them to ascertain to what extent they "can recognize in this text the faith of the church throughout the ages."

Concerning baptism, the document addresses the two practices mentioned earlier. The first controversial point relates to the difference between infant and believer's baptism. The Lima Declaration acknowledges the validity of both baptisms. It states that the difference between them becomes "less sharp when it is recognized that both forms of baptism embody God's own initiative in Christ and express a response of faith made within the believing community."

The second controversial point concerns rebaptism. The declaration states that baptism is unrepeatable. Repeating baptism has a checkered history. At the time of Luther and Calvin, a radical reform movement known as the Anabaptist movement developed. These Christians are called *ana*baptists (which literally means "baptized again"), because they held as invalid the baptism of infants. For the Anabaptists the church is a completely voluntary society of committed believers. Only those truly converted to Christ can be baptized. For them, Mark 16:16 was decisive: "Whoever believes and is baptized will be saved; whoever does not believe will be condemned." Consequently, they insisted on a rebaptism for those baptized as infants.

Both Luther and Calvin opposed the Anabaptists because they argued that infants can participate in the Christian covenant and community. To deny infant baptism is a return to a religion of works (human initiative) and not grace (God's initiative). In addition, Paul taught that the infants of believers were holy and not unclean (1 Cor. 7:14). Today, the issue of rebaptism mainly concerns the sacramental integrity of other churches. A baptized Presbyterian who becomes a Catholic should not be rebaptized. To do so would call into question the validity and the sacramental integrity of the Presbyterian community. At Vatican II, the bishops acknowledged in the *Decree on Ecumenism* the validity of all baptisms when it declared that baptism truly incorporates people "into the crucified and glorified Christ" and "constitutes a sacramental bond of unity linking all who have been reborn by means of it" (n. 22).

At appropriate places throughout this book there will be references to the Lima Declaration of 1982 because this landmark document is a concrete example of the common effort of the churches to reappropriate and confess together the center and limits of the Christian faith, now and as we prepare to enter the third millennium.

3

The Story of Jesus of Nazareth

This chapter covers four areas that are central to the Christian faith: Jesus' resurrection, the four canonical gospels, Jesus' teachings, and his death. Once again there is an exploration of the texts in terms of the precritical, historical-critical, and critical interpretations of the Bible. The process of actualization points up aspects of Christian humanism.

The Resurrection
1 Corinthians 15; Acts 9:1–19; 22:1–16.

The name of Jesus of Nazareth is associated with the name Herod because Herod the Great (37–4 B.C.) ruled when he was born and Herod Antipas (4 B.C.–39 A.D.) was king when he was killed.

Herod the Great was a dictator who ruled the Jews shrewdly and ruthlessly for 33 years. About thirty years before Jesus was born, he conquered Galilee with the help of the Roman army. Consequently, he served at the disposition of the Romans, whose favor he constantly cultivated, especially by collecting the heavy taxes demanded of the area by Rome. Herod was an Idumean by birth, a hellenist by culture, and a Jew by religion. A builder of public works, he constructed fortresses, aqueducts, amphitheaters, buildings, and cities, often in honor of Caesar. One of his glories was Caesarea on the coast, a city Greco-Roman in style and atmosphere (Acts 23:23–35; 25:1, 13). Even more glorious was his restoration and enlargement of the temple. He began this task in 20 B.C. and it was not completed until a few short years before its total destruction in 70 A.D.

Herod was paranoid and did everything possible to make sure that no one took his throne. He executed for treason many members of his family: his second wife and her family, the wife of one of his brothers, two husbands of his sisters, and numerous members of his household. He even had two of his sons strangled, and, finally, on his deathbed he ordered the slaying of his firstborn. He was so fearful of losing power that he mercilessly stamped out any messianic beliefs. If the massacre of the children in Bethlehem and the surrounding region "is legend, it is not for want of willingness on Herod's part" (Steinfels 1976, 50).

Jesus' birth occurred according to the scriptures during the reign of Herod. If it is true that Herod "ordered the massacre of all the boys in Bethlehem and its vicinity two years old and under" (Mt. 2:16), then Jesus was born around 6 B.C. Historians discovered that a monk by the name of Denis the Short proposed in 533 A.D. to reckon years no longer by the foundation of Rome but from the birth of Jesus. He chose the year 754 after the founding of Rome as 1 A.D., a date too late since Herod died in 750 (Brown 1977, 167).

The name *Jesus,* which means "God saves," is Latin for *Y'shua* (Hebrew) and *Iesous* (Greek). No one knows the exact day of Jesus' birth. The December 25 date was chosen because it coincided with a Roman feast of lights. The Romans knew that in winter there was one day that had the least sunlight (the shortest day) and after that the days got progressively longer until June 22 (the longest day of the year). Since their scientific calculations were not precise, they picked December 25 instead of December 22 as the shortest day. Christians adopted this scheme of things and designated December 25 as Jesus' birthday because they professed that, as the light of the world, he brought true light into it.

Like John the Baptist and the great prophets of Israel, Jesus was a religious reformer. Reformers are often persecuted and murdered because they challenge the power and wealth of the power-elite. The exact date of Jesus' death is extremely difficult to determine. After intensive study of all available facts, many scholars conclude that the crucifixion could have taken place on April 7, 30, or April 3, 33. With the present information available, most see no possibility of coming to a final decision (Brown 1994, 2:1373–76).

Jesus' death was a devastating blow to his family, disciples, and friends. But to their utter astonishment and joy, he appeared to them a few days later resurrected from the dead. The disciples never expected the resurrection. There are several reasons for this statement. First, those Jews who believed in resurrection posited a general resurrection of all the dead and not an individual resurrection. "There was no expectation of the resurrection of a single man from the dead, separate from and preliminary to the general resurrection" (Brown 1973, 76). The author of Matthew's gospel unites Jesus' resurrection with the general resurrection. This is the usual explanation for the dead coming out of their tombs when Jesus dies on the cross (Matt. 27:52–54). In Jewish theology resurrection is corporate, that is, both collective and corporeal (bodily). Second, although an afterlife is affirmed in some scriptural passages (Dan. 7:13, 12:2; 2 Mac. 7:9), it is denied in other passages (see Job 14:13–22; Sir. 14:16–17, 17:22–23, 38:21). Even in Jesus' day the Pharisees and Sadducees were divided over this question. Third, the gospels report that after Jesus' arrest and crucifixion, the disciples were afraid they would also be persecuted. There are two stories: in one they remained behind locked doors in Jerusalem and in the other they returned to Galilee to resume their lives as fishermen. In both instances there is no hint that Jesus would be raised from the dead. Fourth, the gospels show no anticipation of Jesus' resurrection. In John (19:39), Jesus is anointed on the day of his death with elaborate care with "a mixture of myrrh and aloes and weighing about one hundred pounds" and buried in a special tomb. In the synoptics, Jesus is not anointed at his burial but the women go to the tomb on Easter Sunday to anoint the body. To their distress, they find the tomb empty.

There is a difference between the resurrection and the resurrection appearances. The resurrection is not a historical event, that is, one which takes place in space and time and is observable by people. It is an **eschatological** event (the word eschatology means the "last things" and the "future"). An eschatological event occurs on the border between this age and the age to come, between this world and the next. Our world is marked by space and time. Everyone and everything are described as being in some place at a particular time. Time and place limit us. We do not know what the next world is like but surmise that God cannot be limited by space and time. We speak of God being omnipresent and eternal. These words are actually negative descriptions. They mean, respectively, that God is not limited by space and time the way we are. At his death Jesus went into God's world and into a new mode of existence. This is called an eschatological mode of existence. In Jewish language, the resurrection is an end-time event. According to Jewish theology there would be a final day in human history that would be followed by a new age when God would fully establish his reign of peace and wholeness. This period—this end-time—would replace the present sinful order of history. For Christians Jesus' resurrection marked the beginning of the end-time.

In order to understand the appearances it is necessary to review the Jewish and Greek understanding of what it means to be human. In Jewish anthropology humans are body-persons. For the Greeks, on the contrary, humans are spirits captured in a body. The worst news you could give Greeks is that they would get their bodies back after death. This explains why some Athenians "began to scoff" when Paul explained Jesus' bodily resurrection (Acts 17:32). For Jews, humans are body-persons by definition. Eternal life with God would be inconceivable if humans were no longer corporeal. In Jewish anthropology a human being is always seen as a physical-psychological unity. For this reason, most scholars think the stories of the empty tomb are historical because it would have been extremely difficult for the disciples to believe in Jesus' resurrection if his corpse remained in the tomb.

Resurrection Appearances Evaluated

The resurrection appearances were historical events. Certain people had these profound experiences at a particular point in space and time and they witnessed to them, often by their death. At his resurrection Jesus made a real and powerful re-entry into history. The appearances involved an irruption of God's time in the midst of human history.

The risen Jesus made several appearances. He appeared to his women disciples first, according to Matthew and John. Mary Magdalene has the primary role among the women recipients of the appearances. In all four gospels she is at the tomb on Easter morning. Paul wrote (1 Cor. 15) that Jesus appeared to groups (the twelve, more than 500 brethren, and all the apostles) and to individuals (himself, Peter, and James). James is called Jesus' brother. Eventually he became the leader of the church in Jerusalem (see Mt. 13:55 and Acts 15:13). Paul's list is interesting, frustrating, and significant. His list is interesting because he does not include the women disciples. It has been suggested that Paul did not include them because in his day women could not appear in court as official witnesses. The list is frustrating because this is the one and only time we hear of some of these appearances. It would be wonderful indeed if we had a narrative about the experience of the 500+: who they were, where and why they were assembled together, what their experience was, and what effect it had on their lives.

The list is significant because some despisers of Christianity attribute the rise of Christianity to the collective hallucination of twelve uneducated fisherman. But Paul insists that Jesus appeared to more than twelve, including himself, a persecuter of the Christian community. The final count realistically comes to about 600 people. This large number is helpful because there is some truth to the idea that it would have been extremely difficult for the church to develop if the witnesses were a mere twelve uneducated fisherman. Jesus appeared to many. The church began with a sizable core of convinced and convincing witnesses.

To return from the dead and to make a real and powerful re-entry into human history is unprecedented. The bodily resurrection is a unique, eschatological event, that is, Jesus comes from the future back into the present. Except for Christianity, no group, nation, or religion makes such a claim. The Christian scriptures insist throughout all 27 books that Jesus in his body-person returned to human history. The resurrection of Jesus is at the heart of Christianity. There would be no Christian church without the resurrection. In 1 Cor. 15, Paul reiterates this three times (verses 14, 17, 19). If Jesus had not risen, faith in both Jesus and their own resurrection was worthless. In fact, Christians would be the most pitiable of all humankind because they had committed themselves and their destiny to a corpse. Can a corpse deliver anything? No king, emperor, or religious leader has been able to provide what every human desires, namely, deliverance from the slavery of sin and death to wholeness and eternal life. This salvation or freedom constitutes the Christian good news, the Christian gospel.

The bodily resurrection of Jesus is so unique that many, including some Christians, deny it happened. These Christians state that the resurrection is a metaphor for the belief that the spirit of Jesus lives on (see O'Collins 1985, 422). They mean what is commonly meant when a deceased family member, friend, or leader is remembered after her or his death. It is said that the ideals, or program, or system that she or he stood for continue to have an impact on those who remember them and try to carry on and personify what they stood for or taught. For example, on January 28, 1986, an American spaceship blew up shortly after takeoff, killing all seven astronauts instantly. On October 3, 1988, when the next launch was safely in orbit, the captain of the crew announced this poignant message to the whole world: "Today, up here where the blue sky turns to black, we can say at long last to Dick, Mike, Judy, to Ron and El, and to Christa and Greg: Dear friends, we have resumed the journey that we promised to continue for you. Dear friends, your loss has meant that we could confidently begin anew. Dear friends, your spirit and your dreams are still alive in our hearts."

While it is true that people live on when we remember them, Christians maintain something very different: the risen Jesus lives on whether or not we allude to him.

A second group of Christians who deny the actual resurrection maintain that the disciples came to an inner conviction of the importance of Jesus for a life of faith in God. Jesus was a man of faith who committed himself without reserve to God, despite the negative response to his reforms from the people and their religious leaders, and despite the horrible death he endured. The disciples came to the conclusion that Jesus of Nazareth, a holy prophet, was *the* Christ, that is, a model of a faithful response to God in all the great decisions of life. In short, the resurrection appearances are psychological projections on the part of the disciples. They are symbols of the new found insight of the disciples into the significance of Jesus for Christian spirituality and life.

It is true that the disciples gained an insight into Jesus' identity, character, and message after his death. But the sacred authors say something more important. Jesus is the Christ because he literally destroyed the forces of sin and death. Christians did not place their faith in an idea about Jesus, but in Jesus himself who appeared externally to them. Many of those who had experienced the risen Christ died for their faith. They did not die for a philosophy of life or an ideology but for a person risen from the dead.

A third group of Christians declares that the term *resurrection* symbolizes that the disciples experienced Jesus' forgiveness for their denial and desertion in his time of greatest need. This forgiveness gave them a new perspective about themselves and provided the basis for their coming together again to continue Jesus' reform movement (ibid., 424).

The scriptures do narrate forgiveness stories (Lk. 22:33; Jn. 21:15–17), but Jesus appeared to some 600 persons and not just the 12. Not all needed forgiveness. Mary Magdalene and the other women were completely faithful to Jesus. Moreover, Jesus conveyed more than *their* forgiveness. The Christian message states that the death and resurrection of Jesus is a sign of God's unconditional forgiveness of all humankind. Finally, the resurrection is primarily about what God did to Jesus and not what happened to the disciples. What happened to the 600 is secondary to what happened to Jesus.

The three explanations just outlined propose that the resurrection appearances took place only in the hearts and minds of the disciples, through either a vision (a mental apparition) or an insight of some kind. But these interior explanations are

quite problematic. We turn, then, to explanations of the resurrection appearances as happenings outside the disciples'
minds. The scriptures state indeed that the disciples actually
saw and heard something. Precisely what?

Some commentators say the disciples experienced Jesus as a
magnificent light (see O'Collins 1987, 319). This is the way the
appearance to Paul on the road to Damascus probably in the
year 36 is described in Acts 9 and 22. Other scholars reject this
answer because they say light (or fire) is a conventional symbol for contact with the divine. This is the way God is
described when he gave Moses both his name at the burning
bush (Ex. 3:14) and the Torah on Mount Sinai (Deut. 5:15).
The Bible reports that when Moses dedicated the tabernacle in
the Sinai desert (Lev. 9:24) and Solomon dedicated the temple
in Jerusalem (2 Chron. 7:1–3) a miraculous fire "came forth
from the Lord's presence and consumed the holocaust." The
priest-prophet Ezekiel described the appearance of the glory of
Yahweh as "a huge cloud with flashing fire" (1:4). The author
of Revelation describes the heavenly Jerusalem: "The city had
no need of sun or moon to shine on it, for the glory of God
gave it light, and its lamp was the Lamb" (21:23). God is
described in 1 Timothy 6:14–16 as "the King of kings and Lord
of lords, who alone has immortality, who dwells in unapproachable light, and whom no man has seen or can see."

Luke's description of the Damascus revelation of the risen
Jesus to Paul is the traditional way of symbolizing that Paul
encountered the divine glory. When Paul writes about his
experience, he says Christ "appeared" to him (1 Cor. 15:8). He
does not use light imagery. To underscore the transformation
that took place in the body-person of Jesus, Paul uses agricultural imagery: a seed is planted and rises as wheat. Jesus was
not a ghost or wraith or phantom. His perishable, weak, mortal and physical body was now imperishable, powerful,
immortal and spiritual. Jesus has been glorified. He now has a
new manner of existence. The best Paul can do is grope for
words to contrast the physical and **spiritual body**. By spiritual
body he does not mean an invisible, incorporeal soul, but a
human form that is not subject to change, corruption, or
death. Paul was faced with the limitations of language
because Jesus had appeared from the other side of death.

A clear and concrete description of these theophanies eludes him—and us.

The 600 people experienced a unique mystery, one which required faith. Thomas Aquinas (1225–74) wrote that "the apostles saw the living Christ after his resurrection with the eyes of faith" (*Summa* III. 55.2 ad.1). The 600 could not "see" and "hear" the glorified Jesus with their natural senses without the aid of faith. Both seeing and hearing are not easy to describe when applied to this eschatological event. The seeing and hearing are not necessarily physical and yet they are more than a purely internal experience (Brown 1973, 108). The appearances "were spiritual events that were impossible to record and unverifiable by means of concrete evidence" (Hill 1991, 201). Consequently, we have to be content with Paul's description in 1 Corinthians 15, with his teaching that the Lord Jesus "will change our lowly body to conform with his glorified body" (Phil. 3:21), and with his conviction that God "was pleased to reveal his Son to me, so that I might proclaim him to the Gentiles" (Gal. 1:16). The resurrection appearances were theophanies similar to those experienced by Abraham, Moses, and some of the prophets, and there are no categories available to make them clear. They defy description. All of us have difficulty trying to explain our own deep human feelings and experiences. Often we are lost for words. What would we do if we did not have cards for birthdays, Valentine's, and Mother's Day? If we do try to convey what happened to us during a peak experience, often there is nothing left for us other than to speak in paradoxes, that is, to link together concepts which in this present life are mutually exclusive. The Swiss priest-theologian Hans Küng explains: "This is what happened in a way in the gospel accounts of the appearances, at the extreme limit of the imaginable: not a phantom and yet not palpable, perceptible-imperceptible, visible-invisible, comprehensible-incomprehensible, material-immaterial, within and beyond space and time" (1976, 350–51). Today at Easter time many Christian churches hang banners bearing the image of a butterfly to symbolize the resurrection and the new manner of existence Jesus now has. The difference between a caterpillar laboriously crawling across a branch and a butterfly flitting easily through trees is offered as a symbol of the startling transformation that took place from a physical to a spiritual body.

Gospel Accounts of the Appearances
Matthew 28; Luke 24; John 20–21.

Paul's emphasis on the transformation from physical body-person to spiritual body-person is radically different from the gospel accounts of the appearances. In the gospels the glorified Jesus is described in physical and realistic terms. He does not seem to be glorified or in a completely new mode of existence. He seems resuscitated. The gospels tell the story of three resuscitations: the daughter of Jairus (Mk. 5:21–43 and the other synoptics), the son of the widow of Nain (only in Lk. 7:11–17), and Lazarus (only in Jn. 11:1–4). These three returned to mundane human life where they had to eat, sleep, wash, work, and so forth—and eventually die again. Jesus was not resuscitated!

Mark's gospel was probably written in Rome by an unknown hellenistic Jewish Christian around 68 while the church suffered persecution from the emperor Nero (54–68). The church considered itself the community of the end-time. Today the gospel canonically (officially) ends at 16:20. In some ancient manuscripts, the gospel ends at 16:8. Verses 9 to 20, called the Marcan appendix, are judged to be additions by another author because the style, vocabulary, and subject matter of these verses are non-Marcan and seem to be based on an editing of Luke 24 and John 20. Nonetheless, the Council of Trent declared 16:9–20 canonical. If we accept the original ending of Mark, then this gospel has no resurrection appearances. An angelic young man in a white robe announces to the women that Jesus will appear to Peter and the other disciples in Galilee.

Matthew has two appearance stories. In the first, Jesus greets Mary Magdalene and another disciple named Mary. Both women recognize Jesus, take hold of his feet, and worship him (28:9–10). In the second story (28:16–20), Jesus meets the disciples on a mountain in Galilee where he authoritatively commissions them to be his church and to teach all nations. The ending of Matthew offers a key to his theology. His church in 85 no longer expects Jesus' imminent return. His return has been delayed because the church's mission to baptize the whole world will require a lot of time.

Luke-Acts was written by an unknown Gentile around 85. Scholars are not sure where. Some point to Asia Minor while others say somewhere in Greece (Brown 1994, 1:9). His church considered themselves the new Israel with a mission to spread the gospel to the ends of the earth (Acts 1:8). Like Matthew's church they no longer expect an imminent triumphal return of Jesus. Luke has two appearance stories. Cleopas and another disciple (24:13–33) are walking toward a village named Emmaus when Jesus joins them. Jesus explains three times that the cross is the pathway to messianic glory. In Luke's second story Jesus appears to the eleven and "those with them" in Jerusalem (24:36–50). Jesus explains why he died, gives his disciples their universal mission, and promises that they will be "clothed with power from on high."

John has four appearance stories: to Mary Magdalene at the tomb where she mistakes Jesus for the gardener (20:11–19); to ten of the twelve disciples in Jerusalem where he imparts both their mission and the Holy Spirit (20:19–23); to doubting Thomas and ten other disciples (20:24–29); and to Simon Peter and six other disciples by the Sea of Galilee (also designated the Sea of Tiberias as in John 21:1–24).

All seven gospel stories have some similarities. At the start Jesus is not present and his absence is either stated or presumed. He makes his appearance and is recognized. His presence is tangible. He actually appears to be resuscitated. For example, in Matthew's gospel, Mary Magdalene takes hold of Jesus' feet, whereas in John's gospel Jesus tells Mary not to touch him even as he encourages Thomas and the other men to do so. Jesus offers the disciples bread, cooks fish for them, and eats with them. The experiences are not merely visual. Jesus speaks at length with the disciples. There is an instruction and a charge. There is a communication of meaning. The appearances are "revelatory encounters" (Fuller 1971, 49).

In all seven stories Jesus seems resuscitated. The evangelists composed these realistic and physical portrayals to dramatize that the person raised from the dead was indeed Jesus of Nazareth. Nevertheless, the real point of these symbolic stories is Jesus' glorification, that is, his transformation from a physical to a spiritual body-person. Although the evangelists describe Jesus eating and talking with the disciples, "it is obvious in the narratives that Jesus now is in an entirely new mode of existence" (Hill 1991, 201). For example, Mary Magdalene, an intimate and faithful disciple who helped anoint Jesus' corpse for burial, did not recognize him because he was completely transformed. Then Jesus says she should not touch him. She cannot touch him the way she did before his death because the primary object of Christian faith (then and now) is not the physical Jesus of history but the risen Christ—the glorified Son of God at his Father's side (Jn. 20:17), and the source of the Spirit. Similarly, Luke's story of the two disciples who walked seven miles with Jesus on the road to Emmaus yet did not recognize him underscores Jesus' spiritual presence with his community in the scriptures and the breaking of the bread. In John's gospel the stories of Thomas and Simon Peter highlight, respectively, that even the (600) disciples needed faith to accept the resurrection appearances and Peter's special roles in the church. Not only is he a fisherman (a missionary), he is also the shepherd (pastor) of the community. In other stories Jesus comes and goes without warning, even through the walls of locked rooms, and he chides the disciples for their lack of faith. Faith is not needed if a physical person is standing before you.

Theological Purposes of the Resurrection Narratives

The resurrection narratives have five theological purposes. **First**, the evangelists proclaim that the Easter event was really experienced by the (600) disciples. There is an apologetic function for the symbolic stories in which Jesus eats with the disciples (Lk. 24:41–43) and lets them verify his wounds (Lk. 24:39; Jn. 20:24–28). The appearances were most real.

Second, they state that the church community, which had its roots in the ministry of Jesus, was now a reality. Jesus established his church community, giving it the task of completing his mission. The appearances are church-founding experiences. In Matthew's gospel, Jesus commissioned the disciples to continue his mission—but their assignment was not restricted as his was "to the lost sheep of the house of Israel" (10:16); it extended to the whole world (28:19). In Luke the universal mission was reiterated (24:47). In John's gospel Jesus told the disciples on Easter evening that he was sending them on mission just as the Father sent him (20:21).

It is difficult to determine how specific and detailed the revelation was. It does not seem that the disciples were given a detailed plan. Their understanding developed. For example, the famous commission in Matthew (28:16–20) contains Jesus' explicit command to evangelize the whole world. And yet the early decades of the church's history as recorded in Acts make it difficult to suppose that the 600 were aware of any such command. It seems that a universal mission is a conviction arrived at only later and by degrees and that it was read back into the resurrection narratives.

Third, the disciples learn that Jesus was still present with them, but now in a new and intimate way. Like all humans, the Jesus of history was limited by space and time. When he was in Jerusalem, he could not be in Bethlehem. When he was in Cana, he could not be in Nazareth or Capernaum. With the resurrection, Jesus was everywhere. He could say to each and every disciple, "I am with you always" (Matt. 28:20). Even while he was exalted at the Father's right hand, he was also present with his disciples when they gathered in his name to read the scriptures and to break the bread. The church was his end-time community.

Fourth, the most important revelation was Jesus' divinity. This perception may not have been instantaneous. The realization probably developed slowly as the disciples struggled to formulate what was revealed. When proclaiming the resurrection, the confession of the 600 was not simply, "We have seen Jesus," but "We have seen the Lord" (Lk. 24:34; Jn. 20:18, 25; 21:7). Lord in Greek is *kyrios*, the word used to translate Yahweh.

In hellenistic culture *Lord* was the most common honorific title used for deities and emperors. Lord was the highest possible title, even higher than king. The title "king" did not convey the idea of absolute and unlimited sovereignty whereas "Lord" did. Herod the Great was king of the Jews but Caesar Augustus (27 B.C.–14 A.D.) was the emperor or Lord. The disciples applied *kyrios* to Jesus since the title meant someone with supreme authority. The title may have been inspired by their post-resurrection meditation on Psalm 110:1: "The Lord said to my Lord: Sit at my right hand till I make your enemies your footstool."

The Christians used Lord in a context where it was always clear that they were not identifying Jesus with God/Yahweh, the Father of all, but relating him to the Father in a unique and special way. *Kyrios* implies divinity.

The disciples had no knowledge of Jesus' divinity until the resurrection (as the Pontifical Biblical Commission taught in 1964 in its *Instruction on the Historical Truth of the Gospels*). The gospels always show Jesus conscious of his dignity, one which involved a unique relationship to God. There is no serious reason to deny that the historical Jesus had knowledge of the mystery of his own identity and his sense of oneness with his Father developed as he matured. He understood it better when he was thirty than when he was twenty or ten. But Jesus could never even hint at his divine identity. His own men and women disciples would have been the first to reject him, not only on religious grounds, but also out of common sense. The Jewish religion underscores God's oneness and transcendence. There is only one God and no images can ever be made to represent the Holy One. God was so holy that often they would not use his special name, Yahweh. Even today many Jews consider Christians to be idolaters because they worship Jesus as Son of God. For Jesus, a Galilean craftsman, to claim divinity would be blasphemy and worthy of immediate death by stoning. How could Jesus ask his disciples to accept his divinity when they knew his family, shared food and prayer with him, watched him sleep, sweat, and wash, and witnessed his struggles, concerns, and faith? They witnessed some of Jesus' miracles, but these are not signs of divinity. Luke-Acts reports miracles by the disciples that are more impressive in number and scope than those of Jesus. For example, when Peter's shadow touched the sick, they were cured (Acts 5:15).

We are back to the problem of how to interpret the scriptures and understand the meaning of the authors. The gospels do indeed contain scenes in which Jesus' divinity is publicly proclaimed. For example, unclean spirits declare that Jesus is the Son of God (Mk. 3:11). Even Jesus openly acknowledges his divinity. In Matthew's gospel (16:16), Jesus asks his disciples what they and others think of him. Peter, spokesman for the others, states that Jesus is "the Christ, the Son of the living God." Jesus declares that Peter's confession was revealed to him by his Father. In John's gospel, John the Baptist testifies that Jesus is the preexistent Son of God (1:30, 34) and Jesus claims oneness with the Father (10:30; 17:21–23).

This chapter has opened with the resurrection of Jesus and not with his birth, teachings, and death. The reason is that the scriptures were written from the perspective of the resurrection. According to the historical-critical method, the books were not written by neutral observers. Rather, they were written by believers in Jesus' divinity *for* believers *to* deepen their faith in Jesus as the incarnate and risen Son of God.

A precritical reading of the gospels tends to regard them as histories or biographies written with the same techniques as modern biography or history. **History** is the accurate recounting of externally perceived events that have taken place in certain places and at a specific time. These events are chosen and interpreted by the historian and then reinterpreted again and again as history unfolds. Later on other historians discern other significant effects and/or patterns. For example, the meaning for the history of the world of the discoveries of Christopher Columbus in 1492 is newly explained in 1892 and then again in 1992, based on what has happened in the intervening periods.

The gospels are based on historical events but they are not written the way modern historians write history. The gospel writers were not concerned with accurate details. The gospels cannot be harmonized because they contain significant discrepancies. For example, the synoptics limit Jesus' ministry to one year whereas John has a three-year period. The gospels also give different times for the same event. For example, in John's gospel, Jesus cleanses the temple at the beginning of his three-year ministry whereas in the synoptics the event occurs during the last week of Jesus' life. Some events are only partly historical (for example, the genealogies of Jesus) and some stories might be imaginary (for example, Jesus walking on water, calming storms, and resuscitating Lazarus).

The gospels are neither modern history nor biography but are a distinct literary genre. They do yield a portrait of Jesus, a historical person, and do provide a broad chronological pattern of Jesus' life, but primarily they are theological interpretations of Jesus as Lord, Savior, Son of God and Messiah.

Those who read the gospels in a precritical way have an understanding of Jesus that goes something like this: Jesus taught, at least in a veiled way, that he was the true and natural Son of God. Jesus' disciples professed their faith in his divinity during their ministry together. Jesus knew he was sent by God to institute and organize a church, that is, a new religion distinct from Judaism. During his ministry, Jesus chose twelve disciples to whom he gave special training to carry on his teachings and way of life. He prepared them for the severe persecutions they would face from family, synagogue leaders, governors, kings, and even Gentiles (Mt. 10:16–22). He also instituted sacraments, especially baptism, Eucharist, and priesthood. Jesus made the twelve priests in this new religion, even appointing Peter to head his hierarchical church.

The historical-critical method defines **gospels** as books which blend symbolic stories of the **Jesus of history** (the time of Jesus from his birth until his death) and the **Christ of faith** (the resurrected Jesus). The precritical method does not differentiate between the Jesus of history and the Christ of faith. The historical-critical method holds that the Jesus of history and the Christ of faith are similar at one level and dissimilar at another. They are similar because they are the same person; they are different because they have a different mode of existence. The Jesus of history was limited by space and time, whereas the Christ of faith is not. When Jesus was is Jerusalem, he could not be in Nazareth or Bethlehem. The Christ of faith transcends all time and space. He is everywhere at one and the same time, especially where his disciples are gathered in his name.

What is important to the evangelists is not the historical Jesus' day-to-day activities, teachings, and miracles, but the presence of the Christ of faith in Mark's community in 68, in Matthew's and Luke's churches around 85, and in the Johannine church in the 90s. The author of John speaks for all the inspired authors when he states that his purpose in writing is explicitly theological: this book is written "that you may [come to] believe that Jesus is the Messiah, the Son of God, and that through this belief you may have life in his name" (20:31). In the four gospels "the message to the present takes the form of stories and sayings from the past" (Perrin 1969, 78). In other words, the evangelists express the present experience of the Christ of faith in terms of the past ministry of the Jesus of history. The evangelists take their post-resurrection beliefs about Christ and insert them into the life of the Jesus of history. For example, the resuscitation of Lazarus is found only in John. Did this event actually take place? If it did, it is quite extraordinary since Lazarus's unembalmed corpse had been buried for four days. Why is this spectacular miracle not mentioned in Paul's epistles and in the synoptics? Is it inserted into Jesus' ministry by the Johannine church in order to symbolically proclaim that those who believe in Jesus never die? Martha says to Jesus: "I have come to believe that you are the Messiah, the Son of God, the one who is coming into the world" (Jn. 11:27).

Sometimes historians use a similar technique. Over forty years ago, Paul Horgan (1903–95) wrote an award-winning, two-volume historical epic about the Rio Grande River. He pointed out that the writing of history is not only a technical craft but also an art. In order to produce a work of art the historian might invoke certain flexibilities of method. "Here's one that I've invoked in order to give the reader an immediate sense of locality in the vastly scattered backgrounds of the river empire. To accomplish this I have in many cases used recent or modern place names in speaking of persons and events belonging to earlier times. For example, *Mexico* properly speaking was not the name of a nation, or a whole national region until 1812, but I use it for events in its area before that date rather than the officially correct designation *New Spain,* because by doing so I hope to give the modern reader a more ready sense of where he is on the map" (1954, 1:viii).

In order to provide their churches with a greater understanding of the divinity of the risen Christ, the New Testament authors struggled to find language to communicate the mystery of Jesus' identity. They explained his divine identity in different ways. In Paul's epistles (Rom. 1:3–4; Gal. 4:4) and in

Acts (2:32, 36, 5:31, 13:32–33), Jesus' divine sonship is associated with the resurrection. But in Mark's gospel, Jesus' divinity is announced at his baptism (1:11). Matthew and Luke explain that Jesus' divine origin begins with his miraculous conception through the Holy Spirit. They have no theology of preexistence and **incarnation** (the Word became flesh, became a body-person). John, as we have seen, knows a preexistent and incarnate Son of God. Jesus has come down to do his Father's will (6:38; 8:23, 38, 42, 58; 16:28). In the second century the conception theology of Matthew and Luke were combined with the preexistence christology of John and became the orthodox explanation of Jesus' divinity: the preexistent Word of God took flesh in the womb of Mary (Brown 1977, 141). The church eventually put its understanding into the Nicene Creed (325), which was given its final form in 381 at the Council of Constantinople (see p. xxxi).

The **fifth** theological purpose of the gospels is to proclaim that the risen Jesus is the Messiah or "the Christ." The risen Jesus is the Messiah because he is the Son of God.

What does **messiah** mean? The Hebrew scriptures do not offer a systematic explanation of the origin and nature of messianic expectations. There were several interpretations of this important symbol.

There was a **dynastic messianism** associated with the family of David (2 Sam. 7:1–17; Micah 5:2; Zech. 9:9). According to Isaiah (9:5–6), one of David's descendants will be the Messiah:

For a child is born to us, a son is given us. . . .

His dominion is vast and forever peaceful,
From David's throne, and over his kingdom,
    which he confirms and sustains
By judgment and justice, both now and forever.
The zeal of the Lord of hosts will do this!

Jesus is sometimes called the Son of David in the scriptures but the early Christians knew that that symbolic title did not adequately describe Jesus the Christ. For example, Paul wrote that Jesus was a descendant of David "according to the flesh, but established as Son of God according to the spirit of holiness through resurrection from the dead" (Rom. 1:3–4; see also Mk. 12:35–37).

After the end of the Davidic dynasty in 587 B.C., there developed a **general messianism**. This perspective held that God would raise up a leader—either an ideal priest or a prophet like Moses—who would bring the Jewish nation from oppression to glory. Isaiah 52:7–10 goes so far as to state that God will save the nation without human assistance.

> How beautiful upon the mountains are the feet of him
>   who brings glad tidings,
> Announcing peace, bearing good news, announcing sal-
>   vation, and saying to Zion, "Your God is King!"
> Hark! You watchmen raise a cry, together they shout for joy,
> For they see directly, before their eyes, the Lord restoring
>   Zion.
> Break out together in song, O ruins of Jerusalem!
> For the Lord comforts his people, he redeems Jerusalem.
> The Lord has bared his holy arm in the sight of all the
>   nations;
> All the ends of the earth will behold the salvation of our
>   God.

A third set of texts speaks of a final age (Isa. 26–29, 40–41; Ezek. 40–48). Some place a Davidic king in the midst of this age but others do not. The Essenes expected two messiahs: one a king and the other a priest.

Many modern scripture scholars believe that the Jesus of history did not understand his mission in terms of the ideal Davidic king. It is generally agreed that the common understanding of messiah in Jesus' day was that of a religious-national king like David who would confirm the Mosaic covenant, deliver Israel from its enemies, and establish a world empire marked with justice and peace. To establish an empire, kings must invest considerable energy, money, and time in instituting laws and engaging in wars. Laws protect the people within the kingdom by providing order, justice, and harmony. Wars protect the people from outside aggressors and enemies. There is nothing in the portrait of the Jesus of history that would indicate that he conceived of himself as a socioeconomic, political, and military leader. Jesus declared that his kingdom is not of this world (Jn. 18:6). He lived a life of voluntary poverty, abhorred violence, and rejected a messianic role and any attempts to make him king.

In Mark's gospel, Jesus tells various individuals and groups not to proclaim him as messiah (1:44, 7:36, 8:30, 9:9). This is sometimes referred to as the **messianic secret**. Does the messianic secret represent the actual approach of Jesus or is it Mark's theological conviction that Jesus' messiahship cannot be appreciated until one accepts the mystery of the cross and suffering in Christian faith?

On the other hand, the scriptures do indeed contain a few scenes in which Jesus is called Messiah. In Mark's gospel, Jesus does accept a messianic role when crowds of people enthusiastically welcome him to Jerusalem, hailing him as the blessed one "who comes in the name of the Lord! Blessed is the kingdom of our father David that is to come" (11:9–10). In John's gospel, Andrew invites his brother Simon (Peter) to meet Jesus with the words, "We have found the Messiah" (1:41). Jesus uses the title for himself twice (10:25, 17:3) and John the Baptist indirectly identifies Jesus as the Christ (1:20, 3:28). The historicity of these Johannine passages is questioned, however, because they could reflect the post-resurrection understanding of Jesus. Nevertheless, there is some evidence that during Jesus' lifetime some of his disciples thought of him as the Messiah and "made that claim/confession . . . to him or to others" (Brown 1994, 1:478). The reasons why he may have been considered the messiah were his Davidic roots and his strong talk of the presence of the kingdom of God in his preachings and healings, which could have led naturally to the thought that Jesus himself was the promised king. The brothers James and John asked to sit on either side of Jesus when he came into his glory (Mk.10:37). Finally, there is no place in the gospels where Jesus denies his messiahship. It is difficult to explain why the post-resurrection disciples would have contradicted Jesus by giving him a title he had firmly rejected.

In conclusion, it must be explained that in giving the title Messiah to Jesus, the disciples radically changed its meaning. The Christians actually shattered the traditional meaning of messiah. First, religious-national king did not fit what Jesus had accomplished. Although Jesus may have aroused messianic expectations, his death on a cross as a common criminal was incompatible with the biblical and contemporary understanding of messiah. There is no "suffering Messiah" in the Hebrew Bible and this is what Christians proclaim. Second, kings attempt to bring their people from evil and death and to wholeness and life by means of law and war. But no earthly king ever achieves these goals, either for his people or himself. Christians claim that Jesus is the Messiah precisely because he conquered sin and death. He alone has made wholeness and life available to humankind. Third, this title signaled the irrevocable ending of one age and the certain beginning of another wholly new one. Jesus instituted a new creation so that "whoever is in Christ is a new creation: the old things have passed away" (2 Cor. 5:17).

The New Creation and the Dignity of Women

As we have seen, the entire Bible is open to a critical or actualization interpretation. Such an interpretation of the *new creation* inaugurated by the resurrection is especially needed today for two areas of great concern for Christian humanism, namely, the dignity and equality of women and the persistence of evil.

Over the centuries the lack of respect for the dignity, intelligence, freedom, and equality of women has caused great suffering, scandal, and anger. Significant steps have been taken to rectify this situation. In chapter one references were made to the international conference sponsored by the 1994 United Nations on population and development. Delegates from 170 countries assembled in Cairo, Egypt. In the two previous conferences—at Bucharest in 1974 and in Mexico City in 1984—women had a minor voice regarding the family-planning programs. At Cairo, on the contrary, the conference was shaped by women's views and voices. The women made sure that the role of women was placed at the center of family planning. They declared that as long as women were mired in illiteracy and oppression, there would be no progress on population-related issues. There are still too many places where women are literally chattels, articles of personal, movable property. For the population and development policies to have any success, the empowerment of women must not be excluded. Consequently, policies were asked for that would

provide women with better health services and better education, and which would spare them such human rights abuses
as forced abortion and genital mutilation. The women of the
world made it clear that they want to bring down the birth
rate on a do-it-yourself basis. They took this position not
because of deforestation or famine or unemployment per se,
but because it is better for their children. The majority of the
poor around the globe are women of color and their children.

Before and during the conference, the Vatican (with support from a number of Islamic and Latin American countries)
filibustered over certain statements concerning abortion, contraceptive birth control, homosexuality and extramarital sex.
At the end of the conference the Vatican representative signed
the final document, expressing reservations only about the
fuzziness of the term "sexual and reproductive health" in a
couple of the chapters.

There were many evaluations of the conference by participants. Ellen Chesler, a director of the International Women's
Health Coalition, a New York-based organization, declared, "I
think this conference can be seen as ending 2,000 years of
ecclesiastical authority or jurisdiction over marriage and
women's lives. Medicine and science, not religion and belief,
will govern family planning" (Crossette 1994). Daniel Maguire,
professor of moral theology at Marquette University, had
another view. He judged (1994, 918) that "in many ways the
conference and its written product are a triumph for the values that define holiness in Judaism, Christianity and Islam as
well as in other religions. Though the word religion seems not
to have made it into the final document, the religiously championed values of compassion, social justice, and reverence for
this generous host of an earth are enshrined in it. Religious
representatives should have been celebrating, not bickering
about disputable issues in reproductive ethics."

What do the scriptures say about the equality and dignity of
women? This question is fundamental to Christian humanism.

We have seen in chapter one that in Genesis 1, Adam and
Eve have equal dignity because they were created at the same
time in the image of God. In Genesis 2, their equality and
unity are symbolized by the rib image: since both are made
from the one human taken from the clay, the man and woman

are bone of bone and flesh of flesh. During his ministry Jesus proclaimed that God is the Father of all persons and desires the salvation of all. Paul taught that the risen Christ shattered the religious, economic, and sexual dichotomies of all societies: "There is neither Jew nor Greek, there is neither slave nor free person, there is not male and female; for all are one in Christ Jesus" (Gal. 3:28). Being one in Christ does not eliminate diversity but integrates it.

On the basis of these principles, the Christian churches should promote and expand the dignity and equality of women. However, in most churches women are systematically excluded from positions of authority and from ministerial posts. The ground of this subordination is **patriarchalism**, a cultural view which fosters male superiority, grounds authority in physical power, and structures society hierarchically. But it was not always so.

During the ministry of Jesus and in the first decades of the church it is clear that, "while women's activities were somewhat limited by what was culturally permissible, many roles which ultimately were associated with the priestly ministry were evidently never restricted to men" (Boucher 1980, 46).

The Christian scriptures do not provide an exact or complete record of the ministry of Jesus and the development of the early church. That is why it is not easy to summarize accurately the role of women during the ministry of Jesus and in the apostolic church. Nevertheless, the scriptures provide enough information to show that women did not have the completely subordinate roles they have today. Many of Jesus' disciples and followers were women, persons like Mary Magdalene, Joanna, and Susanna, all of whom were faithful to the end (Mk. 15:40–41, 47; 16:1; Lk. 8:1–3). Martha declares that Jesus is "the Christ, the Son of God" (Jn. 11:27), a confession similar to Peter's that won him high praise from Jesus (Mt. 16:16–17). It was women who discovered the empty tomb (Mk. 16:2–8; Lk. 24:2–11) and, according to Matthew (28:1–10) and John (20:11–18), it was to Mary Magdalene and other women disciples that the risen Jesus first appeared.

Paul listed the requisites for apostleship: to have experienced the resurrected Jesus and to have received from him a commission to teach the gospel (1 Cor. 9:1–2; Gal. 1:11–17).

Luke added a third requirement: to have accompanied Jesus during his ministry. Women like Prisca and Aquila met Paul's criteria (Rom. 16:3). Mary Magdalene not only met Luke's criteria but she has the special title of "apostle to the apostles" because she was sent to announce to the apostles that Jesus had risen (see Jn. 20:18).

Women were admitted without any qualification to baptism and membership in the church. Women were members of the earliest church and were present at Pentecost (Acts 2:1–4). Women like Prisca were instrumental in founding churches (Acts 18:2, 18–19 with 1 Cor. 16:19 and Rom. 16:3–5). Others like Euodia and Synteche were leaders within communities (Phil. 4:2–3; Rom. 16:1–2, 6, 12). Women participated in public worship (1 Cor. 11:5); taught converts (Acts 18:26); were prophets (1 Cor. 11:5; Acts 21:9); and deacons (Phoebe in Rom. 16:1–2; see also 1 Tim. 3:8, 11).

Unfortunately, however, there are also several passages that seriously detract from this positive picture. First, in 1 Cor. 11:3–6, women are told to wear the customary veil or head-dress when praying and prophesying in church. Paul attempts to ground this rule in the order of creation, but his argument is very obscure so that exegetes disagree on its meaning. Possibly it is a cultural regulation. At any rate, it is no longer observed.

Second, women are told not to speak in church but to get answers to their questions from their husbands (1 Cor. 14:33–35). This rule about speaking publicly contradicts what was said in an earlier section of the letter (see 1 Cor. 11: 5, 13), and could well be a later addition by an editor. Other scholars point out that the verses are found in some of the best manuscripts. Since this is so, it seems better to accept the verses as authentic and then explain why Paul included them in the letter. Madeleine Boucher states that the context of the passage "indicates that the prohibition is against asking questions (11:35) or in some way disturbing the assembly (see 11:28, 30)" (Boucher 1980, 45). Frederick Cwiekowski (1988, 126) suggests that there were cultic gatherings in Corinth and elsewhere in which the roles of women attracted suspicion and criticism because they undermined public order and decency. Paul's directive that women not ask questions in the assembly flowed "from his concern to protect the Christian communities from being confused with secret, orgiastic oriental cults."

Third, 1 Timothy 2:11–15 says women should be submissive and silent, not teach or have any authority over men. The statement not to teach is not in agreement with 1 Cor. 11:5 and with early church practice when women did teach (Acts 18:26). Why this reversal? Why do the Pastoral epistles of Titus and Timothy, written between 80 and 100, have a rather negative attitude toward women? The reason for this mistrust of young widows (1 Tim 5:11–13) and the disdainful attitude toward women (2 Tim. 3:6–7) is that in the Greco-Roman world there were teachings markedly disparaging toward sexuality, marriage, and childbearing. These teachings had crept into some Christian communities and the author of the epistles to Timothy was trying to correct these cultural errors. In so doing, he "gives a strong reaffirmation of the traditional role of women in the only way he really knows: by reasserting that women, who are to understand their lives in terms of their domestic responsibilities, are to be seen and not heard" (Cwiekowski 1988, 163).

Raymond Brown offers a much different explanation. He observes that the churches for whom the Pastorals were written highlighted the role of the officeholders as official teachers commissioned to protect the community of learners from false teachers. Many of the learners could not be trusted to discern true teachings by themselves. Women, particularly, were singled out as excessively gullible. They were "always trying to learn but never able to reach a knowledge of the truth" (2 Tim. 3:7). Brown judged this criticism demeaning. His conclusion: "There was, then, a tendency toward discrimination against women in some New Testament churches, especially in those churches where community functions were more carefully structured" (Brown 1984, 94).

The consensus of many scripture scholars is that, while it is true that the three passages discussed here did limit women's activities to what was accepted in the Greco-Roman world, they were pastoral directives concerning worship that were motivated by social and cultural factors. Nevertheless, today "They can scarcely be taken as permanent theological norms relating to church ministry" (Boucher 1980, 45). Consequently, many churches are taking steps to enhance the dignity of women. For example, some are adopting an inclusive language **lectionary**, that is, the book of prescribed readings from the Bible followed in regular sequence through the church year. Rosemary Radford Ruether, theologian and professor, expressed the thought of many women (and men) when she wrote that "such a lectionary is needed because women in contemporary churches are suffering from linguistic deprivation. . . . They can no longer nurture their souls on alienating words that ignore or systematically deny their existence. They are starved for the words of life, for symbolic forms that fully and wholeheartedly affirm their personhood and speak truth about the evils of sexism and the possibilities of a future beyond patriarchy" (1985, 4–5).

In a number of churches women are assuming ministerial roles. Several Protestant denominations have been ordaining women as ministers or priests since 1944 and as bishops since 1980. But even within some denominations that ordain women this issue is divisive. For example, the Episcopal church in the United States with its 2.5 million members has 100 dioceses, but 4 dioceses bar women from the priesthood.[1] The official Catholic church prohibits the ordination of women. It has consistently taken this position. For example, on May 22, 1994, Pope John Paul II issued an apostolic letter, *Ordinatio sacerdotalis,* in which he declared "that the church has no authority whatsoever to confer priestly ordination on women and that this judgment is to be definitively held by all the church's faithful." Many wondered what the pope means when he said it was "definitive" that women could not now or ever be priests. The Vatican responded to these doubts in a brief statement that was signed on October 28, 1995, but released on November 18, 1995. "Definitive," replied the Vatican, means infallible. The church cannot ordain women priests because this teaching is part of the deposit of faith. Specifically, the document stated that this teaching "is to be held always, everywhere and by all as belonging to the deposit of the faith." This declaration unleashed a new round of debates over the extent of the authority of the hierarchical church and what is included in the church's deposit of the faith.

Over the years the official Catholic Church has offered three arguments against the ordination of women: Christ had male disciples who were his priests; there have not been women priests in the two-thousand-year history of the Catholic church; and priests should be male since they represent Jesus Christ to the community. Those who favor the ordination of women priests accuse the Vatican of a precritical view of the scriptures and a failure to deal creatively with the Christian tradition. They argue that Jesus never ordained the men disciples as priests, that many of his disciples were women, that the church's stance ties it to disciplinary rules that developed out of an outmoded patriarchal culture, and that all Christians, men and women, are christened at baptism to represent Christ.

The Vatican stance has prompted sharp criticisms. For example, Sandra Schneiders, professor of spirituality and scripture, in her comments on the desire of women for ordination declared, "The last time there was such a groundswell that was not heeded was the Protestant Reformation" (see Ostling 1992, 53). In 1994, the Vatican held a month-long international assembly of bishops **(a synod)** to discuss the role of persons consecrated to Christ in the church—religious priests, nuns, and brothers. Only 59 of the assembly's 348 participants were women, even though three-quarters of the "consecrated people" in the church are women. The women participants had a limited chance to speak and no vote. In short, they were observers. This situation provoked some sisters from the United States to protest the synod in St. Peter's Square. Chanting "We shall not be silenced," the sisters raised banners that declared: "They are talking about us without us" and "Women want to be a part, not apart" (Drozdiak 1994).

The Christian churches are divided within themselves and among themselves about the roles of women in ministry and authority. Until the churches can agree on the meaning and consequences of the teaching that in the risen Christ there is neither male nor female (Gal. 3:28), the churches will continue to be divided and a cause of scandal to a world which is increasingly based on the equality of women in principle and in fact.

The New Creation and the Persistence of Evil

Another question that needs a critical or actualization interpretation is the biblical declaration that the new creation inaugurated by the resurrection means that God has saved us from evil, especially sin and death. If this is true, why is there still so much evil? Why are the daily news reports in newspapers and on TV filled with stories of crime, infidelity, cruelty, and murder? The response of Karl Rahner (1904–84), an eminent Jesuit theologian, was written long ago (1968, 80–81), but is worth quoting at length today because it expresses the hope that grounds Christian humanism.

> What we call (Christ's) resurrection and unthinkingly regard as his own personal destiny, is simply, on the surface of reality as a whole, the first symptom in experience of the fact that behind so-called experience (which we take so seriously) everything has already become different in the true and decisive depth of all things. His resurrection is like the first eruption of a volcano which shows that in the interior of the world God's fire is already burning, and this will bring everything to blessed ardor in his light. He has risen to show that that has already begun. Already from the heart of the world into which he descended in death, the new forces of a transfigured earth are at work. Already in the innermost center of all reality, futility, sin and death are vanquished and all that is needed is the short space of time which we call history *post Christum natum* [after the birth of Christ or what we call A.D.], until everywhere and not only in the body of Jesus what has really already begun will be manifest. Because he did not begin to save and transfigure the world with the superficial symptoms but started with its innermost root, we creatures on the surface think that nothing has happened. Because the waters of suffering and guilt are still flowing where we are standing, we think the deep sources from which they spring have not yet dried up. Because wickedness is still inscribing its runes on the face of the earth, we conclude that in the deepest heart of reality, love is extinct. But all that is merely appearance, the appearance which we take to be the reality of life. He has risen because in death he conquered and redeemed forever the innermost center of all earthly reality. And having risen, he has held fast to it. And so he has remained.

Formation of the Gospels

Acts 2:14–40; 3:12–26; 4:1–12.

The Pontifical Biblical Commission's *Instruction on the Historical Truth of the Gospels* in 1964 speaks of the "three stages of tradition by which the doctrine and the life of Jesus have come down to us." Stage one entails what the Jesus of history said and did, and what his men and women disciples saw and heard. Jesus of Nazareth proclaimed through his powerful words and deeds that God is a Father who creates, covenants, loves, and saves. Jesus had a **theocentric kerygma**, that is, a God-centered message. Jesus was a proclaimer of God the Father's loving and judging presence. Jesus did not place himself at the center of his teachings. There is no evidence that Jesus required his disciples and others to adhere to him personally with religious faith. On the contrary, he proclaimed God's reign and love that has been manifested at creation, in the history of Israel, and now in him.

The second stage of the tradition constitutes the period when the first-generation Christians proclaimed and explained the life and words of Jesus, especially his death and resurrection. The eminent Lutheran biblical scholar Rudolf Bultmann (1884–1976) captured this stage in one sentence: "The proclaimer became the proclaimed" (1951, 1:33). The 600 disciples proclaimed a **christocentric kerygma**, that is, a Christ-centered message. Jesus was proclaimed as Lord, Son of the Father, source of the Spirit, and the Christ. The faith *of* Jesus in the immediate proximity of the reign of God in himself became faith *in* Jesus as the source of freedom from sin and death. The kingdom of the Father was now understood in terms of the experience the 600 had of what the Father had done for Jesus and how Jesus responded to his Father's love. The message continues to be ultimately theocentric but by being immediately christocentric.

The significance of this shift in kerygma or message can be illustrated by the way Muslims regard Muhammad, the poet-prophet who proclaimed and celebrated Allah and not himself. After Muhammad's death in 632 A.D., his disciples repeated his message, especially as found in the Qur'an. Muhammad did not become the object of the people's faith. Actually, Muslims are insulted if they are called

"Muhammadans." Jesus, the risen Christ, on the contrary, is central to the Christian religion. Disciples of the risen Jesus are quick to call themselves Christians because the Father made the kingdom present in him.

The best place to see the preaching of the 600 is in three speeches in Acts (2:14–40; 3:12–26; 4:8–12). These sermons are symbolic communication that cover substantially the same ground: the messianic age has come; the new age is here through the ministry, death, and resurrection of Jesus; Jesus is exalted and Lord; Jesus sends the Spirit; the end of human history is at hand; repent and be baptized.

The church's **oral tradition** developed because of its own inner needs and because of its contact with outside forces, such as Judaism and the Greco-Roman religions. We do not have many of Jesus' very words. His message was adapted by the 600 as they gave instruction to converts (Acts 8:26–40; Lk. 4:17–21; 24:25–27), standardized community worship (for example, the Last Supper accounts in 1 Cor. 11; Mk. 24:25–27; John 6), and engaged prospective converts (Mt. 8:1–17; 22:15–46).

As time went on, some of the teachings of Jesus that were shaped by and for kerygmatic purposes were written down, that is, put in some kind of **literary form**. It is believed that sayings, parables, miracle stories, infancy narratives, and resurrection narratives were collected. For example, one significant saying reported in all four gospels declares that "If any man would come after me, let him deny himself and take up his cross and follow me" (Mk. 8:34, Mt. 16:25, Lk. 9:24, Jn. 12:25). This sentence would make little sense in the mouth of the Jesus of history but makes eminent sense in the mouth of the Christ of faith. In the post-resurrection church it must have been extremely difficult for both Jews and Gentiles to commit themselves to a suffering messiah. The study of these various literary forms within the gospels is called **form criticism**. The effort to establish through a study of the oldest and best manuscripts a biblical text as close as possible to the original is called **textual criticism**.

The third stage of the tradition comes with the actual composition of the gospels by sacred authors. The author of Mark was the literary genius who produced the first gospel probably in Rome around 68. He took the oral and written traditions and put them into narrative form. Stories have the effect of catching the reader up into the action and involving her or him in the plot. In the gospel stories Jesus directly addresses the members of the community and their difficulties. For example, it is not easy to be a Christian since the way to salvation involves the cross (self-sacrificing love). Jesus declares that his disciples must take up the cross and follow him (8:34).

It is believed that Mark wrote to console the Roman church during the persecution by Nero (54–68). Mark indicates that the Christians can expect to be "arraigned before governors and kings" (13:9), but the Holy Spirit will guide them. Mark reminds the Christians that suffering and persecution are an important part of discipleship, even if during the ministry of Jesus the disciples and Peter did not always understand that lesson (8:31–35, 9:31–32, 10:32–45). The Christian community also experienced growing estrangement from the Jews: "You will be beaten in synagogues" (13:9). The Christians do not observe the Sabbath (2:23–3:6), Jewish practices of fasting (2:18–20), or the dietary laws (7:19). It also seems that they have relativized the temple (12:33, 13:2). Its destruction is anticipated (13:2) inasmuch as Jerusalem has been under a siege by Roman forces since 66. Mark's community regards itself as the authentic covenant community. It is the new cloth and the new wine, as explained by Jesus (2:21–22).

Mark and the other evangelists were **redactors** (editors) who expressed, interpreted, and explained the kerygma in their gospels. They took the oral and written tradition and molded it for the specific needs of their churches. As we have seen, the **gospels** are books that blend the Jesus of history with the ministry of the risen Christ in and through his church communities. The evangelists are primarily concerned with the identity and mission of their churches. For example, each evangelist sees the church in relation to Judaism. For Mark the church is the community of the new age, for Matthew the true Israel, for Luke the new Israel, and for John the church replaces Israel. **Redaction criticism** is the study of the differences among the gospels. Norman Perrin (1969, 1) explained that "It is concerned with studying the theological motivation of an author as this is revealed in the collection, arrangement, editing, and modification of traditional material, and in the composition of new material or the creation of new forms within the tradition of early Christianity."

For example, the synoptics have statements about *salt* (Mk. 9:50, Mt. 5:13, Lk. 14:33–35). Mark emphasizes preserving peace within the community. In their culture to share salt with someone was to form an indissoluble bond. Matthew emphasizes that the disciples will become ineffective if they lose their savor just as salt is useless if it loses its particular taste. Luke seems to suggest that salt has something to do with the self-denial required of followers of Christ. The synoptics also refer to a lamp (Mk. 4:21, Mt. 5:14, Lk. 11:33). Mark underscores that the reign of God is now hidden from sight but it will ultimately be manifested. Matthew declares that the followers of Christ must be active and visible and not hidden. Luke wants to emphasize that the truth is self-evident to anyone who can see.

When the four gospels are compared, it soon becomes clear that the first three have a similar order and content. All three have Jesus teaching for approximately one year up north in Galilee and then going down to Jerusalem where he is crucified by the end of the week. There is considerable verbal similarity: only 30 verses in Mark do not appear either in Matthew or in Luke or in both. On the other hand, the three gospels have significant differences. The presence of so much material that is the same and so much that is different in the first three gospels is called the **synoptic problem**. The word "synoptic" means "presenting a common view."

Matthew and Luke are different from Mark because the first gospel was eventually inadequate to the needs of their communities. The churches of Matthew and Luke had new and different problems of identity and mission from Mark's community. Jewish Christians had been expelled from the synagogues and there was a greater sense of the universal mission of the church. Matthew and Luke had to provide their communities with more information and clearer symbols for their specific institutional, theological, and devotional needs. For example, Matthew and Luke contain many speeches and sayings about the coming kingdom of God that are not found in Mark. In some 230 verses, Matthew and Luke share material lacking in Mark (Brown 1994, 1:64). These additional teachings or sayings highlight the risen Jesus' role as the authoritative wisdom and moral teacher of their communities. Some of the sayings include such famous statements as the beatitudes: "Blessed are the poor in spirit, for theirs is the kingdom of heaven" (Mt. 5:3); "Blessed are you who are poor, for the kingdom of God is yours" (Lk. 6:20). These additional teachings are called **Q**, from the German word for "source," **Quelle**. This source-document has never been found. "Probably Q came from a Greek-speaking community, predominately Jewish-Christian in outlook, located around the middle of the first century in northern Palestine" (Cwiekowski 1988, 152). Q was probably put together so that the community could continue to live and proclaim Jesus' teachings about the kingdom of God and discipleship—teachings that had been validated by his resurrection.

The gospels of Matthew and Luke, on the other hand, are different from one another, because their authors wrote separately, had different theological purposes, and their respective churches had their own specific needs. It is almost impossible to contend that Matthew wrote knowing Luke's gospel and vice versa. Their infancy narratives have different emphases. Their concern was the theological significance of Jesus' birth (what does it mean?) rather than the historical details (what happened?).

The gospel of Matthew teaches that the church is the true Israel, and Jesus recapitulates the history of Israel. For example, in his infancy narrative he makes Joseph, who lives in Bethlehem, the dominant character. An angel informs Joseph in a dream not to dismiss his pregnant wife because the child will be a son of David. The child is born in Joseph's house. **Magi** (Persian astrologers) pay homage to the child-king and inform the parents that Herod plans to kill the child. The parents emigrate to Egypt. For Luke, Jesus is the savior of all humankind and he places the church within the context of the Roman Empire. In the Lucan infancy narrative, Mary dominates the scenes. She and Joseph live in Nazareth and are forced to go to Bethlehem for the universal census ordered by the emperor, since Joseph is of the family of David. The angel Gabriel tells Mary that her child will be the Son of God. When the child is born in a stable, angels inform shepherds that in Bethlehem a savior who is Messiah and Lord is born.

In a later section (see Chapter 4) attention will be given to the formation of the gospel of John and its distinctive theology.

Jesus the Teacher

For many people the word *teacher* denotes someone hired by a school to instruct students. By definition a **teacher** shows someone how to do something. Anyone who shows another how to write, to eat, to sew, to drive a car, to ride a bike, or to read is a teacher. Jesus was recognized as a teacher even though he lacked formal training and credentials from approved authorities. He is respectfully called teacher some forty-eight times in the gospels, although in Matthew only unbelievers and Judas use the title whereas believers call him Lord. Most teachers work out of one place. Jesus was an itinerant teacher.

We have little knowledge of much of Jesus' life. Matthew and Luke relate his birth. But what of the many years between his infancy and his public ministry? Did Jesus spend those years in Nazareth? There are several reasons to suggest that he was an itinerant craftsman who became an itinerant teacher. **First,** there would not be that much work in a small town like Nazareth, since people in a small town had to be resourceful and do a lot of their own repairs. Jesus had to travel to find work. **Second,** according to tradition Jesus was celibate. Marriage and family were not only expected but they were sacred duties. Celibacy has never been part of the Jewish tradition. It would have been extremely difficult to avoid marriage in a small town. **Third,** Jesus does not have the traits of someone raised in a small town for over thirty years. He was an exceptionally capable man whose range of interests and experiences was much greater than his disciples. Jesus was able to attract disciples and to gather large crowds. People were impressed by his knowledge, style, and message (Mt. 7:28; 13:53). He was aware of the religious and political problems of his day. He knew the teachings of the Pharisees, Sadducees, and John the Baptist so that, in the light of the Torah, he could challenge them.

The gospels do not provide us with the psychological and religious development of Jesus. We know nothing of his inner thoughts and struggles. There is no story of his prophetic call, nor is there any explanation of a development of his **prophetic consciousness**, that is, his conviction that, based on his awareness of his unique relationship with God, he could speak and act for God whom he calls Father. "Father" in Aramaic is **Abba**, a term used by children to address their fathers. Jesus' use of the term is not baby talk, but an intimate and familiar way of speaking to God (Mk. 13:32, 14:36; Lk. 10:21–22, 11:2, 22:42; Mt. 11:25–27, 26:39; Jn. 3:35–36, 5:19–23). Jesus' use of the term was highly unusual, if not unique, in his day. Everything in his life was based on his unique **filial consciousness**, that is, that he was always in the presence of a loving and protecting Father. He taught that God is Father of all and that everyone should have childlike trust in God in the daily experience of the joys, hopes, difficulties and dangers of life. From the very beginning of his ministry in Galilee (Mk. 1:15), Jesus called all people to adopt his filial consciousness and at the end of his ministry in Jerusalem he was crucified on charges growing out of this teaching. The early Christians manifested their filial consciousness when they prayed to God as "Abba" and when they taught this prayer to the Gentiles (Rom. 8:15; Gal. 4:6).

Jesus Teaches the Kingdom of God

The teachings of Jesus are captured in the cultural symbol *kingdom of God*. Although the symbol is found only once in the Hebrew scriptures (Wis. 10:10), the Jews knew its meaning because God is frequently referred to as a king with dominion over all creation, especially in the enthronement Psalms (47, 93, 96–99). The kingdom is not a thing, a people, or a place. It is a relationship.

At the time of Jesus the symbol *kingdom of God* had three interrelated meanings. **First,** God is a creator-king who saves his people from chaos and disorder. The kingdom of God myth states that Yahweh has become king and, as such, he does four things: he creates the world; annually renews the fertility of the earth; sustains his people in their place in the world; and saves the faithful from the forces of evil, frequently personified by sea monsters (Ps. 74:12–14; Ps. 89:10–11).

Second, the kingdom of God referred to the time when God would save the Israelites from their oppressors. The history of the Jews is the history of oppression by one foreign power after another: Egyptians, Philistines, Assyrians, Babylonians, Persians, Greeks and Romans. At some point in time, God would establish his kingdom and put an end to all hostility and oppression. God's power would be manifested to Israel and to all nations.

Third, the symbol referred to "the day of the Lord" when God would save Israel from sin and evil. The Jews looked to a final day in human history when God's reign would be finally and fully established. The day would mark the end of sin and be followed by the end-time: a new age in which Israel would be vindicated and God's justice and order would prevail.

Today since the symbol *kingdom of God* is masculine and also suggests something objectively completed and realized, it is often translated as "rule" or "reign of God." This translation suggests something gender-free, active, and organic. It points to a relationship: the Father-King ruling in human hearts. It is interesting that the metaphor, reign of God, is found in John's gospel only twice (3:3, 5). He prefers *eternal life* or *life*. The reign of God is life with the Father and the Son, now and forever. Christian disciples participate in Jesus' life: "I came so that they might have life and have it more abundantly" (10:10).

When Jesus used the symbol *kingdom of God,* he called people to allow God the Father to reign in their hearts. He taught that nothing compared in value or importance to God, and people should give their whole hearts, souls, and minds to God. Once people accepted God with filial consciousness, the past would be renewed, the present would be marked by a new way of life and by new possibilities, and the future would be the fulfillment of God's new age.

To teach the reign/kingdom of God, Jesus employed four interrelated symbols. **First,** Jesus frequently ate with people, especially tax collectors and sinners **(table fellowship)**. Human and animal eating seem the same at face value, but they are quite different. We call formal human eating *dining.* When we invite others to dine with us, it is a symbol of love and friendship. Jesus was not an ascetic like John the Baptist (Lk. 7:33). He dined so frequently with people that he was denounced as "a drunkard and glutton" (Lk. 7:34). What scandalized his contemporaries was that he dined publicly with those considered sinners. We have seen that groups like the Pharisees shunned those who failed to follow the written and oral Torah. Since Jewish meals always began and ended with prayer, and since they were the condition for the possibility of religious discussions about the Torah and the destiny of Israel, these formal meals were Jesus' very dramatic way of bringing his message of God's love and judgment to people. This was Jesus' way of inviting the so-called sinners to reject their past and to start a new life. Jesus' table fellowship aroused more opposition than his words. Today, many Christian communities continue Jesus' table fellowship by holding a symbolic meal of bread and wine each Sunday, and in some churches, daily.

Second, Jesus taught the reign/kingdom by his prayer. The Jews have the Kaddish prayer, an ancient prayer said daily even today, and especially at times of mourning. It reads: "Magnified and sanctified be his great name in the world that he has created according to his will. May he establish his kingdom in your lifetime and in the lifetime of all the house of Israel, even speedily and at a near time."

Jesus' prayer, the Our Father, resembles the Kaddish, but Matthew (6:5–15) and Luke (11:1–4) have different versions of the prayer. They also provide different settings and reasons for the prayer. In Matthew Jesus teaches the people gathered for the Sermon on the Mount the proper way to pray; in Luke the disciples ask if there is a prayer that is distinctive of their community and Jesus provides it.

Since there are two versions of the Our Father, we cannot be sure which one he actually taught. Nonetheless, the two prayers contain some of Jesus' most important themes, especially the coming of the kingdom and a new life of friendship, love, and community built on forgiveness of all, in imitation of the Father's forgiveness.

Third, Jesus was a miracle worker. His miracles are at the heart of his message about the reign of God. **Miracles** are changes, brought about in people or things by the power of God, which are normally not possible by human means or within the laws of nature.

The word used for miracle in the synoptics is *dunameis,* meaning "acts of power." It was probably Jesus' miracles more than his teachings that at first attracted the large crowds who assembled to hear and see him in Galilee. For those with faith his miracles were signs of God's power and the presence of the kingdom. Isaiah promised that in the day of salvation the deaf would hear, the blind would see, and the poor would rejoice (Isa. 29:18–19). There is, however, a paradox related to miracles. If you truly have faith in God, you do not need a miracle as proof of anything. If you do not have faith, no seemingly miraculous event will persuade you that faith makes sense.

The gospels describe Jesus working four kinds of miracles: **healings** (the blind, lame, lepers), **nature miracles** (changing water to wine, walking on water, calming storms), **exorcisms** (driving out evil spirits or demonic forces that have taken possession of humans or things), and **resuscitations** (restoring consciousness and life to Jairus' daughter, the son of a widow from Nain, and Lazarus). Similar miracles are related in the Hebrew scriptures. Abraham secured through prayer the health of Abimelech's wife and his maidservants (Gen. 20), and Elisha cured Naaman of leprosy (2 Kgs. 5). Elisha multiplied oil for a generous widow (2 Kgs. 4:1–8) and enough bread from twenty barley loaves to feed one hundred soldiers (2 Kgs. 4:42–44). David played his harp to exorcise Saul of an evil spirit (1 Sam. 16). And Elijah resuscitated a widow's son (1 Kgs. 17).

Most Christians firmly believe that Jesus was a miracle worker. He brought the time of salvation when physical and moral evil were overcome. What is in question is the historicity of all the miracle stories. A precritical reading accepts all of them as historical; a historical-critical interpretation suggests that many are symbolic stories to convey deep faith in the identity and mission of the risen Christ.

We have already discussed the difficult questions raised by the resuscitations. They seem to be post-resurrection affirmations that, as risen Lord, Jesus conquered death. The nature miracles are also problematic. They "are often put in a category of their own because of their apparent lack of historicity" (Hill 1991, 97). Many regard them as symbolic stories created to convey post-resurrection christology, namely, that the risen Christ has sovereign power over the forces of nature which were created by and for him. The exorcisms are also debatable. John's gospel has no exorcisms but the synoptic gospels contain a number of them. For example, Jesus' first miracle in both Mark and Luke is an exorcism.

There are reasons why the exorcisms are questioned today. First, in Jesus' day demons were often invoked as the cause of sicknesses that were not easily explained. "Persons afflicted with what we would call today mental disturbances were regarded as possessed because observers were unable to analyze properly the causes of the maladies in question and consequently ascribed them to a demon" (Fitzmyer 1982, 36). For example, there is the story of a boy "possessed by a mute spirit" who was exorcised by Jesus. Modern science would diagnose him as epileptic (see Mk. 9:14–29). Second, the ontological existence of angels and demons is questioned. Those who believe in their actual existence accept the exorcisms literally. They claim that it is almost impossible to understand Jesus' proclamation of the reign of God without understanding at the same time the gospel accounts of the opposition Jesus faced from Satan, a true spiritual Prince of Darkness.

Those who reject angels and demons argue that the Jews adopted the theology of angels and demons from the Persians during their long association with them from 538 to 330 B.C. The official religion of the Persians was Zoroastrianism. Zoroaster (628–550 B.C.), their teacher and prophet, taught a dualistic view of the world, that is, the universe is ruled by two supernatural forces. The powers of good or light were led by Ahura Mazda; the forces of evil and darkness were led by Ahriman, a devil. According to their belief, at the end of time a climactic battle between Mazda's angels and Ahriman's demons would result in the triumph of the good and the destruction of evil. Until then, the two powers would struggle incessantly, with humankind caught up in this cosmic struggle.

The Persian notion of angels and demons helped the Jews find suitable answers to two theological problems. First, how does God communicate with his people? For the Jews the one God is omnipotent and transcendent. The space between an infinite God and his finite creatures is measureless. One sure way this transcendent God can communicate and bridge this chasm between himself and his finite creatures is through angels. God was pictured as a king surrounded by a host of

angels, immortal, spiritual, noncorporeal beings. Our English word "angels" comes from Hebrew and Greek words which mean "messengers." According to the Bible, there are nine species of angels: seraphim (Isa. 6:2), cherubim (Gen. 3:24), thrones (Col. 1:16), dominations (Col. 1:16), virtues (1 Pt. 3:22), powers (Eph. 3:10), principalities (Col. 2:15), archangels (Jude 9) and angels (Lk. 1:13). Second, why is there evil and sin? God is not only transcendent but also all-holy and omnipotent. God cannot be the cause of evil. The only way evil can come into human history is through **demons**, evil angels. In Jesus' day the Pharisees took seriously the reality of angels and demons but the Sadducees denied their existence. The Sadducees probably denied the existence of angels because in the Pentateuch there are stories—including Hagar by a spring in the wilderness (Gen. 16:7, 13), Jacob's dream (Gen. 32:25), and Moses at the burning bush (Ex. 3:2–4)— which begin with an angelic presence suddenly switching to the divine presence. The presence of an angel symbolizes the very presence of God. For example, Jacob named the place where he wrestled with an angel "Peniel" because, as he said, "I have seen God face to face" (Gen. 32:31). Apparently, "the angel of Yahweh" is not an individual spiritual creature but the Creator himself in a form visible to humans. It is only in such postexilic books as Tobit and Daniel that individual angels like Michael, Gabriel, and Raphael are identified with personal names.

There is a major difference between the Hebrew and Christian presentation of the evil one. In the Hebrew scriptures, Satan (which literally means "adversary") is totally at God's disposal. The word *satan* refers to one of the "sons of the gods" *(bene ha Elohim),* those mysterious beings depicted as members of Yahweh's heavenly court (Ps. 89:6–7). Satan had several roles: to patrol the earth (Job 1:7), to accuse Yahweh's people of their failures (Zech. 3:1), and to test the loyalty of Yahweh's subjects, as in the story of Job, God's "blameless and upright" servant (Job 1:1). The term "devil" meaning "the evil one" does not occur in the Hebrew Bible.

In the Christian scriptures, there is a devil, an evil one, who is totally opposed to God the Father-Creator and his Son. As the source of lies, suffering, sickness and death, he is forever on the prowl "like a roaring lion looking for [someone] to devour" (1 Pt. 5:8). In the book of Revelation, Satan is identified with the devil and the Genesis serpent (12:9–12). Jesus defeats Satan by his cross and resurrection. At the end of history, Satan will be placed in "the pool of fire and sulfur," there to be tormented "forever and ever" (Rev. 20:9–10). Many modern Christians deny the ontological existence of angels, demons, and devils because of the background just outlined. They do not deny the existence of demonic forces that create so much havoc for individuals and societies. They regard Jesus' exorcisms as powerful metaphors for the risen Jesus' conquest of the evil, even demonic, forces that undermine all societies and individuals. Nevertheless, the *Catechism of the Catholic Church* (released in October 1992) states that the existence of angels is "a truth of faith. The witness of Scripture is as clear as the unanimity of Tradition" (n. 328).

The healing miracles are another matter. It is generally accepted that these are the miracles that Jesus performed. They pointed to a world in which no one is sick or will die; they anticipated the age to come, the time when God "will wipe every tear from their eyes, and there shall be no more death or mourning, wailing or pain, [for] the old order has passed away" (Rev. 21:4). The healing miracles also dramatized the presence of the reign of God. They provided the sick or disabled a chance to live a new life. In Jesus' times, since disease and disabilities were associated with the demonic, the sick were to be avoided. Jesus mixed with the sick and healed those who asked for a cure in faith. For example, lepers had to live away from healthy people since this disease is contagious. Once cleansed they could rejoin their families and community. Their body-person was recreated, renewed, and sustained, and evil was overcome. Their social and political situation changed. Their religious situation also changed: they could worship in the temple and their synagogue.

In John's gospel, there are seven miracles, four of which are also found in the synoptics. But John does not use the word "miracles" but rather the word "signs" *(semeia)*. The signs do not point to the reign of God but to Jesus himself. The seven signs symbolically communicate the identity and glory of the risen Christ so that his disciples would believe in him (2:11).

Fourth, Jesus often spoke of the reign of God in **parables.** These are stories that compare or link everyday experiences to the kingdom of God. They emphasize the value of the kingdom and what actions should be taken to belong to it. Parables are meant to turn a person's life upside down inasmuch as they challenge a person's lifestyle and purpose. They often have an ending that goes against the conventional wisdom. They shatter worlds. What Jew would expect a Samaritan to save an injured and helpless Jew? How many fathers are prodigal (generous) enough to forgive unconditionally a prodigal (recklessly wasteful) son? Parables force us to ask ourselves if we are giving priority to the important dimensions of life. They surprise like a joke: you either get the point or you do not. For example, Jesus said, " The kingdom of heaven is like a merchant searching for fine pearls. When he finds a pearl of great price he goes and sells all that he has and buys it" (Mt. 13:45–46).

The four methods of teaching are interrelated. Jesus' table fellowship was the enactment of his parables and prayer. The Our Father would have been empty without the other three methods of teaching. The healings complemented the parables. And the parables would have been sterile without the healings and table fellowship.

There is something else about Jesus' teaching of the reign of God. Sometimes preachers and teachers announce that Jesus brought the reign of God. On the contrary, the kingdom brought Jesus. The reign of God began with creation. God has always been in partnership with humankind: with Adam and Eve, Abraham and Sarah, Jacob and his twelve sons, and so forth. What Jesus manifested is that what had been present in a conditional and provisional way became present in an unconditional and definitive way in his incarnation and ministry.

Jesus the Prophet

Jesus the teacher was also a prophet. While it is true that the gospels never describe a time when he received the prophetic vocation, the gospels make it clear that he was a prophetic teacher. His first words in Mark (1:15) are "This is the time of fulfillment. The kingdom of God is at hand. Repent and believe in the gospel." In Luke especially, Jesus speaks and acts as a prophet (4:24–27, 7:16, 9:8, 19, 24:19). Jesus believed his mission marked a decisive moment, a turning point in religious history. He was the prophet of the end-time, as his healings and table fellowship manifested. In short, Jesus had an **eschatological consciousness.** Eschatology refers to the future. For Jesus, the future kingdom is even now present but not yet fully. "The kingdom of God is an event of the future, but it is a future that is virtually present. The relation of dawn to sunrise is analogous to this conception. At dawn we may say that sunrise is yet to come, but dawn is an assurance that it is close at hand. So Jesus announces the kingdom in the way dawn announces sunrise" (Tyson 1984, 247).

There are gospel passages that suggest that the Jesus of history expected the reign of God to reach its final completion during his lifetime or shortly thereafter. In the scene before the transfiguration, Jesus says to some of his disciples, "Amen, I say to you, there are some standing here who will not taste death until they see that the kingdom of God has come in power" (Mk. 9:1). Mark 13 is an extensive eschatological discourse. In it Jesus predicts the destruction of the temple, offers apocalyptic signs of the end of history, and speaks of the coming of the Son of Man. He concludes by declaring: "Amen, I say to you, this generation will not pass away until all these things have taken place" (Mk. 13:30). Scholars suggest that Jesus is the source of these passages and not the early church because it would be most embarrassing to retain them since human history did not end.

Unlike the classical Hebrew prophets, Jesus did not have visions or experience ecstatic states. Neither did he use such traditional formulas as "The word of God has come to me" or "Thus says the Lord God" (see, for example, Isa. 1:24; Jer. 2:12; Amos 3:11). Jesus spoke authoritatively in his own name. What is distinctive of his style is his use of the word **Amen** (which means "truly" or "indeed" or "I tell you this") at the beginning of sentences: "Amen, amen, I say to you . . . " Like the prophets of old he called for a conversion of heart and lifestyle **(repentance)** in view of God's impending reign, and he made a sharp critique of abuses. In Jesus' day there was polarization between men and women, rural and urban, priestly and lay, traditional and hellenistic Jews, and between the Jews and Gentiles.

Jesus spoke against three abuses in Jewish society: exclusiveness, legalism, and ritualism.

The Jews were grateful and proud to be the chosen people. However, many took this to an extreme. Since Gentiles were considered sinful, a faithful Jew should not associate with them. Many Jews also avoided the poor, diseased, and disabled because it was generally agreed that evil and illness were connected. Jesus taught that, since God is Father of all, there should not be elitism. "And if you greet your brothers only, what is unusual about that? Do not the pagans do the same? So be perfect, just as your heavenly Father is perfect" (Mt. 5:47–48).

Jesus conversed with Gentiles and cured those who, in faith, asked for relief. He mixed with sinners, declaring that he came not to call the just but sinners (Mk. 2:17). He ate with tax collectors and prostitutes because "Those who are healthy do not need a physician, but the sick do. I have not come to call the righteous to repentance but sinners" (Lk. 5:31–32). He touched and let himself be touched by the sick, the poor, and the so-called sinners (see Lk. 7:36–50).

Legalism is a danger in any religion, especially one that is an ethical monotheism. A faithful Israelite "delights in the law of the Lord and meditates on his law day and night" (Ps. 1:2). **Legalism** means to obey the letter of the law with little or no covenant love. It is based on a self-righteousness that corrupts the law. Legalism brings God's Torah down to the level of calculating rules and regulations. The classical prophets warned the people that God was unhappy with their heartless, "routine observance," that is, when they drew near to God "with words only" and honored him "with their lips alone" (Isa. 29:13). Jesus taught that we are graciously accepted by God without regard to any system of calculated righteousness. Jesus loved the Torah.

> Do not think that I have come to abolish the law or the prophets. I have come not to abolish but to fulfill. Amen, I say to you, until heaven and earth pass away, not the smallest letter or smallest part of a letter will pass from

the law, until all things have taken place. Therefore, whoever breaks one of these commandments and teaches others to do so will be called least in the kingdom of heaven. But whoever obeys and teaches these commandments will be called greatest in the kingdom of heaven. I tell you, unless your righteousness surpasses that of the scribes and Pharisees, you will not enter the kingdom of heaven (Mt. 5:17–20).

Jesus' contemporaries often placed the oral tradition on the same level of importance as the scriptures. This explains why they complained when Jesus healed on the Sabbath, when the disciples plucked some grain on the Sabbath as they passed through a field, and when Jesus and his disciples did not wash their hands before eating. Jesus asked the Pharisees and scribes, "And why do you break the commandment of God for the sake of your tradition?" (Mt. 15:3). In other words, Jesus displayed "an astonishing freedom toward the law. He imposed no specific formal rules on those who wished to follow him: no novitiate, no vows, no regular exercises, no long meditations, no liturgical directions. And no distinctive garments, no dietary prescriptions, no ritual ablutions, no penal or procedural laws" (Küng 1986, 344).

The most crucial part of Jesus' message is his appeal to fulfill God's will in love. This entails freedom from the law because no law can take into account all the vicissitudes of life or consider all the concrete interests and needs of the individual. Jesus opposed every kind of legalism with his radical love for all, even enemies. As Hans Küng explains, "Jesus measures the letter of the law against God's will itself, thereby liberating and blessing men and women, placing them immediately in God's presence. This is a new kind of obedience to God, not according to the letter, but (as Paul will say) in the 'spirit.' Jesus neither asks for recommitment to the old law nor does he proclaim a new law embracing every aspect of life. He issues neither moral nor ritual regulations spelling out how a person should pray, fast, observe the holy times, and act in the holy places, or even how to live hygienically" (ibid., 64).

Jesus also condemned **ritualism**—performing religious acts but with little or no inner devotion. Jesus taught that God deserves a response of sincere love.

But take care not to perform righteous deeds in order that people may see them; otherwise, you will have no recompense from your heavenly Father. When you give alms, do not blow a trumpet before you, as the hypocrites do in the synagogues and in the streets to win the praise of others. Amen, I say to you, they have received their reward. But when you give alms, do not let your left hand know what your right hand is doing, so that your almsgiving may be secret. And your Father who sees in secret will repay you. When you pray, do not be like the hypocrites, who love to stand and pray in the synagogues and on street corners so that others may see them. Amen, I say to you, they have received their reward (Mt. 6:1–5).

Furthermore, since God is Father of all, a person cannot genuinely pray if a brother or sister is not at peace with her or him. "Therefore, if you bring your gift to the altar, and there recall that your brother has anything against you, leave your gift there at the altar, go first and be reconciled with your brother, and then come and offer your gift" (Mt. 5:23–24).

Jesus also spoke against three abuses that pervade all societies and which are counter to Christian humanism: sexism, greed, and violence.

For thousands of years all cultures have been patriarchal, that is, men dominate societies. Men structure societies for themselves and keep them under their control. Women are not valued in either societies or religions, and they are not protected in the law. Jesus' view of women was based on the theology of Genesis and his filial consciousness. Men and women are equal and made in the image of God. His own disciples marveled that he talked with a woman (Jn. 4:27).

Jesus rarely speaks about sexuality in the gospels. He did speak out against the abuse of women. He also taught that his Father cares for every person, male and female. These teachings allow us to believe that he condemned sexism. In defense of the inviolability of women's bodies, he declared immoral not only external unchaste actions but also unchaste thoughts: "You have heard that it was said, 'You shall not commit adultery.' But I say to you, everyone who looks at a woman with lust has already committed adultery with her in his heart" (Mt. 5:27–28).

According to some of Jesus' contemporaries, a man could divorce his wife even for minor faults or offenses. To protect women from such cruel and demeaning treatment, Jesus condemned divorce. "Everyone who divorces his wife and marries another commits adultery, and the one who marries a woman divorced from her husband commits adultery" (Lk. 16:18).

Jesus condemned greed and reliance on wealth. He lived a life of voluntary poverty, inviting those who would follow him to sell all they had (Mt. 19:21). He taught that people should not be anxious about food, clothing, and shelter because God who feeds the birds and clothes the grass of the field will surely provide for them (see Mt. 6:25–33). Jesus himself cared for the poor and looked after them (Lk. 6:20).

Jesus warned about the perils of riches. People should not be attached to possessions and wealth (Mt. 5:3). Wealth can become a growth-inhibiting obsession that can cause people to cheat and abuse others. Furthermore, since wealth provides security, the wealthy tend to cut themselves off from God. "Do not store up for yourselves treasures on earth, where moth and decay destroy, and thieves break in and steal. But store up treasures in heaven, where neither moth nor decay destroy, nor thieves break in and steal. For where your treasure is, there also will your heart be . . . No one can serve two masters. He will either hate one and love the other, or be devoted to one and despise the other. You cannot serve God and mammon [wealth]" (Mt. 6:19–21, 24).

Finally, Jesus spoke against violence. Since God is Father of all, there is no place for violence by word and/or action. Rather, the reign of God becomes a reality in the exercise of justice, love, and compassion. Jesus said the peacemakers shall see God (Mt. 5:9). He taught that if someone has been victimized, forgiveness is required, even if it means forgiving "seventy times seven" times (Mt. 18:21–22). The unforgivable sin is not to forgive your brother from your heart (Mt. 18:35).

You have heard that it was said to your ancestors, "You shall not kill; and whoever kills will be liable to judgment." But I say to you, whoever is angry with his brother will be liable to judgment, and whoever says to his brother, "Raqa" [imbecile], will be answerable to the Sanhedrin, and whoever says, "You fool," will be liable to fiery Gehenna. . . . You have heard that it was said, "An eye for an eye and a tooth for a tooth." But I say to you, offer no resistance to one who is evil. When someone strikes you on [your] right cheek, turn the other one to him as well. . . . You have heard that it was said, "You shall love your neighbor and hate your enemy." But I say to you, love your enemies, and pray for those who persecute you, that you may be children of your heavenly Father, for he makes his sun rise on the bad and the good, and causes rain to fall on the just and the unjust (Mt. 5:21–22, 38–39, 43–45).

Compared to the classical prophets of Israel, Jesus did not concentrate on the burning social and political issues of his day. For example, he did not denounce Roman taxes and imperialism, or the unhealthy and dehumanizing living conditions of the poor and infirm. Neither did Jesus have a messianic consciousness, that is, he did not directly endeavor to eliminate the socioeconomic and political problems of his people. Nevertheless, Jesus' criticisms of both Jewish and Gentile societies were disturbing, disruptive, dangerous, and subversive (Metz 1980, 80–99, 200–204).

Neither was Jesus an **ethical teacher,** that is, he did not add any new rules of human conduct in order to promote justice and the well-being of society. All of Jesus' teachings can be found in the Torah. Even Jesus' new commandment to his disciples to love one another as he loved them (Jn. 13:34–35, 15:12) is in Leviticus (19:18, 34). What makes Jesus' commandment new is that, until the incarnation, the extent of God's love was not known, that is, that he loves so much that he sends his Son. Jesus did underscore some teachings, such as nonviolence, forgiveness of enemies, and the renunciation of wealth. But Jesus was not an ethical teacher. On the contrary, he was a religious prophet. He discussed ethical issues because ethics is an essential dimension of all religions. His emphasis was on his Father who creates, covenants, loves, and saves. Jesus did not impose a particular pattern of living valid for all times. He taught that God wants us to be open to life and to respond to persons and events in a fitting and proper way. Jesus' teachings are not based on a law-ethic; they are based on a person-ethic. A morality based upon law-observance can meet neither the limitless needs of people and society nor what happens by chance or accident. After the resurrection, the disciples realized that the title "prophet" is inadequate for Jesus when contrasted with Son of God (Jn. 1:17–18) and Christ (Mk. 8:28–29). Jesus never said "The word of God has come to me" because he is the Word (Jn. 1:1).

The Jesus of History and the Historical Jesus

Now that we have reviewed Jesus' life and teachings, we can address again the difficulties in reconstructing the life of the Jesus of history. Over the centuries Jesus has been described in ways considered outside the boundaries of Christianity. John Allegro (1923–88) maintained that Jesus never existed but was a fictional character imaginatively created by a Jewish drug-sex cult that had its commune on the shores of the Dead Sea. According to Hermann S. Reimarus (1694–1768), Jesus was a deluded fanatic who hoped to become Israel's earthly messiah and the founder of a theocratic state. When his messianic mission failed, he died in despair. The French novelist Ernest Renan (1823–92) wrote that Jesus was a pious fraud who used the resuscitation of Lazarus to achieve popularity. Nevertheless, Jesus can be called divine because he "caused his species to make the greatest advance toward the divine." Adolph von Harnack (1851–1930), a church historian, described Jesus as a preeminent ethical teacher who preached the fatherhood of God, the brotherhood of humankind, and the infinite value of the human soul. Albert Schweitzer (1875–1965), musician, theologian, and physician, depicted Jesus as an eschatological and deluded visionary who anticipated and predicted an apocalyptic end-time. When he realized he was mistaken in his predictions, he went to his death hoping that this act would somehow bring about the reign of God. The noted exegete Rudolph Bultmann (1884–1976) declared that Jesus' personality, character, and life cannot be known, but the Christ of the gospels is the model of an existential and authentic life of faith. We are forced to ask how it is possible for academically trained scholars to arrive at such diverse interpretations of the Jesus of history.

One reason is that the authors just listed brought their own assumptions and prejudices to the texts. Allegro and Reimarus, for instance, were intent on discrediting and debunking Christianity and its doctrines about Jesus. Another reason is the nature of the sources available. The primary source is the New Testament, but there are surprisingly few references to the historical career of Jesus outside the four gospels (see Gal. 1:19, 4:4; Rom. 1:3; 1 Cor. 7:10–11, 9:5, 14, 11:23, 26, 15:4–8). The gospels themselves present many challenges because as symbolic communication each has significant material not found in the others (for example, only John has the wedding at Cana and the astounding resuscitation of Lazarus) and because there are major differences between the synoptics and John. In the synoptics Jesus teaches for one year and mainly in parables; in John he teaches for three years and mainly in long allegorical speeches. In the synoptics Jesus begins his ministry in Galilee after the arrest of John the Baptist; in John he carries on a simultaneous ministry with John the Baptist in Judea. In the synoptics Jesus cleanses the temple during the last week of his life; in John this event takes place at the beginning of his ministry. In the synoptics Jesus goes to Jerusalem only once during his ministry; in John he is in and out of the holy city several times. In the synoptics the Last Supper takes place on the first day of Passover and hence is a **seder**, that is, a family meal that re-enacts the passover from slavery to freedom; in John, since the meal takes place on the day before Passover, it is not a seder. In short, it is difficult to access the Jesus of history, because what we can elicit from the gospels is the **historical Jesus**, that is, Jesus as reconstructed by historical research and the historical-critical method.

Despite these problems concerning the Jesus of history and the historical Jesus, scholars still think it is possible to develop some criteria for determining what events and sayings are historical, that is, they reflect the actual life of the Jesus of history. Scholars have developed the following **criteria** (see Perrin 1974, 281–82; Hayes 1976, 36–37; Evans 1993, 21–33; Gibeau 1994, 7).

First, **embarrassment**. Since there are some actions or sayings of Jesus that would have embarrassed or created difficulties for the early church as the apostles proclaimed the gospel, it is unlikely that they would have invented them. We have seen earlier that the evangelists struggle with the baptism of Jesus, the Messiah, by John the Baptist, the messenger. Why does Jesus submit to this ritual of repentance when he is sinless? In all four gospels Jesus is baptized. But the evangelists place the baptism within theological teachings. In Mark, the stress is on Jesus' identity as the Father's beloved Son and one filled with the Spirit. In Matthew, the baptism is to fulfill God's plan for Jesus as the savior of sinners. In Luke's gospel Jesus is not baptized by the Baptist because he is in prison. Luke makes the Baptist the final figure in the first covenant. In John's gospel, the baptism is a revelation to John the Baptist that Jesus is the Son of God.

Second, **distinctiveness**. There are things that are dissimilar to characteristic emphases of both Judaism and the first Christian communities, for example, Jesus' use of Abba and Amen.

Third, **multiple attestation**. There are themes, sayings, or concerns that occur in different literary forms throughout the tradition. For example, Jesus is fully human and fully divine; he spoke of the kingdom of God as at once present and future; he spoke in parables; he was prayerful and taught the Our Father; he dined frequently with those considered sinners; he was a miracle worker; he had a filial, prophetic, and eschatological consciousness; he had men and women disciples; he was crucified, and he was raised from the dead and appeared to many.

Fourth, **consistency**. This criterion presupposes a certain knowledge of the deeds and sayings of Jesus. Consequently, material may be accepted as authentic if it is consistent with material established by the three criteria just outlined. For example, Jesus insisted on forgiveness of enemies, nonviolence, and care of the sick, the poor, and women.

Fifth, **linguistic and environmental tests**. Material is rejected if it is incompatible with the language or environment of the ministry of Jesus. For example, Jesus denounced the divorce of women by men in Luke 16:18, but did not (even could not) say what is in Mark 10:12. Here Jesus says a woman who divorces and remarries commits adultery. Jewish women could never sue for divorce. Mark has adjusted the teaching for his Gentile audience because hellenistic women could divorce.

Finally, it has to be admitted that these five criteria, even when interrelated, are not foolproof. There are several reasons: (1) the gospels are theologically interpreted history; (2) the criteria presume a clear knowledge of the Jesus of history; (3) first-century Judaism was so complex, with its many movements and theologies, that it is not easy to determine precisely if Jesus' sayings are significantly different from Judaism and the first communities, which were composed of Jewish Christians.

The Death of Jesus
Mark 15:16–41; Matthew 27:27–56; Luke 23:26–48; John 19:17–37.

When the Christians defended the awe-inspiring resurrection, they also had to defend the scandalous death by crucifixion, a form of hanging. The latter was no easy task since Deuteronomy 21:23 declares that "God's curse rests on him who hangs on a tree." The gospels give considerable coverage of the arrest, trial, sufferings, death, and burial of Jesus in Jerusalem. These stories are called the **passion narratives**. It is believed that the author of Mark drew on oral traditions that had circulated in the Christian communities about the arrest, trial, crucifixion, and burial of Jesus to compose the first unified account. All four narratives provoke many questions. Here we will cover three questions.

First, what is the theology of each account? It becomes clear when the four narratives are given a careful reading that, while they report the same train of events and often employ almost identical language, the narratives contain some startling and significant differences. It becomes clear that the four narratives cannot be harmonized into a single account. According to the historical-critical method, the symbolic narratives have been shaped and reshaped through preaching, scriptural reflection, theological argument, and the dynamics of storytelling itself into four historical plays. For example, only Mark has Jesus on the cross for six hours; the others have him there for three. Only Luke has the story of the repentant thief. Only

Matthew reports that Judas hanged himself, that Pontius Pilate, the tyrannical governor from 26–36, washed his hands to symbolize that he was innocent of Jesus' blood, and that, at the moment of Jesus' death, the dead rose out of their graves and walked around the city. Only John has Jesus' mother and the beloved disciple present at the cross. The second question: why was Jesus executed? What was the reason or reasons why Jesus was considered so dangerous and disruptive that he had to be eliminated? The third question: how did Jesus view his own death? Why did he accept it? After all, Jesus was a young man of about thirty-eight and was at the beginning of his prophetic ministry.

The Theology behind the Passion Narratives

Each evangelist has a different christology. Mark's crucifixion scene is tragic (15:16–41). The setting is stark. Jesus is isolated, faces his fate in solitary agony, and is the subject of terrible humiliation. An artist like the Dutch painter Rembrandt (1606–69) would paint the scene in very dark colors, especially since "at noon darkness came over the whole land until three in the afternoon" (15:33).

In Mark's gospel, Jesus is sentenced to death by a reluctant Pontius Pilate, denied and betrayed by his male disciples, insulted and tortured by soldiers, mocked by the priests, scribes and even passersby, reviled by the two thieves crucified with him, bereft of his Father's presence, and left alone and without the comfort of his mother and the other women who loved him. The only words Jesus says are from a psalm (22:2): "My God, my God, why have you forsaken me?" Jesus dies in agony and pain with a loud cry, and is buried without appropriate anointing.

The single verse—Psalm 22:2—can be taken in two ways. If it is taken as part of the whole psalm, then Jesus dies in faith and trust in God because the psalm expresses complete faith in God's power, faithfulness, and justice. The psalmist is a persecuted but upright man who trusts Yahweh and finds in him the source of his consolation and ultimate triumph. If the verse is taken by itself, it contributes to the tragedy of the death of a holy and just man. Mark's theology underscores that the cross in all its absurdity and tragedy is the sign that we are called to surrender our whole being to God the Father despite life's absurdities and tragedies. More than any other gospel, Mark portrays the disciples' failure to understand that Jesus had to suffer. Jesus' invocation of Psalm 22 enhances the scandal of the cross. The psalm reflects what Paul meant when he wrote to the Corinthians (2 Cor. 5:20–21): "We implore you on behalf of Christ, be reconciled to God. For our sake he made him to be sin who did not know sin, so that we might become the righteousness of God in him." Jesus endures the bitterest consequences of humankind's sin. By identifying himself with sin and associating with sinners at meals, Jesus liberates humans from sin and death.

Matthew's crucifixion scene is paradoxical (27:27–56). Jesus is a king (messiah) but his royalty is displayed in humiliation. He does not meet violence with violence. Rather, he freely chooses the road of obedience as the way to promote his Father's reign. An artist would paint the scene in dark colors but with shades of purple and scarlet.

There are many ironies and paradoxes in the narrative. Jesus is presented by the priests to Pilate as a criminal, but both Pilate and his wife, two Gentiles, recognize his innocence. Jesus is mocked by the soldiers as king of the Jews, and so he was. Jesus quotes Psalm 22 about being forsaken by God, but his resurrection shows he was never forsaken. Jesus dies as a criminal, but at his death the earth quakes and the dead are resurrected—two eschatological symbols that the messianic age has arrived. The centurion recognizes Jesus as Son of God but the religious leaders of Israel failed to understand him. In short, at the very moment when Jesus is mocked for failing to provide the Jews with his messianic credentials, Jesus inaugurates the true Israel.

Matthew's theology highlights that the cross in all its absurdity and tragedy is a sign that there is power in weakness, joy in sorrow, and life in death. His gospel concludes with Jesus telling the apostles that "All power in heaven and on earth has been given to me" (28:18).

Luke's crucifixion scene is pathetic, that is, it evokes tenderness, pity, and compassion (23:26–48). Jesus is an innocent martyr who is overtaken by "the power of darkness" (22:53). During his sufferings, Jesus is patient and forgiving. He is more concerned for others than himself. He dies peacefully and confidently in his Father's comforting presence. He prays, "Father, into your hands I commend my spirit" (23:46). An artist would paint the scene with dark colors but with light from heaven focused on Jesus.

There are many tender touches in Luke's narrative. Two cruel men, Herod Antipas and Pontius Pilate, find Jesus innocent. Luke downplays Roman responsibility for the execution of Jesus by having Pilate declare three times that Jesus has done nothing deserving of death (23:14, 15, 22). Only Luke relates that women wept for Jesus as he carried his cross and that Jesus addressed comforting words to them. Only Luke has a penitent thief proclaim Jesus' innocence. Priests mock Jesus, but the people do not. The latter watch in silence and return home repentant. Jesus asks his Father to forgive all his enemies because they really did not know what they were doing. The centurion declares that Jesus was innocent. Jesus is not abandoned: at a distance some of his acquaintances and women disciples watch his death and hasty burial. Noticing that the anointing was not done properly, they go home to prepare spices and perfumed oils.

Luke's theology underscores that the cross in all its tragedy and absurdity is a sign that God is present in the church and human history with forgiveness, compassion, and his Holy Spirit.

John's crucifixion scene is triumphant (19:17–37). Jesus moves through this gospel with sovereign self-possession and composure, that is, he dominates every scene, never has to ask a question, and knows everything that is happening. These qualities do not change when Jesus is crucified. Jesus is a sovereign king who reigns from the cross. His royalty shines forth despite his sufferings and humiliation. From the cross he offers light, peace, and strength. Darkness does not cover the land as in the synoptics. An artist would paint the scene bathed in golden colors, with Jesus shining with an inner light, as radiant as the venerated subject of a painting by Raphael (1483–1520), a major Italian Renaissance painter.

There are many indications of Jesus' triumph in John's narrative. Jesus talks at length with Pilate, explaining his kingship and the source of his authority. Jesus' power and supreme inner freedom prompt Pilate to make determined efforts to release Jesus. On the other hand, Pilate seems more on trial than Jesus. Simon of Cyrene does not appear in this gospel. Jesus is able to carry his cross by himself. One of Jesus' garments is a seamless tunic. It could refer to Joseph, one of Jacob's sons and a Christ-figure, who was sold by his brothers into slavery after they had stripped him of his long, many-colored tunic (Gen. 37:23). The robe could also refer to the seamless robe worn by the high priest (Lev. 21:10). Jesus' kingship is proclaimed in three languages and therefore to the whole world. While hanging on the cross, Jesus is not mocked by the priests or passersby. He is surrounded by his mother, Mary Magdalene, other women disciples, and the beloved disciple. Jesus speaks at length. He gives his mother to the care of the beloved disciple, says he is thirsty in order to fulfill the scriptures, and dies, not with a loud cry but calmly announcing, "It is finished." *To finish* is to make something perfect, to bring something to its goal or destiny. Jesus dies aware that he has achieved his Father's purposes. He is buried in cloths that have been diffused with aromatic oils that befit a king.

John's theology highlights the divinity of Jesus and that his death on a cross, despite its absurdity and tragedy, is the sign that Jesus draws all humankind to himself and to eternal life.

Reasons for the Crucifixion

We turn now to the second question: Why was Jesus executed? It is rather clear that the Jewish leaders, specifically the Pharisees (Mk. 3:6), the chief priests, and temple scribes (Mk. 10:33, 11:18) sought Jesus' death. They brought Jesus to Pilate because only the governor could issue a death sentence. Why did the priests seek Jesus' death? A modern Jewish scholar has declared that from reading the gospels "we cannot be certain what Jewish laws, if any, Jesus broke" (Borowitz 1980, 91).

Several explanations have been offered. First, some scholars (Sanders 1985, 1994) believe that what led to Jesus' death was his aggressive action of cleansing the temple, the holy place in the holy city. This dramatic action, reported in all four gospels, was Jesus' protest of the administration of the temple by the priests and those who had a financial interest in the pilgrimage business. Like Jeremiah (7:11), Jesus declared the temple had become "a den of thieves." In Mark (11:18) it says the chief priests and scribes, feeling genuine religious outrage at Jesus' conduct and claims, "were seeking a way to put him to death." At the trial (Mark 14:57–58) some falsely alleged that Jesus said, "I will destroy this temple made with hands and within three days I will build another not made with hands." In the gospels of Matthew and John, it is the high priest Caiaphas who urged that Jesus be put to death. Other scholars (Brown 1994, 1:459–60) believe that Jesus' negative evaluation of temple worship was a partial cause of the Sanhedrin's decision that led to Jesus' death. But they add that the stories of Jesus' activities in the temple have been so shaped by later events in Judea—especially the destruction of the temple and the Jewish rejection of Jesus as Messiah—that they cannot provide secure evidence for the reasoning that led the religious authorities to seek Jesus' death.

Second, some scholars (Fuller and Perkins 1983, 44) say that Jesus was crucified as a messianic pretender. They hold this position even as they grant that the Sanhedrin trial has been colored by the messianic faith of the post-Easter community. The synoptic accounts of the Sanhedrin trial include questions about Jesus' messianic claims. Jesus answers unambiguously in Mark (14:62), "I am." In Matthew (26:64) and Luke (27:67–70) it is not clear whether Jesus accepted the title. We have argued earlier that Jesus did not affirm or deny the role. This leads other scholars (Sloyan 1973, 58) to maintain that the titles used in the trial scenes are titles bestowed on the risen Jesus by the early church and for which the Christians themselves were on trial when the gospels were written. Nevertheless, what seems plausible is that since Jesus was ambivalent about his messiahship—he neither affirmed nor denied it—the chief priests were able to hand him over to Pilate as a would-be king (Brown 1994, 1:480).

Third, some say Jesus was accused of **blasphemy**, that is, he misused the divine name and/or claimed divinity. In John's gospel Jesus makes himself equal to God (5:18) and declares, "I am the Son of God" (10:36). In the synoptics Jesus is asked by the Sanhedrin during his trial if he is the Son of God. As with the messiah question, in Mark's gospel Jesus' answer is unambiguous whereas his response is not that clear in

Matthew and Luke. The Sanhedrin accuse Jesus of blasphemy in Mark (14:64) and Matthew (26:65), but not in Luke. Some scholars (see Vawter 1973, 67; Brown 1994, 1:465–72) contend that these accounts cannot be read precritically because the evangelists read back into the ministry of Jesus charges that the synagogue leaders made against their communities. In the second half of the first century, it is the Christian communities that were on trial for proclaiming that Jesus is the Christ and the Son of God.

What the priests and Pharisees may have objected to is the claim by the Jesus of history to have a special relationship with God, one which would put him above the Torah. Jesus was convinced that he was God's unique and final agent in establishing the reign of God. One text says the priests acted out of ignorance (Act 3:17). They may have judged Jesus to be a false prophet not only because of his bold proclamation of the imminent arrival of the rule of God, but also because of the authority with which he taught and acted as a self-designated spokesman for God. For example, in Matthew's gospel Jesus enters a synagogue on a sabbath immediately after arguing with the Pharisees about the sabbath (12:1–8), and heals a man with a paralyzed hand. The Pharisees were so incensed that they "went out and took counsel against him to put him to death" (12:14). By definition false prophets lead the people to error and the scriptures declared that they should be killed (Deut. 13:5, 18:20). The chief priests and elders may have honestly believed that they were dutifully defending the covenant against any distortion or deviation.

Fourth, some say Jesus was charged with "inciting the people to revolt" (Lk. 23:14) and subverting the nation and the religion (Hengel 1974). The priests may have delivered Jesus to the Roman authorities as the would-be "King of the Jews" because, worried about civic unrest, they sincerely thought that Jesus was politically dangerous. The priests could hardly offer Pilate religious reasons for condemning Jesus. They knew Pilate considered their theological controversies irrelevant. In all four gospels, Pilate concentrates on the charge that Jesus claims to be king. Since Jesus' teachings about a kingdom involve political rhetoric, it would be easy enough to present Jesus to the Roman authorities as one involved with political activities, such as his so-called opposition to the payment of taxes (Lk. 23:2). Nevertheless, in all four gospels Pilate says he does not find Jesus guilty of their political charges. He knew that Jesus had been handed over for trial "out of Jewish zeal and intrareligious fighting" (Brown 1994, 1:387). Notwithstanding Pilate's declarations of innocence, the Jewish authorities persisted. No one in the gospels speaks in favor of Jesus. The people and chief priests condemn him. Pilate relented. "In all the Gospels the mass opposition to [Jesus] is what ultimately forces Pilate to accede to the crucifixion" (Brown 1994, 1:809). Pilate condemned Jesus for high treason against the Roman state, ordering a sign be placed over the cross stating that this criminal was the "King of the Jews."

These four reasons are plausible, but none is satisfactory or conclusive because there is insufficient evidence for each. Many scholars honestly state that we are in the embarrassing situation of not knowing precisely on what charge (or charges) Jesus was executed. Raymond Brown, noted scripture scholar, spent ten years studying and researching the passion narratives. In his two-volume work of over sixteen hundred pages, he concludes that the passion narratives do not provide a conclusive explanation of why Jesus was executed (Brown 1994, 1:544).

Jesus' Own View of His Death

The third and last question concerns how Jesus viewed his own death. Normally, humans find another person's death troublesome, especially because it ends an irreplaceable life. According to the Talmud, when Solomon looked upon the corpse of his father, David, he exclaimed in anguish: "Even a live dog is better off than a dead lion" (see Eccl. 9:4). Normally, humans do not want to die. Since death is shrouded in darkness and mystery, it makes us apprehensive and anxious. Unless one takes a docetist view of Jesus, it is safe to say that for Jesus death was a real event that evoked fear, agitation, and struggle. Mark (14:33) says he was distressed and troubled; Luke (22:44) embellishes the agitation by stating that Jesus' sweat flowed quite profusely, "like drops of blood falling [in quick succession] on the ground." Hebrews (5:7) is most graphic: "In the days when he was in the flesh, he offered prayers and supplications with loud cries and tears to the one who was able to save him from death, and he was heard because of his reverence."

The gospel of Mark reports that Jesus predicted his violent death three times (see Mk. 8:31, 9:31, 10:32–33). A precritical reading accepts these predictions as historical, maintaining that Jesus was aware of his fate through his divine knowledge. The historical-critical method, since it affirms the genuine humanity of Jesus, maintains that Jesus did not have access to knowledge of the future. It interprets these predictions as post-resurrection theology that underscores the centrality of the cross in Christian life. This is not to deny that Jesus could easily surmise that his disturbing and dangerous challenges to the religious authorities put him on a collision course that could result in persecution and even death.

Again we are in an embarrassing situation: we do not know for sure how Jesus interpreted his death. There are two long-standing, scriptural interpretations that are challenged today.

First, there are passages that state that Jesus went to Jerusalem to die because it was what God wanted. The death of the incarnate Son of God had been decreed and preordained as the means of salvation. In Mark (14:21) Jesus concludes his comments about his betrayer by stating that he "goes, as it is written of him." In the garden Jesus prays that the Father remove the cup of death, but says "not what I will but what you will" (Mk. 14:36). Peter declares that Jesus' death "brought to fulfillment what he [God] had announced beforehand through the mouth of all the prophets, that his Messiah would suffer" (Acts 3:18).

A precritical understanding of these texts is based on assumptions about God and the scriptures that are no longer viable. A precritical interpretation of the crucifixion as the result of God's design casts Judas, the high priests, the temple scribes and Pilate as mere puppets, actors in a divine put-on. Instead of freedom, there is fate. In addition, a literal interpretation makes God a sadistic executioner who is not able to honor his covenants with humankind until his own Son suffers a horrible and bloody death. The story in Genesis of Abraham and Isaac declares that God abhors human sacrifice. Furthermore, Jesus' prayerful compliance to his Father's will "is not a passive acquiescence to some pre-ordained divine plan to have him sacrificed. Instead, it is a resolve to carry through his God-given message, even if it has to end in an excruciating death" (Hill 1991, 181).

Today, a critical or actualization reading of the passion narratives states that God does not inflict human sufferings, nor did he decree the sufferings of Jesus. On the contrary, he participates in suffering. The cross points to a God who is so involved in the suffering of the world that he experiences our pain. He is not the executioner but the fellow sufferer. In the cross of Jesus, God once and for all sided with the wretched of this world, especially those who live in situations that appear beyond human hope. To proclaim the cross of Christ means to join God as he places himself with the wretched of the earth and struggles to free men and women from their oppressions.

Second, it is said that Jesus died for our sins. Paul clearly taught this theology (1 Thes. 5:10; Rom. 5:9). He reminded the Corinthians "that Christ died for our sins in accordance with the scriptures" (1 Cor. 15:3) and that he was convinced "that one died for all" (2 Cor. 5:14a). But was this Jesus' reason for accepting his death? The historical-critical method holds that Jesus did not have in his mind dying for us or saving us from our sins in any juridical sense. Several qualifications are offered. First, probably the most we can say is that he died because his love for his contemporaries was so strong that he accepted death at their hands rather than abandon his prophetic mission to invite all to accept themselves as children of God. Jesus' love for his contemporaries can be extended to a love for all of his Father's children. Second, we might also be able to say that Jesus, conscious of his own call to foster the reign of God, died for sin insofar as he accepted his death as part of the triumph of the kingdom of God over sin and death. Third, Paul and the 600 came to realize that Jesus' death had a salvific dimension inasmuch as it conquered sin and death. His resurrection showed that God invites all to a sinless and resurrected life with him.

Connected to Jesus' death as the means of salvation from sin is the biblical concept of reconciliation. Paul wrote to the Corinthians (2 Cor. 5:17–19): "So whoever is in Christ is a new creation: the old things have passed away; behold, new things have come. And all this is from God, who has reconciled us to himself through Christ and has given us the ministry of reconciliation, namely, God was reconciling the world to himself in Christ, not counting their trespasses against them and entrusting to us the message of reconciliation."

Paul is explaining that the death of Jesus was not meant to reconcile God to humankind (that is, to make sinful and hard-hearted humankind more acceptable to his Father), but to reconcile humankind to God.

Reconciliation is a misunderstood word. It is often defined as the act of forgiving a wrong, a misunderstanding or a break in a relationship. It means that persons in conflict become one in heart once again. But more is involved in true reconciliation. For the unity to be complete, the perspective (the mind or the point of view) of the other must be understood and even adopted. Our problem is understanding God's view of life and reality, especially since the world he created is marked by so much evil, purposeless suffering, and death. How, humans ask, can God be a loving, covenanting, and saving Father when human life is filled with so much tragedy, physical and mental suffering, and death? Jesus' faith was that God would vindicate him—even in his death. The resurrection became the sign that God is Father and we should accept him as such with childlike faith. The resurrection also reinforces what was said above about God participating in human suffering and working to defeat it. God is a fellow sufferer. He wants us to accept his gracious presence and to have faith that he brings a certain measure of peace and wholeness now and will eventually complete his victory over all sin and suffering.

If these two explanations of how Jesus understood his own death are inadequate, one contemporary historical-critical interpretation has received significant positive response (see Brown 1994, 1:494–515). Theologians suggest that Jesus went to Jerusalem not to suffer and die for the sake of suffering and death, but to fulfill his mission as a prophetic teacher (Lk. 13:33; Acts 7:52). His mission was to explain the meaning of human life as a life of love for a provident Father, a life that demands trust and service given with radical fidelity and honesty. Jesus' mission was to give faithful testimony to his experience of God as Abba and to invite all to share his filial consciousness. To be true to his prophetic call, he had to prophesy in Jerusalem, the holy city in the holy land. He knew that to fulfill his mission meant he would be in danger of death, as the fate of John the Baptist and the classical Hebrew prophets indicated. Jesus accepted death as the price of fidelity to his conviction that God would vindicate him against those who unjustly regarded him as a false prophet with diabolic power. Jesus' dangerous, disruptive, disturbing, and subversive teachings brought about his death, and his death revealed his final fidelity to his God-given mission. The greatest proof persons can give of their fidelity to their convictions is to die for them. Since Jesus' faith in his Father was so deeply grounded in his filial consciousness, he surely believed his Father would provide ultimate vindication for his life and death. The resurrection became this vindication. Jesus did not go *to* his death but *through* it to the Father. In Mark (14:25) Jesus says at the Last Supper: "Amen, I say to you, I shall not drink again the fruit of the vine until the day when I drink it new in the kingdom of God." This passage is both a statement about his impending death and an expression of certitude that his death will not hinder the triumph of the reign of God.

Dr. Martin Luther King Jr. (1929–1968) modeled his prophetic attack on racism in this country on the Jesus of history. He told his followers in August 1963 that he had a dream and part of the dream included his death. In 1968 he went to Memphis, Tennessee, with his bodyguards to participate in a labor dispute. Surely there must have been times when his advisers and bodyguards persuaded him not to go into some very dangerous situations. But a prophet cannot always avoid dangerous situations. He has to be where the people are. Dr. King knew that, since the liberating effects of his message threatened the enemies of liberty, he would be in great danger of being killed. He went to Memphis anyway. There he was shot and killed on April 4, 1968, having first accepted death as the price of fidelity to his vision for his people and the whole country.

A critical or actualization reading of the death of Jesus flies in the face of the ethos of our times, an age of liberalism in which everyone is said to be in control of his or her own history. To support liberalism and the desire of people to be free from all impediments to their ability to give total direction to their lives, liberal theology has often recoiled from proclaiming the cross. Paul taught that the cross was "a stumbling block to Jews and foolishness to Gentiles" (1 Cor. 1:23). Many years ago, H. Richard Niebuhr (1894–1962), distinguished professor at the Yale Divinity School, criticized liberalism's view of God. He said this theology teaches that "a God without wrath brought men without sin into a kingdom without judgment through the ministrations of a Christ without a cross" (1937, 193). Many people do not want to hear about the cross, that is, about the negative aspects of life and the need for self-sacrifice. For many, self-fulfillment is their goal and self-denial is shunned, even rejected. The death and resurrection reminds us of the paradox of human life: the person who would save her or his life must lose it (Mt. 10:39)—a major challenge as we prepare to enter the third millennium.

4

The Story of the Apostolic Church

The center of the Christian faith is multidimensional. The church community is an important part of this center. The Apostles' Creed declares, "I believe in the holy Spirit, the holy Catholic Church." The Nicene-Constantinopolitan Creed asserts, "We believe in one holy catholic and apostolic Church." This chapter investigates what the scriptures say about the origin, nature, and development of the church. The disciples of Christ report that the holy Spirit led them as a new community to proclaim the good news of Christian redemption. This chapter examines the churches of Peter, Paul, and John. In earlier chapters there were descriptions of the Marcan, Matthean, and Lucan churches.

Pentecost
Acts 2:1–14; John 14:15–17, 25–26; 15:1–17, 26–27; 16:4–15.

Two months after leaving Egypt with Moses, around 1350 B.C., the Israelites arrived at Mount Sinai. Here Yahweh gave the Torah to Moses. The setting of this theophany was remarkable. There were "peals of thunder and lightning . . . and a very loud trumpet blast." Yahweh appeared "in fire" (Ex. 19:16–19, 20:1–17; Deut. 5:1–6), a conventional symbol for the presence of God. The reception of the Torah represents the community's acceptance of the covenant.

Liturgically, the Jews celebrate this event fifty days after Passover (Lev. 23:15–16). The Greek term for the fifty days is **Pentecost**. The day is also called the Feast of Weeks because it is also a festival of thanksgiving for the harvest, celebrated seven weeks (or fifty days) after the beginning of the harvest. The first fruits are offered to God (Lev. 23:10; Deut. 16:9). Pentecost (the Hebrew name is *Shavuot*) "marks the second great historical experience of the Jews as a people—the experience of revelation. Shavuot is the closure of the Passover holiday. On this day the constitution of the newly liberated people, the Torah, was promulgated" (Greenberg 1988, 25–26).

In Jerusalem in the year 33 A.D., 120 disciples, including Mary the mother of Jesus (Acts 1:14), were gathered in prayer and fellowship to celebrate Pentecost. Suddenly, there was a mighty wind and fire (Acts 2:1–4), reminiscent of the first Pentecost at Sinai. The disciples experienced a special outpouring of the Holy Spirit. They began "to speak in tongues." The Greek words for this phrase give us our English word **glossolalia**. To speak in tongues is to utter a prayer in sounds that express feelings of thanksgiving, adoration, and praise that are too deep for normal human words. Sometimes the sounds have no known meaning; at other times the sounds are in a language listeners understand, but they are unknown to the person doing the praying.

The Holy Spirit became their Torah, indicating that Christian life is essentially a response to the Spirit and not to any law or disciplines. For example, Jews are directed to pray three times each day; Muslims are instructed to pray five times each day facing in the direction of Mecca. Christianity has never set down a particular pattern of living based on prescribed laws or disciplines. On the contrary, Christian life calls for openness to the Spirit in the events of each day. It is the Spirit who grounds the church in its identity and mission and guides it into the fullness of truth.

Pentecost is often called the "birthday of the church," because in the person of Peter, the leader of the disciples, the church began its mission to all the nations of the world. The church actually has its roots in the ministry of Jesus when he gathered a community of disciples and celebrated common meals with them. This is not to say that Jesus intentionally organized a new community with its own creed, cult, constitution, and ministers distinct from Judaism. On the contrary, Jesus gathered a community of followers and taught them to live and await the reign of God for Israel. After his death, Jesus appeared to some 600 women and men, making a powerful and lasting impression on them. We have seen that one of the reasons for the resurrection appearances is that they were "church founding" encounters with Christ. Certainly those who had experienced the resurrection appearances could not keep this extraordinary happening to themselves for fifty days. They must have proclaimed to whoever would listen to them that God had made "both Lord and Messiah, this Jesus whom you crucified" (Acts 2:36). In Luke's theology, Pentecost is the "birthday of the church" because through Peter the church officially proclaimed the gospel.

The church exists to proclaim the Father's love and salvation to the whole world. In the crowd that Peter addressed on the first Christian Pentecost, "there were devout Jews from every nation under heaven" (Acts 2:5). In the first visit of a pope to the United Nations, Pope Paul VI in his dramatic address to the assembled delegates on October 4, 1965, made a symbolic reference to the first Christian Pentecost: "We have an awareness of living through a privileged moment—brief though it be—when a wish borne in our heart for almost twenty centuries is being accomplished. Yes, you recall it. We have been on our way for a long time and we bring a long history with us. Here we are celebrating the epilogue to a laborious pilgrimage in search of an opportunity to speak heart to heart with the whole world. It began on the day we were commanded: 'Go, bring the good news to all nations!' You are the ones who represent all nations."

References to the Spirit in the New Testament vary in details, depending on the theology of the inspired authors. For example, Mark and Matthew refer to the Spirit four and five times, respectively, whereas Luke-Acts mentions the Spirit thirteen and forty-one times, respectively. The *Acts of the Apostles* is sometimes called the *Acts of the Spirit* because it is the story of the many interventions of the Spirit into the church's institutional, devotional, and intellectual life.

The scriptures do not provide a systematic theology of the Spirit. However, scholars discern five major, interrelated activities of the Spirit (Brown 1985, 101–13). He distributes

charisms, that is, gifts such as faith, wisdom, understanding, prophecy, teaching, administrating, and speaking in tongues (1 Cor. 12:1–11). Second, the Spirit directs the church's worldwide mission. Third, the Spirit assists the church's officeholders in their task of teaching, governing, and sanctifying the church community. Officeholders exercise authority through the gifts of the Spirit, not through office (1 Tim. 4:14; 2 Tim. 1:6–7). The fourth and fifth functions are highlighted in John's gospel. The Johannine church had a special title for the Spirit, namely, **Paraclete**. This Greek word, which has as its root meaning "to call to one's side," is not easily translated. It can mean lawyer, advocate, helper or counselor—a person who stands at one's side in court to give advice. No one translation captures the complexity of the functions of the Paraclete-Spirit (14:15–18, 15:26–27). The Paraclete has two important roles: he guides each believing Christian to be a faithful disciple (14:25–26, 16:12–15) and he defends the community against those who reject Christ and fight what he represents (16:4–11).

The Basic Structures of the Church

The church is a community. But community is an analogous term: it has many definitions, depending on concrete situations. Today it is used so widely that it can refer to a family, a city, a political party, a voluntary organization, a religious order, and other groups such as a college, a specific college class, blacks, gays, and lesbians. All these groups are the same and yet entirely different from one another. The church, too, is a voluntary association, a society, a family, and an interest group. Nonetheless, it is *sui generis* (unique; literally "of one's own kind"), because its source is Jesus Christ, its ground the Paraclete-Spirit, and its goal the reign of God.

The one and only Church of Christ is divided into thousands of church communities, but it seems that all have four basic, interrelated structures, which they organize differently.

First, the church is a visible society or institution that mediates the risen Christ and his Paraclete-Spirit. The institution has its own leaders, officeholders, laws, customs, rituals, and special teachings or doctrines. The institutional church is regarded as a means of grace; it is a conditional reality subordinated to the reign of God.

Second, the church is an interpersonal community or *communion,* bound together around the living, risen Christ and his Paraclete. All share in the suffering and resurrection of Christ and in the life of the Father, Son, and Spirit. The community enjoys fellowship, prayer, goods in common, mutual concern and love. In a closely-knit community the associates know when members are born, sick, successful, worried, getting married, out of work, or dying. They share one another's joys and fears and participate in one another's hopes, anxieties, and sorrows. The Christian word for communion, *koinonia,* connotes a deep spiritual union, a nuance not captured by our English word community.

Third, the church is a missionary community. Led by the risen Christ and his Paraclete, it shares with the whole world the good news of salvation from sin and death and for wholeness and life. The mission is threefold: *to teach* the kingdom of the God of Jesus Christ; *to witness* the reign of God by its own life of peace, freedom, and justice; and *to serve* the needy and the poor in imitation of Jesus.

Fourth, the church is a community of disciples, that is, it is composed of individual disciples who, at a public baptismal ceremony, make their own personal (not private) commitment to the God of Jesus Christ and his Spirit in faith, hope, and love. Each person has charisms to be used to promote and expand the church and its mission.

Pentecost is called the birthday of the church because on that day the four basic structures were explicitly operative for the first time. Before Pentecost the disciples were bound together as an interpersonal community with their leaders (Peter and others). But the disciples did not become a missionary community until Pentecost.

Churches with a Eucharistic Spirituality

A special way of coming into contact with Christ through the Spirit within the church is by means of **sacraments**, signs and instruments of Christ's presence. The sacraments symbolize one's entrance into the **paschal mystery**, that is, the death-resurrection of Jesus. All Christians celebrate the sacrament of baptism. Anglicans (or Episcopalians), Catholics, and Orthodox churches have seven sacraments whereas the mainline Protestants recognize only baptism and the **Lord's Supper** (1 Cor. 11:20) or what Catholics call the **Eucharist**, because these two are expressly commanded by Jesus in the gospels.

The **Eucharist**, which means in its Greek root "gratitude" or "thanksgiving," is a thanksgiving meal in a sacrificial context. The ritual meal consists in bread and wine. Christians are with Christ like the two disciples who dined with him at Emmaus. Catholics, Orthodox, Anglicans, and Lutherans believe that the bread and wine become the actual body and blood of the risen Christ when the priest or minister pronounces the words of consecration. Catholics call this change **transubstantiation**. Martin Luther taught that Christ is really present in the bread and wine by **consubstantiation**, that is, the bread and wine coexist with the body and blood of Christ. The gift of Christ is given with the bread and wine. Ulrich Zwingli (1484–1531), a former Catholic priest who became a Protestant reformer in Switzerland, taught that the Lord's Supper is only a sign of Christ's sacrificial death. Christ is only figuratively present in the bread and wine of the meal through the faith of the participants. There is only a memorial presence. John Calvin professed that sacraments do not "bring down" grace as Luther and the Catholics taught. Neither were they merely memorial gestures as Zwingli taught. Their main purpose is to feed the faith of the believer who celebrates them. They do that by "lifting up" the faithful to participate in union with Christ and God's grace. The Lord's Supper provides invisible food for the soul through partaking of the body and blood of Christ. However, the bread and wine do not literally become the flesh and blood of Christ. The faithful are "elevated" to heaven to partake of the heavenly body of Christ.

When the community gathers for Eucharist, it is a minister or a priest—an officially ordained person—who presides. The ordained person is the instrument by which the Spirit changes the bread and wine into the body and blood of Christ. When priests and ministers are ordained, they are not given magical powers to make this awesome change. In principle, any Christian can preside at Eucharist; in church discipline, only those officially commissioned can validly do so.

The Christian churches are divided about the importance of the Eucharist. Catholics and Orthodox churches place the Eucharist at the center of a Christian life. For example, at Vatican II in the *Decree on the Ministry and Life of Priests* the bishops declared: "No Christian community can be built up unless it has its basis and center in the celebration of the most holy Eucharist. Here all education in the spirit of community must originate. If this celebration is to be sincere and thorough, it must lead to various works of charity and mutual help, as well as to missionary activity and to different forms of Christian witness" (n. 6). This statement explains why Catholics celebrate the Eucharist daily (usually with a small and steady group of participants) and why they expect all Catholics to celebrate together every Sunday. Protestant communities do not celebrate as frequently as Catholics. Some groups, like the Disciples of Christ, Lutherans, and Anglicans, celebrate weekly. Some denominations celebrate monthly, others quarterly, and some annually. Communities such as the Quakers, Christian Science, Pentecostals, and the Salvation Army do not observe the rite at all.

The Lima Declaration on the Eucharist

The above three paragraphs on the Eucharist are filled with controversial issues such as these five: the Eucharist as sacrifice, the real presence of Christ, the theory of transubstantiation, the priest as presider, and the frequency of eucharistic celebration. The Lima Declaration of 1982 addressed these important matters in order to bring order to the Christian faith and to set boundaries around it.

The first controversial point concerns the Eucharist as sacrifice. The document suggests that "All churches might want to review the old controversies about 'sacrifice' and deepen their understanding of the reasons why other traditions than their own have either used or rejected this term." Specifically at issue here is whether Christ's death on the cross can be repeated or prolonged. That it cannot is the standard Protestant position. Catholics, on the other hand, tend to declare that the celebration of the Eucharist is a "repetition" by the priest of the sacrifice of the cross. Today the Catholic position is that Jesus' unique giving of himself for us **(expiatory sacrifice)** is "made present" in the Eucharist. This theology does not contradict the unique and unrepeatable character of the sacrifice of the cross. The Lima document explains this point: The Catholic tradition of expiatory sacrifice may be interpreted to mean that "the unique sacrifice of the cross is made actual in the Eucharist and presented before the Father in the intercession of Christ and of his church for all humanity." Consequently, Christians who celebrate Eucharist should be able to give their consent to the Lima Declaration: "The Eucharist is the sacrament of the unique sacrifice of Christ, who lives eternally, done in order to make intercession for us. It is the commemoration of all that God has done for the salvation of the world."

The second controversial point concerns the presence of Christ in the forms of bread and wine. Many Protestants once held that Christ's presence depends simply on the faith of the individuals present, whereas Catholics hold that individual faith plays no part at all in the matter of Jesus' presence. Once the ordained priest says the words of consecration, Christ is present. Today, Christians should be able to give consent to this statement from the Lima Declaration: The eucharistic meal is "the sacrament of the Body and Blood of Christ, the sacrament of his real presence . . . The church confesses Christ's real, living, and active presence in the Eucharist . . . Although Christ's real presence in the Eucharist does not depend on the faith of the individual, everyone nonetheless agrees that faith is necessary, in order to be able to distinguish Christ's Body and Blood."

The third controversial point pertains to the transformation of the bread and wine. Catholics hold that the bread and wine are transformed by transubstantiation. In the past they declared that the theory of transubstantiation was the only way to explain the transformation. Most Protestants had regarded this theory as unbelievable. Today, many are not so quick to dismiss it. Some agree with the Lima Declaration: "In the history of the church, various attempts have been made to understand the mystery of the real and unique presence of Christ in the Eucharist. Some have been satisfied simply to give consent to that presence, without trying to understand it. Others regard it as necessary to insist on a change brought about by the Holy Spirit and Christ's words which has the result that they are no longer ordinary bread and ordinary wine, but the Body and Blood of Christ."

The fourth controversial point involves the role of the priest or presider. In the past Catholics claimed that the priest alone celebrated the Eucharist on behalf of the people. No Catholic was offended when a priest said he would remember the needs and intentions of people at "my Mass." Protestants were inclined to dismiss the importance of the ordained ministers, claiming simply that any Christian could celebrate the Eucharist whenever and in whatever way he wanted to. The Lima Declaration transcends these perspectives when it declares principles that all Christians can accept: "It is Christ who invites us to the meal and presides at it . . . In most churches, this presiding function is performed by an ordained office-bearer . . . The minister of the Eucharist is the messenger who represents the divine initiative and who expresses the link between the local community and the other local communities in the universal church."

The fifth controversial issue pertains to the frequency of the celebration of the Eucharist. As we have seen, the churches are terribly divided on this question. The Lima Declaration asserts that the Eucharist should be celebrated "at least every Sunday" and that every Christian should be encouraged to receive the Eucharist frequently.

Churches without a Eucharistic Spirituality

Christian churches such as the Quakers, Christian Science, and the Salvation Army do not foster a eucharistic spirituality because they underscore the human yearning for experiential communion with a saving, loving, and just God by highlighting a subjective, intense, and immediate communion with Christ and/or his Spirit. Some of these churches have their roots in the Methodist church, a community founded in England by John Wesley (1703–91). He called his group the "United Society," but others called them Methodists because of the methodical way they kept their routine of reading, prayer, and study.

Wesley was ordained a priest in the Church of England in 1728. He reports that on May 24, 1738, he had a deep religious experience in London. At a meeting in which he and others were reading Martin Luther's commentary on Paul's epistle to the Romans, he had an overwhelming assurance of his salvation in Jesus Christ. He later wrote: "I felt my heart strangely warmed. I felt I did trust in Christ, Christ alone for salvation. And an assurance was given me, that he had taken away my sins, even mine, and saved me from the law of sin and death."

Wesley taught that God is in constant relation with the world and that we should be in contact with God not only with our minds but also with our whole person through feelings and emotions. God offers **justification** to all, that is, forgiveness of sins. A person must have personal assurance of this forgiveness. Each person then must go beyond "justification by faith alone" to **sanctification**, that is, to a life of "scriptural holiness." Methodists test piety by morality and morality by piety. All members are required to live a disciplined, moral life and to care for society. The Methodists took an active role in the United States against slavery.

A number of churches splintered off from Methodism. These include such churches as the Salvation Army, Holiness churches, and the Pentecostals. Modern Pentecostalism is an American phenomenon that took root in various parts of the country at the beginning of the twentieth century. A famous Pentecostal church was inaugurated in Los Angeles on April 14, 1906, four days before the famous San Francisco earthquake. Rev. William J. Seymour (1870–1922) led a religious revival in a rundown building on Azusa Street. Services went on for days, the mood growing increasingly enthusiastic, drawing hundreds of black and white folks. Those present experienced a major outbreak of glossolalia. So great was the glossolalia that within a week the event was reported in the Los Angeles Times.

Reverend Seymour, a son of former slaves, not only taught himself to read and write but also educated himself in the Bible and theology. His times were marked by intense prejudice around the country against blacks. Nevertheless, he preached the equality of all peoples. This Christian perspective did not prevent him from affirming his own black heritage. He introduced Negro spirituals into his liturgy at a time when this music was considered inferior and unfit for Christian worship. For Seymour, Pentecost entailed more than glossolalia. It meant to love in the face of hate. His actualization of the Pentecost story challenged the whole nation to attend to the Christian gospel of universal love. In his churches white businessmen and black workers, men and women, Asians and Mexicans, white lawyers and black laundry women were equals.

Those who could not understand the revolutionary nature of Seymour's pentecostal spirituality soon took refuge in ridicule and scorn for this "self-appointed Negro prophet." Under the crushing weight of public opinion, many despised the developing pentecostal spirituality because of what they called "its lowly black origins." Soon the heirs of Azusa Street created other denominations, but, unfortunately, the churches segregated along racial lines. It is reported that Seymour died of a broken heart because the new churches preferred the power of influence and money to the power of the Spirit and because his ecumenical and demanding spirituality was ignored, a spirituality that denounced elitism, greed, sexism, and racism.

Pentecostalism is now a worldwide Christian movement, one that is growing dramatically. There are signs that its membership will be larger than both Catholics and mainline Protestants in the early part of the twenty-first century. Some of the better known of the more than eleven thousand Pentecostal churches are the Church of the Nazarene, Assemblies of God, and the Pentecostal Church of God. Like Methodism, these communities teach that "a baptism of the Holy Spirit and fire" should be expected among those who have been converted (justified). Baptism in the Holy Spirit is the single most important factor binding together all of these churches. The pentecostal experience has its own personal religious excitement. Like Methodism, these churches teach that justification should be followed by a dramatic move toward the perfect sanctification the gospel announces. Pentecostals add to justification and sanctification a third sign, namely, **commitment**. They teach that contact with the Spirit should result in the reception of spiritual gifts, especially praying in the Spirit, speaking in tongues, and healing through prayer and faith.

Pentecostal churches are characterized by a strict morality and an emphasis on mission and evangelization. Their worship is not as structured as in the Catholic church and the mainline Protestant denominations. Their spontaneous and informal worship is characterized by spirited preaching, lively congregational singing, free prayer, and personal testimonies. In church services, women can give personal testimonies, sounding like preachers, but many churches bar female pastors.

Pentecostals have grown in numbers in the United States and Latin America. Their converts are often from Catholicism. This development has put a strain on some ecumenical relations. For example, in May 1990, when Pope John Paul II made his second visit to Mexico, the local bishops refused to invite the Pentecostals to an ecumenical meeting with the pope. The Mexican bishops refuse to call them churches, but refer to them as "sects." One Mexican bishop was quoted as saying, "You do not have dialogue with bandits." In one of his homilies John Paul noted that some Catholics had "broken the link of saving grace, joining the sects. No Catholic in Mexico can consider himself exempt from the obligation to bring defectors back to the church." He went on to add, "I would like to meet with you one by one to tell you: come back to the fold of the church, your mother" (Rohter 1990).

The Parousia Myth

1 Thessalonians 4:13–5:22; 1 Corinthians 7:1–9, 27–31; Revelation 22:6–21; Matthew 25:1–13; Luke 19:11–27.

In several sections of the New Testament, the authors make it clear that the first generations of Christians did not expect the church and human history as we know it to last too long. Neither had a long future. To appreciate why they thought this way, some background about their understanding of the future dimension of time will be helpful.

There are three ways all people experience the future: the future flows from or continues what has been happening in the past and the present; the future is anticipated as people make short-range or long-range plans; and sometimes the future is radically better or worse than the present because of a complete and dramatic change that takes place.

The Bible has the same three views of the future. There is **prophetic eschatology,** that is, the future flows out of the past and present. The prophets were future-oriented, telling the people that their faithful God would give them a new land, or a new law, or a new leader. **Proleptic eschatology** denotes the present being affected by one's anticipation of the future. Chronologically, the future has not yet arrived, but psychologically it influences the present. Everyone has an eschatological consciousness. We constantly plan or anticipate future meetings or events. Normally, we live *in* the present but *on* the past and *from* the future. This is proleptic eschatology. Jesus' teachings that the eternal reign of God is even now present but not yet fully is proleptic eschatology.

The third eschatology is apocalyptic. The root meaning of this word is "uncovering" or "removing the veil" or "revealing." **Apocalyptic eschatology** says the future will be radically different from the present. Often the present is considered to be so evil that it must be destroyed and a completely new start made. Even today we associate the word apocalyptic with fire, destruction, and devastation. The Bible contains many apocalyptic sections (see Ezek. 4–24, Zech. 9–14, and Dan. 7–12). In the synoptic gospels Jesus describes the destruction of the world in Mk. 13, Mt. 24:1–24, and Lk. 21:5–36. There will be earthquakes and "tribulation such as has not been since the beginning of God's creation until now, nor ever will be" (Mk. 13:19). Despite the terrifying aspects of these descriptions, their real purpose is to give hope to people facing great dangers and/or persecution.

The time of Jesus was one of heightened apocalyptic eschatology. John the Baptist spoke in apocalyptic terms of "the coming wrath . . . Even now the ax lies at the root of the trees . . . He will clear his threshing floor and gather his wheat into his barn, but the chaff he will burn with unquenchable fire" (Mt. 3:7, 10, 12). Jesus spoke in apocalyptic imagery (Mk. 13). As we discussed in Chapter 3, it is generally thought that Jesus believed the reign of God would be fully manifested either in his lifetime or shortly thereafter (Mk. 9:1, Mt. 10:32, Lk. 23:43,

Jn. 14:3). For example, this statement (Mk. 14:25) by Jesus during the Last Supper is apocalyptic since it implies a period of trial followed by one of vindication: "Amen, I say to you, I shall not drink again the fruit of the vine until the day when I drink it new in the kingdom of God."

After Jesus was raised from the dead, the first disciples were convinced the end-time had begun and Jesus would appear soon to close down human history as we know it. **Parousia,** a Greek word which means "presence" or "arrival" or "coming," was usually associated with the ceremonial arrival of an emperor or some other person with great authority. In the period between 33 and 70 A.D., apocalyptic eschatology played a major part in Christian theology and life. Paul shared with Jewish apocalyptic thought the belief that the present age is dominated by the powers of evil. Nevertheless, he was confident that the reign of God had already begun in the death-resurrection of Christ. When the subjugation of evil is complete, then Christ will appear in triumph. Paul taught the Thessalonians in 51 A.D. that the return of Jesus was imminent (see 1 Thes. 4:13–5:11). Around 55, he said the parousia was so imminent that he recommended to the Corinthians that they not settle into life by getting married but "remain single as I do" (1 Cor. 7:8, 26, 29, 31). With the passage of time Paul did not seem so positive that the parousia would occur in his own lifetime. In a letter to the Philippians written from prison in Ephesus in 56 or 57, he expressed a doubt about staying alive until the end. He said he longed "to depart this life and be with Christ" (1:23).

Mark's gospel, probably written around 68 in Rome, teaches that the parousia is imminent. In one discourse, Jesus said that some of his listeners "will not taste death until they see that the kingdom of God has come in power" (9:1). The community expected the fulfillment of their hopes before "this generation" passed away (13:30). While they did not know the day or hour, they were warned to watch (three times) and not to sleep. The members of the community had such faith in the imminent parousia that they were willing to sacrifice their families, homes, and property for Jesus and "the age to come" (10:30).

Some twenty years later, Matthew and Luke tone down Mark's theology of the imminent parousia. For them it is delayed indefinitely (see Mt. 25:1–13; Lk. 19:11–27; Acts 1:6–8), in part because the church has a worldwide mission to teach all nations (Mt. 28:16–20; Acts 1:8). This is not to say that Christians stopped anticipating the parousia (see 2 Pt. 3:8–10; Jas. 5:7–11). The last book in the Bible, Revelation, indicates that apocalyptic expectations were still a living force in the church until the second century. Written around 90 to 95 during the persecution by Domitian, emperor from 81 to 96, the last chapter of the Bible mentions parousia six times. In fact, the Christian Bible ends with this exchange between the risen Jesus and his disciples: "'I am coming soon.' Amen. Come Lord Jesus! The grace of the Lord Jesus be with all" (22:21–22).

No one knows how human history as we know it will end. Some passages like Mark 13 describe apocalyptic destruction; other texts speak of a new creation in which the "world will be set free from slavery to corruption" (see Rom. 8:18–23).

When the parousia will occur is not known either. Jesus states that neither he nor anyone else knows the day and the hour when the final events would take place (Mt. 24:36, 25:13). Paul says it "will come like a thief in the night" (1 Thes. 5:2). As the year 2000 approaches, the media will carry many stories of predictions of the imminent end of the world. There is a well-known passage in Revelation (20:1–3) that talks of the time of the parousia. "Then I saw an angel come down from heaven, holding in his hand the key to the abyss and a heavy chain. He seized the dragon, the ancient serpent, which is the Devil or Satan, and tied it up for a thousand years and threw it into the abyss, which he locked over it and sealed, so that it could no longer lead the nations astray until the thousand years are completed. After this, it is to be released for a short time." This passage has fascinated many Christians. It has also often led to confusion and fear when given a precritical interpretation. The 1,000 years of peace are called the **millennium.**

Three Views of the Millennium

There are three different understandings of the parousia in relation to the millennium. Roman Catholics are **amillennialists** (no millennium). They believe good and evil will continue to coexist until Christ's parousia. There will be no literal millennium.

Rather, Christ can return at any time to establish the new heaven and new earth. God's ways are not our ways and so our way of reckoning time is not God's time: "But do not ignore this one fact, beloved, that with the Lord one day is like a thousand years and a thousand years like one day" (2 Pt. 3:8).

In principle, Catholics keep the parousia in mind. It is mentioned in the Our Father. Also the parousia is referred to in three of the four **memorial acclamations** that follow the consecration at the Eucharist.

Christ has died, Christ is risen, Christ will come again.

Dying you destroyed our death, rising you restored our life.
Lord Jesus, come in glory.

When we eat this bread and drink this cup, we proclaim your death, Lord Jesus, until you come in glory.

In practice, the parousia does not dominate Catholic thought. Most Catholics probably do not give serious consideration to it until there is talk of war with atomic weapons or some major catastrophe occurs.

Many Protestant groups give serious attention to the parousia. It even plays a part in their political decisions. For example, some Protestant individuals and/or communities, based on their precritical interpretation of the scriptures, are pro-Israel because Israel's survival is crucial in the movement toward the final battle of Armageddon (Rev. 16:16) when Christ will triumph over the Antichrist. **Armageddon** refers to the mountain region of Megiddo, scene of many battles in the Hebrew Bible. According to some Protestant interpreters, the parousia is near and the final countdown began with the Six Day War of 1967, which brought Jerusalem under Jewish control (Woodward 1982, 79; G. Niebuhr 1995b). Israelis who have welcomed the strong financial and moral support of such millennialists are embarrassed when they hear the context of that support.

The eighteenth-century Shakers were **postmillennialists**, that is, they believed the parousia would take place after the millennium. They believed human history would be getting better and better as the kingdom of God was progressively realized. Finally, things would be so good that 1,000 years of peace and prosperity would follow. After that, Christ would return and bring in the new heaven and new earth.

Seventh-day Adventists and some Holiness and Pentecostal communities are **premillennialists**, that is, they maintain that the world is an evil place and keeps getting worse. When evil becomes overwhelming, Christ will return, bind the devil, and establish the 1,000 years of peace. After the millennium, the devil will be loosened for a while to tempt those who might still fall into sin. He and his forces finally will be totally defeated. Then Christ will bring in the new heaven and new earth.

The key question regarding the parousia myth concerns why this is a very firm belief. The answer involves an understanding of divine providence and the reign of God. The God who creates, covenants, loves, and saves must triumph completely over sin and death. The destiny of humankind according to the Christian gospel is community with God marked by love, wholeness, and life. As Paul reminded the Corinthians, Christ must reign "until he has put all his enemies under his feet" and has subjected everything to his Father so that "God may be all in all" (1 Cor. 15:25–28). Since evil "has remained as it was from the beginning of creation," a perennial temptation is to scornfully ask, "Where is the promise of his coming?" (2 Pt. 3:3–4). If there is no parousia, then the birth, life, death, and resurrection of Jesus would have been in vain. If there is no parousia, Christianity would not have a gospel. Its message of ultimate salvation and Christian humanism would be irrelevant.

Paul of Tarsus
Acts 9:1–31; 15:1–35; Romans 1:1–17; 2 Corinthians 5:16–21.

Paul of Tarsus is sometimes called "the second founder of Christianity." We know more about Paul than we do about the Jesus of history or Simon Peter because we have a wealth of autobiographical material in his letters and biographical information in the Acts of the Apostles. This brilliant and holy apostle was born around 10 A.D. into a Jewish family in

Tarsus, a prominent city of Cilicia. We know nothing of his family. He was by birthright a Roman citizen (Acts 22:25–29). His Jewish name was Saul and his Roman name Paul. These two names are not connected, even though in English they are almost identical in spelling. Saul means "desired one"; Paul means "small," probably in the sense of being modest.

Paul was a devout and zealous Pharisee (Acts 23:6) of the tribe of Benjamin (Rom. 11:1) and by trade a maker of tent cloth (Acts 18:3). He was educated in Jerusalem by Gamaliel (Acts 26:4). He never met the Jesus of history (2 Cor. 5:16). In the holy city he attended temple and synagogue and came into contact with the Christians through the preaching of such Christians as Stephen, a deacon. Stephen and other hellenistic Jewish Christians taught that Jesus was the Christ and that, due to the resurrection of Jesus, the temple and its animal sacrifices were relativized. Saul and others found these teachings highly offensive. Stephen was stoned to death (Acts 7:54–60). Saul was present and consented to it, according to Luke (Acts 8:1). After Stephen's martyrdom, a persecution broke out. Saul actively participated, entering the homes of Jewish Christians and dragging them off to prison. So bent was he upon extending the persecution beyond Jerusalem that he gained letters from the high priest and journeyed to Damascus, a city some one hundred forty miles north of Jerusalem.

On the road to Damascus in the year 36, Saul encountered the resurrected Christ. Acts narrates this theophany (revelatory encounter) three times (Acts 9:3–9, 22:6–11, 26:12–18) in order to underscore the extraordinary significance of Paul's call to Christianity. These three symbolic accounts should not be read as verbal transcripts of what actually happened because they contain some factual discrepancies and have theological purposes. For example, in Acts 9 those accompanying Paul stand speechless, whereas in Acts 26 they fall to the ground. In Acts 9 those with Paul hear the voice but see no one; in Acts 22, they do not hear the voice but they see the light. What is essential to all three accounts is the theological significance of Saul's conversion for the spread of Christianity. For Saul, the revelation at Damascus resulted in the collapse of his Pharisaic worldview and lifestyle and the rise of a new worldview as a Christian missionary grounded in a deep personal relationship with the risen Christ.

The risen Jesus revealed himself to Saul. In Acts it was reported that Jesus asked, "Saul, Saul, why are you persecuting me?" This question formed the basis of Paul's theology of the Christian life. Devotion to the risen Jesus of Nazareth was now Paul's way of being a Jew (Acts 24:14). The one God of Abraham, Isaac, and Jacob had a Son and Spirit. Jesus was risen and even now is present with his community. Saul realized he had already encountered the risen Christ sacramentally through and in his community. Consequently, to oppose the community, "the Israel of God" (Gal. 5:16), was to oppose Christ.

The three accounts in Acts also communicate symbolically that the Holy Spirit moved the Gentile mission along by intervening at every crucial stage. Saul the "desired one" was singled out as "a chosen instrument" of Christ (Acts 9:15). God's promise to Abraham that his nation would be the instrument of salvation for all the nations found a measure of fulfillment in the mission of Paul, his coworkers, and other apostles.

Paul the Missionary

It is not possible to pinpoint Paul's activities immediately after his Damascus experience. It seems that he began to preach the gospel in Damascus. Later he went into Arabia, the Gentile district east of the Jordan River and southeast of Damascus (Gal. 1:17). This area was the location of several hellenistic cities. It seems that Paul's mission was not successful because he quickly returned to Damascus. Three years later he went to Jerusalem to visit Peter and James (Gal. 1:18–19). It was Barnabas who introduced Paul to the disciples in Jerusalem. Barnabas was a Levite from Cyprus who had contributed all his money to the common fund in the Jerusalem church (Acts 4:36–37). The fact that Barnabas was placed at the head of the list of prophets and teachers at Antioch (Acts 13:1) prompts some scholars to suggest that Barnabas, "and not either Peter and Paul, was the most prominent leader in the beginnings of the Christian missionary movement" (Cwiekowski 1988, 87).

Paul preached Christ in Jerusalem and argued with the Jews. When it was learned that they planned to kill him, he was forced to flee the city to save his life (Acts 9:28–30). Paul went to Caesarea and from there he returned to Tarsus. Sometime thereafter when Barnabas traveled to the region of

Syria and then Cilicia, he found Paul and brought him to Antioch on the Orontes River. Antioch, located on the best land route between Asia Minor, Syria, and Palestine, ranked behind Rome and Alexandria in importance as a cultural, political, and educational center. It became the capital of the Roman province of Syria in 64 B.C. Here Greek culture and philosophy interacted with oriental religions and culture. It was in Antioch that the followers of Jesus were first called Christians (Acts 11:26).

With the approval of the Jerusalem community, Paul made several missionary journeys. They may not have taken the form of the three neatly defined journeys as narrated in Acts, but the general picture given in Acts is probably correct. Paul was able to move easily around the Mediterranean basin because the Romans promoted and controlled commerce by suppressing pirates and other bandits; there was a common language, Greek; and many diaspora Jews had influenced those friendly Gentiles who sought God.

The first journey was made from 46 to 48 with Barnabas and John Mark (Acts 13:1–14:28). Some scholars believe John Mark of Jerusalem and the Mark mentioned in several passages (Phlm. 24; Col. 4:10; 2 Tim. 4:11; 1 Pt. 5:13) are the same person (Cwiekowski 1988, 143). The trip covered about 1,200 miles. Their first stop was at Cyprus. Here the very first Roman official whom Paul encountered was favorably disposed toward hearing the gospel. In spite of the opposition of "a Jewish false prophet," the proconsul of Cyprus, Sergius Paulus, believed. Paul had similar success with other Gentiles. The ones he had trouble with were the Jews. Paul and his companions regularly went first to the synagogue because they were convinced that it was necessary that the word of God be spoken first to the Jews (Acts 13:36). The chosen people must not have any grounds for complaint or for excusing themselves. Following the violent opposition of "unbelieving Jews," Paul and his party turned to the Gentiles.

The second journey, which covered some 2,600 miles, took place during the years 49 to 52 (see Acts 15:36–18:22). Paul journeyed overland through Asia Minor and its Galatian cities, reached Europe when he traveled into Macedonia and Greece, spending most of the time, about a year and a half, in

Corinth. His coworkers on this journey were Silas, Luke, and Timothy. Timothy, who is mentioned in the introductory salutation of five of the epistles, was sent by Paul on special missions to the churches (Acts 19:22; 1 Cor. 4:17; 1 Thes. 3:2).

Paul's first convert on European soil was a woman, Lydia of Philippi (Acts 16:14–15). She was an educated hellenist and merchant who traded in purple goods, a luxury item. This devout woman was probably a God-fearer, that is, a Gentile who had not converted to Judaism but attended prayer services of the Jews and accepted their basic teachings about the one true God. The church at Philippi began with her conversion and she may well have led the house church which met in her home.

The third journey (Acts 18:23–21:6) covered 1,400 miles during the years 53 to 57. Paul had as many as ten different companions, including Timothy and Silas. Three of the years were spent at Ephesus. Before Paul left that important city, he gave a farewell address to the elders, who had great respect and love for Paul. When Paul had finished speaking to them, "he knelt down and prayed with them all. They were all weeping loudly as they threw their arms around Paul and kissed him, for they were deeply distressed that he had said that they would never see his face again. Then they escorted him to the ship" (Acts 20:36–38).

Paul the Universalist

Between the first and second journeys, there was an important meeting in Jerusalem in the year 49 (see Acts 15 and Gal. 2). In addition to Paul and Barnabas, those present were Peter, John of Zebedee, and James, the brother of Jesus. This apostolic council was the first great turning point in the history of Christianity. The meeting was held to solve the "Gentile question." All present agreed that the gospel was to be offered to all peoples, but the question concerned the conditions to be fulfilled before Gentiles could be admitted to the community. There were four positions.

First, some Jewish Christians, the so-called **Judaizers**, insisted that Gentile converts practice full observance of the Torah, including circumcision. This group originated in Jerusalem and had some success in Galatia and Philippi (Gal. 2; Phil. 3). They held that until a Gentile male fulfilled God's commandment given to Moses, he should not be given any assurance of salvation. Christian baptism was not a substitute for circumcision. Circumcision was *the* sign of membership in the covenant community and the condition of God's love and mercy. Paul rejected this theology. His position is most clearly summarized in his letter to the Philippians. He wrote that what he most desired in life was union with Christ. He wanted to "be found in him, not having any righteousness of my own based on the law but that which comes through faith in·Christ, the righteousness from God, depending on faith" (3:9).

Paul encountered Judaizers, called at times the "circumcision party" (Acts 11:2; Tit. 1:10), on his first missionary journey. He argued with them then and later. In his letter to the Galatians, written around 54, Paul denounced the Judaizers as "false brothers" (2:4), and was so upset with them and their theology of Christian salvation that he wrote: "Would that those who are upsetting you might also castrate themselves!" (5:12).

Paul acknowledged that the Torah and circumcision were within the limits of Christianity, but not at its center. By placing the Torah and circumcision at the center of the faith, the Judaizers eventually found themselves outside the limits of Christianity.

Second, a group was represented by Peter and James. They did not require circumcision but did ask that Gentiles keep some Jewish purity laws, e.g., observance of the dietary laws such as refraining from food with blood in it, and not engage in incest (Acts 15:20). The reason for these strictures was to make it possible for Jews and Gentiles, persons from very distinct cultures, to share a common life and common meals. This group was strong in Jerusalem, Antioch, and probably in Rome, Pontus, and Cappadocia (Acts 2:9–10).

Third, a group was represented by Paul, Timothy, and Silas. They did not require the observance of any Jewish practices, except the laws against incest, which most Gentiles already observed (1 Cor. 5:1). Some of Paul's earliest companions, Barnabas and John Mark, probably left him because they preferred the position of Peter and James (Gal. 2:13, Acts 15:39). Paul did not insist on a break with the cultic practices of Judaism. Jewish Christians could still attend the temple and observe the feasts, and did not have to abandon circumcision and the Torah (Rom. 2:25–3:2).

Fourth, the hellenistic Jewish Christians held the most radical view. They called for the elimination of all Jewish observances: circumcision, the food laws, and the temple cult. This movement began in Jerusalem with Stephen and the other deacons and spread to Samaria with Philip, and eventually to Phoenicia, Cyprus, and Antioch (Acts 11:19–20). The Jews stoned Stephen to death because he downgraded the importance of Moses, the temple, and the law (Act 6:11–13), thereby challenging the theology that tied salvation exclusively to Judaism. Paul was close to this position by the time he wrote Galatians around 54. The theology that Christianity had replaced Judaism is forcefully maintained in both the epistle to the Hebrews (dated in the period 75–90) and the gospel of John (dated around 90).

It was Paul, the church's first religious genius, who saw much more clearly than anyone else what was behind the Gentile question. First, if the position of the Judaizers was adopted, Christianity would have been confined to a sect *within* Judaism. The universal mission of Paul and other apostles would have been set back. Second, Paul knew there could not be peace and reconciliation in community between the Jewish Christians and the Gentile Christians if the Gentiles were forced to live like Jews. Third, and most important, this question posed a threat to the very center of the gospel itself. Paul was convinced that it is God who **justifies**, that is, who accepts sinners as not guilty (Rom. 4:5). In turn, sinners turn to God in faith and accept the unconditional salvation he has offered in the death-resurrection of Jesus. Justification is by faith (Rom. 1:16–17), and not through any human effort to make oneself pleasing to God (Rom. 10:4), whether obedience to the Torah or the performance of good works. If salvation from sin and death was to be won by obedience to the Torah, "then Christ died to no purpose" (Gal. 2:21).

Paul kept in touch with the many churches he founded by letters or **epistles**. Most dictionaries define epistles as letters. Strictly speaking, letters are personal and informal whereas epistles are formal essays. Paul's writings are, to a great extent, letters rather than epistles. They are usually written to people whom Paul knows and loves. They are occasioned by his absence and his desire to offer his love, consolation, and guidance on both personal and communal problems. It is also true, however, that Paul's letters "come close, at times, to the essay form. Romans, for example, though filled with intensely personal passages, is a well-crafted treatise, the greater part of which Paul could easily have sent to any of his churches" (Flanagan 1986, 13–14).

Paul's letters are an important part of the twenty-seven Christian scriptures. Thirteen bear his name, but it is generally agreed that he actually wrote seven—all during the 50s: 1 Thessalonians, Galatians, 1 and 2 Corinthians, Philippians, Romans, and Philemon. Actually, Paul wrote many more letters than we now possess, and he received letters from the churches to which he sent replies. In 1 Corinthians, for example, he mentions his earlier letter to their community (5:9) and the letter that they had written to him inquiring about some community matters (7:1).

Even though parts of Paul's letters are difficult to understand (2 Pt. 3:15–16), they provide the best picture we have of the social, disciplinary, and theological problems (and the resources for dealing with them) in the first generation of the Christian churches. In 1 Corinthians, for example, each chapter or group of chapters deals with a major issue that confronted a Gentile community persuaded that, through Jesus, God's purposes outlined in the Jewish scriptures were being fulfilled. The first two chapters deal with the conceptual or intellectual question of whether the message Paul preached was compatible with human wisdom. Some members in the church claimed a superior wisdom. Paul tried to combat this development by declaring that Christ is both the power of God and the wisdom of God. There is no place in the community for claims of access to secret and superior knowledge. This issue anticipates the late first and early second century problem with Gnosticism.

The letters make clear that Paul's missionary endeavors were not an unmitigated success. There was misunderstanding and opposition that led to persecution, imprisonment, and eventually death. He states (2 Cor. 11:23–28) that as a minister of Christ and his gospel he had to endure much more than other apostles:

. . . far greater labors, far more imprisonments, far worse beatings, and numerous brushes with death. Five times at the hands of the Jews I received forty lashes minus one. Three times I was beaten with rods, once I was stoned, three times I was shipwrecked, I passed a night and day on the deep; on frequent journeys, in dangers from rivers, dangers from robbers, dangers from my own race, dangers from Gentiles, dangers in the city, dangers in the wilderness, dangers at sea, dangers from false brothers; in toil and hardship, through many sleepless nights, through hunger and thirst, through frequent fastings, through cold and exposure. And apart from these things, there is the daily pressure upon me of my anxiety for all the churches.

Paul the Theologian

Paul was not a systematic theologian. Nevertheless, "it is hard to dispute the claim that he was, and remains, the first and most profound of all Christian theologians" (Flanagan 1986, 27). It is beyond the scope of this book to develop all the theological and disciplinary issues that Paul addressed. We have already discussed his teachings on Jesus' resurrection, justification by faith, and the imminent parousia. Summarized here is Paul's thought on several, interrelated topics.

Paul taught that the gospel has universal applicability. No one was excluded from God's salvation and the grace of Christ and his Spirit. In writing to the Galatians he reminded them that in the church all divisions in society had been broken down, whether cultural, economic, or sexual. Paul did not mean that faith in Christ Jesus eliminated diversity and pluralism. On the contrary, it integrated them. "For all of you who were baptized into Christ have clothed yourselves with Christ. There is neither Jew nor Greek, there is neither slave nor free person, there is not male and female; for you are all one in Christ Jesus" (Gal. 3:27–28).

Paul's description of Christians as persons "baptized into Christ" evokes another Pauline theme, namely, grace. Grace is not a thing but a technical term that points to *both* the presence of the triune God *and* the subsequent changes in persons when they respond to God. It is God who loves us first and sends his Son and Spirit to free us from sin and death.

The risen Christ is still present in human history, especially with his church. Christ and his church form the body of Christ. To be a Christian is to be "in Christ" or "with Christ." To be a Christian means to be profoundly shaped and changed by the paschal mystery. It is interesting that the word *disciple* (which means devoted follower or earnest learner) does not occur in Paul's epistles and yet it occurs some 260 times in the gospels and Acts. It seems that Paul envisioned a different and closer relationship than the master-disciple relationship. Ideally, the Christian is another Christ in thought, word, and deed.

Paul also gives considerable attention to the Spirit. The Spirit is present in the community doing the five things mentioned earlier. Of the five functions of the Spirit, Paul emphasizes that the Spirit pours out charisms: wisdom, understanding, knowledge, faith, healing powers, miracles, prophecy, and so forth. However, there were some charismatics in his church communities who misunderstood the presence of the Spirit and the nature and purpose of his gifts. Paul had to address these individuals, offering them four criteria for judging and using the gifts.

First, the Spirit fosters love: "the love of God has been poured out into our hearts through the Holy Spirit that has been given to us" (Rom. 5:5). Consequently, the gifts should not provoke jealousy or arrogance (1 Cor. 13:4–7). Paul insists on the importance and greatness of love (1 Cor. 13). The gifts are not a sign that one has reached perfection. All should "Bear one another's burdens, and so . . . fulfill the law of Christ" (Gal. 6:2).

Second, the Spirit fosters community. The charisms are not for the person's enhancement but for the common good (1 Cor. 12:7). For example, the gifts of wisdom, understanding, and prophecy have been given in order for the charismatics to bring insight and guidance to others (1 Cor. 14:3–5, 16–19). Charismatics are not superior in knowledge to the rest of the community.

Third, the Spirit is the Spirit of Christ: "And no one can say 'Jesus is Lord,' except by the Holy Spirit" (1 Cor. 12:3). The Spirit molds the community and empowers it to be more and more Christlike by being loving and by bearing the cross (2 Cor. 3:18).

Fourth, the Spirit's presence is eschatological, that is, even now present but not yet fully. This means that, although Christians live intimately with the Father through the Spirit, they are still subject to sinful temptations and death. While Christians have the power of the Spirit, nonetheless this power always operates within human weaknesses (1 Cor. 2:1–5).

Those who misunderstood the power, presence, and gifts of the Spirit are technically called **enthusiasts**, based on a Greek word that means "having God within one" or "to be inspired by a deity." In various hellenistic religious groups, miracles, ecstatic phenomena, and superior knowledge were considered to be manifestations of the power of their deities (Perrin and Duling 1982, 151). Some Corinthians carried these ideas into Christianity. They became, according to Paul, "inflated with pride" (1 Cor. 4:18), believing their baptism made them "spiritual" in a way others were not and their Christian wisdom meant they possessed wisdom in a way others did not. These ideas created factions that undermined the unity of the community both religiously and socially. Some Corinthians even believed that since they were truly "spiritual" men, they could be indifferent to things of the body. One form of this indifference was an extreme libertarianism which included the freedom to visit the famous Corinthian brothels (1 Cor. 6:12–20). Paul had to remind the enthusiasts that the power and wisdom of God are manifested primarily in Christ crucified (1 Cor. 1:23) and that their bodies are temples of the Holy Spirit (1 Cor. 6:19).

In addition to the enthusiasts, Paul had to deal with the meaning of the Torah in view of the paschal mystery. As a Pharisee dedicated to the Torah, his new understanding of the law must have caused him great anxiety. He had both positive and negative things to say about the Torah. On the positive side, Paul expressed the highest regard for the Torah. After all it is God's saving teachings given through Moses and affirmed by the classical prophets. Paul wrote: "So then the law is holy, and the commandment is holy and righteous and good" (Rom. 7:12). God gave the law to lead his people to righteousness and a life marked by communal justice, freedom, and peace. The law defines what God desires and what he opposes. Its authority is unquestioned. The point is simple enough: God gave the law and he expects it to be followed as part of the mutual covenant. Paul wrote: "For it is not those who hear the law who are just in the sight of God; rather, those who observe the law will be justified" (Rom. 2:13). Paul encouraged his fellow Christians to do **good works**, that is, to be just, assist others, pray, visit the sick, comfort the sorrowful, forgive and love enemies, feed the poor, and so forth. To be "in Christ" is to treat others the way Christ treated them. The Torah has 613 commandments. Jesus said they are summarized in two: love of God and love of neighbor. Paul reduced the commandments to one: "For the whole law is fulfilled in one statement, namely, 'You shall love your neighbor as yourself'" (Gal. 5:14). To fulfill the law of Christ it is necessary to "bear one another's burdens" (Gal. 6:2).

Another reason why the law is holy and good is that Christ is the end of the law, that is, he is its fulfillment. The ultimate meaning and purpose of the law are manifested in Christ. Sin dominated humankind, controlled the law itself, and led inexorably to death. Jesus, who never sinned, was nevertheless condemned and killed by sinful people. But at that point the Father intervened and raised Jesus from the dead. The resurrection broke the power of sin, showing that death is not the ultimate fate of humankind. Sin became powerless because without the threat of death it was empty. The Torah can now have its intended effect: it can produce life, not because a person lives under it, but because she or he lives in Christ. In the paschal mystery God conquered sin and death. In other words, Christ is both the termination and the fulfillment of the law. Christians have a life in Christ, one that is not bound to law-observance but nevertheless fulfills it.

Paul had some pejorative things to say about the law. Over the years there was included in the law what is called **works of the law**, that is, acts that signify the conditions of Jewish identity and existence. Included in these are circumcision, dietary regulations, and Jewish holy days. Like Jesus, Paul separated these ritual laws and disciplines from the Torah. To him they were opposed to the divine will because they became marks of exclusivism. They placed the Jews inside the law and Gentiles outside it. Paul came to regard the works of the law simply as ethnic practices. They made Jews feel superior to other nations. But the idea of an elitist relationship with God was intolerable to Paul, mainly because he believed a new age had been inaugurated by the paschal mystery in which there was neither Jew nor Greek. God is the God of both Jews and Gentiles. Paul taught that "by works of the law no one will be justified" (Gal. 2:16). Moreover, "For all who depend on works of the law are under a curse" (Gal. 3:10) because there is no way in which they can persevere in doing all the things written in the law. Paul took pains to show that the scriptures did not mandate the observance of circumcision as a requirement for justification. Abraham was accepted by God even though he had not been circumcised (Rom. 4). According to Paul's interpretation of the scriptures, circumcision came later as a seal of God's acceptance of Abraham, not as a condition for it. In short, circumcision, dietary regulations, and cultic holy days form no part of the divine will for all peoples.

Another problem for Paul was that the Torah, although it stipulated God's will, defined sin and became an agent of sin. Because Paul was convinced that salvation came through the death and resurrection of Jesus alone, he taught that the temple, synagogue, and law were nonessential. The law, said Paul, came under the power of sin. Paul asked, "What then can we say? That the law is sin? Of course not! Yet I did not know sin except through the law and I did not know what it is to covet except that the law said, 'You shall not covet'" (Rom. 7:7).

The God-given law has been used by the demonic forces to effect the reign of sin in the world. Paul is not saying that no one ever knew covetousness—whether of things or another person's husband or wife—was wrong until it was given in the law. What the presence of the Torah does is give a person a means to evaluate himself or herself. The Torah reminds us that we are under the power of sin. The Torah enlightens us about the nature of sin, but, at the same time, it cannot diminish the power of sin. Although God intended the Torah to produce justice and order, it often does not do so because this world is dominated by sin. Even God's Torah is used by sin. Only the death of Jesus broke the power of sin because death was not his ultimate fate.

Finally, the most important issue raised about the law is its role in salvation. The law is not a principle of salvation, that is, it cannot free humans from sin and death. Salvation, on the contrary, comes through faith in God's grace and salvation. Christ is the fulfillment of the law and abolishes the law, not as a moral demand, but as an exclusive system of salvation.

Paul provides us with no autobiographical material after his third missionary journey. It is likely that Acts is correct in reporting that Paul was arrested in Jerusalem where his life was threatened because, by bringing Gentiles into the temple, he "defiled this holy place" (Acts 21:28–29). The Roman authorities wanted Paul to be tried by the Sanhedrin, but Paul refused. As a Roman citizen he appealed to be sent to Rome for his own safety and for an imperial trial. In Rome Paul was placed under house arrest. Acts closes on a note of victory: Paul, the saintly missionary, is present at the heart of the Roman Empire, receiving all who come to him, "and with complete assurance and without hindrance he proclaimed the kingdom of God and taught about the Lord Jesus Christ" (28:31).

Acts does not report the deaths of Peter and Paul. According to tradition, both were executed under Nero in the year 67. Peter was crucified and Paul beheaded. Both had spent more than thirty years witnessing to the good news that the Father has saved humankind from sin and death through the death and resurrection of Jesus and in the power of his Spirit.

The Johannine Church

John 1:1–51; 13:22–26; 18:15–16; 19:26–27; 20:1–10; 21:7, 20–23.

Over the past thirty years scholars have produced volumes on John's gospel and epistles. For many reasons, this scholarship has not filtered into the mainstream of Christian teaching and devotion. What is written here still surprises many Christians.

The Johannine church probably originated in Palestine in the 30s and, due to persecution, moved in the 50s to a location in the Diaspora, probably Ephesus. We know about this church through its gospel and three short letters. The gospel was written in the 90s, with final redaction in 100–110; the letters around 100. The community was composed of both Jewish (9:22, 12:42, 16:2) and Gentile Christians (1:38, 41; 12:20–22).

Who was John? Two of Jesus' disciples were the brothers James and John, fishermen and sons of Zebedee. In the synoptics the two brothers and Peter formed an inner circle of disciples. They are present at very special events: the transfiguration (Mk. 9:2–13) and in the garden when Jesus was arrested. In John's gospel there is a disciple who is described six times as "the one whom Jesus loved." In theological literature this clause is shortened to **Beloved Disciple**. Until recently, John, son of Zebedee, was identified as the Beloved Disciple because after the resurrection, John and Peter were associated in Jerusalem (Acts 3 and 4) and in Samaria (Acts 8:14). Irenaeus, the saintly bishop of Lyons (ca. 180), claimed the gospel was written by John, son of Zebedee.

There is, however, internal evidence that John, son of Zebedee, was neither the author of the gospel nor the Beloved Disciple. Three reasons are given: (1) The Last Supper, crucifixion, and tomb scenes in John all have parallels in the synoptics, parallels in which John, son of Zebedee, plays no important role. The sons of Zebedee do not even appear in John's gospel until the last chapter (21:2). (2) John, son of Zebedee, was a Galilean yet John's gospel focuses on Jerusalem. Jesus is there for three Passovers (see 2:13, 6:4, 11:55). Also, the language and imagery of Galilee are missing from the gospel. Jesus does not speak in parables but uses vocabulary associated with Jerusalem and Qumran: light/darkness, love/hate, life/death, from above/below, and truth/falsehood. (3) John and Peter are described as "uneducated, ordinary men" (Acts 4:13). It is unlikely that such a person could be the author of John's gospel, a work remarkable for its insights, artistic literacy, and theological profundity. The author of the gospel "was an unknown Christian living at the end of the first century in a community for which the Beloved Disciple, now deceased, had been the great authority" (Brown 1979, 186).

The synoptics and the gospel of John present very different accounts of Jesus. In the synoptics Jesus has the characteristics of a wisdom teacher. He is called teacher (rabbi), gathers disciples, answers questions about the Torah, works miracles and speaks in proverbs and parables. In John, Jesus is personified wisdom. He has no temptations, is baptized by John the Baptist so that his divine identity can be made public, knows about Nathaniel under a fig tree even before he meets him (1:48), suffers no agony over his death in the garden, has full knowledge of what will happen (13:3), asks no questions, works seven marvelous signs that point to his real identity, reigns from the cross, and is buried with an anointing befitting a king.

Christology is the ascription of titles, honor, and even divinity to Jesus of Nazareth because of what he did for the salvation of humankind and for what he continues to do in his church today as the risen Christ. John's christology is much more profound than that of the synoptics. While it is true the synoptics declare that Jesus is Son of God, Christ, and Lord, these titles are open to misinterpretation. "Son of God" can mean a representative of God, like a king or an angel or even Israel itself. "Christ" can indicate a religious-national king like David. "Lord" can mean emperor but also no more than master. In John, on the contrary, Jesus is the very glory of God and is one with the Father (14:8–11). He is the Word (1:1) who exists before Abraham (8:51–58) and belongs to and comes from a heavenly world (3:13, 31).

If John, son of Zebedee, was not the Beloved Disciple, then who was? Scholars surmise that he was a minor figure whose career during the lifetime of Jesus was magnified precisely because he was the founding father of the Johannine community. His career is dramatized so that he could serve as a model for all disciples and believers. The Beloved Disciple was a historical person: at first a disciple of John the Baptist (Jn. 1:35–39) and later a disciple and companion of Jesus (Brown 1979, 31–32). He is not named because his primary (not sole) importance is as a symbol for discipleship rather than as a historical career. A similar approach was taken by the Essenes, who always refer to their founder as the Teacher of Righteousness.

The Beloved Disciple does not make his appearance in the gospel until chapter 13. He is in six scenes with Peter and in each case the two men are contrasted, with the Beloved Disciple coming off as a more loving and more faithful disciple.

Scene 1: 13:22–26. At the Last Supper it is the Beloved Disciple who rests on Jesus' chest while Peter is at a distance and has to signal the Beloved Disciple for the information he desires about Jesus' betrayer. The Beloved Disciple is the thirteenth disciple.

Scene 2: 18:15–16. After his arrest, Jesus is brought to the palace of the high priest. The Beloved Disciple makes it possible for Peter to gain entrance into the courtyard. The contrast seems to be intended because in the synoptics Peter gets into the courtyard on his own.

Scene 3: 19:26–27. The Beloved Disciple is present at the foot of the cross and becomes Jesus' brother when he is asked to care for the mother of Jesus. Peter had abandoned Jesus (16:32) and even denied three times he was one of his disciples (18:17, 25, 27).

Scene 4: 20:1–10. The Beloved Disciple outruns Peter to the empty tomb. The evangelist states that the Beloved Disciple believed on the basis of what he saw in the empty tomb. The Beloved Disciple believed without seeing the resurrected Jesus and thus is more blessed than Peter. Nevertheless, in some traditions, Peter is the first to see the resurrected Jesus.

Scene 5: 21:7. The disciples are fishing and Jesus is standing on the shore cooking. The Beloved Disciple recognizes Jesus and tells Peter, "It is the Lord." The Beloved Disciple's love has brought him closer to Jesus than Peter.

Scene 6: 21:20–23. Jesus says the Beloved Disciple will remain. Peter jealously inquires about the fate of the Beloved Disciple. Once Peter the fisherman meets the criterion of genuine discipleship by answering the threefold question about his love of Jesus, he is commissioned to assume an additional role, that of shepherd. The role of shepherd is one kind of discipleship; the Beloved Disciple's is another. Peter would eventually give testimony to Jesus by sacrificing his life in martyrdom for Jesus' community (21:18–19). The Beloved Disciple was not a martyr (21:23), but he becomes the quintessential disciple whose testimony is true (21:24).

The History of the Johannine Community

The Johannine community was probably established in the 30s. The Beloved Disciple is the ultimate source of the community's profound theology and writings (Jn. 21:24, 1 Jn. 1:1–3), but not the author of the gospel or the epistles. The authors of these inspired writings were unknown Jewish Christians. They wrote because a half-century after the founding of the community, it was in turmoil. The gospel community faced problems within and from without.

Within the community were some who believed in Jesus but did not openly profess their faith out of fear of expulsion from the synagogue (12:42–43). Others had difficulty accepting Jesus as the bread of life who gives life to his followers. These disciples drew back and no longer associated themselves with the community (6:52–64).

The community faced opposition from without from three groups: the world, the Jews, and the faithful followers of John the Baptist.

The word *world* has two meanings in John. One is benevolent, as in the famous John 3:16: "For God so loved the world that he gave his only Son, so that everyone who believes in him might not perish but may have eternal life." The pejorative meaning of *world* denotes those Jews and Gentiles who reject Jesus, the Light of the World. These persons "preferred darkness to light, because their works were evil" (3:19). Furthermore, not to believe in Jesus is also not to believe in God (5:38, 8:46–47).

Here the word *Jews* does not mean the Jewish people as such. This would not make much sense since Jesus, the twelve, and the Beloved Disciple were Jews. Nevertheless, the language is very strong: Jesus himself says the Jews are children of the devil who "willingly carry out your father's desires" (8:44). The term could derive from the many Samaritans in the community (4:39–40). Samaritans were not Jews and so the hostile expression could have been quite natural to them (Brown 1979, 40). The Jews in turn call Jesus a Samaritan (8:48), a hostile expression for them.

The word *Jews* is used seventy times in John as compared to a half dozen times in each of the synoptics. It denotes the religious authorities, especially those in Jerusalem, who refused to believe in Jesus and desired to kill him. It is believed that Jewish Christians were under great pressure from their fellow Jews for proclaiming Jesus' messiahship and divinity. There are several references in chapter 9 to expulsion from the synagogues. The evangelist highlights that Jesus came to his own—but they did not accept him (1:11). For the Johannine church, Jesus' body replaces the temple (2:19–21) and Jesus replaces the "feasts of the Jews" (5:1, 6:4, 7:2, 10:22). Their temple and feasts have lost their significance because Christianity has replaced Judaism. In the gospels of Matthew and Luke, Christianity is the fulfillment of Judaism.

The Johannine community had trouble with followers of John the Baptist who considered him to be either the messiah or *the* envoy of God. For several reasons, the attack on this group is not so harsh as it is on the world and Jews who preferred darkness to light. First, Jesus, Andrew, the Beloved Disciple, and others had been disciples of the Baptist. Second, the Baptist had been commissioned by God to reveal Jesus to Israel. Third, John the Baptist not only admitted he was not the messiah but he also professed that Jesus is both "the Lamb of God who takes away the sin of the world" (1:29) and the preexistent Word of God (1:15, 30).

The three letters were written by an unknown elder (presbyter) around 100 because there was a schism in the community (1 Jn. 2:19). Some had withdrawn from the community, but traveled to house churches to proclaim their teachings. The author of the epistles, the elder, warned the churches that the secessionists stressed the divinity of Jesus to such an extent that they did not fully acknowledge the reality of Jesus' humanity (**docetists**) or they gave an inadequate acceptance of it (**gnostics**). Docetists and Gnostics accept the incarnation (that the Word became flesh), but they minimize the salvific importance of the life and death of Jesus (1 Jn. 4:2–3, 10; 5:6). Jesus is a source of wisdom rather than a dying-rising savior. Strictly speaking, docetism and gnosticism are second-century heresies. These errors appear in the Johannine community in their earliest forms and hence their proponents are called **protodocetists** and **protognostics**.

The Johannine Theme of Love

At the core of Johannine ecclesiology is love—love for Jesus and the community. The author of the letters denounces those members of the community who believe that, since they already have eternal life due to the resurrection and the presence of the Paraclete, there is little value in doing good deeds and keeping the commandments. The elder reminds them of their ethical responsibility to love one another (1 Jn. 3:23, 4:21; 2 Jn. 5).

The English word *love* is used to express the infinite range of love in all its human and divine aspects. People say they love dogs, ice cream, reading, beer, movies, or sports. The word expresses not only human relationships but also God's concern for his creatures. We often use *love* when we should use the word *like.*

The Greeks were able to make clearer distinctions about love because they had several words for it. Eros, the son of Aphrodite, was the deity of love. The word eros refers to self-fulfilling love. It denotes the natural aspiration or desire we have for the good, true, and beautiful. It is the power which leads people towards self-fulfillment through union with the object of their desire. The gospel does not require an ascetic renunciation of human desire for the good and beautiful things in creation. Christians are encouraged to use but not abuse things like food, drink, music, dancing, sports, and art. The word *eros* is not used in the Christian scriptures because it "had become compromised by its association, in Greek culture, with morbid eroticism and purely carnal sexuality, which pervaded even religious cults" (Küng 1986, 90). This is the case today with our adjective *erotic,* which refers to sexual activity and desire, especially when these are explicit and/or an excessive preoccupation. Nonetheless, we can have an *eros* love for God (loving God for our own sake), because "In him we live and move and have our being" (Acts 17:28).

The word **philia** is used in the New Testament. It usually means friendship-love. The Greek ideal of true friendship was for people to be of one heart and mind and to have all things in common. In other words, friends are equals who seek the good of the other. Christianity challenged the Greek emphasis on friendship-love as the ideal of love by highlighting love for each and every neighbor—even if the neighbor is one's enemy. Furthermore, we can have a *philia* love for God since Jesus' disciples are his friends (Jn. 15:13–15).

The word **agape** means selfless giving or self-sacrificing love. It entails great concern for the other to the extent of self-sacrifice. Agapic love transforms self-fulfilling love and friendship love. In marriage, for example, the couple experiences *philia, eros,* and *agape*—the fulfillment of their loving friend in freedom and equality. The three words are not mutually exclusive.

In the scriptures, the word *agape* means the love which God shows in giving his Son for the salvation of the human race (Rom. 5:8). God's love "has been poured out into our hearts through the Holy Spirit that has been given to us" (Rom. 5:5). The Johannine church offers a profound metaphor for God: "God is love" (Jn. 4:8)—and the one who saves us because of his love (Jn. 3:16–17). The Father loves Jesus' disciples with the same love he has for Jesus (Jn. 17:23–26). The requirement laid upon humankind is the double commandment to love God and neighbor (Mt. 22:37–39). *Agape* love for one another is the sign that one is a disciple of Christ (Jn. 13:35). Above all, many Christians pray that their personal relationship with God will be like the apostle Paul's: "For I am convinced that neither death, nor life, nor angels, nor principalities, nor present things, nor future things, nor powers, nor height, nor depth, nor any other creature will be able to separate us from the love of God in Christ Jesus our Lord" (Rom. 8:38–39).

Peter and the Papacy

Simon and his brother Andrew were Galilean fishermen. They were among the twelve whom Jesus called and appointed to be close to him in his ministry. In the synoptics the disciples are called in Galilee; in John's gospel, Andrew and Peter were disciples of the Baptist in Judea. It is here they became Jesus' disciples. It is said that Jesus gave Simon the name Peter/Cephas, which means "rock." But because the naming is described differently in three of the gospels, we cannot be sure of its historicity. All of the gospels report that Peter had a certain primacy among the disciples. Nevertheless, he denied his master and friend. According to Paul (1 Cor. 15:5) and Luke (24:34), Peter was the recipient of a special resurrection appearance.

Peter's character and personality are not easily described because he is portrayed differently in each of the gospels. In Mark, Peter is like the other disciples: he hardly understands Jesus' ministry, even in his great confession that Jesus is the Messiah (8:27–33). Nevertheless, Peter is the most prominent of the twelve and their spokesman. He is also the symbol of their faith and generosity (they are disciples who preach and cast out demons) as well as their failings (they desert, deny, and betray their master). Jesus predicts that Peter will deny him three times. The rock is a stumbling stone.

Matthew generally follows Mark's account of the scenes in which Peter is with Jesus, except that Peter, while he understands Jesus, lacks a deep faith. Only Matthew tells the story of Peter's attempt to walk on water until his limited faith causes him to sink (14:22–33). Nonetheless, Peter is more prominent in Matthew than in Mark. He confesses that Jesus is not only the Christ but also the Son of God. Also, Jesus changes his name to Peter (which means rock) and declares that he is the foundation stone on which the church is to be built (16:16–18). The rock is a foundation stone.

Luke retains most of the scenes with Peter that are found in the other synoptics. None of Peter's failings are omitted but they are consciously toned down. For example, when Jesus is at prayer in the garden, the disciples are awakened only once and not three times as in Mark and Matthew; when Peter denies Jesus he does so without swearing; and at Caesarea Philippi, Peter does not object to Jesus' prediction of his imminent sufferings and death in Jerusalem (9:22), as he does in Mark (8:32) and Matthew (16:22). Furthermore, Jesus says a special prayer for Peter so that his faith will not fail and Satan will not sift him like wheat (22:31–32). Jesus' prayer is fulfilled because Peter becomes a model disciple, missionary, and shepherd. The rock is firm.

In John's gospel, Peter is in eleven scenes, five without the Beloved Disciple and six with him. We saw earlier that Peter and the Beloved Disciple are not rivals, but Peter is contrasted with the Beloved Disciple, being not as faithful, loving, and insightful. Nevertheless, it is Peter the fisherman who is commissioned to be shepherd of the church. The rock gives support and strength.

The four gospels seem more interested in Peter as a symbol than as a historical figure. In Mark he represents those who do not understand the place of the cross in Christian life, whereas in Luke he is a model disciple. In Matthew and John, he is a symbol of authority in the church and of those authorities who must interpret the Christian message as they face new issues. In short, "the image of Peter was adapted to meet the needs of the church after his death" (Brown, Donfried, and Reumann 1973, 77–78).

After the resurrection, Peter plays a prominent role in helping the young community develop its identity and mission. He is no longer fearful but courageous and bold. He cannot remain silent about the wonderful things he has seen and heard (Acts 4:20), despite the threats from the Jewish authorities. Knowing he had to obey God rather than humans, he "filled Jerusalem" with the gospel of Jesus Christ (Acts 5:28). As he continues Jesus' ministry, extraordinary miracles occur when his mere shadow falls on the sick (Acts 5:15).

Peter is present at the baptism of Cornelius and his family, an event often described as the "Pentecost of the Gentiles." Paul, the apostle to the Gentiles, travels to Jerusalem after his conversion to consult with Peter. Over the years these two pillars of the church were in contact with one another for the good of the church. Peter was a stabilizing force for unity in the midst of the church. According to tradition, Peter journeyed to Rome, the center of the empire, where he was executed during the persecution by Nero in the year 67. "Peter is a bridge figure" in the Christian scriptures (Brown 1984, 147). The word *pontiff* means in its Latin root "bridge-maker." There is no evidence that Peter served as supreme pontiff or pope. Neither is there evidence that the twelve appointed others as their successors. The traditional, institutional understanding of the papacy emerged in the second century, having developed from its scriptural roots under the guidance of the Spirit. Peter is fisherman (missionary), shepherd, teacher, and witness (martyr) (see Mt. 16:17–19; Lk. 22:31–32; Jn. 21:15–17). Even those listed as first-century successors of Peter—Linus, Cletus, and Clement—were probably prominent presbyter-bishops in Rome and did not function as the one leader of the universal church. Modern Catholic and Protestant scholars, having studied the scriptural basis of the papacy, conclude that the papacy is an evolving institution in a living church (Brown, Donfried, and Reumann 1973).

The Lima Declaration and Ministry

The Catholic church declared at Vatican Council I on July 18, 1870, that Christ made Peter the "visible head of the church," and gave him "a primacy of true and proper jurisdiction," and "perpetual successors." Peter's successors have "full and supreme power of jurisdiction." With his full jurisdiction, the pope can be a stabilizing force for unity in the midst of diversity. Unfortunately, papal power has not always contributed to unity. On the contrary, it has often been a significant factor in the major divisions of the one Christian church. The result is that today the only church that accepts the primacy and jurisdiction of the pope is the Catholic church. But the issue of ministry goes far beyond the exercise of the papal ministry. It is quite evident that all the churches are divided about the nature and purposes of **ministry** itself. This word literally means a "service" and concerns officeholders and ministers in the church who publicly preach or teach or administer the sacraments. Because the churches do not mutually recognize one another's ministers, ministry has been the most intensely debated issue among the Christian churches in the twentieth century. The Lima meeting of 1982 addressed the mutual recognition of ministries in its declaration, *Baptism, Eucharist and Ministry.*

The section on ministry is some twenty-four pages, more than twice as long as those on baptism and the Eucharist. Three of the most controversial topics discussed are apostolic succession, the threefold ministry of bishop, presbyter, and deacon, and the ordination of women.

The first controversial point concerns **apostolic succession**, that is, the legitimation of the office and authority of bishops based on their valid derivation from the apostles. The continuity of the church with the original apostles finds profound expression in the successive laying on of hands by each generation of bishops. Some churches claim strict apostolic succession. However, apostolic succession is but one expression of the apostolic tradition. Other churches do not claim a chain of bishops going back to the first century. These churches, called **nonsuccession churches**, have either ordained ministers with an apostolic content to their ministry or an apostolic ministry that takes various forms without using the title "bishop." The Lima Declaration asked those churches with apostolic succession to recognize the apostolic dimensions of the nonsuccession churches and, at the same time, it asked the nonsuccession churches to consider the value of the successive laying on of hands by bishops. This religious ceremony is a symbol that could "strengthen and deepen" their own continuity with the apostolic tradition.

The second controversial point relates to the threefold ministry of bishop, presbyter (priest), and deacon, as found in the Anglican, Catholic, Lutheran, and Orthodox churches. The Lima Declaration stated that, while there is no one pattern of ministry presented in the Christian scriptures, the threefold ministry may serve "as an expression of the unity we seek and also as a means for achieving it." For the threefold ministry to be more widely accepted and implemented, churches maintaining it "will need to ask how its potential can be fully developed for the most effective witness of the church." Those churches without the threefold ministry "will need to ask themselves whether the threefold pattern as developed does not have a powerful claim to be accepted by them." This suggestion is very delicate because the nonsuccession churches are uncertain about how the three categories of ministry—especially that of bishop—are to be understood.

The third controversial point is the ordination of women, a topic discussed earlier in chapter 3. As is well known, some churches are vehemently opposed (Catholic and Orthodox) while others are already ordaining women as ministers, priests, and even bishops (Anglican and Lutheran). The Lima Declaration realizes that this difference in policy and discipline raises "obstacles to the mutual recognition of ministries." Nevertheless, it asks that such doctrinal and disciplinary differences "must not be regarded as a substantive hindrance for further efforts toward mutual recognition. The Spirit may well speak to one church through the insights of another."

The members of the Faith and Order Commission believed in 1982 that it was the Spirit that had led them to this special time "when sadly divided churches have been enabled to arrive at substantial theological agreement." The purpose of the Lima Declaration is to lead the Christian churches to unity by clarifying the center and boundaries of the Christian faith and life. Unfortunately, the churches are still "sadly divided." The next chapter studies these divisions and the attempts to reunite the thousands of churches into the **one and only Church of Christ**, that is, one community with one God, one Lord, one Spirit, one baptism, and one faith, hope, and love.

5

The Story of the Major
Church Divisions and Ecumenism

Jesus wanted his community of disciples to be "one flock, one shepherd" (Jn. 10:16). He prayed that his community would be one in heart and mind just as he and the Father are one, so "that the world may believe that you have sent me" (Jn. 17:21). Without such unity, the creedal phrase "the one holy catholic and apostolic church" would be hollow and Christian humanism would be building on a shaky foundation.

The author of Acts (2:44) portrays the apostolic church as a living model of the unity Jesus prayed for: "All who believed were together and had all things in common." In the letter to the Ephesians (4:1–6), the unknown author has Paul address the community about its "seven unities": "I, then, a prisoner for the Lord, urge you to live in a manner worthy of the call you have received . . . one body and one Spirit, as you were also called to the one hope of your call; one Lord, one faith, one baptism; one God and Father of all, who is over all and through all and in all."

Unfortunately, the one Church of Christ has not been "the seamless robe of Christ" throughout its history. The scriptures show clearly that right from her very beginnings there arose in this one and only Church of God certain rifts (see 1 Cor. 11:18-19; Gal. 1:6-9; 1 Jn. 2:18-19). However, in 1054 there was a major rift between the churches of the West and East;

and in 1517, a devastating division within the church in the West. Today the one and only Church of Christ is in disastrous disarray because it is divided into thousands of churches or denominations. Christianity is like a precious stained-glass window that has been shattered almost beyond repair. One can go through the alphabet and name a church: Anglican, Baptist, Congregationalist, Disciples of Christ, Evangelicals, Friends, and so forth. All these churches are deeply divided over the inner core and the outer limits of the gospel. There is considerable controversy over the church's identity and mission, the interpretation of the Bible, authority, moral issues, women priests, and many other issues. These divisions are a shameful contradiction of the nature of the one church and a stumbling-block to its mission. A divided church scandalizes the world and divided Christians become unconvincing messengers of Christ's peace, justice, and fellowship. This chapter reviews two themes: the major divisions in the Christian church, divisions based in good part on different interpretations of the scriptures; and ecumenism, the task of reconciling all the churches in the one and only Church of Christ.

East-West Schism
1 Corinthians 12-13.

Pope Leo IX (1049-54), a man of spirituality, gentility, and courtesy, was a reformer and disciplinarian. As a bishop he tried energetically to raise the moral standards of monasteries and clergy in his diocese of Toul in Alsace Lorraine. As pope, this able man was more a bystander than an actor in the tragic schism that took place on July 16, 1054, because he had died on April 19, 1054, and his successor, Victor II, was not elected until April 13, 1055. Nevertheless, since Leo's legates were acting in his name, the East-West division is attributed to his pontificate. The word **schism** means in its Greek root "to split" or "to divide." It is a formal separation or division based on different understandings of a teaching, discipline, and/or authority. The division centers on authority. Those involved seriously question the authority of those who determine teachings and/or disciplines that are binding on all. The ultimate meaning of a schism is that those who effect the schism "set up a rival altar."

Leo IX wanted the churches of the East to help him control the growing power of the Normans, who raided the papal state from southern Italy. He appealed for help to the Patriarch of Constantinople, Michael Cerularius (1043-58), but the patriarch refused to get involved in the pope's political problems. The patriarch then added fuel to the estrangement by imposing the Eastern rite on Latin churches in Constantinople and by condemning several western practices. To seek reconciliation, Leo sent legates to Constantinople under the leadership of the Lombard, Archbishop Humbert of Mourmoutiers. By all reports, Humbert was a fiery competitor with little charity of spirit. He hated Greeks and could hardly communicate in their language.

Michael Cerularius was an arrogant, ambitious, yet popular leader who despised Latins and was concerned for the ecclesiastical supremacy of Constantinople. In 1053 he shut down the Latin churches in Constantinople and launched a violent attack on western religious practices, such as the use of unleavened bread in the Eucharist. With their sophisticated liturgy, theology, and spirituality, the Greeks felt superior to Rome. When Cerularius and Humbert met, the two irreconcilable personalities clashed. In addition to geographical, linguistic and cultural differences, the Latins and Greeks were divided over disciplinary practices; for example, the Greeks fasted on Saturdays instead of Fridays, used leavened bread in the Eucharist, and allowed married men to be ordained as priests. At the level of theology and the interpretation of scripture, however, their differences were more significant.

The Greeks taught that "the Spirit of Truth . . . proceeds from the Father" as stated in John 15:26. This was the wording in the Nicene-Constantinopolitan Creed adopted in 381 by the ecumenical Council of Constantinople. The Latins, relying on the saintly Augustine of Hippo (354-430) and a local council held in Toledo, Spain, in 589, said the Spirit proceeds from the Father *and the son (filioque)*. Rome adopted the *filioque* theology around the year 1000 and added it to the Nicene-Constantinopolitan Creed without consulting the Greek communities.

Filioque is theological theory. Who can ever know the essence (the inner life) of the triune God? And are not all descriptions of God symbolic communication? The Greeks preferred "from the Father" because, since the Father alone is the principle, source, and cause of all things, the Spirit does not proceed from the Father "after the Son" but rather "with the Son" (Pelikan 1989, 5:22). The Latins preferred *filioque* because it expresses the communal and dynamic sense of God's three-in-oneness and mutuality. The Greeks held that *filioque* was too rational. It diluted the essential incomprehensibility of God by making God one with three aspects of being.

Today most ecumenists agree that *filioque* might be a better explanation of the eternal, ontological bond among the Father, Son, and Spirit than the one based on John 15:26, but it is still a symbolic interpretation of the dogma of the trinity and the imaginative refinement of an idea and as such does not belong "in a creed intended to express the common faith of the East and West" (Kilmartin 1979, 57-58). At the Lima conference in 1982, the delegates discussed at length the need and the possibility of reaching a common expression of the apostolic faith. It was suggested that all Christians should accept the Nicene-Constantinopolitan Creed as an expression of the apostolic faith. The delegates acknowledged that the ancient creed does need a common explication for the contemporary needs of the church. They did not consider it necessary to design a new creed to replace the Nicene-Constantinopolitan Creed as the ecumenical symbol of the apostolic faith. It is interesting that the Nicene-Constantinopolitan Creed the committee proposed to use was the original Greek text accepted at Constantinople in 381. This text does not contain the *filioque* that was later added in the Western church at the beginning of the eleventh century (Dulles 1982, 128).

Back in 1054, there lurked beneath the cultural, theological, and scriptural differences the question of ecclesial authority. Who can authoritatively explain the nature and mission of the Spirit? The Spirit is central to the Christian scriptures, church doctrine, and creeds. However, the creeds reveal little about the Spirit. Therefore the theological and historical facts have prompted Raymond Brown to say "with permissible exaggeration" that the Spirit "has been the most divisive feature in the history of Christianity" (1985, 102).

The authority issue also involved the interrelationship of conciliar and papal authority. The Greeks questioned the extent of papal jurisdiction, arguing that ecumenical councils that included all the bishops were the one sure source of inspired doctrinal authority. Their model was the church's first councils. For example, after lengthy deliberation, the Jerusalem church in 49 (Acts 15) announced its understanding of its mission in consultation with Peter, James, and Paul: "It is the decision of the Holy Spirit and of us . . . " This process carried over to the deliberations and decisions of the first ecumenical councils, which "had been held in the East and not under any direct papal authorization" (Pelikan 1989, 5:249).

This account of the personal, political, theological, ecclesial, and disciplinary differences among the delegates is the background to the heated exchange that took place between Humbert and Cerularius in full view of the congregation in the Santa Sophia on July 16, 1054. Humbert placed on the altar a decree, excommunicating the patriarch and his supporters. Cerularius responded with his excommunication of Humbert on July 24.

Conventionally, if somewhat inaccurately, the East-West division is dated 1054. Actually, some of the successors of Leo IX attempted reconciliation with the patriarchs. Most of the patriarchs of the East were better disposed toward Rome than toward Constantinople. But two events solidified the division. In 1098, the Greek patriarch of Antioch was expelled from the city and replaced by a Latin patriarch. There still might have been reconciliation, but the ruthless sack and pillage of Constantinople by crusaders in 1204 ended all hopes of reunification.

The Eastern churches that were excommunicated are called **Orthodox**, a term which means "right praise" or "holding the correct faith." There are many Orthodox communities: Greek, Russian, Rumanian, Bulgarian, and so forth. Many of these churches have branches in the United States. At the beginning of 1996, the total world membership of the Orthodox churches was estimated at 225 million.

Over the centuries there have been many efforts to reunite the Orthodox churches and the Catholic Church. A major step took place on January 5-6, 1964, when Paul VI and Patriarch Athenagoras of Constantinople met in Jerusalem on a common pilgrimage, praying that "this meeting may be the sign and prelude of things to come for the glory of God and the illumination of his faithful people." On December 7, 1965, the day before the closing of Vatican II, the two leaders mutually lifted the excommunications of 1054. Since Christian unity was one of the goals of Vatican II, this act was a dramatic symbol of the intent of the Catholic Church to achieve Christian unity. In 1967, the two leaders exchanged visits, July 25 in Constantinople and October 26 in Rome. These religious encounters helped smooth the way for many productive Catholic-Orthodox dialogues, which continue to this day. There are many issues needing clarification and discussion. For example, they should agree on a common date for the celebration of the resurrection. Protestant and Catholic communities now reckon the date on which Easter falls by one calendar, Orthodox communities by another, and it is rare when the two Easters happen to fall on the same date. The fact that not all Christians observe Easter on the same Sunday is a continuing sign of the divisions within the one Church of Christ. A consensus among Christians to celebrate Christ's resurrection on a common date would be a small but tangible sign of the quest for visible unity.

Martin Luther and Reformation
Romans 1:1-17.

Martin Luther (1483-1546) is one of the most dominant figures in the history of Christianity. Probably more books have been written about him than anyone else except Jesus. He started the Reformation, but he was not the first who urged the church to reform. **Reform** entails a process to remove defects, to correct what is wrong, or to improve by alteration in order to steady a thing, a person, or a place on its course. A **reformation** consists in a radical transformation of a person, thing, or place, in order to correct what is wrong and to remove defects. It brings about not only something new but also a new self-understanding. Those who joined Luther viewed Christianty's inner core and outer limits quite differently from those who opposed him.

Reform Movements before Luther

The church had needed reform at all levels of its life for centuries and for many reasons. Many of the popes were not devoted vicars of Christ. The papacy moved to Avignon, France, in 1309 and remained there until 1378. Here the popes served as tools of French interests. From 1378 to 1417 the **Great Schism** occurred. During this time there were two and sometimes three men who claimed to be the lawful pope. Various councils were held to correct this situation. Then, almost as soon as the schism was healed, the papacy fell into the hands of popes who were more fascinated by the glories of the **Renaissance** than the gospel.

The Renaissance, a cultural movement concerned with art, architecture, and literature, emerged in the fourteenth century and flourished in the fifteenth and sixteenth centuries. It rejected medievalism and called for a return to the classical humanism of Greco-Roman culture. The ideal of the Renaissance was to control the natural world and to create a perfect society through knowledge. The Renaissance was spurred on by the flood of scholars who fled Constantinople after it was captured by the Muslims in 1453. These scholars brought manuscripts which contained different views about humankind, life, and society from those common in the West. These manuscripts alerted scholars to the many changes and interpolations that had taken place in the copying and recopying of ancient texts. New philosophical outlooks were introduced. The Greek language became more common among western scholars. This made it possible for them to compare the Greek text of the Bible with the Latin version. There developed a great concern for returning to the sources of the Christian faith. The scriptures took on more prominence, being regarded as more authoritative than church doctrines and practices.

At the time of Luther, the pope from 1513 to 1521 was Leo X (Giovanni de'Medici). By all reports he was a polished and devious politician but an irresolute, lax, and incompetent pope. His long career in the church's power structure began at the age of thirteen when he was made a cardinal by Innocent VIII (1484-92). Leo was a true Renaissance pope, but was unconcerned about the church's spiritual welfare; he was unaware of the intellectual ferment brought on by the printing press invented by Johann Gutenberg in 1455; and he was insensitive to the widespread desire for reform of the corruption, ignorance, and doctrinal confusion in the church. It is reported that when he was elected pope he remarked, "Let us enjoy the papacy which God has given us." His papal court was a continuous round of festivities, banquets, theatrical shows and hunting parties. Leo also immersed himself in literature, the arts, and music, and, consequently, was generous to artists and scholars because of his interest in furthering humanist culture. The result of his lavishness is that he damaged the papal finances. To recoup his treasury and in order to build St. Peter's Basilica in Rome, he permitted the sale of indulgences and sold church offices and pardons.

An **indulgence** is the partial or full remission by the church of punishment due to sins which have already been forgiven. Based on the merits of Christ and the saints, the church reasons that it can grant indulgences drawn from the treasury of merits available to help sinners on earth or in purgatory. Luther did not denounce indulgences but their sale.

Many of the bishops were also corrupt, avaricious, and indolent. **Simony**, that is, the buying and selling of ecclesiastical offices and pardons, was common. Many bishops had jurisdiction over several dioceses that they had purchased. From them large sums of money poured into their hands. Often bishops were absent from their dioceses, which meant they could not fulfill their roles as teacher, sanctifier, and administrator. They placed in charge those willing to pay for administrative positions.

Such corrupt leadership set the tone for many of the lesser clergy, monks, and nuns. The educational requirements of the clergy were practically nil. Celibacy was openly flouted. Many priests proudly fathered children and then secured funds to support them. Monasteries relaxed their rules of discipline and prayer, becoming centers of leisurely living instead of houses of penance and prayer. Many monasteries that had been famous centers of learning were no longer such.

Part of the reason for the terrible state of the church is that society was going through a great transition at many levels. Explorers like Christopher Columbus (1451-1506) were discovering new worlds beyond the western horizon. Scientists like Nicholas Copernicus (1473-1543) were making great advances in astronomy, physics, mathematics, and medicine. The **feudal system**, an economic, political, and social system that had been in place since around 850, was coming to an end. In this system, people had different rights based on their political and economic status. The economic situation depended on a local agricultural structure with the estate or manor as its basic unit. The lord of the manor parceled out land in return for services, dues, and an oath of loyalty. There was a hierarchy that determined how much land was owned: from king to prince, counts, dukes, knights, squires, and serfs or peasants. The peasants were exploited by the landowners. Most of the poor received little or no support from the church. On the contrary, many bishops and clergy were landowners who supported the feudal system. From time to time the peasants revolted and called for a new order. There was a major revolt from 1524 to 1526, in which the people applied the principles of the Reformation to their situation.

Replacing the feudal system were powerful monarchs who forced the nobility and clergy to serve the ends of the nation as a whole. The kings of France, England, and Spain were soon quite powerful. They were aided in their nationalistic enterprises by the rise of the various vernacular languages and the decline in the use of Latin, which earlier had been a common bond for much of western Europe. The Christian world was unraveling.

Two famous reformers before Luther were John Wycliffe of England (1328-84) and John Huss of Bohemia (1369-1415). Wycliffe, a priest-theologian, attacked the teaching of transubstantiation and held that the scriptures were the sole criterion for any action taken by the church. To make the Bible accessible to the English people, he translated it into English. Wycliffe also taught that only a church that imitated Christ's humility and poverty was the true church. He supported the policies of the English government to restrict papal powers of ecclesiastical appointments and taxation. He urged the king to disendow the church and divest it of its property. Wycliffe was condemned as a heretic in 1382 but, unlike many other reformers who were persecuted and killed, he was left undisturbed in his retirement.

Huss, a popular preacher and theologian, called for freedom of preaching, communion in both bread and wine, and civil punishment for mortal sin. He taught that the church should not own property or wealth. He was condemned by the Council of Constance in 1414, a council called to reform the church. Huss was burned at the stake. His ashes were spread on a lake to prevent his followers from using his "relics" to further his cause.

By the time Luther appeared on the scene, the church and society were ripe for a much-needed reformation. The Reformation took place not because Luther decided that it would, but rather because the ecclesial, cultural, economic, political, and social factors converged to make it possible. The conflict between Luther and Rome started as a protest in the name of the scriptures and salvation. Because of a whole series of factors—some political, some economic, some the result of ignorance, stubbornness, and poor communication—the church of the West was divided beyond the imagination of any of the participants. Luther never intended to shatter the church of the West. His revolution is probably the most devastating event in the history of the church. The devastation continues because new denominations spring up almost weekly as various groups break off from their mother churches to start their own.

Luther's Life and Personal Struggles

Luther was born on November 10, 1483, in Eisleben, Germany, and baptized the following morning on the feast of St. Martin. His father, Hans, was of peasant origin and first worked as a copper miner. Later he moved into the middle class, becoming the owner of several foundries. As a father he was so strict that Luther reported that he did not have a happy childhood. His first experiences at school were no better than those at home. Luther disclosed that he was whipped for not knowing his lessons. Luther's father wanted him to be a lawyer so he could help with the legal matters that affected his foundries. He spared no efforts to provide his son the necessary education. But Luther had no desire to become a lawyer and so in July 1505, just short of his twenty-second birthday, he joined the Augustinian monastery at Erfurt.

There were several reasons why Luther made his decision. He was drawn to the religious life by the death of a good friend in a duel. Another reason is that he was caught in a thunderstorm and thrown to the ground by a bolt of lightning. He felt so overwhelmed by the fear of death and hell that he promised St. Anne, the patroness of miners, that he would become a monk. Ultimately, Luther was led to the monastery by a concern for his own salvation. The theme of salvation and damnation permeated both church and society. Most people believed completely in Satan and his demons. Innumerable evil spirits roamed the earth, seeking to bring people into sin and hell. One must be always on guard against Satan. People imagined themselves caught in a tug of war between God and Satan. Luther's father even suggested that it was Satan who hurled the lightning bolt that drove his son into the monastery.

Luther entered wholeheartedly into monastic life. He was ordained a priest in 1507 at the age of 24, and, in general, found peace and happiness in the monastery. Nevertheless, below the surface he was in terror. He entered sincerely into the monastic spirituality which involved frequent prayer, fasting, participation in the sacraments, especially the sacrament of penance, devotions to Mary and the saints, and the discipline of silence and reserve. Nevertheless, he was not convinced that he was doing enough to be saved. God seemed like a severe judge, like his father and his early teachers. Despite his best outward efforts he found himself inwardly overwhelmed by sinfulness, unworthiness, and alienation from God. His deep concern for his salvation brought on health problems such as constipation. In short, Luther's central question was the same for everyone: How can I find a gracious God? He wanted certainty about his salvation and a firm sense of God's real concern and favor in his regard.

Luther's spiritual advisor recommended that he read the great teachers of **mysticism**, those who had lived a life of intense prayer. The mystics affirmed that all one had to do was to love God and that all the rest would follow as a result of this love. But Luther soon discovered that loving God was not an easy matter, especially since he associated the just God with the very demanding judgments of his father and teachers.

When a life of deep prayer did not work, Luther's advisor directed him to study the scriptures not only for himself but also to prepare himself to teach scripture at the University of Wittenberg, recently founded in 1502. Since Luther had received a doctorate in theology in 1512, he knew the Bible quite well. Nevertheless, in 1513, at the age of 30, he began to study and teach the Psalms. He read them from the perspective of the Jesus of history. He soon realized that Jesus shared humankind's agony of being separated from God, as in Psalm 22: "My God, my God, why have you forsaken me?" While he found consolation in the sufferings of the Jesus of history, this did not suffice to cure him of his own anguish and despair.

The great discovery probably came in 1515 when Luther began lecturing on the epistle to the Romans. Paul addresses God's justice in 1:16–17: "For I am not ashamed of the gospel. It is the power of God for the salvation of everyone who believes: for Jew first, and then Greek. For in it is revealed the righteousness [justice] of God from faith to faith; as it is written, 'The one who is righteous [just] by faith will live.'" Luther realized that "God's justice" should not be taken literally in a precritical way whereby it refers to God as an angry judge dispensing rewards to the good and punishments to the unjust. For the apostle Paul, God's justice refers to the saving intervention of God, that is, to God's love, mercy, and forgiveness whereby in Christ Jesus he purifies people of evil, frees them from their sins, and declares them innocent of injustice. A person does not have to find a gracious God. The gracious God has already found us. All one has to do is accept this love and forgiveness in faith. Luther was so overjoyed by this insight that he later wrote: "I felt that I had been born anew and that the gates had opened before me into Paradise."

Heiko Oberman, a foremost Luther scholar, refers to Luther's experience of the saving justice of God as "the tower experience." According to tradition, Luther was in the toilet when he realized the true meaning of Romans 1:16–17. "'According to monastic piety of the times, a monk was not supposed to spend more than three minutes at a time in the toilet because that was where, it was thought, Satan was at his most powerful. Linger too long in the water closet and the devil, it was believed, might pull you by the anus into his power.' Satan, in other words, was identified with man's lowest bodily functions and Luther, with all his problems of elimination, must have been forced to spend undue amounts of time sitting on Satan's throne" (Woodward 1983, 14).

Indulgences had been sold for years. The particular sale that prompted Luther's protest had been authorized by Leo X. Bishop Albert of Brandenburg was already in control of two dioceses but hoped to acquire the most important diocese in Germany, that of Mainz. He agreed to pay the pope the sum of ten thousand ducats. Since this was a considerable sum, the pope also authorized Albert to announce a great sale of indulgences in his territories, on condition that half of the proceeds be sent to Rome. Leo wanted some of the money to complete building the great Basilica of St. Peter, which had been begun on April 18, 1506, under Pope Julius II (1503–13).

The Dominican John Tetzel (1465–1519) was put in charge of the sale of indulgences in Germany. An unscrupulous man, he made scandalous claims in order to promote the sales. He told his audiences that an indulgence made the sinner who made the purchase "cleaner than when coming out of baptism," and "cleaner than Adam before the fall," and that "the cross of the seller of indulgences has as much power as the cross of Christ." Those who bought an indulgence for a deceased loved one were promised that, "as soon as the coin in the coffer rings, the soul from purgatory springs."

Luther and others were distressed by the way Tetzel and his associates misrepresented the church's gospel by their appeal to the ignorance and superstition of the people, and by the deep corruption of the church's highest officials. According to Luther, if people sin they should personally repent and change their ways. Buying indulgences is not true repentance. On the contrary, it is a corruption of the biblical teachings about God and his justice. Also, if it is true that the pope is able to free souls from purgatory, he ought to use the power, not for trivial reasons like building a church, but simply out of love and freely. In truth, the pope should give the money to the poor, even if it were to require selling the Basilica of St. Peter. Luther nailed a paper, written in Latin, containing ninety-five theses against the selling of indulgences on the church door in Wittenberg on October 31, 1517. The impact of this act was so great that that date is usually given for the beginning of the Protestant Reformation.

Printers soon spread copies of the ninety-five theses throughout Germany, both in the original Latin and in a German translation. Luther sent a copy to Albert of Branden-burg, who in turn sent a copy to Leo X. The pope asked the Augustinian order to deal with the matter. As far as he was concerned, the controversy between Luther and the sellers of indulgences was merely "a monkish squabble." The following examples are illustrative of the ninety-five theses (Rupp and Drewery 1970, 19–25):

1. When our Lord and Master, Jesus Christ, said, 'Repent . . . ,' he meant that the whole life of believers should be one of penitence.

2. The word cannot be understood as referring to the sacrament of penance, in other words of confession and satisfaction, as administered by priests.

20. Therefore the Pope, by his plenary remission of all penalties, does not mean 'all' in the absolute sense, but only those imposed by himself.

21. Hence those preachers of Indulgences are wrong when they say that a man is absolved and saved from every penalty by the Pope's Indulgences.

79. It is blasphemy to say that the cross erected with the insignia of the Papal arms is of equal value with the cross of Christ.

80. Bishops, curates, and theologians who authorize such preaching to the people, will have to answer for it.

81. This wanton preaching of pardon makes it difficult even for learned men to redeem respect due to the Pope from the slanders or at least the shrewd questionings of the laity.

It is not necessary to detail the rest of Luther's controversy with the church, various emperors and governments, and rebellious peasants. For the purposes of this book it is enough to add that Leo eventually condemned Luther for teaching heresy in 1520 and excommunicated him on January 3, 1521. **Heresy** (the Greek root means "to choose") is the denial of church teaching, often by choosing only one aspect of the teaching to the systematic exclusion of all others.

In the twentieth century the possibility of lifting Luther's excommunication to further the goals of ecumenism has been discussed several times. In 1970, a group of German Lutheran bishops stated that the excommunication had already become history and that historical facts could not be abolished retroactively by formal legal acts. In 1980, when Cardinal Joseph Ratzinger was archbishop of Munich, he concurred with the Lutheran view, saying that he was "in principle against such posthumous cleansings of history."

Luther's Theology

Martin Luther was a man of violent temper, rough manners, and coarseness of language. At the same time, this complex man was a well-educated, intelligent, honest, and devout priest with extraordinary powers of persuasion, both written and oral. Luther proposed three interrelated principles which he found in the Pauline epistles to bring the church of Christ back to its basic holiness and integrity.

First, Luther taught that humans are saved **sola gratia**, that is, by grace alone. God's salvation in the death-resurrection of the Jesus of history is God's gracious gift (Gal. 2:20–21). Luther's tower experience convinced him that he went through a door opened by God. God had made the way possible. There is no way in which sinful creatures can earn or **merit** God's salvation. Christ alone saves us and not Mary, the saints, pilgrimages, or indulgences.

Second, humans are saved **sola fide**, that is, by faith alone (Gal. 2:16). Humans are totally incapable of any kind of self-justification because of the sinfulness inherited from the first parents. There is no work, even one of love, which can dispose God to justify—to look kindly on—humans. Salvation is always a gift to be accepted in faith. The church underscored works: buying indulgences, going on pilgrimages, having masses offered for oneself without personal involvement. Luther rejected this approach.

Third, humans are saved **sola scriptura**, that is, by scripture alone. The church presented itself as the authoritative interpreter of God's will. Luther emphasized that the church itself is judged by the scriptures. The word of God is a window to God. We do not look at the window but through it. The Bible gives a more trustworthy witness to the word of God than that of the pope's corrupt church. Luther was so anxious to get the Bible into people's hands that he translated it into very readable German.

Luther's theology can be summarized in one sentence: humankind is saved (justified) by the grace of God alone through scripture alone, appropriated by faith alone.

The Counter-Reformation

The response of the Catholic church to the Lutheran reformation is called the Counter-Reformation. At its center was the ecumenical Council of Trent, which held many sessions from its opening in 1545 to its closing in 1563. Trent consolidated and reformed the church's laws, liturgy, disciplines, and doctrines. The bishops gathered at Trent disagreed with the theology of Luther because he overemphasized his position—as his reliance on the word *alone* indicates. The bishops decreed that Luther neglected certain truths that are central to Christianity.

Luther's theology of "grace alone" acknowledged that people enjoy the presence of God's grace. But Luther held that at heart humans remained sinners. Grace was the divine response to utter human depravity. Justification, for Luther, was extrinsic, that is, God's grace never really healed the intrinsic core of people. The justified remain sinners because of the effects of sin. There is no way humans could merit God's love or had been intrinsically changed. God simply looked on his creatures "with rose-colored glasses." Luther was so taken with the sinful inclinations of humans that he taught that, left to themselves, people can only will evil. They can not even will to do good. No human act is truly good. That is why Luther claimed that Christians are simultaneously justified and sinners *(simul justus et peccator)*. These teachings collided with those of the Catholic church: It teaches that humans are basically good. The Fall has blemished us but not corrupted us. Grace is divine assistance to a humanity that has not been totally perverted by sin.

The Catholic bishops disagreed with Luther's theology of "faith alone" because he made humans totally passive in their response to God's offer of salvation. God seems to come into an empty room. Humans have nothing to contribute to the relationship. They simply accept God's saving presence in faith. Catholics, on the contrary, taught that there is no justification *without* faith, but there is justification *through* faith. Augustine of Hippo expressed it well: "God who created you without your consent will not justify you without your consent." Faith, say Catholics, involves our subjective response to God's objective salvation. Faith is not a cause of justification but is a condition for its presence.

The bishops disagreed with Luther's theology of "scripture alone" because, by stating that the word of God is the only authority over a Christian, he disavowed the authority of tradition, the church's officeholders (especially the pope and bishops), and the ecumenical councils. The church acknowledged that the scriptures are normative for the life of the church, but insisted that the living, teaching church is the principal interpreter of God's word. Moreover, the Catholic Church maintains that the pope and bishops are the official interpreters of the Christian faith and scriptures. The Spirit does not speak through the scriptures in such a way that individual readers could indiscriminately challenge the teachings of the officeholders. Although both Luther and John Calvin taught that "the Spirit speaks through the scriptures *in the church,"* some of their followers later taught that the Spirit speaks "so *individually* in the heart of every Christian that the Bible read in a personal way, without church tradition or church setting, is an adequate guide" (Brown 1985, 103). The ecumenical movement is going to have to take seriously the thought of Ernst Käsemann, a Lutheran scripture scholar: "The New Testament canon does not, as such, constitute the foundation of the unity of the church. On the contrary, as such, it provides the basis for the multiplicity of confessions" (Toolan 1982).

Today most Lutherans and Catholics agree that Luther and the Catholic Church were arguing about two sides of the same coin: grace and merit, faith and works, scripture and church officeholders. Neither side saw the other side. Today, since both communities agree that the two sides are necessary, many wonder if both churches can indefinitely justify a continued separation.

Ecumenism

John 17; Ephesians 4.

Thomas Stransky (1986), a Catholic priest and leading ecumenist, explained that the main flaw in the present ecumenical movement is an inadequate understanding of the nature of ecumenism. A faulty understanding of ecumenism can only create fear and further divisions. **Ecumenism** is the quest of Christians for full visible unity for mission through personal and church renewal and reform. The Greek root of the term means "the inhabited world." Ecumenism, then, points to the whole world and wholeness. This meaning prompted Arie Brower, a former deputy general secretary of the World Council of Churches and former general secretary of the National Council of Churches, to state in 1986 that ecumenism "is the shaping and nurturing of the whole person committed to the whole ministry of the whole gospel through the whole church for the whole world."

The phrase "full visible unity" assumes that since all Christians are disciples of Jesus Christ, a real but imperfect union already exists among them. However, this view of unity can point to an invisible and spiritual union, whereas the union should also be visible and juridical (having the same laws and administration). Christians should have the same altar, a shared life, a common worship, a single mission, a universal or catholic outreach, and be grounded in the apostolic faith of the first-century church. This does not mean that there must be uniformity of doctrines and disciplines. On the contrary, this apostolic faith must be articulated in such a way that it will be "open to the pluralism, the mutual surprise and joy of discovery which belong to an adequately diversified unity" (Deschner 1986).

This unity should occur for the purposes of mission. The church has a **threefold mission**: to teach the reign of God as Jesus did; to witness in word and deed to this kingdom; and to serve the reign of God, especially by care for the poor, sick, and oppressed.

Ecumenism is a commitment to the unity of the one Church of Christ in order that it can fulfill its mission. Mission is "the obligation of the whole church to proclaim, by word and act, the whole gospel to the whole world" (Stransky 1986). Some theologians fear that our ecumenical pedagogy is weakest at the point of mission. It would seem that few Christian persons or groups enter the ecumenical movement because of a commitment to the unity of the church-in-mission. Most get involved in specific common ministries (e.g., social justice projects, Bible study, or prayer services), but in doing so they often miss the wider implications of their specific projects: the proclamation to the whole world of the good news that God the Father has saved us in the death-resurrection of Jesus the Christ.

Renewal and reform are conditions for the possibility of unity. Christians cannot bring about the one and only Church of Christ by their own efforts. This is the work of the Spirit. Nonetheless, all Christians are obliged to work with the Spirit for unity, until it is fully accomplished by the Spirit. This work, which should be a priority, requires the continual reformation of the church's institutional, intellectual, and devotional dimensions. For example, deficiencies in church discipline (institutional) and the formulation of doctrines or laws (intellectual) need to be rectified. At the devotional level, this reformation begins and develops with a change of heart—which can occur through study and dialogue. A change of heart and holiness of life, along with public prayer for the unity of Christians is called **spiritual ecumenism**, and is regarded as the soul of the whole ecumenical movement. Spiritual ecumenism formally began in the United States through the efforts of Paul Francis Wattson (1863–1940) and Lurana Mary White (1870–1935). They were Episcopalians when, in 1898, they founded in Garrison, New York, the Society of the Atonement, a Franciscan community of friars and nuns with a special ecumenical dedication. This little group was corporately received into the Catholic Church on October 30, 1909.

In 1908, they had initiated eight days of prayer—from January 18 to 25—for church unity. They called this the Church Unity Octave. For some time, this octave focused firmly on reunion with Rome. The prayers were rather sternly phrased. For example, on January 20, prayers asked for "the submission of Anglicans to the authority of the Vicar of Christ." On January 22 the prayers asked "that Christians in America may become one in union with the chair of St. Peter."

The Vatican approved the octave in 1909, and then extended its observance to the universal church in 1916. In the early 1960s, the name of the week of prayer was changed to the Chair of Unity Octave. Finally, in 1966, in keeping with a greater ecumenical awareness, the present name was given: the Week of Prayer for Christian Unity. The title changes are significant for two reasons: Catholics had learned to pray with others and not simply for them; the emphasis was no longer church reunion but Christian unity.

The Modern Ecumenical Movement

At the beginning of the twentieth century there were moves to bring the churches back together. In 1902 Patriarch Joachim III of Constantinople sent an encyclical to all the Orthodox churches, expressing concern about possible rapprochement among those who believe in God as Trinity so that the union of all Christian churches might eventually come about. The patriarch hoped for two things: a union of Orthodox churches and programs whereby the Orthodox could make contacts with other Christian churches.

It is plausible to date the beginning of the modern ecumenical movement to the World Missionary Conference held at Edinburgh, January 13–23, 1910. There were 1,200 delegates from the Protestant missions from around the world, except Latin America and Africa (Desseux 1983, 46). The main concern of the delegates was their common task: the evangelization of the world. One of the conference's eight commissions was designated to study cooperation and the promotion of unity. Several speeches alluded to the regrettable absence of Roman Catholic and Orthodox observers.

The organizer and president of the conference was the American Dr. John Raleigh Mott (1865–1955), a Methodist layman, who later received the Nobel Peace Prize in 1946. In his first address he asked, "Has it not humbled us increasingly as we have discovered that the greatest hindrance to the expansion of Christianity lies in ourselves?" Nonetheless, the meeting was an optimistic and unanimous affirmation of their task to evangelize the world.

During the conference, Bishop Charles Brent (1862–1929), a Canadian Episcopal bishop in the Philippines, was disturbed because questions of faith and church order were considered to be outside the competence of a missionary conference. He argued that Christians could not be content with merely cooperative efforts. In addition to cooperation, a forum was needed so the churches could study the causes of division with the purpose of removing them. Brent was to be the chief instrument in bringing about the Faith and Order Movement. A committee was approved, eventually set up in Geneva, and the first world conference was held in 1927.

On January 10, 1919, the Orthodox Patriarch Germanos of Constantinople called for all Christian churches to form a "league of churches." The Orthodox "became the first church to call for a permanent organ of fellowship and cooperation between the churches" (Rusch 1985). In January 1920, the Orthodox sent an encyclical to all the churches of the world, calling for the formation of an ecumenical council of churches (Visser't Hooft 1982, 1–2).The encyclical recognized both the new opportunities and the dangers of the times. It underscored the need for discussions at the practical level, insisting that doctrinal differences did not doom the enterprise to failure. By taking common action, it was stated, the churches would gain knowledge, eliminate prejudice, and create a spirit of trust that would militate against mutual disagreements and distrust. Unfortunately, the document did not receive wide circulation. Yet it was a significant contribution.

Meanwhile, Protestants were organizing an interchurch and international forum to examine the doctrinal causes of disunity. In May 1919 they sent a delegation to Pope Benedict

XV (1914–22) inviting him to attend. He politely declined, but said he would pray for the success of the conference and, especially, that "those who participate in it may, by the grace of God, see the light and become reunited to the visible Head of the church, by which they will be received with open arms" (Tavard 1960, 117).

In 1927, Protestant emissaries preparing for the first ecumenical conference on Faith and Order to be held at Lausanne, Switzerland, visited Pope Pius XI (1922–39), seeking his blessing and cooperation in the search for Christian unity. Pius declined any interest in the "distinctive witness" they sought to bring intact into "the coming great church." Rather, the pope politely reminded them that their search could be immediately finalized right there on the spot by a return to the Catholic Church.

After the visit, the Holy Office announced in July 1927 that Catholics could not take part in the Faith and Order Conference at Lausanne. Just after the Lausanne conference, Pius issued his encyclical *Mortalium animos* in January 1928 in which he denounced ecumenical congresses, meetings, and addresses because they led to **indifferentism**: the belief that one religion (or church) is as good or as bad as any other. Catholics could not take part in these assemblies, he wrote, nor should they encourage or support them, since "the unity of Christians can come about only by furthering the return to the one true Church of Christ of those who [had] separated from it." Furthermore, since the other Christians are themselves so divided in belief on many points, the encyclical wondered how, with their wide variation of opinions, they "can open up the way to unity of the church when this unity can be born of but one single authority, one sole rule of faith, and one identical belief."

Another ecumenical conference—Life and Work—was organized in 1919 and held its first preparatory conference at Geneva in 1920. Nathan Söderbloom (1866–1931), Lutheran Archbishop of Uppsala, Sweden, was the organizer and leader. This outstanding Christian was to receive the Nobel Peace Prize in 1930.

The purpose of the organizers of the Life and Work conference was to relate the Christian faith to the social, political and economic problems of society. They believed that the churches should first unite and then discuss doctrines. Their motto: "Service unites; doctrines divide." Their first meeting was held at Stockholm in 1925, with six hundred delegates from thirty-seven countries. Some consider it the first ecumenical conference because it was composed entirely of delegates who were representatives of their churches (Visser't Hooft 1982, 10).

The ecumenical movement that began among the Protestant churches in 1910 reached a major landmark in 1948. Within both the Faith and Order and the Life and Work movements there grew an awareness that their concerns were so intertwined that they needed to be brought together in a single council. In 1937, these councils met at Edinburgh and Oxford, respectively. Both recommended unity in a World Council of Churches.

World Council of Churches (WCC)

A provisional WCC was set up at Utrecht, Holland, with Willem A. Visser't Hooft (1901–85) as its general secretary. He gave the council its name and is considered "the supreme architect of the ecumenical movement" (Thompson 1985a).

World War II prevented the WCC from holding its first meeting until August 22–September 4, 1948. The meeting in Amsterdam attracted 351 delegates from 147 churches from 44 countries. Visser't Hooft was elected the first general secretary, a post he would hold until 1966. Geneva was chosen for the headquarters.

The WCC theme was "Man's disorders and God's design." Right from the first meeting, concern for church unity and for social questions were inextricably linked; they are two sides of the same ecumenical coin. For example, the most controversial statement made in the Amsterdam assembly was its criticism of laissez-faire capitalism and Marxist communism. "The Christian churches should reject the ideologies of communism and laissez-faire capitalism and should seek to draw men away from the false assumptions that these extremes are the only alternatives. Each has made promises which it could not redeem."

At Amsterdam, the delegates committed themselves to stay together, having defined themselves as "a fellowship of churches which accept our Lord Jesus Christ as God and Savior." The last two words in the statement were never defined. Incarnation (Christ is God's incarnate Son) and atonement (Christ saves on the cross) were underscored, but each church was free to interpret them in its own way.

The WCC does not pretend to be or become a "super church." It is an instrument for the union of the churches; only particular churches can choose to unite with others. The WCC provides a forum for speaking and acting together, hoping to create the conditions for the possibility of visible union. The WCC "is not a church but a confederation of independent churches, each of which remains free to disassociate itself from any WCC position or statement" (Rausch 1985).

The second WCC assembly was held in Evanston, Illinois, in August 1954. There were 502 delegates from 161 member churches. Their theme was "Jesus Christ—the hope of the world." They committed themselves not only to stay together (as had been agreed at Amsterdam) but also to grow together. They stressed service to the world and said less about evangelization and missionary activity than had been said at Amsterdam.

The WCC held its third assembly at New Delhi in 1961 with 577 delegates from 197 member churches. Its theme was "Christ, the Light of the World." The delegates affirmed their intention not only to stay together and to grow together, but also to assume new tasks together. They revised their self-definition as presented at Amsterdam: "The WCC is a fellowship of churches which confess the Lord Jesus Christ as God and Savior according to the scriptures and, therefore, seek to fulfill their common calling to the glory of the one God, Father, Son, and Holy Spirit."

Four Orthodox churches—Russian, Romanian, Polish, and Bulgarian—became members. This gave the Orthodox more influence in ecumenism. Their presence, said Visser't Hooft, did not make the ecumenical task easier, but did enrich it. John XXIII approved Roman Catholic observers at the New Delhi meeting, leaving Cardinal Bea to choose the delegates.

The fourth assembly was held at Uppsala, Sweden, in July 1968, with Eugene Carson Blake as general secretary

(1967–72) (see Thompson 1985b). The assembly met against the background of the many challenges of the 1960s: the ambiguity of new scientific and technological progress, the growing gap between poor and rich nations, and racism. Its theme was "Behold I make all things new" (Rev. 21:5). There were 704 delegates from 235 churches and 84 countries, one-third from the third world. The largest group of delegates came from Orthodox churches. The Catholic church sent fourteen observers and nine theologians joined the Faith and Order Commission.

The fifth assembly was held in Nairobi in 1975. There were 676 delegates from 285 member churches. The general secretary was Philip Potter (1972–84). The delegates agreed that in addition to staying and growing together, they would struggle together. Their theme was "Jesus Christ frees and unites." The delegates declared that faith in the triune God and socio-political engagement, conversion to Jesus Christ, and active participation in changing economic and social structures belong together and condition one another. They wrote a major amendment into their constitution, declaring that the churches are called "to the goal of visible unity in one faith and in one eucharistic fellowship expressed in worship and in common life in Christ, and to advance toward that unity in order that the world may believe." New Delhi (1961) had called for the unity of all in each place; and Uppsala (1968) had underscored the depth and extent of catholicity. Nairobi (1975) complemented those two meetings by acknowledging there can be unity-in-diversity and diversity-in-unity.

The WCC held its sixth assembly at Vancouver, July 24–August 10, 1983 (see Rausch 1984). There were 847 delegates from 301 member churches from 100 countries. Twenty Roman Catholic observers, including six bishops, were approved by the Vatican. The theme of the assembly was "Jesus Christ—the life of the world."

The WCC has been a controversial body because it deals with controversial issues in which theology and ethics impinge on political, economic, and socials policies. Its Vancouver meeting was as faithful as previous assemblies had been to the ecumenical pioneers who emphasized the importance of the work of Christian unity not in a political or social vacuum, but in relation to the continuing worldwide struggle for a greater measure of justice, peace, and human dignity. The delegates were reminded that peace and justice belong together with baptism, Eucharist and ministry. These two strains must mutually reinforce one another rather than become parallel tracks which might split apart. Keeping them together is no easy task.

Pope Paul VI visited the WCC in Geneva on June 10, 1969, a visit unthinkable in 1948. The visit proved his esteem for the work of the WCC, and yet he made it clear that the Catholic church was still reluctant to enter fully into the organization.

There are several reasons for this reluctance. First, the Catholic Church is so hierarchically and solidly structured and organized that it would be very difficult to diffuse its identity and independence of action within another organization. Second, there are theological and jurisdictional problems that must be considered, especially those concerning the future role of the papacy. Third, the sheer size of the Catholic Church is such that it would so overwhelm the WCC as to call into question its very identity. The Vatican believes that for these three reasons it is "inopportune" for the Catholic Church to join the WCC.

The seventh assembly was held at Canberra, Australia, in 1991 from February 7 to 20. The president of the assembly was Emilio Castro of the Evangelical Methodist Church of Uruguay, elected the fourth general secretary of the WCC in 1984. The 842 voting delegates from 100 countries represented 311 churches—a major increase over the 147 churches present in 1948. In 1983, thirty-one percent of the delegates were women; in 1991, women constituted thirty-five percent. Present also were twenty-three Vatican-delegated observers.

For the first time the theme focused on the Spirit: "Come, Holy Spirit, renew the whole creation." This was also the first time the theme was formulated as a prayer.

The assembly was held while the Persian Gulf War was being waged and it affected the deliberations. For example, Emilio Castro, disappointed that all could not celebrate one Eucharist, hoped all the delegates would unite at the eucharistic table at the next assembly to be held in Harare, Zimbabwe, in 1998, the fiftieth anniversary of the founding of the WCC.

He asked how the presidents of warring countries could ever unite in peace if the churches could not unite around the Eucharist. This plea raised the perennial question: Is the Eucharist the expression of unity or a means to unity?

Some of the ecclesial questions that were debated included the relation of men and women and women's ordination; the theological perspectives, particularly that of northern nations versus that of southern nations; cultural limitations of biblical language (particularly the dominance of male metaphors for God); and the inevitable tension between ecumenists and social activists. The former focus on the nature of God and church unity; the latter emphasize peace and justice. However, this tension reached a most critical point at Canberra because "it became apparent that the quest for Christian unity, and so issues of faith and order, were no longer the major concern of many of the delegates. If this is true as well of the churches they represented, then something significant has happened in the ecumenical movement" (Putney 1992, 633). Orthodox participants were disturbed by some of the presentations, especially that of the Korean theologian Chung Hyan-Kyung, which seemed to equate the action of the Paraclete-Spirit in Jesus with the spirits of nature, ancestors, or social movements. They warned that they might withdraw from the organization if it deviated from basic Christian beliefs by accepting as valid theology ideas they considered to be "apostasy" and "syncretism."

On June 24, 1985, the seventy-fifth anniversary of the World Missionary Conference, a meeting was held in Edinburgh with some five hundred delegates present. The meeting was not a triumphalist celebration. A delegate from Nigeria reminded the assembly that "there were Christians in Africa before they were in Edinburgh." Emilio Castro, secretary general of the WCC, did not spare his predecessors. In his address to the assembly, he criticized the way they had married missionary activity with colonialism, and noted the irony that by 1914 the armies of the missionary countries were killing each other. Finally, he observed that the regions whose representatives dominated Edinburgh in 1910—the United Kingdom and western Europe—had reached the point in 1985 where they now needed re-evangelization. In fact, to the dismay of many, neither the Church of England nor the Church of Scotland had sent delegates.

Finally, it should be noted that Konrad Raiser was elected the fifth general secretary of the WCC and assumed office in January 1993. An ordained minister in the Evangelical Church in Germany and a professor of ecumenical theology, Raiser had been deputy general secretary of the WCC from 1973 to 1983.

Catholics and Ecumenism

Ever since the schisms of 1054 and 1517, the Catholic church had taken a defensive and unfriendly attitude toward the other Christian communities. They were considered heretics and schismatics. They were separated from the Catholic Church, which Pope Pius XII (1939–58) declared in his encyclical *Mystici corporis* (1943) was the one and only Church of Christ. As the true church, the Catholic Church had the four marks of the true church as stated in the Nicene-Constantinopolitan Creed, namely, it was one, holy, catholic, and apostolic. The Catholic church's stance was ecclesiocentric: the way to unity is for all Protestant and Orthodox churches to return to the Roman Catholic Church.

Meanwhile, the world had gone through major changes as a result of the rise of modern science in the seventeenth century. There was less stress on authority (those in power determine all the rules and processes) and on tradition (there are ways things have been done and these should not be tampered with). The emphasis in the modern world was on freedom, equality, community, dialogue, and democracy.

When Pope John XXIII (1958–63) called for Vatican Council II (1962–65), he gave as one of his reasons the unity of all Christians. When the bishops met they underscored what the churches had in common. They realized that there could not be dialogue and sharing unless the bishops approached the other churches as equals. The bishops called the other churches "separated brethren" and "sister churches." Since all Christians believe Jesus is their Lord and Savior and are baptized in his name, then there already exists a real but incomplete unity among all the churches. This perspective is christo-centric: Jesus Christ and his Spirit unite all Christians.

The bishops summarized their teachings on ecumenism in the *Decree on Ecumenism,* promulgated on November 21, 1964. This document was new because it acknowledged that both sides were responsible for the divisions and because it overcame the simple identification of the one and only Church of Christ with the Catholic Church, as had been claimed by Pius XII. Nevertheless, the council reaffirmed the special claim of the Catholic church to be *the* Church of Christ: "For it is through Christ's Catholic church alone, which is the all-embracing means of salvation, that the fullness of the means of salvation can be obtained" (n.3). This meant that the way to unity is for all the churches to be regrafted into the one and only Church of Christ, especially as this is manifested in the Catholic Church. The bishops stated that the Church of Christ "subsists in" the Catholic Church.

The phrase "subsists in" has been controversial since the council. In March 1985, the Vatican's Congregation for the Doctrine of the Faith, in criticizing a book by a Latin American theologian, argued that the authentic meaning of "subsists in" was that "only elements of the church" exist outside the "visible structure" of the Catholic Church. In May 1987, Cardinal Jan Willebrand, president of the Secretariat for Christian Unity, questioned this interpretation of the Congregation for the Doctrine of the Faith. Avery Dulles, a prominent American Jesuit theologian, concurred, insisting that "subsists in" is quite different from "is" and that the phrase "subsists in" was "an expression deliberately chosen to allow for the ecclesial reality of the other Christian communities" (1989, 430). Gregory Baum, a distinguished Canadian Catholic theologian, had already written along these lines in 1972: "Whoever speaks of the Catholic church as the one true church must qualify this doctrine by the complementary teaching that the one true church transcends the Catholic church and cannot be simply identified with it."

Since the council in the 1960s, the modern world has put even greater value on the need for all people to enjoy equality, freedom, community, dialogue and democracy. The result is that the present focus of ecumenical theology is the mission of the church to proclaim, manifest, and expand the reign of God and the gospel of Jesus Christ. This mission should be directed to all, especially the poor. This is a theocentric view of ecumenism. Furthermore, the Catholic Church's claim to possess fully the marks of the church has been questioned. The Catholic Church is certainly one, but there are also serious divisions about such issues as the ordination of women, married priests, and contraceptive birth control. The church is indeed holy but every Catholic must honestly acknowledge his or her sinfulness. The church is catholic—it has a universal thrust—yet in many instances it remains too clerical, too masculine, and too western. The church is apostolic—faithful to the teachings, discipline, and mission of the apostolic church—but it often seems more concerned for its own maintenance than its missionary outreach.

Ecumenism and the Future

The ecumenical movement has achieved a measure of success at the executive levels, especially through the WCC and the many interchurch dialogues that have taken place. More work has to be done at the parish and congregational levels. For some ecumenists, the parish level is "the most crucial area for future development of ecumenical life . . . Ultimately it is here that Christian unity will or will not happen" (T. Horgan 1990).

Unfortunately, not all Christians and/or churches favor the ecumenical movement. For example, in 1988, when John Paul II addressed the European Parliament in Strasbourg he was denounced as "the antichrist" by Ian Paisley, militant Northern Ireland Protestant leader.[1] In 1990 a group of Welsh Presbyterians protested the week of prayer for Christian unity held by Anglicans at their Westminster Cathedral. They told reporters that "the ecumenical movement comes directly from hell."[2] On September 7, 1994, a group of directors of the Southern Baptist Convention's Home Mission Board issued a statement of dissent concerning efforts to promote Roman Catholic and evangelical cooperation. This statement was a response to an unofficial document issued by some Southern Baptists which outlined some common ground for Catholics and conservative

Protestants in their struggle against abortion, pornography, and other social and political issues. The dissenters contended that the evangelical-Catholic document not only undermines mission efforts by subordinating doctrine to a political cause, but it also represents Roman Catholicism as "a legitimate form of discipleship."[3]

Despite such pockets of negativity, ecumenists insist that the future of ecumenism involves two principles that should govern all proposals for Christian unity. First, unity should be visible, with the spiritual dimensions incarnated in the church's forms and structures: all the Christian churches should unite to manifest the holiness of the triune God and to worship this God. Unfortunately, the reports of too many ecumenical meetings read "like negotiations waiting for concessions rather than accounts of meetings seeking common worship" (Van Beeck 1985, 70). Denominational power games that inhibit unity have to be eliminated. Second, visible unity should be such that each church can maintain its distinctive identity, and none would be absorbed by others or all leveled into a synthetic hybrid. At Vatican II the bishops stated in their document on ecumenism that "in order to restore communion and unity or preserve them, one must impose no burden beyond what is indispensable (Acts 15:28)" (n.18). There is growing support for the model of church unity advocated by Cardinal Joseph Ratzinger and others: reconciled diversity (Hebblethwaite 1993; Rusch 1985, 118).

Reconciled diversity would protect and foster the distinctive charisms, disciplines, and style of each church. An example of such reconciled diversity exists in the United States. All fifty states respect and obey the Constitution and the Bill of Rights. Nevertheless, California has its own style, laws, and traditions. California is not New York anymore than New York is New Mexico or New Jersey or New Hampshire.

Reconciled diversity will not take place unless the churches respond fully to the gift of the Holy Spirit. Response to the Spirit is our task. No one has addressed this point—that ecumenism is at once a gift and a task—more dramatically than Raymond Brown (1984, 61–74).

In an explanation of Luke-Acts, Brown points out that "the distinguishing feature" of Luke's ecclesiology is "the overshadowing presence of the Spirit." He explains that the Acts of the

Apostles is the story of the many interventions of the Spirit. For example, the Spirit directed Peter to the house of Cornelius, inspired Paul and Barnabas to seek out Gentile converts, helped the church reach a decision about circumcision for Gentile converts, and led Paul to decide he must go to Rome. But Brown wonders if this account of the many interventions of the Spirit leads easily "to a *deus ex machina* concept of the Spirit," especially with regard to ecumenism. He agrees that the ecumenical movement—from 1910 to 1948 to 1962 to 1982 to the present—is the work of the Spirit. But he points out that we cannot "assume that the Spirit will bring the work to a triumphal conclusion." Brown shows that the Bible is filled with stories of how the people of God failed to respond to God's providence and paid the price for their failures (e.g., the twelve tribes were reduced to two; religious institutions such as the monarchy and priesthood failed; and "Israel learned more about God in the ashes of the Temple destroyed by the Babylonians than in the elegant period of that Temple under Solomon"). He then concludes with this disturbing question: "If in the next two decades the churches do not seize the opportunity, if a union between two major churches does not take place as a sign of what may be possible, and if consequently Christianity enters the third millennium much more divided than it entered the second millennium, is it not possible, and even likely, that the opportunity will never come again?"

6

Christians and Society

God and the Poor
Amos 8; Micah 6.

The world God created has an abundance of potable water, vegetables, and fruits as well as birds, animals, and fish suitable for human food. God made humans stewards of the world and its material goods. If the goods of the earth were evenly distributed, there would be enough land, food, and water for all people to live comfortably. Presently, people fall into one of four general categories in terms of their possession of the material goods of the world. Many people have or can acquire a sufficient amount of these goods for their families and themselves. Some—the rich—have a superabundance of these goods. Unfortunately, far too many live in **involuntary poverty**, that is, they do not have adequate food, clothing, housing, medicine, or education to live a life fitting and proper to their human dignity. In short, they are destitute. The fourth category is sometimes called a life of **voluntary poverty**. This means that some people freely choose to live simply, with little or no material goods (exterior renunciation) but (in their interior attachment to God) to use food, shelter, and money in a spirit of detachment and gratitude. Jesus lived such a spirit of poverty during his public teaching ministry when he had "nowhere to rest his head" (Mt. 8:20).

Religious communities have been formed to live the ideal of voluntary poverty. But the lifestyle prescribed by their vow of poverty does not hold the suffering, deprivations, and humiliations of those forced to live in involuntary poverty. Even those religious men and women in very ascetical communities have what is necessary for human life: a solid roof over their heads, a steady, healthful diet, sufficient clothing, and proper medical care. For religious communities, the virtue of poverty, not chastity, is the most difficult virtue to live. Poverty actually encompasses the voluntary renunciation of sexual intimacy, family life, and control over one's workplace and mission.

God the Creator wants people to enjoy his gifts. Involuntary poverty is contrary to human dignity and stunts human growth and maturity. It is the opposite of Christian humanism. Being wealthy, on the other hand, is not wrong, provided the wealth is not used selfishly. The rich are called to care for the poor and to be "poor in spirit" (Mt. 5:3). God also wants the rich ultimately to trust him rather than their riches. During the reigns of Saul, David, and Solomon, the Jews tried to imitate the standards of wealth and power honored by their rich neighbors. When the kings and people turned to riches rather than Yahweh and his covenant, the consequences were disastrous.

Jesus' attitude toward material comforts and goods is complicated. On the one hand, he enjoyed table fellowship, especially with the poor (Lk. 5:29, 7:33–50, 15:1), and, on the other hand, he did not approve the sectarian puritanism of the Essenes or the aristocratic lifestyle of the Sadducees. In his teachings he reiterated the concern of the prophets for outcasts, the involuntary poor, and those on the margins of society (Lk. 14:13, 21; 15:1–2; 17:11–19; 18:1–14). When the messengers from John the Baptist came to Jesus to discover if he was the one who is to come or should they look elsewhere, Jesus replied: "Go and tell John what you have seen and heard: the blind regain their sight, the lame walk, lepers are cleansed, the deaf hear, the dead are raised, the poor have the good news proclaimed to them" (Lk. 7:22).

Perhaps Jesus' most formidable teaching about wealth is that there is an irreconcilable antinomy between God and money. He said, "No one can serve two masters. He will either hate one and love the other, or be devoted to one and despise the other. You cannot serve God and mammon" (Mt. 6:24). *Mammon* is an Aramaic word which means wealth or property. It includes more than money. It also includes all the things money can buy: comfort, security, success, power, and prestige.

In summary, concern for the involuntary poor pervades the scriptures. God is often portrayed as being on the side of the oppressed and the outcasts. A paradigm of God's care for such people is the Exodus of the Hebrew slaves from the clutches of the pharaoh under Moses. Yahweh elected the Israelites to be his chosen people, leading them from slavery in Egypt to a promised land of plenty. The Jewish prophets, especially Amos and Micah, challenged the priests and people to care for the sick, orphans, and widows; they also announced messianic promises when God would bestow peace and prosperity. Jesus is also paradigmatic. He was poor and fulfilled his mission among the marginalized, oppressed, and the destitute (Lk. 6:20). His life as critic of injustices brought him ridicule. In Luke's gospel, after Jesus declared that one cannot serve God and mammon, there is a sentence (16:17) not found in the other three gospels: "The Pharisees, who loved money, heard all these things and sneered at him." The sneering eventually turned to persecution and a death sentence.

Christian Social Teachings

Since there are so many Protestant churches, it is almost impossible to summarize Protestant social teachings. In general, it begins with the presupposition that the individual and society are in conflict or competition. There is a dialectical relationship between the individual over and against the person as a social being. The individual strives for freedom and independence; society strives to constrain the independence of the individual for the common welfare. This conflict can be moderated by individuals working to produce a healthful, harmonious social unit. The state is established by individuals out of enlightened self-interest because only institutional force can keep individuals from destroying one another. Otherwise, a political community is neither essential nor intrinsic to the human condition.

Catholic social teaching, on the other hand, has developed in stages over many centuries and so its principles are clearly enunciated. It begins with two insights, one theological and the other political.

First, God's providence—his care and concern for humans and their daily lives—tells us human life is good and should be of quality for all. In order that life be of quality for all, more is required than charitably providing food, housing, or medicine. People seek justice. The meaning of **justice** is captured in the ancient phrase *suum cuique*—to each what is due. There are three complementary forms of justice: commutative, distributive, and social. **Commutative** or individual justice concerns private claims between individuals or groups. It entails such things as fidelity to agreements, contracts, and promises. **Distributive** justice specifies that all persons have some share in those goods that are essentially public or social, such as education, housing, health care, and a minimum income. **Social** justice concerns the realization of distributive justice. Both are based on the assumption that people are social by nature. Social justice directs all citizens to aid "in the creation of patterns of societal organization and activity that are essential both for the protection of minimal human rights and for the creation of mutuality and participation by all in social life" (Hollenbach 1977, 220). For example, all citizens should contribute to the common good by paying taxes, performing jury duty, and by opposing structures that abet racism, classism, and sexism. In view of this description, social *in*justice is the structured exclusion of people from access to those things required by their dignity as human beings.

Second, self and society should be viewed from a **sacramental consciousness**, that is, everyone and everything can be a sign of God's presence, love, or judgment. Self and society are not necessarily opposed but, rather, are interconnected. In fact, the formation of a state or a political community is a natural and necessary law of survival and maturation for humans (Maguire 1986, 20–21).

The most basic principle of Catholic social thought is the dignity, goodness, and inviolability of the individual. It opposes collectivist tendencies or systems that leave individuals, especially the poor, vulnerable to oppression of any kind. Its aim is the growth of a fully integrated human being—what we have been calling Christian humanism.

Catholic social teaching places the dignity of the individual within the context of society, which it views as an organic, supportive network of overlapping and interlocking yet hierarchical relationships that work toward social well-being or **the common good**. The common good is the result of responsible citizens acting in a way that leads to mutual respect for rights and dignity. The bishops at Vatican II discussed the common good in the *Decree on the Apostolate of the Laity*. They declared: "Catholics should try to cooperate with all men and women of good will to promote what is true and just, whatever is holy and worth loving (cf. Phil. 4:8)" (n. 14). "The common good, since it is founded on mutual dignity, is not in opposition to human rights, but rather their guarantee" (Hollenbach 1979, 61).

Traditional Catholic teaching reasoned that the common good of society encompassed more than the sum of the private goods of individuals. The common good embraces the institutions, laws, and values that regulate in terms of justice the interaction of individuals and groups in society and protect them from exploitation or oppression by the powerful and resourceful. In this perspective, the private good of individuals is subordinated to the good of the whole society. Personal freedoms have their clearly defined limits. The task of government is to enhance the common good by protecting the common values, institutions, and laws, and by resisting any individualism that would elevate an individual's own private good over the common good (Baum 1979).

This organic and supportive society is also decentralized. Healthy societies need to be built upon strong neighborhoods and local communities. Villages, towns, and cities have formal political and social power and authority. The **principle of subsidiarity** applies. This principle states that things should not be done at a higher level that can be done at a lower level. This principle holds that, since choice is of the essence of human freedom, basic political choices must be left in the hands of those most affected by decisions.

This organic and decentralized society is also pluralistic. A plurality of cultures is necessary since there are many ways through which an individual can pursue wholeness.

Finally, the Catholic tradition is unwilling to separate civil and political rights from social and economic rights. **Civil rights** rule out discrimination based on race, sex, color, or religion. **Political rights** include freedom of speech, assembly, and movement; and rule out arbitrary arrest, torture, and an unfair public trial. **Social rights** include the right to access such needs as food, shelter, basic health care, and education. **Economic rights** include a living wage, private property, and the right to form labor unions. The Catholic Church teaches that all four rights are indivisible and that violations of any of these rights are due to selfishness and greed. Right order and social justice can be reestablished in society if each and every person undergoes an intellectual and moral conversion to greater love, accepts the norms of justice, and strives to serve the common good.

At times the Catholic Church has not always been true to its own social teachings. For example, two nineteenth-century popes, Gregory XVI (1831–46) and Pius IX (1846–78) condemned economic, religious, and political liberalism and, at the same time, denied civil rights. Their justification for their decisions was threefold: the liberal political philosophy of the day promoted individualism and undermined the social cohesion of traditional society; total freedom of religion promoted **indifferentism** (the belief that one religion is as good as any other) and relativized the question of the truth of religion; and the economic liberalism of those times demanded that the government allow maximum freedom of production and trade. The popes feared the poor would be exploited.

The Latin American Bishops

No church group has done more to help the poor and foster Christian humanism than the Latin American bishops. They have done this in part through their **CELAM** meetings. **CELAM** is the acronym for *Conferencia Episcopal Latinoamericana.* The bishops represent twenty-two nations.

The first conference was held in 1955 in Rio de Janeiro. Inasmuch as it preceded Vatican Council II (1962–65), it lamented the shortage of indigenous priests and condemned both Protestantism and communism. Its condemnation of communism was its only reference to the socioeconomic and political context of Latin America. The perspective of Vatican II about the church's involvement in the modern world rendered **CELAM I** obsolete.

At Vatican II, the 531 Latin American bishops introduced the term **church of the poor**. This phrase denotes a church that denounces impoverishment caused by sin and injustice, preaches and lives spiritual poverty, and binds itself to voluntary poverty as a commitment. Not all 531 bishops were enthusiastic about the term and its consequences. Those who were, leaders such as Helder Camara, archbishop of Recife in northeast Brazil and "architect of Medellín" in 1968 (Wirpsa 1993), were passionately concerned with the social and economic development of their peoples (Hebblethwaite 1989).

CELAM II at Medellín became the "new Pentecost" for the Latin American church. It was the bishops' opportunity to apply Vatican II to Latin America. It produced sixteen documents of uneven quality and without a unified conclusion. Nevertheless, the conference surpassed the Vatican Council in many respects. Summarized here are five of its principal themes.

First, immediately after Vatican II, leaders such as Helder Camara had proposed that economic development was the solution to the problems of Latin America. Now the bishops stated that the era of development was actually over. They regretfully agreed that it was not possible for the underdeveloped countries of the south to become like the developed countries of the north, because the socioeconomic situation in the north had not changed a bit. The developed nations continued to prosper at the expense of the poorer ones. The organic networks of society had broken down. The rich and poor were in a serious conflict, and the bishops identified the main areas of oppression: "a situation of injustice that can be called institutionalized violence"; "internal colonialism" whereby a rich minority (oligarchy) dominates power; and an "external neocolonialism" of powerful, foreign nations. The true solution is liberation for the poor, the voiceless, and the oppressed. The bishops questioned the church's traditional alliance with wealthy, oligarchical establishments, and called for radical structural changes. Vatican II had declared a change of hearts (inner, personal transformation) as the way to achieve social justice. As people grow in virtue, political commitment would emerge and social justice would follow, they believed. Medellín, on the other hand, called for both a transformation of individuals and a transformation of the structures of society. However, some of the bishops said transformation of society must come first. Evil societies must be overcome first. In fact, they said, personal growth and holiness truly occur when people combat evil. Also, without the transformation of structures, the transformation of persons is extremely difficult. In the end the bishops compromised and called for both transformations because they were divided over which transformation would be more appropriate for the different countries of the continent (Baum 1984a, 85).

Second, the bishops encouraged **conscientization**—helping people understand that they become responsible for injustice if they remain passive. That is, if people out of fear of the personal risk involved do not take courageous and effective action to bring about necessary changes, they, by their passivity, perpetuate the injustices. .

Third, the bishops declared that **evangelization**—the proclamation of the gospel—cannot take place except within the context of a commitment to the struggle against the systems of domination.

Fourth, Medellín condemned **social sin**, something never mentioned at Vatican II. The bishops reinterpreted the classic doctrine of sin by stating that people need liberation not only from their personal sins but also from the social sin of oppressive social structures. Social sin has a powerful hold on people. It results from our past personal choices for injustice that form into systemic institutions of socioeconomic and political oppression and deprivation. Social sin has to be identified and eliminated.

Fifth, the bishops declared that personnel and resources within the church must be redistributed so as to give effective "preference to the poorest and most needy sectors." This expression would be rephrased as the "preferential option for the poor" at **CELAM III** in 1979.

The preferential option for the poor is not exclusive, but it does require two commitments from the church: to look upon society in all its dimensions from the perspective of the poor, and to give public witness to the church's solidarity with the poor. It is through criticizing injustices that the church can express in a practical way this solidarity. This criticism should never be expressed through violence.

The phrase "preferential option for the poor" has provoked considerable controversy. Donal Dorr noted that it "became the most controversial religious term since the Reformers' cry, 'Salvation through faith alone'" (1983, 1).

The church has always taken care of the poor because involuntary poverty is dehumanizing. The church sponsored almsgiving (see 1 Cor. 16:1; Gal. 2:10) and approved communities of monks and nuns who committed themselves to serving the poor, uneducated, and sick. Nevertheless, in its perennial care of the poor over two thousand years it never proclaimed a preferential option for the poor. Why was this call not heard in the past—or why was it not heard in the same way as at Medellín (Baum 1986b)? There are two reasons. The first concerns the scriptural basis for this stand. The phrase "preferential option for the poor" is not found as such in the Bible. It is grounded in biblical teaching, but it was formulated by concerned Christians using the critical or actualization method of biblical interpretation. The mindset of our times is called the "new humanism" or **historical consciousness**—that humans are the subject of their own history. In today's world the major sign and need of the times is to care for those who are victims of massive suffering and oppression; many people do not have access to many of the basics of human life. When the scriptures are read from this perspective, it becomes clear that God is calling us to care for the poor.

A second reason why the idea of a preferential option for the poor moved to the forefront is due to the way theology developed after Vatican II. Until the Council, the church had a state-of-siege mentality. It withdrew from direct engagement with the social, economic, and political orders, viewing itself as separate from the world. The popes protested injustices, but the effect of their teachings often gave a measure of legitimation to the status quo. This defensive posture was captured in the phrase "in the world but not of it."

With Vatican II Christians found themselves "released from the world for the world." This perspective sees the church as part of the world but aware of its evils. The church must be released from the pretensions, delusions, and sin of the world, but at the same time it "should be released for the world *as it really is:* arbitrary, contingent, ambiguous, loved by God and by the Christian" (Tracy 1981, 48).

Involvement with the world, especially the world from which Christians must be released, entails interpretation. It is impossible to take a neutral position. Everyone views history, the historians inform us, from a particular value perspective. The Medellín bishops read history from the perspective of the involuntary poor. They realized that the conflict between the powerful rich and the powerless poor was one of the world's major problems, especially in Latin America. The bishops realized that their people had to be released from the deadly evil of the violence of poverty. The opponents of the bishops accused them of reading history with a Marxist perspective. But choosing the poor is not Marxist. Marx promoted a preferential option for the workers, the industrial proletariat whose toil fueled the economy. For Marx, the unemployable had no destiny in society. He called them *Lumpen,* the German word for "hoodlum."

Gregory Baum maintains that the church's commitment to a preferential option for the poor is definitive and irreversible. This option was adopted and developed by the Synod of 1971 on social justice; by national episcopal conferences, including the United States bishops in their pastoral letters of 1983 on peace and 1986 on the economy; and by both Paul VI and John Paul II. Baum regards the turn to the poor begun at Medellín "as an extraordinary happening, possibly of world historical importance" (1986b, 30). It has made a major impact on Catholic social teaching. Instead of viewing society as an organic network of interlocking relationships, Catholic social teaching now evaluates society from a critical, conflictive perspective. This perspective sees that a society is divided by structures of oppression, and believes that the church should ally itself with the poor, the workers, and the unemployable. By struggling together with the poor, the church can transform the social order (Baum 1984b). Eventually, and ultimately, the transformation sought would be the Catholic ideal: an organic, supportive, decentralized, and pluralistic society marked by peace and freedom.

The Medellín documents represent compromises; not all the bishops favored the preferential option for the poor. One group that was fiercely anti-communist favored the establishment of a **neo-Christendom**, that is, a society and culture aided by the moral and material support of the state and ruled by the Catholic Christian faith and tradition. These bishops insisted that society's principal enemy is the **secularization** encouraged by the growing industrial developments. Secularization denotes a mindset that, out of concern for the well-being of people in their daily lives, gives little or no attention to the presence of God and religion in civil, social, and economic affairs. The Latin America bishops in favor of a neo-Christendom feared their area of the world was in danger of losing its soul and so must defend its homogeneous culture against secularization by becoming industrialized, but without following the example of the West. These bishops maintained that the primary task of the church, therefore, is to promote a cohesive Latin American culture, adapted to the requirements of industrial society yet faithful to its original values, including the Roman Catholic faith. The primary thrust of the church's pastoral projects is religious. Concern for justice will follow from the transformation of people.

The other group—the bishops who dominated at Medellín—viewed the Latin American scene differently. They believed that injustice and oppression are the principal social evils in Latin America. Furthermore, they claim that a homogeneous Latin American culture has never existed; and that the concept is an ideology that disguises the structural injustices in Latin American society (Baum 1983).

The Latin American bishops met in 1979 for **CELAM III** at Puebla, Mexico, from January 28 to February 13. Pope John Paul II opened the conference with a speech to the bishops on January 28, 1979. He did not use the term liberation theology, but he did speak of liberation. "The church," he said, "feels the duty to proclaim the liberation of human beings; the duty to help this liberation become fully established; but she also feels the corresponding duty to proclaim liberation in its integral and profound meaning, as Jesus proclaimed and realized it." He reminded the bishops that Jesus "identified with the deserted," was committed "to the neediest," and was "never indifferent to the imperatives of social reality" (Brockman 1979, 180–83).

The address "was couched in abstract, traditional and highly nuanced language" (ibid.). The *New York Times* interpreted some of the pope's sentences about liberation and "political involvement" as a rejection of liberation theology. However, most commentators believed he rejected extreme forms of liberation theology, particularly the kind that made "the gospel into political ideology" or which called for "all-out class warfare, and even [Fidel] Castro-style revolution, as the only way to achieve social justice" (Peerman 1979).

The first thing the bishops reflected on was the socioeconomic conditions of their countries. They reported that, unfortunately, the social situation had severely deteriorated since Medellín in 1968. Most Latin American countries had become more impoverished, more debt-ridden, and more repressive. The bishops addressed the needs of their people in a lengthy and rich document that reaffirmed the direction set by Medellín. Summarized here are four of their principal points.

First, Medellín, they declared, "adopted a clear and prophetic option expressing preference for, and solidarity with, the poor." "Preferential option for the poor"—the title of one of the chapters in their document—became the catchword of Puebla and captured its spirit. The bishops expressed concern for many groups—the poor, youth, elderly, and ill-housed city-dwellers; and those involved in liturgical, educational, and social services. All of these persons or groups are to be viewed in light of the option for the poor. This means the preferential option for the poor "is not itself optional—it is not one of several theological or pastoral tendencies among which Christian ministers or constitutions may pick or choose."

Second, the bishops expressed appreciation for the **base communities** and encouraged their growth, calling them "one of the causes for joy and hope in the church." Base communities are small, voluntary associations of lay Catholics who, for the most part, are poor persons who aim to liberate themselves from their socioeconomic and political oppression. The groups meet on a regular basis to deepen their knowledge of the scriptures, to reflect upon community needs and seek adequate solutions to those needs, to celebrate the Eucharist, and to learn ways to spread the gospel. In 1979 there were some forty-one thousand such communities in Brazil alone. By 1986, it is estimated that there were some sixty to eighty thousand groups with a total membership of two to three million (Hewitt 1986, 81).

Third, the bishops explained the crucial difference between evangelization and partisan politics, and they denounced violence of every kind.

Fourth, the bishops called attention to the problems of two exploited groups: the indigenous people and the women of Latin America. Medellín did not discuss either of these two groups. By focusing on them, the bishops indicated that gender and ethnic differences are aspects of the rampant poverty and oppression.

In March 1979, John Paul sent the Latin American bishops a letter with a ringing endorsement of their conference conclusions.

CELAM IV was held October 12–28, 1992, in Santo Domingo, Dominican Republic. The time was chosen to mark the fifth century of evangelization in the western hemisphere. The place was chosen because here the first Catholic diocese in the western hemisphere was established. In announcing the conference, John Paul declared that this meeting should pay particular attention "to a renewed evangelization of the continent, which will penetrate deeply into the hearts of individuals and into the culture of peoples." The theme of the conference was "New Evangelization, Human Advancement and Christian Culture."

During the preparations for the conference two interrelated concerns surfaced. First, active defenders of the option for the poor among Latin American bishops were now in a minority since many bishops appointed by John Paul since Puebla were chosen because of their fidelity to John Paul's ideological and ecclesiological guidelines. Those who had attended

Puebla had fond memories of the successes achieved there but they were "not expecting great things" (MacEoin 1991). Rome still favored a preferential option for the poor but it claimed also that "part of the problem is that the poor lack a work ethic" (MacEoin 1992a).

Second, there were rumors that there would be a shift in focus regarding the process of evangelization: from the poor to "the Catholic culture" of Latin America. This shift was deemed necessary, it was said, because in many Latin American countries, Pentecostal and evangelical churches had grown rapidly. For example, in Guatemala in 1991, the evangelical churches claimed thirty percent of the people in this traditionally Catholic country. In Brazil, eighty-eight percent of the people identified themselves as Catholic in 1980, but in 1991 the number was less than eighty percent. When John Paul had visited Brazil in October 1991, the Brazilian bishops addressed these words to the pope: "We look forward to this conference in Santo Domingo and are glad to join with the church in this call to evangelization. But we would like to know who will be evangelized, how they will be evangelized and who will do the evangelizing." Many Latin American bishops feared that "Catholic culture" was simply a code word for the reimposition of a European model of church. These bishops insisted that the poverty of millions of their people should remain the starting point for their reflections on the theme of new evangelization.

John Paul was in Santo Domingo for six days, October 9–14. In his homilies and lectures he reiterated the preferential option for the poor: "We must feel other's poverty as our own and become convinced that the poor cannot wait." He praised the Latin American women for being the guardian angels of Christianity in their countries. Although he chided activist priests and nuns not to be blind to their primary religious role, he encouraged them to take up the program of Christ's beatitudes, especially as it affects the poor and the downtrodden. He emphasized that the evangelical churches were like "rapacious wolves . . . causing division and discord in our communities." Finally, despite the fact that he was aware of the bitter disputes over Columbus's legacy, he thanked God for "the abundant fruits of the seeds planted over the last 500 years by [the] intrepid missionaries" (French 1992).

John Paul inaugurated the episcopal conference attended by 307 voting bishops from twenty-two nations on October 12. In his lengthy address, he asked pardon for the church's offenses, past and present. Nevertheless, he stressed that the Catholic Church had acted as the "untiring defender of the Indians, the protector of the values that existed in their cultures and supporter of their humanity in the face of the abuses committed at times unscrupulously by the colonizers." He also called for continuity with the Medellín and Puebla meetings, especially their preferential option for the poor (Wirpsa 1992a).

The sixteen-day conference was marked by serious debate about the future of the church (Wirpsa 1992b). The two most important issues were poverty and the indigenous cultures. The bishops acknowledged that the major problem facing the Latin American church was the growing poverty. During the pope's visit, protesters had called Columbus "the exterminator of a race" and they denounced the "500 years of hunger and massacre." The bishops also acknowledged that in many of their countries "races and cultures [were] reasserting themselves—indigenous, blacks, mestizos—many of them impelled by spiritualities far older than Christianity that came to them across the water." The majority of the bishops believed that the gospel can flourish in a variety of cultures. Other bishops, however, talked about spreading and deepening the Christian culture which they viewed "as a monoculture, European style" (Peerman 1993, 184). The bishops who opposed this direction for evangelization did so "not only because of its recolonizing content, but also because it relativizes and reduces to a subordinate position the many cultures of the hemisphere, indigenous, African-American, mestizo, all of them with multiple variations" (MacEoin 1992b).

The bishops produced a sixty-one-page document, "Jesus Christ, Yesterday, Today and Tomorrow." It breaks very little new ground in its sections on such topics as human development, new evangelization, Christian culture, and neoliberal economic policies. It does contain a strong statement on ecology, an emphasis missing from the 1968 and 1979 documents.

It reaffirms the Christian base communities as a way of actualizing the church for their countries and the "irrevocable but not exclusive" option for the poor. The bishops emphasized the "new faces of poverty." Special attention, they maintained, must be paid when the rights of "children, women and the poorest groups in society—peasants, Indians and Afro-Americans—are violated." By linking these people to the ecological issues, the bishops revealed their sensitivity to the relationship between the oppression of the poor and the abuse of the natural resources.

The impact of **CELAM IV** will probably not be realized for years to come, but it represented another major step by the institutional church to oppose, in the name of Christ the liberator, the social, political, and economic forces that dehumanize everyone, especially the poor.

The Nature of Liberation Theology

Liberation theology began to emerge in Latin America, Africa, and Asia at the same time in the 1960s and for the same reasons—because Protestant and Catholic liberation theologians were involved in the lives of the poor, and Vatican II's concern for the poor had a positive influence on many bishops, priests, and nuns (Ferm 1986, 1988). Liberation theology consciously attempts to change history through a struggle for social justice.

Before liberation theology was written in the late 1960s in Latin America, there were liberation movements. The most famous example is the case of Camilo Torres (1927–66), a young, charismatic Columbian priest and social activist. He abandoned the clerical state and in early 1966 joined a guerrilla movement, only to be killed a few weeks later on February 15 in his very first skirmish with the army. His death had a profound symbolic impact. It was an unmistakable sign of a new mood in the Latin American church.

The cause of liberation has continued. Hundreds of thousands have been martyred as they struggled in the name of Christ against injustice. Most go unnamed and unnoticed. Nevertheless, some of the murders have been reported worldwide, drawing attention to the ruthlessness of the military rule in some nations. In El Salvador's civil war, for example, there have been shocking assassinations of church people. On March 24, 1980, Archbishop Oscar Romero (1917–80) was shot while presiding at the Eucharist. Four women missionaries from the United States were brutally raped and murdered on December 2, 1980: Jean Donovan and three nuns, Dorothy Kazel, an Ursuline, and Maura Clarke and Ita Ford, both of Maryknoll. On November 16, 1989, six Jesuit priests, their housekeeper and her teenage daughter were ruthlessly tortured and executed. The two army officers responsible for this crime were sentenced to thirty years in prison on January 24, 1992. The civil war ended a week later on January 31, 1992.

Liberation theology is a term that covers, sometimes rather loosely, a variety of theologians and activists. What they share is a common starting point and an ultimate vision.

For a century before Vatican II, the church tended to remain aloof from the social and economic problems of society because it had witnessed the collapse of European Christendom and the rise of secular states in many European countries. It was a case of the church against the world. One of the reasons for having the Council was to overturn this perspective. As a result, the point of departure of conciliar theology was the problems of modernity and the social locus of the developing countries of the West. This theology directed the church into the modern world in order to connect with its scientific and technological enterprises for the promotion of human, political, social, and economic development. However, Leonardo Boff explained that the conciliar theology evaded "the basic question, the question of the profoundly unequal relationships that prevail among nations and between classes, and the price others have to pay for the benefits of accelerated development in the central countries." Liberation theology's point of departure is "the people, the social locus of the popular, oppressed classes. It strives for the liberation of these classes and seeks to win them a voice in the historical process" (1989, 54).

The ultimate vision shared by liberation theologians is of a salvation that achieves total liberation from both personal and social sin. Beyond this shared goal, there are many differences among liberationists, differences that are conceptual and strategic. For example, some denounce class conflict because it can lead to armed violence and guerrilla warfare.

Some of the leaders include such Catholic and Protestant theologians as Gustavo Gutiérrez of Peru, Juan Luis Segundo (1925–96) of Uraguay, Hugo Assmann and Leonardo Boff of Brazil, Enrique Dussel and Jose Miguez Bonino of Argentina, Segundo Galilea of Chile, Jose Miranda of Mexico, and Jon Sobrino of El Salvador.

The most famous of the group is Gutiérrez. This Catholic priest-theologian is often called the "intellectual father of liberation theology" (Lernoux 1989, 105) because he first proposed the term in July 1968 (Molineaux 1987) and because of his 1971 book, *A Theology of Liberation*. Many see Gutiérrez as a deeply spiritual man whose vision of the "church of the poor" teaches and inspires them as they face the overwhelming task of helping the poor. His critics attempt to portray him as a man who foments violence in society and infidelity to the church (Nickoloff 1993).

The word that dominates liberation theology is the word *new*. This theology originates in a new experience of God that results in a new spirituality that is explained and guided by a new theology. In the past God was often imagined as detached from people's socioeconomic and political lives. It also offers a new self-understanding, new social structures, and a new future.

Liberation theology begins with a new experience of God, one which Gregory Baum believes "differs from other religious experiences which Christians have treasured over the centuries" (1985). Those who have this new experience are either Christians "born into subjection" or Christians who recognize this struggle for freedom and self-determination as the significant sign of the times and believe they cannot grasp the Christian message apart from this sign. They see that the poor are "inhumanly poor precisely because the rich are so inhumanly rich" (Scharper 1978, 397). They experienced God on their side in solidarity with them, summoning them to justice. Christ is not encountered primarily as the sacrament of his Father or as the servant of the world, but as the divine liberator and protector of humanity who blessed "those who hunger and thirst after justice."

The new experience of God moved people beyond a **privatized** or **pietist spirituality** that underscored a personal, even private, relationship with God. **Spirituality** concerns people's response to God's attempts to promote and expand his own presence in our daily history. A privatized spirituality had dominated the Protestant and Catholic churches during the nineteenth and twentieth centuries. Conversion took on new dimensions. A change of heart had to affect more than one's personal relationship with God. It also should include entry into a critical perception of society, especially an awareness of the existence of the structures of sin. The response to God required a response to others.

Sorrow for sin encompasses more than repudiation of one's personal transgressions, according to liberation theology. What also must be taken into account is social sin, those structures of oppression that are the consequences of personal sins. Pietist spirituality taught salvation in terms overly individualistic and overly otherworldly. Liberationist spirituality revealed the illusion of individualism, created "a sense of solidarity with others, especially the poor, and [made] people aware that they [were] imbedded in a conflictual social matrix, the liberating movement of which is part of the mystery of divine redemption" (Baum 1987, 126).

Christian spirituality is built on faith. The new experience of God modifies the three traditional components of faith: conviction, commitment, and confidence (trust). Love and hope have always been acknowledged as dimensions of faith. Faith as commitment borders on love; faith as confidence borders on hope. But since love and hope have a justice dimension, the liberationists recognized that faith and justice are joined in an indissoluble way. The God who calls us to conviction, commitment and confidence also calls to us through the poor and their unjust situations. A "faith that does justice" not only makes people critics of the present order, but it also promotes the cause of liberation and justice. "Faith, therefore, is more than intellectual assent, more than hope in what God will do without us; it is also a present participation in the work that God is doing—that is to say, in the task of bringing forth justice to nations" (Baum 1984a, 77).

This faith that does justice is deep within the Bible. It is the nature of Abraham's faith. When Abraham learned that God planned to destroy the city of Sodom for several reasons, that is its violation of hospitality through homosexual rape (Gen. 19:5), its failure to help the needy and poor (Ezek. 17:49), and its inhospitable, even violent, treatment of strangers (Gen. 19:9), he argued with God on behalf of the people. Abraham asked, "Will you sweep away the innocent with the guilty? . . . Should not the judge of all the world act with justice?" (Gen. 18:23, 25). Abraham, the model of faith, was honored for his generosity (Gen. 13:8–11), hospitality to strangers (Gen. 18:1–5), and his sense of justice (Gen. 18:23–33).

In many Latin American countries, but particularly in Brazil, this faith-justice spirituality is lived out in base communities *(comunidades eclesiales de base)* (Welsh 1986; Hewitt 1986). These communities actually grew out of the liberation movements in the 1960s and so they had a parallel but distinct history of development with liberation theology (McGovern 1989, 588).

For Christians, the base-community churches are a new way of actualizing the church. As a matter of fact, such churches are as old as Christianity—the so-called "house-churches" of the primitive church (see 1 Cor. 1:16, 16:15; Rom. 16:10–16; Phil. 4:22). But they are a new structure in this era. These "popular" churches differ from the "hierarchical" churches or parishes, but like them they should serve as sacraments of the coming kingdom of God. In these base communities the gospel is proclaimed from the perspective of the poor in order to convert the rich and the powerful. The members serve the world by denouncing injustice and promoting social transformation. Together the members study the Bible and celebrate Eucharist. The Eucharist is "de-privatized" because it is no longer perceived simply as spiritual food for individual disciples on their journey. Rather, it creates community among the participants; it is a symbol of the banquet where all will have enough to eat; and it is the presence of Christ the liberator, himself oppressed and killed but now vindicated by God (Baum 1987, 115–16). Finally, the murder of Archbishop Romero and thousands of other Christians indicates that martyrdom has been given a new dimension in Latin America. In the past when martyrs refused to renounce their faith in Christ, they were imprisoned and killed soon after; in Latin America men and women live in fear and face the threat of death at any moment of day or night for their commitment to the struggle for Christ's peace and justice. A favorite motto of terrorists is "Kill one, terrify thousands."

What is also new about liberation theology is that many of its proponents critically used certain terms derived from Marxist or neo-Marxist social theory. Thus it is that liberation theology connects "the biblical idea of the deliverance of those who are in bondage or suffering and the Marxist hope for freedom from class oppression" (Kolden 1984, 123). But why the atheist Marx? When Gutiérrez was asked that question he promptly replied, "Because the people do." What he meant is that the Marxists had reached the poorly-paid workers before the church had reached them.

Karl Marx taught that over the course of history some people have dominated others. The conditions of feudal society gave rise to the **bourgeoisie** (the property-owning class who possess both capital and the means of production) who took power from the landed aristocracy and established capitalism. But the conditions of bourgeois capitalism have given rise to the **proletariat** (wage earners possessing neither capital nor the means of production, who earn their living from hard work). It is the proletariat who are destined to take power from the bourgeoisie and abolish further class distinctions, the unequal distribution of goods, and structures of domination.

To support his thesis, Marx proposed many teachings that are at odds with Christianity. Marxism is atheistic; denies humanity's spiritual dimension; denies such economic rights as private property and such political values as subsidiarity and the common good; encourages armed revolution; teaches the inevitability of class conflict; neglects those living in involuntary poverty; and singles out the economic condition as the significant factor responsible for the transformation of society. Liberation theology not only rejects these teachings but it also ultimately (and ironically) attacks Marxism and any form of atheism "that perpetuates social structures which deform the image of God in human beings" (McDade 1991, 437). In other words, liberation theology opposes whatever in Marxism is contrary to Christian humanism.

On the other hand, Marxist social analysis also has several strengths. Marx explained the existence of ideologies. Liberation theology realized that traditional theology can be ideological. It can, for example, legitimize injustice and inaction. The classical Hebrew prophets denounced the ways in which religion was used by some priests to support unjust kings (Jer. 5:31).

Marx showed that evil is systemic. There can be no reform within an unjust system; the whole system has to be changed. For example, impoverished women are the most oppressed group in society and the church. This situation will not change until the machismo ideology and the patriarchical structures that pervade both society and the church are transformed.

For Marx, humans are creative workers. He analyzed industrial or manual labor as the source of multiple alienations for workers and denounced it. He said labor caused a threefold alienation. First, it alienated a person from nature because the factory treated the worker's body like a machine, making the worker's own body a stranger to him. Second, it alienated a person from himself because it removed the product of his hands from him. Third, it alienated the worker from his fellow workers because his relationship to others was completely determined by his place in the industrial process (Baum 1975, 21–39).

Finally, Marx had challenged the Aristotelian understanding of the process of gaining knowledge: first theory, then application. This is the order used in the physical sciences. First medicine is studied in a theoretical manner, then it is applied to the sick. According to Marx, the relation between theory and practice (praxis) should be quite different for the human sciences. Marx believed that commitment and solidarity precede the true perception of reality and, in turn, this true perception of reality leads to action that transforms society (Baum 1976). Praxis is too often understood as mere practice. Actually, **praxis** is critical action done reflectively. Theory and practice dialectically influence each other and transform one another. Furthermore, praxis reminds us that theoretical activity is itself a praxis—and one to be tested by the practice it serves (Tracy 1987, 10).

The liberation theologians make praxis the touchstone of truth or authenticity. They say the Christian faith must be lived before it can make any kind of theological sense. Solidarity with the poor is the presupposition for the authentic grasp of the gospel. You know you are a disciple of Christ if you are in solidarity with the poor. This theory of knowledge is captured by the following paradox: We get our most objective knowledge by subjective participation.

Many critics of liberation theology focus on its use of Marxist ideas and its espousal of socialism. From the previous paragraphs it should be clear that many of the works written in the 1970s did indeed use Marxist social and economic-political analysis. Moreover, the fact that some liberationists did use Marxism imprudently made it easy for the critics of liberation theology to link them with the criticisms leveled at radical groups. For example, Helder Camara reported, "When I feed the poor, I am called a saint. When I ask why they are poor, I am called a communist." Similarly, it is true that the late 1960s and early 1970s were a time of great revolutionary ferment and some liberation theologians called for a revolutionary overthrow of the military dictators who kept themselves unjustly in power. For many of these theologians it seemed an obvious right and duty to rise up against them. However, books on liberation theology in the 1980s hardly contain any treatment of Marxist social analysis. This is not to imply, argue Arthur F. McGovern and Thomas L. Schubeck, two United States Jesuit priests, that the earlier writings can be labeled their "Marxist phase" (1988). Even in the early 1970s, Gutiérrez and others distanced themselves from Marxist options and warned against Christianizing any revolutionary ideology. In February 1988, McGovern and Schubeck began a three-month study of liberation theology in Latin America that took them to eight countries. They found liberation theology working in a new context and taking new directions. There was some use of Marxist critique of capitalism "but liberation theologians used its concepts only at a very general level to describe exploitation by wealthy owners, the dominance of northern capitalist countries in the world economy, and the use of ideology to maintain and justify the tangentially status quo" (1988). In a two-week course in Peru under the direction of Gutiérrez, the two Jesuits said they heard no mention of Marxism in any of the talks they attended. Finally, McGovern and Schubeck report that the liberation theologians are quite aware that classic Marxist analysis does not adequately deal with the problems of indigenous peoples, racism, and the oppression of women.

The Contribution of Liberation Theology

Liberation theology has significantly influenced society, theology, ecumenism, and spirituality. Its impact on society has yielded mixed results. On the positive side, it has drawn the attention of the world to the plight of the involuntary poor. It has reminded Christians that care for the poor is central to Christianity. On the negative side, its direct political significance remains small. Even in Brazil where its force seems greatest, its impact comes more from the strength and leadership of the episcopal conference that constitutes a strong voice in that country. Liberation theology enjoyed some influence early on. Now it seems that "the present historical situation in Latin America eliminates any hope for the success of liberation movements . . . [It may have to] moderate its aims and work together with the progressive sector of the bourgeoisie to stabilize civilian, democratic rule and assure the protection of civil liberties" (Baum 1989, 123).

Liberation theology has changed theology. Theologians have traditionally written to and for those people who neither know Christ nor are Christian. For example, Hans Küng discussed in a best-selling book the two great challenges for Christianity as he perceived them: the world religions and secular humanism (Küng 1976, 25–116). Küng's analysis is very helpful and accurate in many ways. In the past, theology has addressed three groups: those within the church—in order to help them clarify their faith; those who belong to other religions and churches—in order to dialogue with them about the God revealed in Jesus Christ; and those indifferent or antagonistic to religion—in order to dialogue with them about the ultimate meaning of life. Today, however, liberation theologians and theologians influenced by them have gone beyond Küng. Included are such Protestant theologians as Harvey Cox (1980), Schubert Ogden (1980), and Robert McAfee Brown (1980).

These theologians do not deny the serious challenge from the world religions and secular humanism, but they argue that there is a more primary challenge, namely, the call of God to us through the poor, the oppressed, and the hungry. Millions of people live a life that is so minimally human that Gutiérrez referred to them as **nonpersons**, that is, "people who are not considered human in our society" (Gibeau 1976). Schubert

Ogden explains the term more clearly: a nonperson is "one who, being excluded from the existing order in one or more respects, is to that extent unfree, a passive object of history instead of its active subject" (1980). All theology must be put within the context of the needs of the nonpersons.

Why this shift of focus whereby Küng's nonbelievers are put within the wider context of liberation theology's nonpersons? The reason is that nonbelievers question our religious world, but usually share our socioeconomic outlook. Like us they have a deep regard for human life and yet, at the same time, they contribute to the plight of the poor by being part of the power elites. Like us they foster the dominant, unchristian ideologies of our society. On the other hand, the poor and the oppressed challenge not only our religious world but our socioeconomic and political worlds as well. Their poverty and hunger challenge our consumerism, racial and sexual prejudices, and comfortable lifestyle. In short, liberation theology says there is a specifically Christian way to view society and to do theology—from the viewpoint of the nonpersons. The poor need a chance to live an authentic Christian life.

Liberation theology has also advanced ecumenism even though not all Catholics and Protestants have accepted it. Nevertheless, liberation theology, as Gary MacEoin explains (1984,12), "is the first common theological movement of Catholics and Protestants since the sixteenth century Reformation . . . In a real sense, this marks the end of the Reformation and Counter-Reformation; and it is significant that it originated in and has taken deepest roots in Latin America, Asia and Africa, regions for which the Reformation as a European historical phenomenon was irrelevant." This means that liberation theology, which began as a movement *in* the church is now almost a new movement *of* the one Church of Christ, albeit a minority movement.

Liberation theology has also influenced the development of spirituality. Before liberation theology, Christian spirituality was predominantly pietist or privatized. Christians held that they and the church stand over against the world in an attitude of defense and offense. In this mindset there are two histories: sacred and secular. Christ is the light of the world—a world immersed in darkness and evil. God remains outside of secular history but will save us in the next world. These

Christians are otherworldly. God reigns in individual hearts. Sacred history operates through the church and this is a place of special encounter with God. A precritical interpretation of the Bible is central to this spirituality. This privatized spirituality does not evoke a keen sense of mission to the world.

But privatized spirituality does not mean that these Christians do not serve others. The spiritual and corporal works of mercy are encouraged. Much good is done through schools, orphanages, and hospitals. But changes in society, it is thought, will flow from personal transformation. For example, people on welfare are told that they have to take total responsibility for their own socioeconomic situation. Welfare is the result of moral evil. Little consideration is given to factors like limited education and sexual and racial prejudice that prevent people from getting jobs and getting off welfare.

Donal Dorr suggests (1984, 199) that "at its worst, this [privatized] spirituality was ghetto-like, individualistic and escapist. But at its best it gave people a sense of God's transcendence . . . [and] a sense of security; there was little need for agonizing, since all knew their place and how they were expected to act." It is also important to add that it is just possible that the worst dimensions of this fortress spirituality "are just the fossilized relics" of a spirituality that at first challenged Christians in a world where many were atheistic, materialistic, anti-Christian and antichurch, to preserve not only God's transcendence and providence, but also the significance of baptism and a personal commitment to Christ.

Liberation spirituality is built on faith-justice. Those involved in the liberationist movements realized that the socioeconomic developments that they had optimistically anticipated never materialized. This failure resulted in new questions for the Christians: "When you set out to serve the world, whose world are you serving? Is it the world as structured by the rich and powerful, a world built on the dominant values of competition and success at all costs? Or is it the world as God wants it to be, one in which structural poverty and powerlessness are challenged, and the poor are privileged agents of God in bringing about the kingdom?" (ibid., 202).

This faith-justice spirituality is, in Leonardo Boff's apt phrase, a "church in the subworld" (Boff 1989, 12–13, 191–94).

It underscores that we have a history marred by structural injustices and grinding poverty. God is on the side of the poor in their efforts at liberation. Christ's disciples serve Christ the liberator and the world by overcoming injustice. Full participation in the liturgy includes both celebrating God's saving interventions and answering his call to alleviate and eliminate injustices. Using the critical method of interpretation, they read and study the scriptures from the perspective of the poor. This liberationist spirituality calls Christians to solidarity with the poor and to disentangle themselves from unjust structures. Such moves are not easy to make because our social, economic and political lives are so interrelated that we are immersed in a huge interlocking system where almost all our actions play a part in maintaining structural injustice. We may be forced to make some compromises.

Compromises should not create guilt. There are several reasons they are necessary. First, although the Sermon on the Mount calls us to selfless love, it is not clear in our day-to-day living what this love requires of us. Compromise is possible because our vocation to be as holy as our heavenly Father cannot be identified with a clear and precise kind of moral perfection. Second, the proper spiritual response to our entrapment in structures of sin is mourning. The biblical word is *lamentation,* especially as found in the writings of Jeremiah (9:10, 18), Ezekiel (19:1, 14), and Amos (8:10). Mourning is part of the process of conversion. "Mourning unites those in the middle class with the victims of society who also mourn, even if for different reasons" (Baum 1989, 119).

In addition to mourning, something can be done in small Christian communities, especially among the poor. Christians committed to the faith-justice spirituality will have to band together because they exist as a minority in the church. Nevertheless, they can be a countervailing current. Minorities sometimes find an appropriate strategy. Gregory Baum (1984a, 104) offered an imaginative and encouraging proposal, one that is quite necessary as we prepare to enter the third millennium.

Imagine for a moment that in a city there were five just Christians in every parish, involved in local projects and joined in a lively network, what impact would such an active minority have on the church and on the city! The advantage of this minority strategy is that it does not depend on the cooperation of those in charge of the . . . institutions, even though their cooperation is of great consequence. Thanks to such a minority strategy, moreover, there is always something we can do. We are not caught in total impotence. We can always find others with whom to promote the countervailing current of social justice, knowing that this is not a waste of time, but a contribution that in the long run prepares significant social change.

Finally, human history reminds us that significant social changes may not occur in this world. The Catholic bishops reminded Christians of the necessity of an eschatological vision in their *Constitution on the Church in the Modern World*. They wrote: "We do not know the time for the consummation of the earth and humanity. Nor do we know how all things will be transformed . . . the expectation of a new earth must not weaken but rather stimulate our concern for cultivating this one. For here grows the body of a new human family . . . For after we have obeyed the Lord, and in his Spirit nurtured on earth the values of human dignity, brotherhood and freedom . . . we will find them again, but freed of stain, burnished and transfigured . . . when Christ hands over to the Father a kingdom eternal and universal" (n. 39).

7

Christians and Sexual Ethics

Principles of Ethics

According to Genesis, God made us body-persons, female and male. Everything that God created is good: the body is good and sexuality is good. Sexuality is central to every person's identity. **Chastity** is the proper use of sex. Everyone is called to be chaste in heart and mind and to live chastely, whether single (celibate) or married, young or old, healthy or disabled, rich or poor.

Christianity teaches that there are principles that govern human sexuality and chastity. The purpose of these principles is to ensure that human sexuality is marked by love, order, law, justice, and freedom, rather than by hate, disorder, lawlessness, injustice, and repression. In order that chastity prevail, most Christian communities propose some fundamental moral principles. (1) There exists an objective moral order in which some sexual actions are good and others are bad. (2) Humans can know this objective order. (3) The objective moral order applies universally to all sexual encounters. Actions objectively morally evil are always objectively morally evil. (4) Unfortunately, many persons do not always realize their fundamental ability to know the objective order (see Keane 1982). The existence of an objective moral order does not cancel the subjective factors in determining morality, such as motives, circumstances, purposes, and the special subjectivity of each person. In fact, the objective and subjective factors should not be considered separately as if they do not affect one another.

Christianity also teaches that there are three characteristics or criteria on which sexual activity depends for its integrity:

1. Sexual activity has the potential first and foremost of being linked with love in a relationship with another person.
2. It has the capacity of procreation.
3. It is accompanied by an intense pleasure which reaches its peak at orgasm.

These three—physical satisfaction, interpersonal intimacy and parenthood—"are not three separate 'variables,' or *possible* meanings of sex which we are morally free to combine or omit in different ways. Sex and love as fully *embodied* realities have an intrinsic moral connection to procreativity and to the shared creation and nurturing of new lives and loves" (Cahill 1990). In short, sexuality is a relational gift.

Legalism

If these principles are true, then the objective moral order cannot be achieved by either of two extremes—legalism and relativism. **Legalism** is strict, literal adherence to law. Under this view sexual morality becomes simply a matter of obedience to the laws promulgated by the authorities, especially a precritical interpretation of scripture. One simply checks what actions and thoughts the scriptures establish as chaste or lewd and indecent.

Both the Jewish prophets and Jesus condemned legalism (Mt. 15:1–20) because it changes radically the original purpose of the law, which is proper concern for and response to God's loving covenant. Legalism turns God into an exacting lawgiver and makes obedience to law the ultimate sign of faith and the principal means to holiness. In the past many Christians showed legalistic leanings in their views of sexual thoughts and fantasies, masturbation by the young, premarital sex, and other sexual issues.

This critique of legalism does not mean churches, society, and individuals do not need law. **Law** is a regulation of reason for the common good. Since we are not completely free nor entirely conformed to the inspirations of the Spirit, laws can serve two purposes: they instruct us about what is good for the individual and the common good of society, and they can correct our inconstancy in doing what is just, chaste, and good. To deny the relevance of laws fostering chastity would be to deny all the wisdom laboriously acquired during the course of human history.

Relativism or Situation Ethics

The other extreme view of objective moral order is called **relativism** or **situation ethics**. Situation ethics is more an issue today than legalism, especially since the publication in 1966 of the influential book *Situation Ethics* by Joseph Fletcher (1905–91). Fletcher was an Episcopal priest, professor of ethics, and a founder of the field of biomedical ethics.

Relativism or situation ethics bases all judgments on individual preference or feeling. It holds that whatever the individual thinks is morally right is in fact objectively right or good and for that very reason. A good example of such relativism was the theory of "values clarification" introduced into the public schools in the late 1960s. Teachers proposed a question for classroom discussion. For example, "Does premarital sex have some meaning in my life, or is its prohibition by church and society nothing more than an outmoded tradition and custom?" Teachers acted not as instructors but as moderators. They were just another person in the room with their own values. They were even encouraged not to hide their own questions and confusion. But researchers soon discovered that values clarification was not having its intended effect. It was not making students more moral—or less moral. It quickly faded from schools, although relativism remains deeply imbedded in the culture.

Since relativism bases judgments on individual preference, it rules out interference in a person's sexual life by the scripture, the state, or anyone. It holds that the damage done by sexual repression needs to be combated. Situation ethics maintains that there is no moral good all can agree on (**ethical agnosticism**), and, therefore, everyone ought to have as much freedom as possible to pursue her or his notion of chastity. This perspective presumes that each person is an autonomous source of value, especially when motivated by love. Fletcher wrote: "The classic rule of moral theology has been to follow laws but do it *as much as possible* according to love and according to reason. Situation ethics, on the other hand, calls upon us to keep law in a subservient place, so that *only* love and reason really count when the chips are down!" (1966, 30).

It must be stated that relativism has some positive dimensions. First, it is founded on an appreciation of the importance to morality of the subjective component, including individual free choice. Second, it is also true that we are always conditioned by cultural and historical circumstances, and some sexual practices are culturally relative (for example, how, when, and where to kiss). But this does not make all practices relative. While it is true that certain values can be appreciated only by one culture, there are values that are valid for all cultures. For instance, persons are more important than things and life is more valuable than a person's convenience or luxuries.

Ultimately, relativism or situation ethics is unacceptable because it is individualistic, totally subjective, and is based on ethical agnosticism—a view incompatible not only with the view that goodness and badness can be measured by objective reality, but also with the social nature of humankind. It should be noted that Fletcher did not totally eliminate objective laws of morality. He agreed that there are valid general moral rules that help people make moral judgments in particular cases. However, he argued that those general rules are not universal and absolute. The situationist, Fletcher wrote, "enters into every decision-making situation fully armed with the ethical maxims of his community and its heritage, and treats them with respect as illuminators of his problems. Just the same, he is prepared in any situation to compromise them or set them aside *in the situation* if love seems better served by doing so" (ibid., 26).

Fletcher's 1966 book had one positive effect. It forced Christian moralists in the United States to reaffirm that all morality, properly understood, is situational, that is, it must take account of circumstances, motives, and the subjectivity of the moral agent. In general, however, Fletcher's theory was roundly rejected because European theologians (and the Vatican) had already encountered it. The theory of situation ethics actually arose in Germany after World War II when there was serious questioning about why so many Christians had failed to protest the injustices of the Nazis, why they had permitted, or at least tolerated, the war with its atrocities and disregard for human dignity and life. Some tried to explain those political and social situations by basing morality on circumstances rather than on universal moral norms (Gallagher 1990, 225-35).

Karl Rahner exemplified the Catholic response when he wrote in 1964 that "a situation ethic carried to its logical conclusion would become an ethical and metaphysical nominalism in which the universal could never actually bear upon the concrete with binding force" (1964, 53). Other theologians and thoughtful people wondered what there was about the situation that suddenly enabled a person to choose wisely if no decision was valid outside the concrete situation. The experience of most people is that it is precisely in moments of passion and/or crisis, when it is difficult to mobilize their powers of reflection to make a prudent choice, that they need guidelines, that is, values, ideals, aims, and purposes.

The Sexual Revolution

In addition to dealing with the perennial issue of legalism and the pervasive issue of relativism or situation ethics, contemporary Christian sexual morality has been put into a new context because of two factors: one sociological and the other theological. The sociological is the **sexual revolution** of the 1960s; the theological is the emergence of a new method of moral argumentation based on some findings of modern science and also the historical-critical method of scriptural interpretation. It is called **revisionism** or **the relational-responsibility model**.

First, in the 1960s the Western world went through a so-called sexual revolution that had been spurred on by such factors as significant economic development, the contraceptive pill, the increase in numbers of women in the work force and professions, the destabilization of traditional values during the Vietnam War (1961–75), and a new societal emphasis on self-fulfillment.

On its positive side, people were no longer afraid to openly discuss sexual matters. Some of the constructive power of sexuality was released and gains were made in sexual justice and equality. Most importantly, there was a significant shift in appreciation of marriage. Sexual intimacy and friendship were firmly combined. Previously, people tended to keep them separated. The conventional wisdom was that the purpose of sexual intercourse was procreation of children; friendships were often to be found elsewhere.

The positive dimensions of the sexual revolution were scientifically confirmed in late 1994 when the University of Chicago's National Opinion Research Center issued a landmark study of adult sexual behavior, *The Social Organization of Sexuality: Sexual Practices in the United States.* This study by Edward O. Laumann and others paints a picture of sexual conduct in the United States that is overall far less libertine than many might have supposed. It shows that society has not capitulated to a permissive sexual ethic. For example, adultery is the exception in this country, not the rule. Almost 91 percent regard an extramarital affair as almost always wrong. According to the study, 75 percent of married men and 85 percent of married women say they have remained faithful to their spouses. Furthermore, it is monogamous couples who not only have the most sex (40 percent of married couples have sex twice a week) but are also most pleased with their sex lives (almost half say they are "extremely pleased and satisfied"). The study also reports that the median number of sexual partners over a lifetime for American men is six, for women two.

On its negative side, the sexual revolution has placed society's traditional values about chastity in turmoil. Sex has been trivialized and exploited for ideological and economic reasons. There is more tolerance of prostitution, homosexual activity, divorce, and cohabitation. Nudity in the media and theater has increased. Pornography has proliferated. Abortion has been legalized. Sexual activity among teenagers has increased—a fact verified by the number of pregnancies among the young. People have been exploited and many seriously harmed by the epidemic spread of venereal diseases and AIDS. Between 1981 and through 1994, people with active cases of AIDS or those who have died of the disease exceeded one million worldwide. The United Nations World Health Organization stated that the true figure is probably more than four times that high because of underreporting and underdiagnosis in developing countries.[1]

The sexual revolution has also thrown the churches into turmoil. There have been so many reports in the media of church groups attempting to draw up a churchwide policy statement that many people began to think that churches have sex on the brain. The churches have often been forced to abandon their policy statements because of lack of consensus or inadequate communication of the issues. For example, the Evangelical Lutheran Church of America (ELCA) released a draft document in October 1993. Most Lutherans heard about the document in a story that had been leaked to the Associated Press rather than from their clergy or other congregational channels. The newspaper story began with this startling statement: "Masturbation is healthy, the Bible supports homosexual unions and teaching teens how to use condoms to prevent disease is a moral imperative." Although church officials denounced the newspaper report, the damage was done.[2] Then on November 4, 1994, the ELCA released a new draft document, one mailed directly to its members. The new statement steers clear of any definite opinion on the question of gay and lesbian sexual relations and avoids reference to masturbation, which the first draft statement called a "generally appropriate and healthy" practice. Throughout, the new draft extols the traditional themes of fidelity in marriage, sexual abstinence outside marriage, and the essential goodness of human sexuality. The church's leaders expect a progress report at their 1995 churchwide assembly and a possible vote, at the earliest, at the 1997 assembly.[3]

Other churches, like the Catholic Church, have issued many very clear churchwide policies, but these have often been greeted with vociferous dissent, even scorn—as will be exemplified throughout the rest of this chapter. It is clear that in many instances the churches have not been able to produce convincing arguments for chaste conduct that all reasonable people can accept.

A New Methodology in Moral Theology

The second factor affecting contemporary sexual morality is the institution of a new moral methodology, particularly in the Catholic community.

Right after Vatican II a revolution was set in motion in Catholic moral theology. It began with a seminal essay on the principle of double effect by the German Jesuit Peter Knauer (1979, 1–39). **Double effect** means that an intended action can sometimes have two effects, one good and one evil. The principle stated that an evil result can be permitted so long as it is not directly intended, is not the means of achieving a good result, and is not out of proportion to the good effect. An example would be performing an abortion in order to save the life of the mother.

At the heart of Knauer's essay was the question of whether some of the most important rules of morality, such as those forbidding masturbation, premarital sex, and contraceptive birth control, were to be considered absolute (no exceptions) or whether exceptions were possible. Those who follow the church's traditional teaching on these matters are called **traditionalists**. Those who advocate another methodology, a **relational-responsibility model**, are called **revisionists** (or proportionalists).

Traditionalist Principles

The traditionalists maintain that morality is based on absolute moral norms and fear that the revisionists leave the door open for moral compromise and breakdown when they say there are few absolute norms and even these are not infallible. The revisionists argue that emphasis on absolute moral norms eliminates morally important elements from consideration such as circumstances, consequences, and motive. Revisionists accept **formal norms**, statements which inform us of values and of the kind of behavior that should be avoided. For example, the injunction not to kill recalls the value of life; the commandment not to steal informs us about the right of private property; and the commandment against making idols instructs us that God can not be confined to space and time.

Actually, revisionism and traditionalism are not two mutually exclusive models of moral theology, but are generic terms to indicate different forms of moral argumentation. Both models are committed to an objective moral order. However, the methodology of the traditionalists is deductive, comprehensive, and certain, whereas that of the revisionists is inductive, partial, and conditional. Revisionism is more a loose tendency than a school of thought, and many of its proponents believe that the kind of weighing of circumstances and motives that traditionalists say is impossible, has in fact long been characteristic of Catholic moral analysis.

The background of this debate is the clash between a classical and historical consciousness. **Classical consciousness** underscores the objective, the unchanging, the universal and abstract, and advocates a uniform approach to moral attitudes and principles. It regards the Bible as a moral code with ready-made normative laws and answers. **Historical consciousness**, on the other hand, looks to the subjective, changeable, particular, and practical. It accepts a certain pluralism in moral theology. The Bible is read in light of the historical-critical method, suggesting that what often seem like universal laws are actually conditional prohibitions.

The foreground of this debate is different understandings of absolutes and principles. The way absolutes are understood has bearing on four aspects of morality: acts as intrinsically evil, the principle of double effect, the natural law, and the ability of church authorities to teach morality.

Many Christian churches have labeled certain acts as **intrinsically evil**, that is, evil in their very nature and, therefore, admitting of no exceptions. Some of these acts are abortion, contraceptive birth control, rape, bestiality, and incest. Other actions are ruled immoral or sinful (e.g., killing another person or an animal) because a person acts against a basic moral good. However, since these prohibitions are conditioned applications of general moral norms or rules for specific situations, exceptions are always permitted when proportionately greater goods or evils come into play (e.g., killing a person in self-defense or an animal for food).

Traditionalists also acknowledge the principle of double effect. As we have seen, it often happens that an intended action can have two effects, one good and one evil. For example, it is wrong to directly take the life of an innocent person even if doing so would save the lives of thousands—as the priest Caiaphas decided about Jesus. It might be permissible, however, to take innocent lives indirectly, as occurs when civilians are killed when bombs are dropped on military targets. The traditional formulation of the principle of double effect requires that an evil effect could be permitted to follow from an action if four criteria were present: the action itself must be intrinsically good or indifferent; the good effect must be the intended effect; the evil effect must not follow directly from the action, only indirectly (the good effect cannot come about by means of the evil); and the good effect must proportionately outweigh the evil effect (Dwyer 1987, 152–61).

Natural law also plays a part in morality, traditionalists believe. The **natural law** is a law implanted by God within every being; it is part of the being's very essence or nature. Traditionalists, relying on a classical consciousness, often reduce the natural law to the **order of nature**, that is, they identify the demands of the moral law with biological and physical processes. Nature's norms are applicable always, everywhere, and for all. There is a blueprint in nature that needs to be uncovered and properly deciphered. The universe is a static structure reflecting the mind of God. All humans, despite variations of culture and history, are the same. There is an eternal law implanted in our rationality that is unchangeable and that can be known by natural reason. Humans can rebel against this law, but it never changes.

Finally, traditionalists stress the teaching role of the official church. They uphold its ability to determine which actions are objectively wrong.

Revisionist Principles

The revisionists use a methodology that draws upon human experience and historical developments for their explanation of evil acts, the principle of double effect, natural law, and church teaching.

As for the idea of evil actions, the revisionists dislike labeling certain human acts as in themselves intrinsically immoral. Such an approach, they maintain, neglects morally important factors such as motive and significant circumstances. They argue that a distinction must be drawn between the kind of evil that the act as such involves in its physiological structure and the kind of evil which the person intends without proportionate reason. Evil intrinsic to the action can only have a meaning in a **premoral** sense.

Revisionists do not say that premoral evil is morally neutral. "To the contrary," as Lisa Sowle Cahill, professor of Christian ethics at Boston College, explains, "it is regarded as something generally not fulfilling from human nature, and indeed harmful to it. It always counts as a negative factor in a total moral evaluation. But taken by itself, it is not morally decisive" (see McCormick 1985, 62–63). **Moral evil** occurs when the person intends the premoral evil without a proportionate reason.

Our human situation is filled with premoral evil, that is, with disvalues that conflict with the values already there. Values such as the dignity of persons, honesty, and chastity must always be protected. We are informed about values through formal moral norms and principles. For example, "You shall not lie" is a formal norm that tells us about the importance of truth in relationships, personal and social. But everyone also experiences such disvalues as error, fatigue, ignorance, and violence. These disvalues are inevitable and unavoidable, due to the limitations built into our human situation. These we may cause but not intend while pursuing some course of action. These premoral actions become moral evils when willed without proportionate reason. For example, the American Indians were shocked when they witnessed white men wantonly killing buffalo for some small part of the carcass. They knew instinctively that this was wrong. The Indians did not want to kill the buffalo—whom they regarded as their brothers—but were forced to do so for food and clothing for their families. They knew they were right but regretted the killing. Similarly, premoral evil is present when a doctor amputates a limb, or motorists accidentally collide, or a hunter shoots a deer for his family's dinner.

The revisionists deny that acts can be labeled intrinsically evil, but they admit the existence of moral norms that are **virtually exceptionless**. That is, they insist that certain acts are clearly wrong. Their examples include cruelty to children, slavery, rape, direct killing of noncombatants in war, and not assisting persons in dire distress. But it cannot be proven with the sharpness of syllogistic logic that no exceptions could ever occur.

The traditionalists argue that in relativizing the notion of acts as intrinsically immoral by subsuming them under the criteria of intention and proportionate reason, the revisionists have stripped the world of any distinctively moral character. If things cannot be known as morally good in themselves, then moral knowledge has been relativized. After all, one can marshall proportionate reasons to justify whatever one wishes.

Further, the revisionists reject the principle of double effect with its third condition that the good effect must not be produced by means of an evil effect. It is positive and proportionate consequences that justify the means used. Revisionists would say Caiphas probably acted with a clean conscience when he wanted Jesus out of the way because he honestly judged him a threat to the safety of all the people and the temple. Jesus warned his disciples that they would be killed by those who would regard their death as a way of "offering worship to God" (Jn. 16:2). Revisionists insist that we can judge whether an evil effect follows directly or indirectly from our formally willed actions, depending on the presence or absence of a proportionate (commensurate) reason. Revisonists actually reject the distinction between directly and indirectly intending the evil effect. They maintain that the key factor is the overall purpose in mind. In many cases the exceptions of the traditionalists are the result of involuted, unconvincing logic. For example, the traditionalists' description of an abortion to save the life of the mother as indirect killing does not seem consistent. In cases like this, actions are justified, based on an estimate of all the values and disvalues involved in the total consequences.

The revisionists also question the extent of the influence of the natural law. The relational-responsibility approach to morality is more dynamic than that of the traditionalists. They do not deny human continuity amid human change. But they insist that the abiding and unchangeable structures of the human person are fewer and more general than previous ages liked to believe. The revisionists root the natural law in the **order of reason** and discerning love. This means that, with the use of reason, humans subordinate and adapt the biological and physical facts of life to reach humane ends. Reason reflecting on the total human experience and not simply the order of nature becomes the guide for human well-being. Biological processes become subservient to the total well-being of human life.

Due to the findings of the human sciences, we have a better sense of the complexities of human nature. The structure of morality is not a static set of regulations constitutive of human nature. Although the term "natural law" indicates that we have impressed in our being tendencies which reflect the order God wishes for us, nevertheless we realize that we are involved in the human social experience of history. Humans grow more truly as they assume more consciously their responsibility for the future of humankind and the world.

The revisionists' view of church teaching is less absolute than that of the traditionalists. The revisionists are accused by the traditionalists of dismantling the teaching authority of the church in moral matters. If there is no objectively definable set of evil actions and consequences, say the traditionalists, then the official teachers are reduced to exhorters and counselors.

While not dismantling the authority of church officials in moral matters, many theologians today give critical attention to Vatican documents. Several have warned that these documents should not be considered the final word, a view that would stifle further theological discussion and that would label those who questioned them as disloyal. To see the documents as unquestionable "would be theologically erroneous, pastorally tragic and practically harmful to both the theology of sexuality and the moral magisterium of the church" (McCormick 1976).

Revisionists Distinguished from Relativists
Revisionists can seem like relativists, but there are several reasons why they are not. First, while revisionism seems to deny the existence of concrete universal norms, it does accept the principle of universality in moral theology. Once an action is understood to be objectively immoral, it will be so whenever and wherever it occurs. Some examples that are virtually exceptionless: deliberately calculated homicide, apostasy for temporal advantages, perjury in order to ruin another, defrauding workers of their just wages, and misusing funds given for the support of the helpless, such as orphans and widows.

Revisionism also seems to lead to **consequentialism**, that is, the belief that actions are right or wrong depending solely on the consequences. This conclusion seems correct especially since revisionism rejects some of the language of double effect, particularly directly and indirectly intending the evil effect. The revisionists say, however, that they are not consequentialists because they ask if there is a proportionate reason for the action, and proportionate reason includes more than weighing the good and bad results of an act. It also looks to norms and principles, as well as the values and disvalues in the total consequences.

Revisionism seems individualistic. However, the revisionists insist that an action does not become moral simply because someone thinks it is moral. Furthermore, as a person forms his or her conscience by weighing the values and disvalues involved in an action, the priority of the community and its objective moral judgments remains in place. Christians can not neglect investigating the teachings and the judgments of officials (like popes and bishops), theologians, tradition, the sense of the faithful, and scripture. However, even here the revisionists remind the traditionalists that authoritative structures can never be final or absolute. "Not only must they continually recommend themselves by their reasonableness to the persons they are meant to serve, but, like all other human devices, they too stand in need of constant criticism and constant improvement" (Johann 1968, 66).

Revisionism seems to some to be chaotic and a cause of moral breakdown. The revisionists insist, however, that for all the vagueness of its objectives, which make it appear a threat to right order, there is an order to their method: our orientation to God and our abiding vocation to participate in God's work of promoting and expanding his kingdom. If relational-responsibility means anything, "it means determining before God the appropriate response to a situation and acting accordingly" (ibid.). The touchstone for distinguishing better from worse is intelligent recognition. Since all of us are by nature open to God, then "we all share a common light by which to judge whether steps proposed are really improvements, or not" and "we all share a common calling to move beyond where we are if we are going to be true to ourselves" (ibid., 67). We may not have metaphysical certitude about moral matters, but **moral certitude** is possible on specific moral matters, and on such matters, moral certitude is enough. Moral certitude is based upon strong likelihood or firm conviction, rather than upon actual evidence.

Masturbation

Genesis 38:1–10; Matthew 22:23–33.

Masturbation is "the pursuit of induced sexual pleasure with or without orgasm, usually solitary but sometimes mutually, frequently involving the genitals but sometimes involving other orifices of the body" (Dominion and Montefiore 1989, 27).

The Bible contains no clear, explicit moral prohibition of masturbation. There is only one instance of masturbation, the famous story of Onan (Gen. 38:1–10). According to Jewish tradition and law (Deut. 25:5–10), a deceased man's brother (or nearest male kin) was required to marry his brother's widow and so continue his family. This was called a **levirate marriage** (see Mt. 22:23–33). The Latin word *levir* means "a husband's brother." Onan refused to consummate a levirate marriage with the wife of his older and wicked brother. Instead, "whenever he had relations with his brother's widow, he wasted his seed on the ground, to avoid contributing offspring for his brother" (Gen. 38:9). God was so displeased, he took Onan's life. Scripture scholars believe that it is primarily Onan's violation of the levirate law rather than the masturbation that "greatly offended the Lord."

The Christian community has always regarded masturbation as a serious moral wrong. According to some modern sociological studies, masturbation is not uncommon. In fact, the conventional wisdom maintains that virtually all males and most females masturbate at some time during their lives. These studies conclude that masturbation is normal, not immoral, not harmful, and relieves sexual tension. The Christian churches, and especially the Catholic Church, have addressed this contemporary evaluation.

The Vatican's Congregation on Catholic Education issued an instruction in 1974 in which it called masturbation a youthful dysfunction but cautioned that "fears, threats, or spiritual intimidation are best avoided" when dealing with this conduct. The Vatican encouraged counselors and parents to aim at helping young people form a balanced sexual attitude. Then, in 1975, the Vatican's Congregation for the Doctrine of the Faith published its *Declaration on Certain Questions Concerning Sexual Ethics* in which it declared that masturbation is objectively a grave sin because it is "a deliberate use of the sexual faculty outside normal conjugal relations . . . that contradicts the finality of the faculty."

This 1975 document evoked considerable response. Many viewed it as theologically inaccurate, psychologically harmful, and pedagogically counterproductive. Häring, for example, granted that, on the one hand, some theologians had gone too far in reaction to an earlier rigorism concerning masturbation by simply dismissing it, but, on the other hand, he warned that a too facile judgment of mortal sin in sexual matters harms the faithful. "It must never for an instant be forgotten," he wrote, "that conversation about mortal sin, especially the mortal sins of children, is conversation about God" (see McCormick 1981, 676).

Charles Curran, who had previously written that masturbation is wrong because a person fails "to integrate sexuality in the service of love" (Curran 1970, 175–6), disagreed with the judgment that masturbation is an intrinsically and seriously disordered act. He said individual masturbatory acts, when judged in the context of the person and the meaning of sexuality, "do not constitute such important matter . . . providing the individual is truly growing in sexual maturity and integration" (see McCormick 1981, 677).

Richard McCormick evaluated masturbation by first locating it within the totality of a person's moral life. He wrote that, since the heart of morality is the individual's relationship with God, then the moral life "consists of a deepening of our fundamental orientation. It consists of a growth process whereby we stabilize, deepen and render more dominant the love poured into our hearts by the Spirit" (McCormick 1968, 770). What the revisionists emphasize is that, in addition to our freedom to make decisions about individual actions, we also have the power to decide about ourselves and our lives. This self-determination starts at our inner core and becomes more and more external inasmuch as it includes our multiple relationships with the triune God, neighbor, and the created world. This self-determination is called the **fundamental** option. We can make decisions that reenforce or reverse this fundamental option. This option explains in part why Bernard Häring (1979, 2:503, 560) strongly urges that single acts of masturbation be evaluated against the developmental process and the person's life-context. Consequently, he wrote that it is wrong to propose that masturbation is always a mortal sin and a reversal of one's fundamental option, and only then consider the difference between masturbation by adolescents, young adults, and a married person. Ethicists, said Häring, must "look first to the diversity of the phenomena" and "only then" ask about the moral meaning or possible sinfulness of the individual phenomenon (ibid.).

Jack Dominion, a British psychiatrist, noted that according to sociologists, masturbation is very common among both males and females, especially during adolescence. He believes that although masturbation is narcissistic, it is a necessary part of growing up since it helps people discover new dimensions of their body and it prepares people for heterosexual relations. He does not believe it is a sin for adolescents. However, it lacks two of the three criteria for integral sexual activity (listed at the beginning of this chapter), since both interpersonal love and procreation are absent.

Philip Keane wrote that masturbation involved premoral evil, which had to be weighed against a variety of factors, depending on circumstances. He was hesitant to declare it a moral evil for adolescents, but he said people should move to a higher stage of sexual maturity. For adults, the premoral evil is more serious. Masturbation can signal a moral disorder. Individual evaluation is required and the person may need counseling if the masturbation is used compulsively as a substitute for more rewarding, interpersonal relationships. When Keane and many other theologians discuss self-stimulation for sperm-testing for the treatment of infertility, they are inclined to accept it as a moral act that is quite different from masturbation as generally understood (1977).

Richard McCormick, while he respects the sociological, psychological and theological reasons for not imputing serious sin to adolescent masturbation, cautions that the young can stagnate their sexual development if, knowing the perspective of mature adults and professionals, they decide to continue the habit of masturbation. For adolescents simply to indulge the habit is to feed and strengthen "the underlying causes of such symptomatic behavior" and to compromise their growth toward maturity. McCormick says he would tell adolescents two things: first, meet the challenge to become genuinely mature and free in sexual expression; second, the habit of masturbation is a serious challenge to growth that requires a serious response, a response that is "a resolute and adult attitude. As long as you maintain this, you are on the right path and responding properly to the challenge" (McCormick 1981, 175).

Premarital Sex

The Hebrew Bible fosters chastity but does not contain a prohibition against premarital intercourse as such. The Greek word *porneia* covers a whole range of sexual activity. It can mean fornication as well as incest, adultery, lewd conduct and prostitution, both secular and religious. The passages in the Christian scriptures that condemn fornication are often condemnations of loveless sexual intercourse, especially with a prostitute. Jesus said virtually nothing about sex. He promoted chastity, especially by condemning all deliberate unchaste thoughts: "I say to you, everyone who looks at a woman with lust has already committed adultery with her in his heart" (Mt. 5:28).

In contemporary society premarital sex has become common and quite general (that is, it is not confined to a small group)—as indicated by the large number of women across ethnic, economic, and religious lines who have had abortions. It is reported that only 20 percent of Americans regard premarital sex as always wrong, whereas 48 percent state it is not wrong at all (McClory 1994). Based on these statistics, it is easy to see why some groups go so far as to offer guidelines to teens to assess their readiness for a sexual relationship. They offer a five-point checklist for good sex: "consensual, non-exploitive, honest, pleasurable and protected." Most Catholics do not subscribe to this list because sexual relationships call for commitment and love—two words absent from the checklist. Nevertheless, Andrew Greeley, priest-sociologist of religion, reported in 1992 that there is a definite decline among Catholics in their acceptance of the institutional church's teaching on this topic. In his report he indicated that "only one of six American Catholics thinks that premarital sex is always wrong" (1992, 345). Other Christian churches are also divided on this issue. For example, an Episcopal bishop argued recently that "life-giving" premarital sex can be just as "holy" as marriage (Spong 1988).

The Catholic Church has maintained that sexual intercourse should be limited to publicly committed married partners. Is there any enduring and universal reason why this is so? Some argue that moral theologians have yet to produce convincing proof why sexual intercourse must be matched in *every* case by a total covenant of love that can be expressed only in marriage (Kosnik 1977, 152–58; see also Cahill 1985, 89–90; Mahoney 1990, 203).

The official church resolutely rejects premarital sex for several reasons: First, the partners have not committed themselves to one another in a stable and definitive way and, therefore, their sexual intercourse is a lie. It does not express exclusive fidelity. In the Catholic tradition, passion and commitment go together: "commitment needs passion to sustain it over the long haul, and passion needs commitment if it is to keep its flame" (Greeley and Greeley Durkin 1984, 109). Second, the procreative character of sexual intercourse demands that the couple be ready and able to secure the education of the possible child. Premarital sex does not involve an adequate context for this value.

In order to give a solid reason why premarital sex is wrong, theologians like Richard McCormick begin by discussing the values found in a Christian marriage. Sexual intercourse is commonly called "the marital act." By so speaking, we indicate that sexual intercourse "has a sense and a meaning prior to the individual purpose of those who engage in it, a significance which is part of their situation whether or not the partners turn their minds to it" (McCormick 1981, 365–67). The *sense* that is prior is that sex should be restricted to the marriage relationship; the *meaning* that is prior is that sex is the expression of love and friendship that is permanent and exclusive. Both the sense and meaning derive from centuries of human experience. Humans have learned "that unless this type of intimacy is restricted to the marriage relationship, the integrity of sexual language is seriously threatened" (ibid., 27–31, 447–462). Marriage is a covenant relationship built on friendship and it is friendship that generates fidelity, loyalty, and constancy.

There are different patterns to premarital sex. It occurs between a client and a prostitute; during the one-night stand; in the temporary, semi-committed relationship; between cohabitating couples; and between the engaged. All of these are different human and moral situations. All have a premoral dimension; those involved in each of these situations will have to determine before God the extent of their immorality.

The status of those engaged to be married has received special attention because there is a serious pledge of permanence and, in a sense, the church's sacrament is involved. The sacrament of marriage has three distinct elements that normally take place in this order: the consent of the baptized partners, the consent of the church, and consummation. These three elements are not an instantaneous action, but a process that takes time. Engaged couples sometimes put the consummation before the consent of the church for different reasons. This is sometimes called "preceremonial intercourse." Some would argue this is not always immoral because the couple is in a state of committed love. Some ask about the relationship of the formal engagement to the sacrament itself. Are not catechumens who prepare for months for baptism to some extent already Christians before the actual baptism? Does marriage begin when the couple becomes formally engaged? Can the concept of "marriage" be so extended?

Despite these theoretical questions, premarital sex for the engaged has its own special, practical difficulties. For one thing, the intention to marry can be, and frequently is, revoked. If the engagement is broken, one of the partners can feel manipulated, used, abandoned, and dishonored. Second, McCormick observes that "the intention to marry is, indeed, part of the process leading to marriage. But the process leading to marriage cannot be converted that easily to read marriage-in-process" (ibid., 458). Third, the significance of the social and ecclesial dimensions of the marriage should not be disregarded. The "public ceremony seals a commitment in as full a human way as possible" (Dominion and Montefiore 1989, 34). The ceremony is meant to safeguard the commitment. "Treating the ceremony as if it were *merely* a ceremony . . . is an unhealthy symptom of an eventually destructive individualism" (McCormick 1981, 458).

Finally, probably the strongest argument against premarital sex is the following: since physical expressions of intimacy express the person, then sexual actions "must correspond to the existing relationship of the persons" (McCormick 1966). According to the Bible, sexual intercourse is limited to the married because this is the only context in which faithful love can find enduring expression, especially when children are the fruit of this love. Single persons, even if engaged, should avoid sexual intercourse because it signifies total personal commitment. Incest, adultery, and fornication are condemned because they fall outside the marriage covenant. Incest and adultery intrude upon, jeopardize, or even sever other prior relationships (parent and child, brother and sister, wife and husband). Fornication involves sexual gratification at the expense of a faithful and committed relationship, thereby discounting the sacramentality of self and the other.

Contraceptive Birth Control

The world is going through a population explosion. Demographers know that at the time of Jesus the world population stood at some 250 million. Today the earth gains as many people in two years. In 1830, during the Industrial Revolution, the population reached one billion; by 1975, there were four billion. By the year 2000 the population could be over six billion. No one with any sense is against birth control and responsible parenthood. No one wants human beings to be born into situations where they begin and end their lives as nonpersons. From the perspective of some Christian churches, and especially the Catholic Church, the problem is contraceptive birth control.

The Catholic Church's first worldwide condemnation of contraception took place in December 1930 when Pius XI issued the encyclical *Casti connubii*. He wrote because on August 15, 1930, the Anglicans meeting for a Lambeth Conference in Canterbury, England, approved contraceptives "in those cases where there is such a clearly felt moral obligation to limit or avoid parenthood."

From 1930 to 1960, no Catholic moral theologian openly espoused the position that contraceptives could be used in good conscience in some circumstances. But, in the late 1950s, the whole context of contraceptives changed when a Catholic doctor, John C. Rock (1890–1984), and his associates developed, popularized, and championed the anovulant pill (McLaughlin 1982). Rock and his supporters maintained that, in arresting the ovulation process, the pill does not violate the structure of the act of sexual intercourse. Use of contraceptives is an intervention into the marital act; the anovulant pill is an intervention into the generative system. Rock and others did not see it as any different from use of the infertile periods—those times when couples can engage in sexual intercourse without achieving conception because no fertile egg is available.

In the 1960s, Western culture expressed great confidence in the social promise of contraceptives, especially the anovulant pill. Advocates of contraception argued that it would improve marriages, reduce unwanted pregnancies and abortions, and free women to make decisions about their marriages, pregnancies, and families.

Shortly before his death in June 1963, Pope John XXIII appointed a high-level international committee of thirteen to investigate the threat of overpopulation and the morality of contraceptives. In fall 1964, during the second session of Vatican II, several influential bishops asked for a study of the means of contraception other than total or periodic continence. These interventions were applauded by the majority of the bishops, but Pope Paul VI removed the issue from the council's agenda and assigned it to the international commission previously set up by John XXIII. During the council, the bishops referred briefly (and vaguely) to the church's teachings and simply reaffirmed them in the *Constitution on the Church in the Modern World*. The bishops said that members of the church "may not undertake methods of regulating procreation which are found blameworthy by the teaching authority of the Church in its unfolding of the divine law" (n. 51).

In December 1964, Paul VI appointed forty more members to the commission of thirteen. In spring 1966, he further enlarged the committee by adding seven cardinals (including Karol Wojtyla, the future Pope John Paul II) and nine bishops, bringing the group to sixty-nine. However, Karol Wojtyla never attended any of the decision-making meetings. In 1967, the active committee of sixty-eight members voted to change the church's teaching that all use of contraceptives is immoral. The vote was sixty-four to four. Despite the vote, Paul VI published his famous encyclical *Humanae vitae* on July 25, 1968. He feared that contraceptives "could open the way to marital infidelity and a general lowering of standards" of chastity (n. 17). He reaffirmed the traditional teaching that contraceptive birth control was intrinsically disordered (*intrinsece inhonestum,* n. 14).

Many bishops, priests, theologians, doctors, lawyers, and organizations like the Knights of Columbus accepted the encyclical in 1968 and do so now. Some theologians even argued that the traditional Catholic teaching on birth regulation, as found in the encyclical, is infallible.

The encyclical was greeted in many other quarters not as an infallible teaching but with vociferous dissent and ferocious debates. Since the bishops of the world had not been consulted, some episcopal conferences were forced to issue statements that clearly modified the papal position. The Dutch bishops directed their people to form their consciences in light of the encyclical, but also to consider such factors as "mutual love, family condition and social circumstances." The English bishops said that they rejected a subjective conscience that will not accept ecclesial documents. Nevertheless, they stressed the primacy of conscience and insisted "neither the encyclical nor any other document of the church takes away from us our right and duty to follow our conscience" (Haughey 1968). The United States' bishops issued the statement *Human Life in Our Day* on November 15, 1968, calling on the priests and people to form their consciences in light of the encyclical. Some people interpreted this general statement as a blank check to choose another course of action than that set down in the encyclical. But the bishops were quick to reply that, whereas people form their own consciences, they must also form correct consciences (ibid.).

The Debate over Contraceptives

There seem to be three major points of disagreement on the morality of contraceptive birth control. First, those who reject the use of contraceptives say nothing should interfere with the biological integrity of sexual intercourse. This position is in accord with the understanding of natural law as an order of nature. The morally good must be in accord with nature. Contraceptives prevent the finality of the sexual act. Every conjugal act must be open to the transmission of life. Any interference in the nature of the act is intrinsically evil.

The counter argument asks why humans cannot intervene in human affairs. Proponents of this argument acknowledge that contraceptives involve premoral evil since they preclude procreation. However, it is argued that humans often have to sacrifice one value for another. Couples know marriage has both a unitive and procreative purpose but deny that contraceptives are the first step on the road to marital breakdown and social chaos. On the contrary, it is enforced abstinence that could endanger the unitive purpose of the marriage, that is, the couple's covenant love. Also, there are often other values to consider. For example, the couple may presently have the number of children they can support spiritually and economically.

Second, those against the use of contraceptives say the unitive and procreative goals of marriage are inseparable. The unitive cannot exist independently. To separate the two goals would leave no case against anal intercourse, bestiality, and other forms of sexual activity.

The counter argument centers on the "Catholic method of birth control," namely, the rhythm method, or natural family planning. This method was forbidden until Pius XII announced in 1951 that it was permissible for a couple with "serious motives" to use natural family planning to limit births.

The rhythm method relies on the approximately six to nine days during the monthly cycle when the woman can conceive. During these times the couple practicing the rhythm method express their love in other, less physically intimate ways than sexual intercourse. Those who advocate the rhythm method report that it increases communication, fertility awareness, self-control, and increased intimacy. It can often prove to be quite dependable when its purpose is to achieve pregnancy. But those who disapprove of the method argue that rhythm is not a perfect method. It may work moderately well for some people, but it is not even an option for many others. In other words, many couples say the method has its dark side (Finley 1991). It creates stress. Some find it psychologically harmful, that is, they cannot grow together when they have to structure their married lives around a method and a calendar. They recall that Paul warned the Corinthians against prolonged abstinence "so that Satan may not tempt you through your lack of self-control" (1 Cor. 7:5). Finally, the most important argument against the method is that it forces the church to be inconsistent in its explanation of the purposes of sexual intercourse. The rhythm method allows sex despite the teaching that the conjugal act must always be open to procreation. There seems to be no difference between using the "safe period" and using contraceptives. In actual practice, the rhythm method is contraceptive by scheduling the intercourse.

Third, those against the use of contraceptives maintain that this is the infallible teaching of the church with a history going back to the third century. The church cannot admit error on this point without irreparably damaging its indefectibility, the belief that the church will never lose its fundamental grasp of the gospel. The counter argument holds that this teaching was never defined as infallible. The church has made errors in the past and corrected them. Such, they maintain, is the case here. Also, Catholics have much to learn from other Christian communities, some of whom permit contraceptive birth control to limit or avoid parenthood. For example, two weeks before his first meeting with John Paul II on May 12, 1992, George Carey, Archbishop of Canterbury, blasted the Catholic church's ban on contraceptive birth control, charging that *Humanae vitae* "actually stopped theological thinking." The context of the archbishop's comments was the worldwide preparations for the United Nations Conference on Environment and Development, to be held in Rio de Janeiro in early June. Carey said the church's teachings on contraceptives would inhibit discussion of population control. He was distressed because population control was not even on the conference's agenda, and he warned that "the moment the pope actually says this is a dogma, it creates a very big problem for the Church of Rome. That's their problem. It's also ours, in the sense that all of us are caught up in it."

Pope John Paul II firmly upholds the teaching of the encyclicals of 1930 and 1968. For example, in *Familiaris consortio,* an apostolic exhortation issued in 1981, he explained that his defense of the church's teachings against contraceptives was in continuity with the living tradition of the ecclesial community throughout history regarding marriage and the transmission of life. It was this stance, he stated, that led him to reaffirm the teaching of Vatican II and *Humanae vitae,* "particularly that love between husband and wife must be fully human, exclusive, and open to new life" (n. 29). The pope then called on theologians to help the hierarchical magisterium make this teaching "truly accessible to all people of good will" by "illustrating even more clearly the biblical foundations, the ethical grounds, and the personalist reasons behind this doctrine" (n. 31).

Despite these exhortations, debate and dissent continue within the Catholic church and among the Christian churches. The glaring discrepancies between the official teaching and the beliefs and practices of Catholics are unhealthful for the church and its institutional, intellectual, and devotional life.

Abortion and Infanticide

The Jewish and Christian scriptures underscore the immorality of murder, the worth of each person, the sacredness of life and the existence of inalienable human rights that transcend any legal order. Abortion and infanticide deny all of these ethical norms.

The Bible declares that, while humans do not know "how the breath of life fashions the human frame in the mother's womb" (Eccl. 11:5), they do know that life in the womb is precious, even if sometimes their appreciation is expressed negatively. For example, Hosea hoped God would curse the tribe of Ephraim for their unfaithfulness by giving them "an unfruitful womb" (9:14). Isaiah reported that God was stirring up the warlike Medes to attack the Babylonians (13:18). Isaiah's readers knew the treachery of the Medes, warriors who neither spared "the fruit of the womb" nor had "eyes of pity for children." Similarly, Amos (1:3) declared that the Ammonites were condemned for their brutal murders, especially because, when extending their territory, "they ripped open expectant mothers in Gilead."

The Bible also holds that life is God-given, beginning even before it starts in the womb. Jeremiah (1:5) and Job (31:15) declare that God knew them before he formed them in their mother's wombs. Job, in the midst of his many trials, wished he had died in the womb and that the doors of his mother's womb had never opened (3:11). John the Baptist leapt in the womb of his mother Elizabeth when he heard the greeting of Mary the mother of Jesus (Lk. 1:41). The "fruit of the womb" of Mary of Nazareth was Jesus, the world's Messiah and God's Son.

Infanticide (the murder of an infant) is condemned. Moses, the most prominent Israelite, and Jesus, the most prominent Christian, were almost killed as babies. Moses was saved from the cruelty of the pharaoh in Egypt (Ex. 1:16); Jesus was saved from Herod's infanticide of the Bethlehem children (Mt. 2:13).

Infanticide is a serious problem worldwide. In some countries where female babies are unwanted, many are killed. Occasionally, the media report isolated and lurid instances of parents who kill their children because they are unable to give self-sacrificing love and cope with the demands of parenthood, or shocking instances of children being killed by other children. According to a report in 1992 from the Children's Defense Fund, two children younger than five are murdered each day in the United States.[4]

These statistics fly in the face of Jesus' memorable words about children when his disciples asked who is greatest in the kingdom of God: "He called a child over, placed it in their midst, and said, 'Amen, I say to you, unless you turn and become like children you will not enter the kingdom of heaven. Whoever humbles himself like this child is the greatest in the kingdom of heaven. And whoever receives one child such as this in my name receives me'" (Mt. 18:2–5).

Abortion is the removal or expulsion of a fetus from the uterus, deliberately procured or induced. There are three kinds: **natural** (when the fertilized egg does not get implanted in the uterus); **therapeutic** (when the fetus is removed for medical reasons); **elective** (when a person chooses to have the fetus removed).

Annually, there are more than 25 million elective abortions worldwide. The United States has one of the highest abortion rates, at approximately 1.5 million annually. These are the cause of ceaseless political, legal, moral, and ecclesial battles, especially since the Supreme Court decision that legalized elective abortion, *Roe v. Wade,* January 22, 1973. The court decreed that abortions are allowed up to the third trimester. They are allowed beyond the third trimester when the life or health of the mother is threatened. The debate has reached a stalemate inasmuch as two values are locked in opposition: life and freedom. Prolife advocates argue for the rights of the unborn. Prochoice advocates argue for a woman's right to make her own decision about her own pregnancy. Abortion is really about powerlessness and power. In the United States and in many parts of the world, women have no power over their bodies, especially about pregnancy. For many men, sexual intercourse is an exercise of sexual gratification and/ or prowess.

The Catholic Church and Abortion
The Christian churches have different teachings about abortion. Some communities permit abortion in cases of rape, incest, or danger to the mother's health or life. The Catholic church's teachings on abortion are crystal clear. It declares all elective abortions immoral. The basis of this teaching is that human life begins at conception. There is no scientific proof for this statement—but one can never prove the contrary. The church declares that the presence of the soul is probable, that is, quite possible. Elective abortion involves the risk of killing a human because human life begins with fertilization. Therapeutic abortion is allowed when killing the fetus is indirect and is done to save the life of the mother.

The Catholic Church has issued many statements condemning abortion. At Vatican II in 1965, the bishops declared in the *Constitution on the Church in the Modern World* that abortion and infanticide are "unspeakable crimes" (n. 51). In November 1974—and probably in response to the Supreme Court decision—the Vatican's Congregation for the Doctrine of the Faith published a *Declaration on Procured Abortion.* This detailed and authoritative document asserts that human life must be given equal protection at all stages from fertilization through adulthood. Speaking of the fertilized ovum, the Vatican document states that the fertilized ovum "would never be made human if it were not human already."

In November 1983, the Catholic Church issued its revised code of canon law. In this document the official church declared abortion to be so serious an offense that it is one of only six offenses punished by excommunication. Canon 1398 states that "a person who procures a completed abortion incurs an automatic excommunication." In 1988 Vatican authorities clarified the legal definition of abortion to include new drugs and surgical procedures. They said that any method used to terminate a human life from the moment of conception until birth is an abortion. For an excommunication penalty to go into effect, one must know there is a pregnancy, and there must be a free choice to abort.

The Vatican attracted worldwide attention before and during the September 1994 United Nations International Conference on Population and Development held in Cairo, Egypt, when it mounted an aggressive diplomatic campaign against the legitimization of abortion. The purpose of the conference was to chart a twenty-year global plan to stabilize the world's population growth. The delegates wanted all nations to commit themselves to hold world population under 7.8 billion by the year 2050. To plan for control of population growth—a complicated web that entails women's rights and dignity, education, employment, consumption, poverty, health care, and development—the delegates had to discuss such topics as "reproductive rights," "reproductive health," "family planning" and "safe motherhood." The Vatican was joined by some radical Muslim states such as Iran and Libya in opposing these slippery terms because they could include abortion. Actually, while the sixteen-chapter draft document did not explicitly rule out abortion, the word abortion appeared only once. The document urged all nations and persons "to deal openly and forthrightly with unsafe abortion as a major public health concern." It was reported by Albert Gore, Vice-President of the United States, that more than 200,000 women worldwide die annually from medically unsafe abortions (1994).

The Vatican had leveled bitter attacks on the Clinton-Gore administration for the role it played in helping shape the United Nations document. "The Vatican consistently criticized the document for promoting an atmosphere of immoral sexual license, weakening the family and advocating homosexual relationships" (Fox 1994). Pope John Paul II charged that the United Nations' plan tended to "promote an internationally recognized right to access to abortion on demand." The position of the United States was that "abortion should be safe, legal, and rare." Based on this stance, the forty-five member United States delegation walked a delicate line, resisting attempts to include language that specifically ruled out abortion but not endorsing abortion as a method of family planning. The Vatican underscored several points. First, it declared there is no such thing as a "safe abortion" inasmuch as an abortion results in the death of a human life. Second, it objected to all suggestions that abortion is a universal right or any implication that abortion has any role in the care of women, family planning, or the politics of population. (The United Nations delegates did state that "in no case should abortion be promoted as a method of family planning"). Third, it also rejected any understanding of sexuality that removed it from interpersonal responsibility, moral considerations, and communal contexts. Nevertheless, at the closing session on September 13, 1994, the Vatican signed the document as a whole, expressing reservations only about the fuzziness of such terms as "sexual and reproductive health" found in chapters 7 and 8.

Christians Divided over Abortion

The views of Christians (including Catholics) on abortion are not radically different from those of other citizens. In general there are three responses to the Supreme Court's 1973 legalization of unlimited abortion on demand: some call for total rejection; others advocate total acceptance; some advocate a middle position, arguing that some legal restrictions are reasonable and necessary.

Many Christians reject the ruling of the Supreme Court because they regard elective abortion as a grave moral evil that denies human life and dignity to the unborn. Many express their opposition to the Supreme Court's decision by participating in such organizations as the nondenominational National Right to Life Committee (founded in 1973) and Operation Rescue (founded in 1987 by Randall Terry, an evangelical Protestant). The latter organization derives its name from Proverbs: "Rescue those who are being dragged to death"(24:11). Thousands join well-organized marches on Washington each January 22, and/or write letters to government officials. In 1994, for example, President Bill Clinton's proposed universal-health-care plan came under strong attack because it would fund abortions in the name of health care. The Christian Coalition, founded by evangelical broadcaster and political activist Pat Robertson, promised to spend 1.4 million dollars to defeat the president's bill.[5] Some radical opponents of abortion have taken the law into their hands by violent protests at abortion clinics and, in some cases, by murdering abortion doctors and clinic personnel. The response of church leaders was mixed. For example, after two workers at a Boston abortion clinic were shot to death in December 1994, the Catholic archbishop called for a moratorium on sidewalk protest vigils outside abortion clinics. The Catholic archbishop in New York City said he was prepared to call for a moratorium only "on condition that a moratorium be called on abortions" (G. Niebuhr 1995a). On the other hand, many church leaders denounced the violence, even offering arguments to refute the violent and murderous actions.

Catholic bishops have spoken out forcefully against the Supreme Court decision on a number of occasions. Individual bishops have publicly excommunicated Catholics who direct abortion clinics and some bishops have publicly denounced specific Catholics in political office who refuse to support antiabortion legislation. In May 1990, the United States bishops hired on a temporary basis a reputable and expensive public relations firm to spread the church's message that all elective abortions are immoral. Building on the prochoice theme of choice, the bishops urged all citizens to "exercise the natural choice—choose life." They also interpreted the injunction in Deuteronomy (30:19) in a critical way: "Choose life, then, that you and your descendants may live."

There are many Christians who take the middle position: they accept the legalization of abortion but argue that some legal restrictions are reasonable. They maintain that the federal government should not have complete control of this issue. Individual states also have to exert their interest in protecting (and even promoting) fetal life. The states should be able to act in ways that prefer childbirth to abortion. An example of this approach is the action in 1994 in the state of Pennsylvania, led by Governor Robert P. Carey, a Catholic Democrat. The Pennsylvania legislators passed a law that, in part, requires women to receive counseling from a doctor about the risks of and alternatives to abortion, and then wait a day before getting one. Single girls younger than eighteen must get the permission of one parent or a judge.

Some Catholics accept legalization of abortion in our pluralistic society because the medical, scientific, and legal communities continue to debate two important issues. The first concerns the moment individual human life begins. Does it really begin at the moment of conception? The second concerns when the developing fetus is a "person" under the law. Does the fetus deserve the same legal protection as a child? Some Catholics declare the Catholic Church's stand that every elective abortion is an unspeakable crime needs more dialogue since many Catholics give different answers to these two questions. For example, a full-page ad with just that message appeared in the *New York Times* on October 7, 1984. Among the ninety-seven signees were twenty nuns. All of the nuns were threatened with expulsion from their communities if they did not remove their names from the statement. Two Notre Dame sisters, Barbara Ferraro and Patricia Hussey, refused, based in part on their extensive work with women who were victims of rape, verbal and physical battering, incest, and abortion. They continued to argue for their position until 1988 when, under considerable direct pressure from

Rome, they withdrew from their community, vowing to continue "loyal, authentic dissent." In 1990, they published their views in a book, *No Turning Back.*

In the spring of 1990, Archbishop Rembert G. Weakland of Milwaukee was the subject of the international media when he issued a report on abortion. The Archbishop held hearings with women in his diocese to gather their views on abortion, especially so he could understand the views of those who disagree with the church's teaching. His report on the meetings was widely publicized. The archbishop upheld the church's teachings but warned that the antiabortion movement was driving away potential supporters, including Catholics, who viewed its focus as narrow, its tactics as aggressive, and some of its rhetoric as "ugly and demeaning." He also urged that politicians trying to face the abortion issue with respect for life should be given "as much latitude as reason permits." The frank discussions with the women affected Weakland so much that he declared he could never again be glib when talking about "the moment of conception" or talk facilely about bringing the baby to term and then "just giv[ing] it up for adoption" (Steinfels 1990; Martinez 1990).

There are some Catholics who accept the legalization of abortion and reject the official Catholic teaching that all abortions are immoral. A group called Catholics for a Free Choice (CFFC) endorses abortion rights. This organization, founded in 1970, was the force behind the *New York Times* ad of October 7, 1984 (Doerflinger 1985). The United States bishops spoke out against CFFC on November 4, 1993. The bishops stated that "there is no room for dissent by a Catholic from the church's moral teaching that direct abortion is a grave wrong." The bishops declared that CFFC "has no affiliation, formal or otherwise, with the Catholic church. [It] can in no way speak for the Catholic church . . . Because of its opposition to the human rights of some of the most defenseless members of the human race, and because its purposes and activities deliberately contradict essential teachings of the Catholic faith, we state once again that Catholics For a Free Choice merits no recognition or support as a Catholic organization."

Daniel Maguire, an active board member of CFFC and moral theologian at Marquette University, maintains that some theologians and a majority of Catholics do not consider abortion immoral under a range of circumstances: rape, risk of health, genetically damaged fetus, physically handicapped woman, teenage pregnancy, a mother on public aid who cannot work, and a married woman who already has a large family (1983, 1984).

The Prolife-Prochoice Debate

In light of the previous discussion, listed here are the key points made by prolife and prochoice advocates in the elective abortion debate. The prolife arguments are the following: (1) The fertilized egg has a right to life, which begins at conception and is paramount. (However, not all Christians agree that individual human life begins with conception. Richard McCormick describes the embryo during the first two weeks as "nascent human life," but he does not consider it an "individual human life" until later [1981, 108–9]. During the first two weeks, the new life does not exhibit the stable and determining character necessary for considering it a distinct individual or a person with human dignity. Many scientists maintain that **hominization** cannot possibly be said to occur before fourteen to twenty-two days after conception [Diamond 1975]. Hominization denotes the progressive development of human life to higher and higher levels of individuality and consciousness. For example, twinning is no longer possible after the first fourteen days.) (2) Elective abortion is murder. (3) When a woman makes a choice to have sexual intercourse, she knows that pregnancy is a possible result. (4) Those who advocate abortion do not appreciate what an abortion is and they need to be informed about its realities. (5) Abortion can be an unsafe medical procedure. (6) Adoption is a "loving alternative" to abortion and that there are many couples who wish to adopt children. (7) A woman's right to choose has been made more important than the choice itself. Furthermore, the choice is portrayed as if it were morally neutral. But it is not. Abortion inflicts such harm on the fetus and its right to life that it cannot be considered a private issue but should be a matter of legitimate government regulation.

The prochoice arguments are the following: (1) All too often women have no choice about either sexual intercourse or pregnancy. They are controlled by men who use them for their own sexual gratification. Even if a man uses a contraceptive, these can fail, putting a woman at risk of an unwanted pregnancy. (2) Women have a moral right to decide whether and when to become mothers. In addition, many persons believe human life begins at the time it can be sustained outside the womb. (3) Science indicates that there are stages in fetal life. These help us distinguish the fertilized egg from a human being and fetal rights from those of a human being. A fertilized egg is not a human being (As we saw above, theologians agree there are different stages of human life, but they still claim that an abortion of this "nascent human life" is tragically justifiable only on very limited occasions.) (4) Women know what an elective abortion entails and to force on them information they do not require is punitive. (5) Abortion is a very safe procedure. (6) Women are not obliged to provide babies for those who cannot conceive on their own. (7) Abortion is a private issue best left to individual conscience and without the interference of law.

Despite the fact that there are arguments on both sides in the debate, the reality in the United States is that the pro-abortion forces have won, that is, the woman's right to privacy—to choice, to an abortion—has become absolute while the claims of the fetus have been lost to public consideration and to legal protection. In other words, prolife advocates are almost always portrayed in the media as reactionaries who impede freedom. Therefore, Christian churches have a major challenge on their hands before this complex and emotional issue and its far-reaching effects on sexuality, dating, courtship, and family life can be resolved in a rational, humane, and religious way.

Marriage and Divorce

The creation myths have as their high point the creation of Adam and Eve. The man and woman were given to one another in partnership or covenant. They were told to be one flesh and to produce offspring. In the Jewish tradition, marital intercourse is holy because it expresses unity with the transcendent other (ultimately God, whose love the partners express to one another) and, therefore, is a profound expression of faith, hope, and love. For the Jews marriage accompanied by procreation is the peak covenantal moment of personal life. This explains in part why the people and even kings and queens like Ahab and Jezebel (1 Kgs. 21:25) frequently turned from Yahweh to such fertility deities as Baal. The classical prophets capitalized on the significance of the marriage covenant by appropriating it as a metaphor for God's loving and saving covenant with Israel (Jer. 3:8; Isa. 62:1–5; Ezek. 23:19). Israel's faith is based on the belief that God is a jealous God who tolerates no rivals (Ex. 20:5; Deut. 4:24). The image of a marriage covenant was also used to describe the unfaithfulness of Israel. Hosea compared the nation to a woman who became a harlot: "the land gives itself to harlotry, turning away from the Lord" (Hos. 1:2). He called the people from their "spirit of harlotry" (5:4) to a life of steadfast love (6:6).

Divorce was rare among devout Jews. The older Jewish tradition—that "a man leaves his father and mother and clings to his wife, and the two of them become one body" (Gen. 2:24)—forbids divorce. In the Jewish scriptures there is only one text about divorce, a passage that presupposes rather than authorizes it:

> When a man, after marrying a woman and having relations with her, is later displeased with her because he finds in her something indecent, and therefore he writes out a bill of divorce and hands it to her, thus dismissing her from his house: if on leaving his house she goes and becomes the wife of another man, and the second husband, too, comes to dislike and dismisses her from his house by handing her a written bill of divorce; or if this second man who has married her, dies; then her former husband, who dismissed her, may not again take her as his wife after she has become defiled (Deut. 24:1–4).

The phrase "something indecent" is vague. It could mean adultery or "immodest conduct"—another vague phrase. As will be explained below, at the time of Jesus the rabbis had two divergent explanations of Deuteronomy 24.

The Christian scriptures present an uneven picture of marriage. On the positive side, Jesus reiterates the teachings of Genesis. In the letter to the Ephesians, Christ's love for his church is compared to a marriage (5:25). (It must be stated that many modern women find the comparison problematic because throughout the section women are subordinate to men.)

A negative view of marriage comes from Paul in 1 Corinthians 7:32–35:

> I would like you to be free of anxieties. An unmarried man is anxious about the things of the Lord, how he may please the Lord. But a married man is anxious about the things of the world, how he may please his wife, and he is divided. An unmarried woman or a virgin is anxious about the things of the Lord, so that she may be holy in both body and spirit. A married woman, on the other hand, is anxious about the things of the world, how she may please her husband. I am telling you this for your own benefit, not to impose a restraint upon you, but for the sake of propriety and adherence to the Lord without distraction.

Paul's view often found acceptance in those denominations that institutionalized a celibate clergy, monks, and nuns. The consequence is that this understanding helped foster anti-sexual, misogynist theories and practices in the Christian churches. These beliefs undermined the gospel message that the spouse is "the first and most obvious focus of that love of neighbor which Jesus likened to love of God" (Mahoney 1990, 319). The book of Genesis describes God as essentially related to his creation and especially humankind, the creatures made in his image. The triune Christian God is essentially relational. "God is love" (1 Jn. 4:8). Today, there is greater appreciation of the psychological and social fact that the fullness of personal identity is to be found only as interpersonal identity. At Vatican II in the *Constitution on the Church in the Modern World,* the bishops underscored marriage as a "covenant of conjugal love." They wrote:

> The biblical Word of God several times urges the betrothed and the married to nourish and develop their

wedlock by pure conjugal love and undivided affection . . .
This love is an eminently human one since it is directed
from one person to another through an affection of the
will. It involves the good of the whole person. Therefore
it can enrich the expressions of body and mind with a
unique dignity, ennobling these expressions as special
ingredients and signs of the friendship distinctive of marriage. This love the Lord has judged worthy of special
gifts, healing, perfecting, and exalting gifts of grace and
of charity . . . This love is uniquely expressed and per-
fected through the marital act. The actions within marriage by which the couple are united intimately and
chastely are noble and worthy ones. Expressed in a manner which is truly human, these actions signify and promote that mutual self-giving by which spouses enrich
each other with a joyful and a thankful will (n. 49).

Catholic View of Marriage
Christianity has always defended marriage. Some churches
sacramentalize marriage, others do not. The Catholic Church
teaches that a sacramental marriage has three dimensions: the
consent of two baptized persons to live together in love until
death, the consent of the church through the witnessing
priest, and consummation.

In a sacramental marriage the couple are baptized. This
should not be understood in a juridical way. A sacramental
marriage entails a commitment to be Christian disciples who
publicly witness the covenant love of God through Jesus
Christ and his Spirit. This is no easy commitment, and some
theologians wonder just how many couples are ready for it
(Cahill 1987).

The priest witnesses the ceremony, symbolizing the ecclesial and social dimensions of a sacramental marriage.

Consummation, too, must not be understood juridically, that
is, occurring at least once after the church ceremony. Consummation involves more than this. It requires a lifelong commitment and struggle to deepen intimacy and love. A lifelong
commitment rules out adultery—also forbidden by one of the
ten commandments (Ex. 20:14), which is reiterated in the
Christian scriptures (Mt. 5:27; Rom. 13:9; Jas. 2:11). In Jewish

tradition, adultery was punishable by death (Lev. 20:10); in earlier Christian tradition it was grounds for excommunication and severe punishment. The Catholic Church dropped excommunication as a penalty when it published the Code of Canon Law in 1917. In some places the severe punishments continued. For example, in 1884 the Catholic bishops in the United States made a law that denied divorced-remarried persons a funeral mass and Christian burial because their second marriage was considered an "adulterous union." Pope Paul VI removed all of these penalties in 1977.

The Catholic Church grants an annulment when it declares that a marriage was not a sacramental union in the first place. The church does this when, after examining the evidence, it has moral certitude there was no marriage. This annulment does not mean the couple were not legally married or that the children are illegitimate.

Annulments in the Catholic community have increased considerably since the early 1960s. In the United States there have been approximately 45,000 to 50,000 annually from 1984 to 1994 (Edwards 1994). Some believe this astounding growth is because the annulments are granted easily and hastily. Others claim that what is called an annulment is actually in many instances a "Catholic divorce." On the other hand, some defend the annulments, regarding them as evidence that the understanding of indissolubility can change over time. Today church officials are taking seriously what modern science has to teach us about the ability to consent to a lifelong decision.

Divorce: A Theological Issue

Divorce has long been allowed in the Western world. Malta is the only European country retaining a ban on divorce. Ireland had a constitutional ban on divorce that was narrowly voted down in November 1995. Although the rate of marital breakdown in that country had been lower than in other Western countries, nevertheless, thousands of couples had separated and many went to other countries where divorce is legal in order to terminate their marriages. In the United States divorces have nearly quintupled since 1940. In 1940 there were 131 million Americans and 250,000 divorces; in 1990, there were 250 million people and 1,190,000 divorces.[6]

What is the modern theology on the indissolubility of marriage? Some theologians maintain that it is an absolute norm that rules out divorce (Palmer 1975). Others argue that indissolubility is an ideal that often is not reached so that divorce is allowed (Kelleher 1973, 1975; Curran 1974). In most divorce cases, the couple's sacramental marriage began well and then over time and for many reasons the marriage deteriorated and then fails. There are also many cases when a sacramental marriage right from its very start is not a true Christian marriage, except in a canonical sense. For instance, some marriages are dead on arrival because one or even both partners are unable to sustain the duties and obligations of marriage due to lack of knowledge, mental ability, or maturity to comprehend or consent to what a valid sacramental marriage entails. In the words of Stephen Kelleher, a Catholic priest and canon lawyer, the marriages just described have become "intolerable," that is, those "in which it cannot be realistically foreseen that the couple would be able to continue or to resume a common life" (1968). He recommended that each person should decide "in his own conscience whether or not he is free before God from one marriage and free to enter another" (1975). The bond no longer exists when love, commitment, and other signs that visibly manifest a marital relationship have been irretrievably lost. He recommended that the church eliminate its **marriage tribunals**—church courts which both decide the validity of sacramental marriages and grant annulments. He also advised that the church replace the marriage tribunals with a system of marriage commissions to assist individuals and the church to reach responsible decisions on marital status. Kelleher had always maintained that the church could not grant divorces but it could acknowledge that a marriage had dissolved.

Some considered Kelleher's proposals about marriage tribunals as impractical, too subjective, and vague. Others maintained that his views of the intolerable marriage were merely common sense. Even before the sexual revolution people had become quite tolerant of divorce among their loved ones. There was less stigmatization and ostracism and more support in putting together a new life, even when this entailed a second marriage without church approval. Also, after Vatican II there had emerged a new pastoral theology of the Eucharist as a meal of reconciliation. This theology made possible the authentic (although unspoken) reunion of many divorced-remarried Catholics to full communion in parish communities.

Divorce in the Christian Scriptures

What did Jesus teach about divorce and what would he teach today? In Jesus' day a man could divorce his wife, but not vice versa. Since all of Jesus' teachings appear in the context of his proclamation of the kingdom and his radical call to conversion and discipleship, he based his divorce teachings on the heart of the Torah. In this case, Jesus taught the older tradition of Genesis 2:24 which states that God created Adam and Eve so that "the two of them become one body." Jesus forbade divorce for any reason because "what God has joined together, no human being must separate" (Mk. 10:9). He considered Deuteronomy 24 a concession by Moses because of the "hardness of heart" of Jewish men (Mk. 10:5; Mt. 19:8). His words in Luke 16:18 are very clear: "Everyone who divorces his wife and marries another commits adultery, and the one who marries a woman divorced from her husband commits adultery."

Mark repeats Luke but adds that if a woman "divorces her husband and marries another, she commits adultery" (10:12). Scholars indicate that Mark's gospel was written around 68 in Rome, a gentile context. In the Greco-Roman world women could sue for divorce. It seems that the author of Mark has extended Jesus' prohibition to women, thereby reaffirming Jesus' strong prohibition of divorce.

Paul, writing in the 50s, reiterated Jesus' prohibition against divorce in 1 Corinthians 7:10. But then he adds this teaching (7:12–15):

> To the rest I say (not the Lord): if any brother has a wife who is an unbeliever, and she is willing to go on living with him [cooperating in forming a home], he should not divorce her; and if any woman has a husband who is an unbeliever, and he is willing to go on living with her, she should not divorce her husband. For the unbelieving wife is made holy through the brother. Otherwise your

children would be unclean, whereas in fact they are
holy. If the unbeliever separates, however, let him separate. The brother or sister is not bound in such cases;
God has called you to peace.

Like Mark, the passage mirrors the hellenistic world where
both the wife and husband had the freedom to divorce. There
may have been some in the Corinthian community who
wanted to forbid Christians to retain their unbelieving
spouses. Paul says such marriages are permissible and can
be redemptive. However, if the unbelieving partner desires
to separate, the couple can divorce because the loving God
wants Christians to live in peace. Peace (the Hebrew is *shalom*)
is more than domestic harmony. It has a theological meaning,
referring to right order and harmony, which for Christians
consists in the new creation initiated by the death-resurrection
of Christ. Paul indicates that "since we have been justified by
faith, we have peace with God through our Lord Jesus Christ .
. . [and] the love of God has been poured out into our hearts
through the Holy Spirit that has been given to us" (Rom. 5:1,
5). Paul is teaching that if a nonbeliever will not live with the
Christian spouse, then the marriage has ceased to be a sign
and instrument of grace.

Matthew, writing around 85, has two references to divorce:
5:32 and 19:1–12. Both texts contain an exception clause
(5:32; 19:9)—an exception quite different from Paul's. The
translations vary. Some say divorce is prohibited "except on
the ground of unchastity" while others state "unless the marriage is unlawful." The exception has given scripture scholars
a lot of trouble and has affected the discipline of some
churches. For instance, in Orthodox churches the exception
has been taken to mean adultery and declared grounds for
divorce. In these churches remarriage is permitted twice. The
second and third marriages are regarded as concessions to
human weakness.

Today the consensus among exegetes is that the Greek
word for "unchastity" or "unlawful" *(porneia)* was interpreted
by the first-century rabbis to cover not only the forbidden
degrees of kinship regarding incest in Leviticus 18:6–18, but
also other forms of sexual immorality. Included, explains John

R. Donahue, a Jesuit scripture scholar (1981, 116), are such cases as "marriages between a Jew and a proselyte prior to conversion, a freed slave, or a woman guilty of cohabitation outside of marriage . . . If *porneia* has these connotations in Matthew's exceptive clause then Matthew is giving a number of grounds by which divorce may take place even after the marriage was in existence." In short, like Paul, Matthew offers exceptions to Jesus' prohibition against marriage.

As a result of examining the Pauline and Matthean texts, scholars ask if Jesus' most firm prohibition in Mark and Luke was an absolute law applicable to all times and all cases or does it represent a conditioned prohibition? Did Jesus teach that divorce was impossible—or that it was wrong? The opinion of many scripture scholars (McKenzie 1980, 1985, 40–50; Fitzmyer 1981; R. Collins 1993) is that divorce is wrong but possible. Jesus did not proclaim an absolute law admitting no exceptions. On the contrary, as a man of compassion, he spoke against divorce in order to protect women from being cast out of their families. During his time, some rabbis allowed divorce only for adultery, whereas others permitted divorce for whatever reason a wife displeased her husband. It could be that the first group equated divorce with the words "something indecent" (Deut. 24:1), while the second group equated "whatever displeased a husband" with the evasive word "dislike" (Deut. 24:3). It seems that Jesus' prohibition of divorce, said John L. McKenzie (1980, 303), "may be rooted in a culture in which women, from birth to death, were secure only as long as they were the property of some man—father, husband, and in their old age, a son." Furthermore, the exegetes point out that the exceptions made by the Pauline and Matthean churches to Jesus' prohibition demonstrate that first-century Christians experienced a need not only to hand on Jesus' teaching on divorce, but also to adapt it to ever new circumstances. It is a fact that marriages fail for many reasons. Scripture scholars suggest that Jesus in his wisdom and compassion would not forbid divorce in our context—although most reluctantly because he accepted the ideal found in Genesis 2:23–24: God wants conjugal unions to be permanent.

Until now, most churches have maintained an "inhumane rigidity" regarding divorce by making it an absolute law based on a precritical interpretation of Jesus' words. The opposite extreme would be an "amoral relaxation" or relativism that paid mere lip service to the teachings of Jesus. Between these two extremes there should be a position which would balance fidelity to Jesus and his church with flexibility, that is, a position that would allow each individual to decide how best to live the life of peace, wholeness, and grace to which God calls her or him (1 Cor. 7:15).

The Divorced-Remarried and the Sacraments

Many Christians get divorced, do not remarry, and continue to participate in the life of the church, including complete participation in the sacraments. On the other hand, many Christians get divorced and enter a second marriage through a civil ceremony. For many the second marriage is a chance to start a new life, particularly if they had attempted to save their first marriage but could not, or if they were unjustly abandoned by their spouses. An important part of their rehabilitation is deepening their Christian spirituality by participating in the sacraments. The traditional practice of some churches, particularly the Catholic Church, is that the divorced-remarried cannot receive the sacraments, including the Eucharist.

Rome maintains this position quite firmly and did so once again on October 14, 1994. The background of the latest Vatican document is a joint pastoral letter written by three German bishops on July 10, 1993. The bishops offered a theological approach to this delicate and painful problem and provided some guidelines for cases in which the divorced-remarried might be admitted to the sacraments. The cases they addressed concerned those persons who honestly believe that the first marriage was not truly sacramental but were unable, for any number of reasons, to obtain an annulment (Grabowski 1994). Neither the issue nor the arguments surrounding this controversy are particularly new. There are both traditionalist and revisionist understandings of the question.

The traditionalist position assumes the existence of a permanent bond of marriage, one that lasts until death. Since the bond is permanent, the traditionalists conclude that the remarried must either separate or live as brother-sister. They have three reasons for this conclusion. First, the couple is living in sin or at least a proximate occasion of sin. They are not disposed for the sacraments of reconciliation or Eucharist because a firm purpose of amendment or change is required. The Italian episcopal conference stated in 1979 that this will to change "does not exist if the divorced-remarried remain in a condition of life that is contrary to the will of God. How is it possible at the same moment to choose the love of God and disobedience to his commandments?" Second, the remarried couple is in a state of imperfect unity with Christ and not eligible to receive the Eucharist. The International Theological Commission said in 1978: "From the incompatibility of the state of the divorced-remarried with the command and mystery of the risen Lord, there follows the impossibility for these Christians of receiving the Eucharist, the sign of unity with Christ." Third, scandal would result if the remarried were admitted to the sacraments. Others would conclude that it is not wrong to remarry after divorce and that the church approves second marriages.

The revisionists state that there is "a virtually unanimous theological opinion that some divorced-remarried may be admitted to the sacraments" under certain circumstances (McCormick 1981, 120). They do not advocate a blanket admission to the sacraments because to do so would compromise the church's fidelity to Christ and/or its discipline regarding annulments. Charles M. Whelan, Jesuit specialist in church-state relations, lists four criteria: if the first marriage is irretrievably lost; if the circumstances that allow official reconciliation (for example, an annulment or the death of a spouse) are not available; if the couple have indicated by their lives that they desire to participate fully in the life of the church; and if there are solid grounds for hope of stability in the second marriage that in all other respects is a Christian marriage (Whelan 1974).

The revisionists reject the traditionalists' arguments. They doubt that the bond of marriage still exists if the marriage is existentially and psychologically dead (McCormick 1981, 119–24). They think the traditionalists' view that the remarried can receive the sacraments as long as they live like celibates is absurd. How, they ask, is the principle of indissolubility not threatened by a second marriage without a sexual life but with sacramental participation, while it would be threatened by a second marriage with a sexual life and sacramental participation (McCormick 1981, 550)?

The revisionists offer three reasons why some of the divorced-remarried may be admitted to the sacraments. First, the life of the couple often does not reflect a state of sin. Also, when children are involved, the church has frequently urged the remarried couple to remain together and to deepen their Christian life. Second, to exclude the divorced-remarried from the Eucharist on the basis of incompatibility with the unity between Christ and his church that the Eucharist signifies involves a static and "perfectionist" notion of the sacraments. Everyone who approaches the Eucharist, including the priest, admits unworthiness. Also, the Eucharist has another function: it is a means of grace. All Christians, including the divorced-remarried, need the grace of Christ. Third, if people are properly instructed, scandal need not follow from admitting the remarried to Eucharist. People should be able to weigh the pre-moral evil involved, namely, that remarriage undermines the stability of marriage, but understand that in this instance the Eucharist would be good for the Christian life of those involved.

Homosexuality

Homosexuality designates the psychosexual inclinations of the person who prefers sexual activity with persons of the same sex. Alfred Kinsey (1894–1956), a biologist at the University of Indiana, reported in 1948 in *Sexual Behavior of the Human Male* that ten percent of the male population is exclusively homosexual. This figure has been challenged in the 1990s. According to *The Social Organization of Sexuality*, about 2.8 percent of men identify themselves as gay and 1.4 percent of women identify themselves as lesbian. Kinsey's figures are close to being accurate for gay males in the country's twelve largest urban areas but not for the country as a whole (Laumann 1994).

In the United States especially, self-avowed homosexuals have become increasingly visible and even militant in their demand to be socially accepted as homosexuals and for freedom from discrimination. There is even a church that comprises mostly gay and lesbian members, the Universal Fellowship of Metropolitan Community Churches, a denomination that in 1992 had 50,000 participants in 264 congregations around the country (Hevesi 1992).

In society there is a widespread and deep-seated **homophobia**: bigotry against homosexuals and homosexual conduct that arises from an irrational fear of homosexuality. This homophobia causes many instances of social, legal, and religious discrimination against gays and lesbians (Nugent 1981). The advent of AIDS has only heightened this fear.

At present there is no consensus among Christian churches or theologians on moral questions about homosexuality and homosexual behavior. The Universal Fellowship of Metropolitan Community Churches applied in 1983 and again in 1992 for formal ties with the National Council of Churches, the nation's largest ecumenical organization. On both occasions its application was tabled. On November 11, 1992, the vote of the top policy-making body of the National Council of Churches was 90 to 81 against (Hevesi 1992).

Some churches refuse to ordain homosexuals; others will ordain but insist on a life without any homosexual activity. The United Methodist Church, which prohibits the ordination of homosexuals, has been unable to provide a churchwide definition of the term, "a self-avowed practicing homosexual." It ruled that each of its sixty-eight annual conferences must define the term for itself.[7] The Presbyterian Church (U.S.A.) will not ordain homosexuals who are open about their orientation. Jane Spahr, a lesbian Presbyterian minister, has been at the center of a divisive national debate over the ordination of homosexuals. She was ordained before she went public with her homosexuality and is one of the most prominent critics of her church's policy.[8]

Some churches bless same-sex unions while others do not. Even within the same church community there are divisions. For example, the official teaching of the Episcopal church is that homosexual activity is inherently wrong. However, in January 1995, the Episcopal Diocese of Washington defied the teaching and declared that gays and lesbians who live together in monogamous relationships should be "honored." By a vote of 134 to 32, the delegates adopted this statement: "Those who know themselves to be gay or lesbian persons and who do not choose to live alone but forge relationships with partners of their choice that are faithful, monogamous, committed, life-giving and holy, are to be honored" (Spohn 1995).

John McNeill, a Jesuit priest and an avowed chaste homosexual, wrote a book in 1976, *The Church and the Homosexual*. He argued that homosexuality is part of God's plan for the world. Homosexual orientation in itself is a precondition for the affirmation of the homosexual lifestyle. For McNeill, gay love is morally good, even holy, when it is mutual, faithful, and unselfish. He disagrees with those who maintain that homosexual acts are permissible as the least offensive among objectively "evil" alternatives. McNeill declared this view to be demeaning. He asked his readers to reconsider the condition of those homosexually-oriented individuals who regard themselves as Christians. These persons, he wrote, say they can express a relationship of shared love, fidelity, and responsibility. Together they can fulfill their identities as Christians-in-community and as persons-in-the-world, summoned to relate themselves in justice and love to all reality. John Giles Milhaven reviewed the book and asked the key question: "And how does one step from 'healthy and loving' to 'morally good'?" (1976, 127).

Without due process, McNeill was given an ultimatum by the Vatican to keep silent on the question of the morality of homosexual activity or face dismissal from his community. Right after the publication of the Vatican document *On the Pastoral Care of Homosexuals* on October 1, 1986, and after thirty-eight years as a Jesuit, McNeill withdrew from the Jesuit community because he could no longer keep silent about the Catholic Church's attitude toward homosexuals (McNeill 1986).

The 1986 Vatican document said too much had been made of the distinction between homosexual orientation and behavior. The orientation of the homosexual, the Vatican said, "is not a sin, it is a more or less strong tendency toward an intrinsic moral evil, and thus the inclination itself must be seen as an objective disorder" (n. 3). The document reiterated the teaching on the objective immorality of homosexual acts because they lack the sexual complementarity and potential fruitfulness demanded by heterosexual marriage. Readers of the document were quick to notice that it misunderstands homosexuality as an orientation. Ordinarily, the term refers to a psychosexual attraction toward one of the same sex, but the Vatican document described it as a tendency toward evil acts. John McNeill and others did not feel that the document provided pastoral care.

Four Interpretations of Homosexual Behavior

In the Christian churches and society there are four views about homosexuality: that it is a perversion, a disease, an irreversible orientation, or a normal alternative to heterosexuality.

Those who view homosexuality as a perversion condemn all homosexual activity as immoral, intrinsically evil, unnatural, and contrary to scripture. The scripture, they maintain, is unambiguous in its condemnation of homosexual practices, in all five biblical references to homosexual activity (Gen. 19:4–11; Lev. 18:22, 20:13; Rom. 1:24–27; 1 Cor. 6:9–10; and 1 Tim. 1:9–10). Homosexuality is not mentioned in any of the gospels. The clearest condemnation of homosexuality is in Leviticus: "You shall not lie with a male as with a woman; such a thing is an abomination" (18:22). "If a man lies with a male as with a woman, both of them shall be put to death for their abominable deed; they have forfeited their lives" (20:13).

Once again it is necessary to differentiate between a precritical and historical-critical interpretation of the scriptures. Proponents of the historical-critical method stress three points. First, the scriptures are ambiguous because the biblical authors had no doctrine on homosexuality and certainly did not address the question of an irreversible orientation. The concepts of "constitutionally homosexual" and "homosexuality" are unknown during the biblical periods. It is modern science that has proposed that some persons are not homosexual by choice or preference.

Second, throughout the Bible, the Genesis description of male-female relationships is taken for granted as the standard or norm. All people are heterosexual and their genital activity would reflect this point. However, whenever people turn from God and his created order, all kinds of disorders and depravities would follow, not only homosexual actions by heterosexuals but also adultery and lying (see Jer. 23:14), and pride, gluttony, and arrogance (see Ezek. 16:49–50). The two texts from Leviticus are part of chapters 17–26, known as the **Holiness Code** because they emphasize Yahweh as the source of holiness and the laws that Israel must observe to acquire a holiness appropriate to the chosen people. This code explicitly bans homosexual conduct but it also prohibits the blind and lame from offering food to God (21:17–18); priests from marrying anyone but a virgin (21:13); fortune-tellers (19:31); tattoos (19:28); adultery (20:10); and sexual intercourse during a woman's menstrual period (20:18).

Third, in biblical times, homosexuality was related to temple services and therefore adoration of false deities (R. Collins 1986, 172–74). This is the context of Leviticus 18. In this text God commands the Israelites not to "behave as they do in the land of Egypt where you once lived, nor shall you do in the land of Canaan where I am bringing you" (18:3). This concern for cultural purity suggests that homosexuality would reflect the male and female prostitution common in Middle East religious cults. This prohibition, as well as those in such passages as Deuteronomy 23:18 and 1 Kings 14:24 and 15:12, suggests that homosexual activity was prohibited because of its intimate association with idolatry (Coleman 1987).

Genesis 19—the story of Sodom and Gomorrah—is not a condemnation of homosexuality as such, but of the violation of the sacred duty of hospitality, according to Luke 10:10–13, and failure to care for the poor, according to Ezekiel 16:49–50. The passages in Romans, Corinthians, and Timothy are condemnations of the dehumanizing pederasty that was widespread in the Greco-Roman culture of the first century. These passages cannot be used to establish that homosexual acts are intrinsically disordered and can in no case be approved. It is generally agreed that none of the biblical authors knew homosexuality as an orientation. They saw it as a human choice, and, as such, a perversion which they condemned along with other unchaste or immoral actions. For example,

Paul asked the Corinthians (1 Cor. 6:9–10) this question: "Do you not know that the unjust will not inherit the kingdom of God? Do not be deceived; neither fornicators nor idolaters nor adulterers nor boy prostitutes nor practicing homosexuals nor thieves nor the greedy nor drunkards nor slanderers nor robbers will inherit the kingdom of God."

Scripture scholars continue to examine the question of homosexual practices and the challenge they place upon our understanding of scripture and God's grace. Luke Timothy Johnson, professor of the New Testament at the Candler School of Theology, Emory University, writes that, as the church leaders determine whether they "can recognize the possibility of homosexual committed and covenantal love, in the way that it recognizes such sexual/personal love in the sacrament of marriage," it is incumbent upon them to listen to "narratives of homosexual holiness" (1994). He suggests that this issue might be analogous to the one facing the Jewish Christians after Gentiles started being converted. Peter, James, Paul, Barnabas, and the others present at the Jerusalem assembly in 49 A.D. wondered whether male Gentiles could be accepted into the church just as they were or should they be obliged to obey all the ritual demands of the Torah, including circumcision. Johnson points out how serious were the stakes. The Gentiles "were 'by nature' unclean, and were 'by practice' polluted by idolatry." As such, they were unfit to participate in table-fellowship. The decision of the church to let the Gentiles in "as is" and to establish a radically new form of table-fellowship "came into direct conflict with the accepted interpretation of the Torah and what God wanted of humans." The decision was not easy to reach. Similarly, Christians are forced today to ask about the compatibility of homosexual love and holiness of life. "The church can discuss this only on the basis of faithful witness. The burden of proof required to overturn scriptural precedents is heavy, but it is a burden that has been borne before."

The attentive reader is aware that Johnson is using the critical method of interpretation of the scriptures to the present situation. The situation in 49 in Jerusalem does not illuminate what is happening in the 1990s. On the contrary, since most Christians have been baptized as infants, they have little appreciation of the nerve-racking struggle of Peter and Paul to understand the bearing of the Mosaic covenant on Gentile converts. The fact that today many Christians condemn homosexuals because of their nature (their orientation) and their practice (same-gender love) can help us understand the anguish and search for the truth of the apostolic church.

A second view of homosexual orientation is that it is a disease. It results from a pathological constitution or is a psychological dysfunction caused by harmful behavioral patterns in the familial or immediate social environment. It can be cured by depth therapy, they believe.

Modern science rejects this view. The American Psychiatric Association moved in 1973 to drop its official diagnosis of homosexuality as a mental illness (Hansen 1986). The organization declared that homosexuality "implies no impairment in judgment, stability, reliability, or general social or vocational capabilities." Similarly, the World Health Organization did not list homosexuality in the 1993 edition of its International Classification of Diseases.

A third understanding of homosexuality differentiates between homosexual activity and orientation. A person's sexual orientation is a given rather than a chosen or preferred condition. This distinction was popularized by Alfred Kinsey in 1948. What causes the orientation remains an unanswered question. Various explanations are offered: heredity or genetic factors or erratic behavior patterns in the family or the social environment.

In 1973, the Catholic bishops in the United States issued *Principles to Guide Confessors in Questions of Homosexuality.* The bishops acknowledged that people do not choose their sexual orientation, but they reiterated the Catholic teaching that "homosexual acts are a grave transgression of the goals of human sexuality and of human personality." Priests were encouraged to help homosexuals work out an ascetical plan of life with a view to controlling their sexual activity.

In December 1975, the Vatican *Declaration on Certain Questions Concerning Sexual Ethics* made the distinction between behavior and orientation. The document observed that some homosexuals are "innately" constituted as such and thus their "constitution" should not be thought "curable"

(n. 8). Nevertheless, the document stated that homosexual acts necessarily involve objective moral evil inasmuch as they "lack an essential and indispensable finality" (n. 8).

In 1983 the Vatican issued another statement on homosexuality entitled *Educational Guidance in Human Love*. It encouraged sex education. However, it did not make the distinction between behavior and orientation in condemning homosexuality. It declared that homosexual activity "impedes the person's acquisition of sexual maturity." Without condoning this kind of sexual activity as a likely path to personal and sexual integration, it did instruct educators not to disturb people who were troubled in these ways with accusations of guilt. Robert Nugent, a priest who co-founded in 1977 a support organization for homosexuals called New Ways Ministry, insisted in his commentary on the document that balance is needed in dealing with the question. "Homosexual *people* should not be reduced to their *orientation;* nor should the homosexual orientation be reduced to sexual *behavior*" (1984, 488).

In response to this Vatican literature, theologians spoke out. Gregory Baum offered this advice to homosexuals: "If it is true that some people are constitutively homosexual and that homosexual relations allow for mutuality, then, from the viewpoint of Christian theology, it is the task of homosexuals to acknowledge themselves as such before God, accept their sexual orientation as their calling, and explore the meaning of this inclination for the Christian life" (1974). Baum does not say explicitly whether homosexual behavior between homosexual persons who were growing in friendship and covenant faithfulness was morally justifiable. Philip Keane, a priest-theologian, took another perspective. He said homosexual acts always involve a significant degree of premoral evil since they are not open to procreation, the heterosexual ideal. Yet they are not necessarily an objective moral evil (1977, 87). For other commentators, both the homosexual orientation and overt acts are not in themselves good for people and therefore not generally right, but they are not necessarily immoral in all cases, especially if the persons are in a stable, loving relationship and if for them neither celibacy nor marriage is a realistic alternative. For example, Charles Curran offered a "theology of compromise": "One may reluctantly accept homosexual unions as the only way in which some people can find a satisfying degree of humanity in their lives" (1972, 217).

A fourth view of homosexuality is that it is a variation within the human condition and not something contrary to nature. As such, it is a fully normal alternative to heterosexuality. They support sexual expression by gay persons that is humane and humanizing, that is, it is "loving, life-giving and life-affirming." For over twenty years "homosexual marriages" have been reported in the media. Those involved insist that their domestic partnerships are the equivalent of traditional marriages.

Some churches have addressed the issue of liturgical rites for blessing same-sex unions. The national Episcopal Church tried this but had to put off a decision until the theological and pastoral issues were resolved and clarified for all the members.[9] Some Christians have called for the legitimization of homosexual marriages. For example, in the early 1970s, a group of Catholic homosexual men and women formed an association in Los Angeles to give witness to the church that it is possible to be both Catholic and gay. John McNeill was a charter member. They call themselves Dignity. However, Dignity gets little support from the Catholic bishops.

Another person receptive to homosexual marriages is Sidney Callahan, a Catholic mother and theologian (1994). She acknowledges that society "must support and privilege procreative families," but sees no reason why this positive support necessitates forbidding the marriages of gay couples. She wonders why it is intrinsically disordered for homosexuals to act on their sexual orientation. This orientation for many is not freely chosen but given. She contends that homosexuals who eschew promiscuity and desire to regularize and ritualize their loving commitment to one another "should be allowed to marry." She argues that there has also been a "rigid overestimation of gender" in Catholic teaching. Gender can sometimes be a minor consideration when a heterosexual couple, in considering their struggle to achieve loving unity, recognizes that there are so many other differences between them that often have more significant bearing on their relationships, such factors as "temperament, intelligence, taste, talents and moral maturity." Her conclusion is that we must affirm embodiment and respect for the symbolic language of the body. She regards "the rejection of loving gay erotic expression as a rejection of embodiment, and another form of resistance to the goodness of sexual desire and pleasure."

It is not just individuals or special-interest groups like Dignity which have lobbied for homosexual marriages. At a meeting of the European Parliament in Strasbourg a vote was taken on February 8, 1994, to support homosexual marriages. A resolution was passed that gave the same rights to homosexual couples—including that of adopting children—as to married couples. The Vatican's semi-official newspaper, *L'Osservatore Romano,* protested at once, declaring that "to promote homosexual tendencies means violating the natural order fixed by God from the moment of conception." On February 22, the Vatican issued a long letter on family values titled "Letter to Families" by Pope John Paul II. This letter had been signed on February 2 in order to coincide with the United Nations' Year of the Family and shortly before the meeting (and decision) of the European Parliament. The papal document declared that homosexual unions were "a serious threat to the future of the family." The Pope explained: "Marriage, which undergirds the institution of the family, is constituted by the covenant whereby a man and a woman establish between themselves a partnership for their whole life. Only such a union can be recognized and ratified as a marriage in society. Other interpersonal unions which do not fulfill the above conditions cannot be recognized, despite certain growing trends which represent a serious threat to the future of the family and society itself."

It is clear from this chapter that the churches, individually and collectively, have a long way to go before they can determine the core and the boundaries of the gospel's understanding of what it means to be human and chaste. This is a major challenge as the churches prepare to enter the third millennium.

8

Christian Humanism
and the Meaning of Life

Humanism—attention to human beings, their origin, interests, achievements, development, and goals—can be either nonreligious or religious. Some aspects of the "new humanism" and Christian humanism were discussed in chapter one and in other sections of this book. This chapter focuses on what Christian humanism maintains about the meaning of human life. It does so by examining two issues. First, human life is like an ongoing drama, still unfinished and full of surprises. But the story line often breaks down because life seems insignificant. We wonder if it has any underlying or long-range significance and rationale. Second, since the ongoing drama includes the entire created realm of things and nonhuman creatures, we ask about our own originality and distinctiveness.

The Problem of Meaning

Clifford Geertz, a cultural anthropologist, published an essay entitled "Religion as a Cultural System," in which he analyzed the problem of the meaning and worth of life. He observed that most humans experience alienation from the Ultimate Reality. He identified three aspects of this problem, maintaining that chaos threatens us when we find ourselves "at the limits of [our] analytical capacities, at the limits of [our] powers of endurance, and at the limits of [our] moral insight." These three situations, especially if "they become intense enough or are sustained long enough," are radical "challenges to the proposition that life is comprehensible and that we can by taking thought, orient ourselves effectively within it" (1968, 653). Christianity attempts to cope with these basic problems.

Humans have always wondered if their existence matters since ordinary life often seems so unsubstantial. This problem of bafflement is exacerbated today by the fact that modern science continues to provide massive evidence of the immense sweep of time and the vastness of space. For example, astronomers have produced evidence that "there are as many galaxies in the sky as there are stars in our own galaxy" (Wilford 1996). Our galaxy—the Milky Way—has some 50 billion stars. Within this context, an individual human life can seem as insignificant as a grain of sand on a beach. An individual can easily imagine that he or she is but an accidental, impermanent, and inconsequential speck of dust, hardly visible to the naked eye. The Christian vision of human life rejects such a conclusion. On the contrary, in its defense of the dignity of the person, it places each individual within the history of creation and all human history. Each person is important and can contribute to God's plan for creation through Christ and in the power of his Paraclete-Spirit. Furthermore, since a Christian commits himself or herself to Christ in faith, then this commitment explicitly makes the Christian a part of Christ's history and meaning. In Christ we attain cosmic significance because the Creator "chose us in him, before the foundation of the world, to be holy and without blemish" (Eph. 1:4). The Christian message is one of hope. It says that you can have confidence in yourself and your life because both are anchored in Christ.

Humans have always suffered physical and mental pain. Sometimes suffering can be beneficial. As a result of suffering, some people mature, develop character, and compassionately open their hearts to others who suffer. Suffering in its negative aspects can often be purposeless, that is, it conforms to no logic that we can grasp or rely on. Often suffering is inflicted on innocent people. It sometimes destroys character. The media are filled with stories of people suffering from the greed, sexism, and violence of others. And people often bring suffering on themselves by their own immoral thoughts, words, and actions. In the midst of these negative aspects of suffering, many cry out, "Where is God now?"

Christianity, like other religions, offers a means to cope with suffering and, in the face of it, attain an affirmation of the meaning and worth of life. Because of the massive suffering of the twentieth century, notably the two world wars, the Holocaust, and AIDS, Christian theologians such as Jurgen Moltmann of the Reformed Church and Edward Schillebeeckx of the Catholic Church have struggled to reconcile the fact of evil and suffering with faith in the Father of Jesus Christ (E. Johnson 1992, 120–27) because "the New Testament gives no systematic treatment of why suffering occurs" (Hauser 1995, 19). These theologians point to the cross, the Christian symbol, because it reveals in a powerful way the tension between the Father and sinful humanity. In the drama of Jesus' life, he was an innocent victim of human sinfulness, ignorance, and rejection. The Father never abandoned his Son but was present, near but silent, in compassionate solidarity with him. In John's gospel this compassion was given visible manifestation through those loved ones who remained around the cross, especially Jesus' mother, the Beloved Disciple, and Mary Magdalene. The Father did act to overcome death by raising Jesus to eternal life. Consequently, Christian humanism declares that the Father of Jesus Christ is intensely aware of our suffering, is compassionately involved in it, and is actively working to overcome it. "While God does not preserve us *from* all suffering, he does preserve us *in* all suffering" (Küng 1992, 607). Christians in turn are called to acknowledge the massiveness of suffering and, despite their limited resources, to struggle against it, transform it, and work in solidarity with suffering people.

Humans have always struggled with existence because sometimes it seems pointless and evil. Today, we are surrounded by a trend, present in politics, in literature, in art, and in the personal conviction of people, that the world is necessarily an evil place, that reality is not only evil but that it must be evil and always will be evil. This worldview looks upon life as basically meaningless. For example, the Pulitzer-Prize writings of both Albert Camus (1913–60) and Jean-Paul Sartre (1905–80) are still fairly popular today. Both of these men insist that the ongoing drama of life comes across as absurd, that is, without sense or structure, rhyme or reason. Any hope for lasting individual and social transformation is regarded as unrealistic. The myth of Sisyphus and his essentially meaningless task of rolling a great rock up a hill each day is a capsule description of this viewpoint. Christian humanism, on the other hand, maintains that reality is essentially good and sacred because God is always redemptively present to us. Transformation, openness, growth, and grace are always available. Each human life has a meaningful place within history as a whole. Each person has a part in the great scheme that began with creation and will reach fulfillment when God in his wisdom and love closes down history as we know it at the end of time. In short, the Christian contribution to humanism is its teaching that each person has inviolable dignity and is irreplaceable.

What Makes Us Distinctively Human

We turn now to the second point: what makes us distinctively human. The merely material things (air, water, fire, earth, sun) carve out a space for themselves by neutralizing opposing forces. They seek their own physical integrity. All contacts and interactions with other things—and even persons—are purely functional. Fire and water react according to their nature with whatever they contact. The fact that contact is with a person as opposed to a thing means absolutely nothing to them.

The "living material" things (plants, trees, birds, fish, and other animals) are nonhuman, sentient, and organic. They have the characteristics of the merely material, but because they are alive, they also seek growth, development, and self-renewal. Plants and animals get nourishment from other things, even converting other things into themselves. They absorb the other, not only for their own survival but also for the offspring they reproduce. They are quite indifferent to the other's existence as valuable in and for itself. The other is valuable for the sustenance it provides.

Human beings are like the merely material because we too are subject to the physical laws of the universe. We also share a lot with the living material because we too draw nourishment from other things and convert them to ourselves. What makes us distinctively human is that each individual is a distinct, created, rational, and historical body-person. Our spirit is not added to our body nor above it, but, rather, at its center. We have freedom, that is, the capacity to fulfill our deepest aspirations by consciously choosing the true and the good. We are transcendent, that is, we are able to go beyond our environment to a certain degree. Although we are not totally independent of the world of nature, we can step back from it and its laws, and by thought, reflection, and language know the world and change it. All persons are different from each other because right down to our own distinct fingerprints, everyone is a body-person who can communicate with others. Some animals know things, but only humans know they know and can communicate this knowledge.

Since Charles Darwin, humans realize that from a biological point of view they make up only a small part of the animal world. Nonetheless, although actions like eating and sexual intercourse have their counterparts in the animal world, they do not have their equivalents. Animals do not dine (have table fellowship) and human procreation has the real potential for being the expression of intimacy, love, and friendship. Not all Christians have such a positive view of human dignity, especially with regard to sexuality. This has been a perennial problem. The apostle Paul had to explain the dignity of the body in his first letter to the Corinthians. He reminded the Christians that "The body is not meant for immorality, but for the Lord, and the Lord for the body" (6:13). Paul addressed those who held that what a person did with one's body did not matter as long as one was a "spiritual" person, as long as one had been saved (6:15–18). Others refrained from sexual relations with their spouses in the interest of spiritual purity (7:5). It seems that even the great apostle Paul had difficulty getting some of his disciples to shape their sexual morality by faith in Jesus as God's incarnate self-gift. Christians do not adequately appreciate that the Word took on human flesh, genitals included.

We saw in the chapter on sexual ethics that, although the teachings of the Christian churches have been quite uneven regarding the dignity and sacredness of the body and sexuality, nonetheless, the churches have generally opposed dehumanizing and unchristian views of human sexuality. They have shown their opposition by fostering the virtues of chastity and fidelity, the holiness of marriage, responsible parenthood, the sacredness of human life, and the profundity of conjugal friendship and love. Today, many Christians realize that sexuality and spirituality are part and parcel of each other, because not only is the body a temple of the Spirit, but also Christ, the Word incarnate, continues to become flesh and dwell among us. For example, in his reflections on the so-called sexual revolution of the 1960s, James Nelson (1987, 189) reported that "The sexual revolution helped convince many Christians that an incarnationalist faith embraces the redemption of alienated sexuality as well as other estranged dimensions of our lives. *Justification by grace* signifies God's unconditional, unmerited, radical acceptance of the whole person: God, the Cosmic Lover, graciously embraces not just a person's disembodied spirit but the whole fleshly self—the meanings of which theology is only beginning to explore."

What also makes us distinctively human is that we are social by nature. Some animals have group activity (a herd, a pack, a flock), but they are not social in the way humans are. The social dimension is absolutely central and constitutive of our personhood. Theologically, its basis is the triune God and the reciprocal self-giving and receiving that marks the relationships of the three divine persons. Philosophically, there have been two divergent explanations of what it means to be social by nature. One view states that a person is an individual substance of a rational nature, complete and incommunicable who can subsequently enter into relationships with others. This description stresses what is given by nature. Popularized by Greek philosophers, it found a secure home in the writings of such thinkers as Boethius (475–525) and Thomas Aquinas. They explain that an individual substance has existence in itself. Each person has what is essential to human nature: a body and a spirit which can think, will, and imagine. The person is complete because he or she has what is necessary and universally present in all humans. Basically, the person has an unchangeable core. The future has little bearing on this core because, since it does not yet exist, it is slightly unreal. Each person is incommunicable, meaning that each person should never be dissolved in a collectivity. Each person is irreplaceable and has inalienable rights.

This Greek description of our social nature, while it can serve to highlight our dignity as made in the image of God, is too static, identifies the perfection of people in terms of knowledge and wisdom, and views history as extrinsic, meaning that it affects people only in an accidental way. Due to the rise of the modern sciences, both physical and social, this view of our social nature has given way to a different model.

Today, based on the philosophies of phenomenologists and existentialists, our social nature is considered to be dynamic. We emphasize a person's special characteristics and personality. We note how people differ from one another by race, color, sex, language, religion, and so forth. Freedom is more important than knowledge, especially since there has been an overwhelming knowledge explosion. We believe persons can achieve a special kind of perfection when they consciously and deliberately commit themselves in the face of the unknown. Change is at the heart of all reality and must be dealt with as it comes. We live in a relational world. Modern anthropology defines persons in terms of their openness to their many worlds. Instead of regarding persons as substantial entities capable of entering into relations, persons are regarded as beings who are constituted by their physical, cultural, familial, socioeconomic, political, and religious relationships. In other words, there is a constant dialectic between the personal and social, but the social is the matrix of development and fulfillment. Before I am a self, I am a sister or brother (daughter or son, wife or husband, mother or father, and so forth). I am a related person with a certain measure of independence rather than an independent person who can enter relationships. My identity is a combination of social gift and personal achievement.

The Greek view that the human is what is given by nature is in sharp contrast with the existentialist view that the human is constantly being developed historically and relationally. The existentialist view reflects the Christian understanding of the human, especially as it is expressed in a faith-justice spirituality. As we have seen, this spirituality underscores community, rejects the treatment of anyone as a nonperson, stresses God's involvement in history, especially with the poor and oppressed, and accentuates the redemptive presence of the Spirit who enables and requires us to change history by cooperating and communicating with one another for the common good. It promotes the common good by opposing both selfish individualism and totalitarian systems that trample on the rights of the individual person. A faith-justice spirituality fosters Jesus' teachings against elitism, legalism, ritualism, sexism, greed, and violence. Obviously, human life would be much more just, peaceful, and humane if these disvalues were eliminated.

We have seen that secular humanists like John Dewey, behaviorists like B. F. Skinner, and scientific naturalists like Carl Sagan view humankind as simply a part of nature. For them, human life is fully reduced to quantitative categories. Human problems and the solutions to these problems belong to the order of quantity that can be objectively measured and reduced to a mechanical cause-and-effect chain. Human problems can be carefully measured and more easily solved once better instruments have been devised.

Christian humanism rejects this reduction of human life to natural, scientifically-controlled processes. It maintains that there is more to the human than the natural because there are profound issues and questions that affect human integration and happiness. Humans are qualitatively different from the world of nature because humans struggle with their finitude, contingency, and transcendence. We also have an insatiable thirst for a greater grasp of truth, goodness, love, courage, and freedom. All of these values point to the one we call God. "One does not live by bread alone, but by every word that comes forth from the mouth of God" (Deut. 8:3; Mt. 4:4).

More exactly, Christian humanism declares that what actually makes us specifically and distinctively human is our destiny to be one with God, now and after death. The technical term for this relationship is **supernatural**. The word denotes our destiny—life with God—and the fact that it is beyond any human power to achieve this destiny apart from the grace of God. It is **grace**—God's loving and enabling presence—that makes it possible for us to seek and respond to God. "And no one can say, 'Jesus is Lord,' except by the Holy Spirit" (1 Cor. 12:3).

This supernatural dimension is not a "superstructure" added to our created, rational, social, and historical nature like a penthouse added to an apartment building. On the contrary, the supernatural modifies all these dimensions. There is no such thing as a "pure nature" to which the supernatural is added. Humans are not free subjects created by God who can then be related to God. Human consciousness and freedom consist precisely in being God-directed from the very moment of existence. As the philosopher Robert O. Johann explained "The Infinite, the Absolute, and the Eternal all enter [our] very definition. The Infinite is [our] horizon, the Absolute [our] norm and the Eternal that endless moment through which all [our] moments pass. In short, to be a person is to be seized by Being itself as its own advocate and spokes[person], indeed as its very promoter, in a world of fact and limit where it seeks always a fuller presence" (1968, 78).

Maintaining a Christian identity and mission are crucial today because secularized society claims that such things as money, politics, power, sex, and technology are to be taken more seriously than our supernatural origin and destiny.

Christian Humanism and the Holy Spirit

Christian humanism holds that our supernatural self is nurtured and enabled by the Paraclete-Spirit. Naturalists, behaviorists, and secular humanists propose that what Christians call the "holy Spirit" is merely an imaginative description of the natural force that helps a person remove all of the fearful thinking that covers over his or her inner perfection. Christians declare the Spirit is real, is personal and is experienced in several ways. The ordinary experience of the Spirit takes place in the deepest part of the human psyche where persons make their most fundamental decisions. This principle has been examined by Karl Rahner. His explanation (1967, 86–87) merits extensive quotation:

> Have we ever actually experienced grace? We do not mean by this some pious feeling, a sort of festive religious uplift, or any soft comfort, but precisely the experiencing of grace, that is, of that visitation by the Holy Spirit . . . which has become a reality in Christ through his becoming man and through his sacrifice on the cross . . .
>
> At this point we would like to say from the very start: let us try to discover it for ourselves in our experience; and to aid this, one can merely tentatively and cautiously point out certain things.
>
> Have we ever kept quiet, even though we wanted to defend ourselves when we had been unfairly treated? Have we ever forgiven someone even though we got no thanks for it and our silent forgiveness was taken for granted? Have we ever obeyed, not because we had to and because otherwise things would have become unpleasant for us, but simply on account of that mysterious, silent, incomprehensible being we call God and his will? Have we ever sacrificed something without receiving any thanks or recognition for it, and even without a feeling of inner satisfaction? Have we ever been absolutely lonely? Have we ever decided on some course of action purely by the innermost judgment of our conscience, deep down where one can no longer tell or explain it to anyone, where one is quite alone and knows that one is taking a decision which no one else can take in one's place and for which one will have to answer for all eternity? Have we ever tried to love God when we are no longer being borne on the crest of the wave of enthusiastic feeling, when it is no longer possible to mistake our self, and its vital urges, for God? Have we ever tried to love him when we thought we were dying of this love and when it seemed like death and absolute negation? Have we ever tried to love God when we seemed to be calling out into emptiness and our cry seemed to fall on deaf ears, when it looked as if we were taking a terrifying jump into the bottomless abyss,

when everything seemed to become incomprehensible and apparently senseless? Have we ever fulfilled a duty when it seemed that it could be done only with a consuming sense of really betraying and obliterating oneself, when it could apparently be done only by doing something terribly stupid for which no one would thank us? Have we ever been good to someone who did not show the slightest sign of gratitude or comprehension and when we also were not rewarded by the feeling of having been selfless, decent, etc.?

Let us search for ourselves in such experiences in our life; let us look for our own experiences in which things like this have happened to us individually. If we find such experiences, then we have experienced the Spirit in the way meant here.

The Paraclete-Spirit is also experienced through the charisms or gifts that only the Spirit can confer (1 Cor. 12–13). In addition, the Spirit also operates in each person's **conscience**. Conscience is the most secret core of a person. There a person is alone with God. For Christians, conscience, which means "with knowledge," is a permanent natural disposition that summons us to seek the good and to avoid evil. It is not an impersonal oracle that confirms or negates our decisions. Rather, it is the result of hard, honest, and practical thinking about a particular decision. Conscience is a process in which human reason applies to individual situations both moral principles and the teachings that come from a plurality of complementary authorities: scripture, tradition, church leaders (like popes and bishops), the whole community, and theologians.

Christian Humanism and Prayer

Another way the Spirit is present is in our prayer. Paul wrote that "we do not know how to pray as we ought, but the Spirit itself intercedes with inexpressible groanings. And the one who searches hearts knows what is the intention of the Spirit, because it intercedes for the holy ones according to God's will" (Rom. 8:26–27).

Anyone who accepts the risen Christ's glorious re-entry into history engages in prayer. Prayer, whether liturgical, communal, or private, entails not only entering into Christ's prayer to his Father but also listening to God and dialoguing with him. Prayer is not easy, yet it is at the heart of the Jewish and Christian traditions.

Prayer was essential to the life of the Jewish priests, prophets, and people. Abraham offered sacrifice to God in faith. The Pentateuch contains rules for religious rituals and ceremonies. Many of the psalms are credited to David, a man of prayer. First Solomon and later Zerubbabel built the temple, the holy place of prayer in the holy city in the holy land. The prophets often learned the word of God at prayer. The Maccabees struggled against hellenization because it was destroying Jewish prayer life. They were able to rededicate the temple after it had been desecrated.

In the gospels, Jesus encouraged prayer and is identified as a prayerful person. He cleansed the temple because it lacked the conditions for prayer and experience of his Father. In Luke's gospel especially, Jesus is depicted at prayer at crucial moments of his life (3:21, 5:16, 6:12, 9:18, 23:46). He taught his disciples the Our Father. He prayed in the garden before his arrest and while on the cross. The prayer of Mary the mother of Jesus is called the Magnificat (Lk. 1:46–55). It is a source of inspiration and consolation to many as they struggle against injustices.

All religions teach that prayer is to religious life what breathing is to human life. But many people ask how it is done. "We find in the Bible no summons to observe, describe, and analyze mystical states and experiences, no ladder of mystical prayer leading up to ecstasy, no stress on any prayer that presupposes special religious gifts" (Küng 1986, 424). Consequently, there are probably as many ways of praying as there are people. Prayer, like all human activities, becomes easier and easier with practice. At one time it was a struggle for us to dress, or to eat, or to hold a pencil and write. Now we do these things effortlessly.

Modern writers suggest that we simply review our day and bring the events and especially our feelings to God. Prayer can be a time to focus on the ongoing drama of life. One author (Hamm 1994) suggests a method of five steps.

First, pray for light. Review the last twenty-four hours. This is not mere reminiscing, but looking for what the Spirit is enabling and requiring me to be and to do. I need "graced understanding." The Spirit of truth will provide illumination about my identity and mission.

Second, review the day with gratitude. Many people begin prayer by asking for forgiveness. But such an emphasis on sin negates the many loving initiatives of God the Father of Jesus Christ. It is the Father of Jesus Christ who creates, covenants, loves, and saves. Human life is a response to what he has done. The opening prayer in Paul's epistles is always one of thanksgiving. We have seen that the central prayer of Christianity is the death-resurrection of Jesus. This is called Eucharist, meaning "thanksgiving."

Every day there are gifts from God: existence, relationships, food, sleep, work, and challenges. Review the day by walking from hour to hour, from place to place, task to task, person to person, thanking the Father of Jesus Christ for his gifts.

Third, review the feelings that surface in the replay of the day. "Our feelings, positive and negative, the painful and pleasing, are clear signals of where the action was during the day." Feelings are an accurate index to what is happening in our lives. Recall the feelings of the day. We all experience a whole range of them: anticipation, anger, admiration, boredom, compassion, contentment, confidence, desire, disgust, delight, doubt, envy, faith, fear, gratitude, hope, impatience, love, pride, regret, resentment, and so forth.

Fourth, choose one of those feelings (positive or negative) and pray from it. Choose the feeling that most caught your attention because this feeling is a sign that something important is going on. React spontaneously to this feeling by expressing the appropriate response: praise, adoration, thanksgiving and/or petition for help or healing or forgiveness.

Fifth, look toward the next day. What is on your calendar? How do you feel about your schedule? How do you feel about the tasks, meetings, and appointments that you anticipate? Turn the feelings into a prayer, asking for strength, or healing, or insight so that the day will be lived in a Christian way.

It must be emphasized once again that prayer, whether liturgical, communal, or private, is possible "because the love of God has been poured out into our hearts through the Holy

Spirit that has been given to us" (Rom. 5:5). Despite this fundamental teaching, many Christians think and pray as if everything depends on them. Many are taught a spirituality that says, "Do your best and God will do the rest," or "God helps those who help themselves." A few years ago a very popular book on prayer by Malcolm Boyd (1965), an Episcopal priest, seriously tried to undermine this kind of spirituality. He gave his book the title *Are You Running with Me, Jesus?* Theologically, he knew this was a poor title, but he explained his choice in the preface.

> It has been asked by some persons why this book is not entitled *Am I Running with You, Jesus?* The question overlooks the fact that my prayer life, as the state of my spirituality, is neither very respectable nor quite correct. Needless to say, I am a self-centered man, sinfully immersed in my own welfare and concerns, attempting to manipulate God, and often lost in my own self-love and self-pity. *Are You Running with Me, Jesus?* more accurately reflects the grounding, motivation, and style of my prayer life and spirituality as I grapple with imperfections and ambiguities in myself and my society.

Christians should pray, knowing that everything they undertake begins with the Paraclete-Spirit's inspiration, continues with his help, and reaches completion under his guidance. In 1977, Malcolm Boyd produced another book on prayer, *Am I Running with You, God?*

Christian Humanism and Death

Christian humanism has something important to say about death and immortality. Death, that time when our part in the ongoing drama ends, is mysterious and frightening. Jesus wept when he heard of Lazarus' death. He was so filled with dread in the garden of Gethsemane when he anticipated his own death, that "he offered prayers and supplications with loud cries and tears to the one who was able to save him from death" (Heb. 5:7). The reality of death, this time of ultimate helplessness, is a problem for everyone, but it is probably a special problem for those naturalists, behaviorists, and secular humanists who profess that there is no life beyond death.

In 1969, Elizabeth Kübler-Ross, a doctor, published *On Death and Dying,* a book which made a major difference in the ordinary regard people have for this common and mysterious reality. Her book grew out of her experiences with dying people who were asked to speak freely and frankly about their experience with the process of dying. According to Kübler-Ross, people can go through all or some of five stages when confronted with the reality of their own deaths: denial that death is imminent, anger at its destructive finality, bargaining in order to delay it, depression because of the loss of cherished persons and things, and acceptance. Kübler-Ross never recommended that people accept death as a prelude to another form of life. She argued that death is as natural as birth. Both are part of life. She maintains that acceptance of the fact of death is realistic and the ideal response to it. People can learn to move beyond denial, anger, bargaining, and depression.

Christians agree that death is implicit in our finitude and is to be accepted as unavoidable and inevitable. But Paul linked death to sin: "Therefore, just as through one person sin entered the world, and through sin, death, and thus death came to all, inasmuch as all sinned" (Rom. 5:12). Christians do not link death exclusively to sin. But the relationship of sin and death makes death a powerful, premoral force. If death were not premoral (inevitable and harmful), then the resurrection of Christ would be stripped of its true significance. Christians accept death because it leads to resurrection. Paul reminds the Corinthians that God has given us the victory over death through Christ (1 Cor. 15:57).

Christians confess in the Nicene-Constantinopolitan Creed that the victory they anticipate is "the resurrection of the dead, and the life of the world to come." But how do Christians understand and explain these words? It seems that today many hold with Greek philosophy that humans are made up of a body and a spirit, with the body being the cruder part of the duality. The body is actually a tomb in which the soul is encased until its liberation at death. This after-death state is superior to the unfortunate embodied soul, once trapped in mortal flesh. But this ancient explanation is not consonant with Paul's literal description of Jesus' resurrected body. Paul insists that God raised up Jesus to a transformed life, one which includes the body. The risen Jesus became a spiritual body-person. He was not freed from his corporeal nature but in and with it. Christian humanism proclaims that the transformation he experienced will also happen to us at death. We do not know what this heavenly life will be like or what it will feel like; we cannot even imagine it. However, it is not Christian teaching that a soul escapes the body to go somewhere better, leaving all material being behind, to live as a pure spirit in a better place. Because of the incarnation and resurrection of Jesus, Christians believe their body is holy. While it is true that our body-person has been wounded by sin and must endure death's temporary triumph, "resurrection of the dead" means we will live on as spiritual body-persons. Just as Jesus died and was raised to the Father's glorious life, so will the Father bring us to his glorious life with Christ, his Paraclete-Spirit, and all the people of God. The ongoing drama will still be unfinished and full of surprises—but all of them joyful.

Postscript: The Center and Its Boundaries

Over the course of Christian history there have been many statements about the center or nucleus of Christianity. Some New Testament declarations are brief (see Eph. 4:4–6; 1 Tim. 3:16; 1 Cor. 15:3–5) and some are long (see 1 Thes. 1:2–10). After the New Testament period, statements of the faith often took the form of creeds, official professions of the faith, usually promulgated by an ecumenical council and used in the liturgy. The Apostles' Creed, considered to be a faithful summary of the apostles' faith, was proclaimed at baptisms in the churches of Rome. The Nicene-Constantinopolitan Creed, which stems from ecumenical councils in the fourth century, is prayerfully recited by Catholics during the Eucharist on Sundays and major feast days, and by Eastern Catholics and the Orthodox communities at every Eucharist.

Creeds draw a line between essentials and nonessentials. In Vatican II's *Decree on Ecumenism,* the bishops called attention to the fact that there exists an "order or 'hierarchy'" of importance among church doctrines, "since they vary in their relation to the foundation of the Christian faith" (n. 11). A majority of Christians would agree that the following teachings are central and foundational for Christianity: the Trinity, the incarnation of the Word of God, the death and resurrection of Jesus of Nazareth, the Paraclete-Spirit, the primacy of God's grace, the divine origin of the church, the importance of baptism and other ecclesial sacraments, the resurrection to eternal life, and the parousia. All of these teachings are in the Nicene-Constantinopolitan Creed. The Lima Declaration of 1982 proposed that all Christian churches accept this creed as an expression of the apostolic faith. However, nearly every major Christian community would want to add to the doctrines listed above. "Lutherans would presumably want to highlight justification by faith and perhaps, in some sense, the sufficiency of scripture. Episcopalians would insist on the episcopal office and the early creeds; the Orthodox, on tradition and the Eucharist; and Roman Catholics, on the papacy" (Dulles 1986, 34). We have seen, nonetheless, that due to many enlightened interconfessional dialogues, there is a growing theological refinement and consensus on all these issues.

Creeds are usually nuanced by the contemporary social, cultural, and religious situation. Paul and his Corinthian community in the early 50s might have endorsed this creed that summarizes their past, present, and future:

> We believe that God the Father of Jesus Christ has freed us from sin, the law, the flesh and death and for authentic human existence in Christ through his Son's death and resurrection. The resurrected Christ has established his church, the Israel of God, through the presence, gifts, and power of the Spirit.
>
> We believe that in this time of Roman imperialism, Greco-Roman culture, interreligious tensions and conflicts, and widespread slavery, poverty, and immorality, that all people, including slaves, women, and Gentiles, who profess the gospel that Jesus is Lord and Christ and are baptized by the Spirit into Christ's death are saved and can participate in his community, a community of faith, peace, unity, love, hope, and service.
>
> We believe that Jesus is the way to the kingdom of God and his parousia is imminent.

The Nicene-Constantinopolitan Creed was written to meet the religious situation of the fourth century. Arius, a popular and influential priest of Alexandria, taught that since the scriptures never stated that Jesus is the *eternal* Word of God, then at some point in time the Father created him. The Council of

Nicea in 325 A.D. confessed that the Son is God and is not a creature; he is "eternally begotten of the Father, God from God, Light from Light, true God from true God." Athanasius, bishop of Alexandria, explained that while the phrases in the creed "are not in so many words in the scriptures, yet they contain the sense of the scriptures."

Creeds, since they are summaries of the center of the faith, require considerable explanation. But the explanations can and do change, and not everyone ratifies the interpretation. It is not easy to set boundaries. Nevertheless, boundaries are indispensable. For example, we have seen that the theology of the parousia has received many interpretations over the course of Christian history. Even Paul in the late 50s no longer confessed that the parousia was imminent. Nonetheless, at the center of the Christian faith is the conviction that God will ultimately triumph over the forces of evil (sin and death). It is simply not logical to believe in the death-resurrection of Christ and not believe his death has already achieved a decisive victory over death and sin (1 Cor. 15:56–57).

The church's creeds do not speak directly to Christian humanism. This theology is latent in both the doctrines and the pronouns *I* or *we,* which form the subject of the creeds. Christian humanism has been given many different expressions and meanings over the centuries. For the author of Hebrews, Jesus is the quintessential Christian humanist because he is "the leader and perfecter of faith" (12:2) and is like us in all things except sin (4:15). The Pauline understanding of Christian humanism is quite clear: put on the mind of Christ (Phil. 2:5). To be "in Christ" means to be another Christ in thought, word, and deed. Christians strive to live a life of faith, hope, and love in Christ through the Spirit.

We have seen that not all Christians understand or live Christian humanism in the same way. Some explanations and lifestyles fall outside the boundaries of Christianity. Paul's enemies, the Judaizers, maintained that Christian humanism must first be solidly grounded in Jewish humanism. Their position was rejected by the apostolic assembly in Jerusalem (Acts 15). The second-century Gnostics limited humanism to an elite who would eventually be freed from the restrictions of the material world in order to live an angelic existence. In the sixteenth century Luther and Calvin taught that the Fall so corrupted and depraved human nature that Christian humanism was beyond our grasp. The grace of God merely camouflaged the fact that humanity is mired in sin. In the early part of the twentieth century the Pentecostals' heightened sense of human dignity based on the presence and charisms of the Spirit was almost shattered when some of the churches divided along racial lines. Catholics, too, have at times lost sight of the meaning of Christian humanism. For example, on January 25, 1995, the Catholic bishops of Germany stated that Catholics share responsibility for the massacre of Jews by the Nazis. January 25 was the fiftieth anniversary of the liberation of Auschwitz, where almost one million Jews were brutally executed. The bishops deplored the failure of German Catholics to resist the racist anti-Semitism of the Nazis. In Christ Jesus "there is neither Jew nor Greek" (Gal. 3:28). Other Christian communities have also succumbed to racism at times. On June 25, 1995, the Southern Baptist Convention adopted a resolution renouncing its racist roots and apologized for its defense of slavery at the time of the Civil War. In Christ Jesus, "there is neither slave nor free person" (Gal. 3:28).

Secular humanists reject religion and Christian humanism. But, ironically, some of them highlight aspects of human dignity that are central to Christian humanism. Albert Camus declared that life was meaningless and yet in his novels (e.g., *The Plague*, 1948), he endorsed the unconditional values of honesty and compassion. Jean-Paul Sartre (1957) rejected the existence of any unconditional values, but he consistently and unconditionally affirmed the value of freedom.

One conclusion to this study is that the center of Christianity can be found in the official creeds, but explaining this center and setting its outer limits have always been problematic because we are dealing with a great mystery that has been "made known to all nations to bring about the obedience of faith" (Rom. 16:26). When the Faith and Order Commission met at Lima in 1982 and proposed that all churches accept the Nicene Creed as an expression of that apostolic faith, it also called for a common explication of the creed for the contemporary situation and it recommended steps towards composing a contemporary creed that would be subject to the ancient creed as a criterion. In view of these perspectives, I propose the following creed for contemporary Christians as we prepare for the third millennium.

We believe that God, Creator of all things, raised up the Israelites from the nations through Abraham, Sarah, Deborah, Ruth, Moses, David and the prophets to be a holy and loving people, faithful to God, the sacred Torah, the temple and the covenants.

We also believe that the God of Israel and all people has manifested himself in a definitive way in the life, death, and resurrection of Jesus of Nazareth, through the power of the Spirit. We believe that the one, holy, catholic, and apostolic Church of Christ, despite its divisions, sinfulness, parochialism and self-centeredness, has been proclaiming and manifesting the God who creates, covenants, loves and saves.

We believe that at this time of widespread involuntary poverty, extensive violence, ecological crises, interreligious tensions and conflicts, scandalous church divisions and secular humanism that Jesus of Nazareth, the risen Son of God and Messiah, teaches us through the Paraclete-Spirit these "seven unities": that life is from God (God creates), that life is ultimately good (God covenants), that life is gracious (God loves), that the good will triumph over evil (God saves), that life's meaning transcends this world (Christ's cross), that we can be sisters and brothers living in peace and love (Christ's Eucharist), and that each human life has dignity and purpose (Christ's Paraclete-Spirit).

We believe that the resurrected Christ will fully establish the reign of God at the parousia. However, since we do not know when or how this will occur, our mission in the power of the Paraclete-Spirit is to unite with the risen Christ as he continues his threefold mission of teaching, witnessing, and serving the reign of God throughout the entire world.

Notes

Chapter 1

1. An editorial, "The Big Thirst," *Commonweal* 121 (25 March 1994): 3–5.
2. A report, "Mandela's Address: 'Glory and Hope,'" *New York Times,* 11 May 1994.

Chapter 2

1. See letter to the editor by Jane M. Friedman in *New York Times,* 16 March 1995, in response to an article, "Tomb of Ramses II's Many Sons Is Found in Egypt" (front page, May 16).
2. A news notice, "Stadium Postponed," *Christian Century* 96 (12 September 1979): 842.

Chapter 3

1. A news notice, "Episcopal Bishop Blasts 'Feminist' Lobby," *Christian Century* 111 (2 November 1994): 1009–10.

Chapter 5

1. A news notice, "Paisley vs. the Pope," *Christian Century* 105 (2 November 1988): 978.
2. A news notice, "Protesters Denounce Anglican Archbishop over Ecumenism," *National Catholic Reporter* 26 (2 February 1990): 9.
3. A news notice, "More SBC Dissent on Accord with Catholics," *Christian Century* 111 (5 October 1994): 889.

Chapter 7

1. A news notice, "World's AIDS Cases Top a Million, U.N. Reports," *New York Times,* 4 January 1995.
2. A news notice, "Lutherans Abandon Sexuality Study," *Christian Century* 111 (2 November 1994): 1007–8.
3. A news notice, "ELCA Issues New Sexuality Report," *Christian Century* 111 (23 November 1994): 1105.

4. An editorial, "Investment in Children Is Sign of Evolutionary Insight," *National Catholic Reporter* 29 (12 March 1993): 28.

5. A news notice, "Health Care Reform and Neighbor Love," *Christian Century* 111 (23 March 1994): 305–6.

6. An editorial, "America Doubled," *New York Times,* 1 April 1990.

7. A news notice, "Defining *Homosexual* Elusive for UMC," *Christian Century* 111 (23 November 1994): 1106.

8. A news notice, "PCUSA Cancels Appearance by Spahr," *Christian Century* 111 (23 November 1994): 1105–6.

9. A news notice, "Sex Issues Are Central at Episcopal Meeting," *Christian Century* 111 (12 October 1994): 920.

Glossary

Aaronites: The older brother of Moses was Aaron. He and his four sons were anointed by Moses to start Israel's priesthood (Num. 3:1–3). Priestly descendants of Aaron's family were called Aaronites. The wife of Zechariah, the mother of John the Baptist, was herself of the lineage of Aaron (Lk. 1:5).

Actualization, Process of: (see critical method).

Angel: From the Greek *angelos,* which translates a Hebrew word meaning "messenger." Angels were commonly conceived in biblical times as emissaries from God who symbolically communicated his will to select people. Many scholars suggest that Israel's angelology derives from close contacts with the Persians from 538 to 333 B.C.

Apocalyptic: From the Greek *apokalypsis,* meaning "an uncovering" or "a revealing." Many biblical authors claimed that God had "uncovered" for them (revealed to them) his message (Gal. 1:12). The term "apocalyptic eschatology" refers to the time when the future will be brought about by terrible destruction. Both John the Baptist and Jesus spoke in these terms.

Apocalypticism: This is a comprehensive name for a style of thought and writing that emphasized signs, visions, and predictions of future events brought about by divine power. The years from approximately 200 B.C. to 100 A.D. were marked by this phenomenon. Thus in the gospels Jesus is asked for signs but says none will be given but the sign of Jonah (Mt. 12:39–41). The Book of Revelation (6:12–14) states that before Christ returns there will be signs in the heavens, in the stars, moon, and sun.

Apocrypha: From the Greek *apocryphos,* meaning "hidden." The word is used to denote those books that were not accepted into the final canon of the Hebrew and Jewish scriptures.

Apostate: From the Greek *apostates,* meaning "deserter" or "rebel." It denotes those who abandon or reject their religious faith. These persons cease to profess and practice their religion, often for material advantage, e.g., to get an education, to retain a job, or to escape persecution and even death.

Apostle: From the Greek *apostolus,* meaning "messenger" or "envoy" or "one who is sent." The word was used to describe missionaries in the apostolic church. The word is not coextensive with the twelve disciples.

Aramaic: This was the language of the Arameans, Syrians who dwelt in parts of Mesopotamia from about 1000 B.C. Jews spoke the language after the Babylonian exile in 587 B.C. A Galilean dialect of Aramaic was probably the language spoken by Jesus. Two of his words are *Abba* (father) and *Amen* (truly or indeed).

Babylonian Exile: From 587 to 538 B.C., many Jews were held captive in Babylon. After Cyrus of Persia conquered Babylon in 539, Jews who wished to do so were encouraged to return to their Palestinian homeland.

Base communities: These informal, action-oriented lay circles received encouragement and the stamp of approval from the Latin American bishops at their meeting in 1968 at Medellín. Base communities are small, voluntary associations of lay Catholics who, for the most part, are poor people who seek to free themselves from oppressive circumstances, especially those that are socioeconomic and political. The communities meet on a regular basis to reflect upon community needs and seek fitting solutions to those needs. The groups devote much of their time to religious activities. They study the scriptures, celebrate Eucharist, and seek ways to spread the gospel.

Beatitudes: Jesus begins his Sermon on the Mount with a list of blessings (Mt. 5:3–12). Luke has a variation of these pronouncements in his Sermon on the Plain (Lk. 6:20–23).

Blasphemy: This means a person speaks lightly or carelessly of God. The second commandment says one should not misuse God's name. Jesus was accused of blasphemy (Mt. 9:3, 26:65; Lk 5:31; Jn. 10:33).

Caiaphas: As high priest from 18 to 36 A.D., he presided over Jesus' trial. He declared that it would be better for Jesus to die than that the whole nation be destroyed (Jn. 11:49–53). His father-in-law had been high priest from 7 to 14, having been appointed by the Roman governor.

Calvary: This is the place outside the walls of Jerusalem where Jesus was crucified. The actual location is unknown. The word derives from the Latin word *calvaria,* a translation of the Greek *kranion,* which means "skull." The Aramaic word for skull is *Golgatha* (see Mt. 27:33; Jn. 19:17).

Canon: From the Greek *kanon,* which means something made of reeds. It came to be used of an authoritative list which serves as a "measuring rod." The books accepted as authoritative scripture are called the "canon." In some Christian churches the term "canon law" refers to a list of laws, disciplines, and regulations.

Catholic: From the Latin *catholicus,* meaning "universal" or "general." It is used of the church as a whole as distinct from one particular part of the church, e.g. the "Latin American church." After the Reformation it distinguishes the Roman Catholic Church from the Lutheran Church and other Protestant churches.

Centurion: This is the name given to a Roman officer in charge of one hundred soldiers.

Christology: From the Greek *christos,* meaning "anoint," which translates the Hebrew *messiah.* Christology is the ascription of titles, honor, and even divinity to Jesus of Nazareth, because of who he is and what he has done (and continues to do) to bring freedom from sin and death and for wholeness and life to all humankind.

Church: From the Greek *ekklesia,* meaning "the assembly called out." It can refer to the universal or international church as well as individual churches or congregations.

Corinth: This seaport city was a center of trade and commerce in ancient Greece. It was the home of a large population of hellenistic Jews and, under the leadership of Paul and his associates, became a Christian center.

Covenant: From the Hebrew *berith,* meaning either "to fetter" or "to eat with," which would signify mutual obligation (1 Sam. 17:8). It denotes the various contracts or compacts made between God and his people. The Israelites had covenants with God through Abraham, Moses, and David. Christians say Jesus formed a new covenant or testament (Mt. 26:28; 2 Cor. 3:6), one which encompasses all people.

Critical Method: This is a method of interpreting texts that moves from the meaning intended by the author to the meaning found by the reader. The Pontifical Biblical Commission referred to this method as a "process of actualization." "Actualization" means that the significance of the biblical text as God's word is applied to contemporary circumstances. This method can be used with all classical texts, religious or secular, because words have a life of their own and the nature of classical texts is such that they have a wealth of meaning, which gives them a value for all times and all cultures.

Deacon: From the Greek *diakonos,* meaning "servant." It indicated those in an order of the Christian ministry. They had an important role in the apostolic church (Acts 6:1–8). Paul used the term for himself (1 Cor. 3:5) and told Timothy how to be a good servant/minister (1 Tim. 4:6). The Greek word is used of a woman, Phoebe (Rom. 16:1). Many churches still ordain deacons.

Devil: From two Greek words with different meanings: *diabolos,* "the accuser" (Jn. 8:44); *daimonion,* one of the evil spirits who was thought to cause diseases (see Mt: 10:25; Mk. 3:22; Lk. 11:14–16). In the Hebrew scriptures, Satan is the "adversary" or the "opponent," as in the Book of Job. His role in this book is to test Job's fidelity to God in the midst of adversity. In Revelation 12:9, Satan is identified with the devil, Lucifer (chief of the fallen angels), and the serpent of Genesis. The Devil is traditionally understood as being engaged in a worldwide and age-long struggle against God, ever seeking to defeat God's plans by seducing people to commit evil.

Diaspora: A Greek word meaning "a dispersion" or a "scattering." It denotes the communities of Jews living outside their ancestral homeland, Palestine (Israel).

Docetism: From the Greek *dokein,* meaning "to seem" or "appear." This was an early teaching which held that Jesus was only divine and only "seemed" to have a human body.

Doctrine, Development of: This denotes the process whereby official teachings are revised in accordance with changes in historical circumstances and understanding.

Elohist: Sections of the Pentateuch are so designated because their anonymous author favored the use of *Elohim* (a Semitic term for a divine being) to denote the Hebrew deity. The word is actually plural and referred to foreign deities (Ex. 15:2). Nevertheless, the Elohist used the word for the God of their nation.

Encyclical: From the Greek *enkuklios,* meaning "in a circle" or "circular." It is an official and major letter written by a church authority that is "circulated" throughout the whole church and (more recently) beyond the church to all people of good will.

End-time: In Jewish theology this term refers to the new age that will follow the final day in history. The end-time is a central theme in apocalyptic literature such as the books of Daniel and Revelation. At the end-time, God will fully establish his kingdom. From the very first, Israel's faith had been oriented toward the future—toward the fulfillment of the promises God made to Abraham. For the Jews, history is not spinning in circles, like the cycle of the seasons. History is a great drama which, under the direction of God, is moving toward a final consummation when God's victory over the powers of evil will be completed.

Ephesus: This wealthy hellenistic city was the site of the famous temple of Artemis/Diana (Acts 19–20) and probably the center of the Johannine church.

Eschatology: From the Greek *eschatos,* meaning "furthest," and *logos,* meaning "word" or "teaching." Literally, it means "the study of the last things." It refers to a study of the last things or the end of human history as we know it. It also refers to the future events we plan that already have an impact on the present. Jesus spoke of the kingdom of God as even now present.

Evangelist: From the Greek *evangelion,* meaning "good news." It refers first of all to the authors of the four gospels. It also denotes those preachers who traveled from place to place proclaiming the gospel (Acts 6:1–5).

Exegesis: A Greek word which means "to show the way." It denotes the method of those trained to give a critical analysis or explanation of the scriptures, especially the original author's intent and meaning.

Exodus: A Greek term meaning "a going out" or "departure." In the Hebrew scriptures it refers to the escape of the Israelite slaves from Egypt under the leadership of Moses. This event is considered Yahweh's crucial saving act in their history (Ex. 15).

Exorcism: The act of expelling a demon or evil spirit from a person or place. Jesus performs many exorcisms in the synoptic gospels but none in the gospel of John.

Fall, The: The disobedience of Adam and Eve (Gen. 3) resulted in their alienation from God and their loss of innocence. According to some interpretations of Paul's theology (especially Rom. 5:12–21; 1 Cor. 15:45–49), the fall of the first parents brought on their death and a self-alienation that subsequently has affected the response of all humankind to God's many loving initiatives.

Form Criticism: The term is a translation of the German *Formgeschichte,* which literally means "form history." It is a study of the various literary forms used in the scriptures, namely, myths, parables, poetry, hymns, miracle stories, and so forth. This method of scriptural study attempts to uncover the oral tradition of the first Christians, which made its way into the gospels. This teaching took the form of prayers, hymns, and narratives as the Christians introduced people to the core and outer limits of the Christian faith.

Fundamentalist: It refers to any religious person or group that interprets its scripture and official doctrines without considering their historical formation, literary form, and the meaning intended by the author. It is opposed to the historical-critical method of interpretation. In the United States the term refers to a movement among Protestants in the nineteenth century who insisted on the literal sense of the scriptures inasmuch as they are the inspired and inerrant word of God.

Fundamental Option: This term refers to the radical orientation of a person's whole life (personal, social, economic, and so forth) toward or away from God. This concept has been stressed in modern moral theology in order to counteract the strong focus of previous teachings on the morality of individual acts. In the past, many immoral acts were considered so objectively evil that the person committing the actions was declared to be automatically and completely alienated from God.

Galilee: The word is from the Hebrew term *Glil ha-goyim,* meaning "circle of the Gentiles." It referred to a section of northern Palestine lying west of the Jordan River. It is here that Jesus grew up in the town of Nazareth (Mt. 2:23).

Gethsemane: It denotes the site of an orchard or garden on the Mount of Olives where Jesus took his disciples after the Last Supper and the place where he was arrested (Jn. 18:1–14).

Gnosticism: From the Greek *gnosis,* meaning "knowledge." In the second century there were elite communities in the Greco-Roman world who believed that salvation was attainable through special knowledge by those initiated into its mysteries. This thinking infiltrated the Christian community and became quite widespread. The official Christian community rejected this teaching because it denied the salvation achieved by the life, death, and resurrection of Jesus. In 1945 a collection of Gnostic writings was discovered in Egypt. These writings may have been written as early as the last part of the first century.

Gospel: From the Middle English *godspell,* meaning "good spell," i.e., "good news." Originally, it referred to the good news of what God had done in the life, death, and resurrection of Jesus. Later it designated the four literary forms composed to narrate and proclaim the Christ-event.

Hellenization: From the Greek *hellenismos,* meaning "imitation of the Greeks." It denotes the spread of the Greek culture in the world conquered by Alexander the Great. Due to increased association, people adopted Greek language, art, architecture, and so forth.

Heresy: From the Greek *hairein,* meaning "to choose." Literally, it means a "choice" of some teachings rather than the official teachings of the community.

Historical-Critical Method: This is a method of biblical studies employed to uncover what actually happened and what the author meant. It includes the search for both the original words and deeds of Jesus and the literal meaning intended by authors of the scriptures. This method is based in part on a theological and philosophical mentality that is attentive to the impact of history on all aspects of human life and thought.

Indifferentism: This is a theological outlook that holds that one religion or ecclesial body is as good (of equal value) as any other.

Indulgence: The partial or full remission of the temporal punishment still due to sins which have already been forgiven.

James: There are three men with this name in the Christian scriptures.
  a. The son of Zebedee, brother of John, and a Galilean fisherman who was one of the twelve (Mk. 1:19–20). He was beheaded during the persecution of the Jerusalem church (41–44 A.D.) by Herod Agrippa.
  b. The son of Alphaeus and Mary (Mk. 16:1). He was one of the twelve and sometimes called "the less" or "the younger" (Mk. 15:40).
  c. The elder brother of Jesus (Mk. 6:3). It seems that he first opposed Jesus (Mk. 3:31–35), but was apparently converted by a special resurrection appearance (1 Cor. 15:7). He later became the leader in the Jerusalem church (Acts 15:13–34; 21:18–26).

Judaism: The name given to the religion of the people of Judah ("the Jews") after the northern kingdom of Israel was defeated by the Assyrians (721 B.C.).

Kerygma: The Greek word for "proclamation." It is used to denote the preaching of the central message of the Christian gospel as a whole or of any part of it. Jesus' proclamation (*kerygma*) centered on his Father, whereas the early Christians proclaimed what God had done in and through Christ.

Liberation Theology: The Bible abounds with calls for the liberation of people from their spiritual, psychological, political, and socioeconomic oppression. Liberation theology emphasizes the motif of liberation by identifying with those in need and by critically interpreting the scriptures and church doctrines in terms of freedom. Liberation theology emerged in the 1960s in Latin America, Africa, and Asia, areas of the world where many, many people suffer from a lack of spiritual and material goods necessary to live a human existence.

Literary criticism: The study of the various literary types found in the Bible: myth, parables, infancy narratives, resurrection narratives, and so forth. Scholars attempt to determine the sources of these texts, the stages of composition from oral to written form, and the kind of editing they received by the inspired authors.

Mary: The Hebrew is *Miryam* (Miriam) and the Latin and Greek is *Maria*. There are six women with this name in the Christian scriptures.
   a. Mary the mother of Jesus. She was the wife of Joseph. She was present at Pentecost (Acts 1:13–14).
   b. Mary Magdalene was from the town of Magdala. Jesus cast seven demons out of her (Lk. 8:1–2). She was a faithful disciple who was probably the first to see the resurrected Jesus (Mt. 28:9).
   c. Mary, the sister of Martha and Lazarus. Jesus was a close friend of this family and frequently visited their home in Bethany (Lk. 10:38–42).
   d. Mary, the wife of Cleophas. She was a witness of Jesus' death and burial. She also saw the resurrected Jesus (Mt. 27:56–61).
   e. Mary, the sister of Barnabas and the mother of John Mark. Her home in Jerusalem was a meeting place for the disciples (Acts 12:12).
   f. Mary, an anonymous woman mentioned by Paul (Rom. 16:6).

Nicene-Constantinopolitan Creed: This is a formal summary of the Christian faith that was accepted by the bishops at the ecumenical Council of Nicea in 325 and confirmed at the Council of Constantinople in 381. It has been known by its present name since the seventh century. (See p. xxxi)

Oral tradition: Material passed from generation to generation by word of mouth before being given written form. Much of Israel's early history, customs, and laws were so transmitted. The apostolic teachings were first proclaimed. Later these teachings were written in the gospels and the other books that form the Christian canon.

Papacy: see pope.

Parable: From the Greek *parabole,* meaning "a placing beside" or "a comparison." It is a short fictional narrative that compares something familiar to something unexpected. Jesus uses this form in the synoptics to teach about the kingdom of God.

Paraclete: From the Greek *paracletos,* meaning "one called alongside to help." It is a legal term, hence it is translated as "advocate" or "counsellor," that is, one who supports a defendant at a trial. This title for the Holy Spirit is special to the writings of the Johannine church (Jn. 14:12, 16–18; 1 Jn 2:1).

Parousia: It is the Greek word for "presence," "arrival," and "coming." For the Greeks it was a technical term to denote the visit to a city or a province of a high official, especially an emperor or king. In the New Testament it came to be used of the expected arrival of Christ in glory to bring the kingdom of God to completion.

Pascal Mystery: From the Hebrew *pesah* and the Greek *paska,* meaning "passing over." For the Jews it refers to their passing from slavery to freedom during the exodus with Moses. For Christians it denotes the whole redemptive "passing over" of Jesus from human existence marked by sin and death to the life of God. Jesus passed over both sin and death through his life, death, and resurrection. Christians participate in this mystery through baptism, the Eucharist, and the other ecclesial sacraments.

Peter: He was the most prominent of the twelve disciples. He was also known as Simon, which was probably his surname. He is also called *Cephas,* which is the Aramaic equivalent of *petros,* meaning "the rock" or "stone" (Jn. 1:40–42). He was the son of John or Jonas (Mt. 16:17; Jn. 1:42, 21:15–17). He and his brother Andrew were fishermen from Bethsaida, a fishing village on the Sea of Galilee (Jn. 1:44).

Pleroma: A Greek word meaning "fullness." Christians used the word to denote the divine realm.

Pope: From the Latin *papa,* meaning "father." This title was used by priests and bishops in the early church but in the eleventh century it was reserved to the bishop of Rome. Catholics consider the pope the "father" or spiritual leader of the church community. His role is to unify the church and strengthen its faith. He is regarded as the successor of Peter. Pope John Paul II is the 264th successor of Peter.

Precritical Method: See Fundamentalist.

Psalm: A song or poem used in praise or worship of God. There are 150 psalms in the Book of Psalms.

Q: An abbreviation for *Quelle,* the German word for "source." Many scholars believe there was a document that contained a collection of Jesus' saying. The theory of its existence was formed to explain material common to both Matthew and Luke but absent from Mark.

Qumran: There was an Essene community located near the northwest corner of the Dead Sea that was destroyed by the Romans around 68 A.D. Near these ruins are caves in which the Essenes hid their scrolls. Some of their documents were discovered in 1947. They are important because they provide ancient versions of much of the Hebrew scriptures and also writings by the Essenes themselves about their community, customs, and beliefs.

Rabbi: A Jewish title meaning "teacher" or "master." It was used for scholars learned in the Torah. Jesus was frequently addressed by this title. In Matthew's gospel, however, Jesus' followers call him "Lord"; nonbelievers call him rabbi.

Redaction Criticism: It is the translation of the German *Redaktionsgeschichte,* which literally means "redaction history." It is the study of the editing of traditional material as it is transmitted or used. It is the attempt to define the purpose(s) of the editors or redactors.

Revelation: From the Latin *revelare,* meaning "to unveil" or "to make known." It means to make known what has heretofore been kept secret. For Christians it denotes God's self-disclosure or self-communication through creation, covenants, events, and persons, especially the life, death, and resurrection of Jesus.

Salvation: From the Latin words *salus* and *salvare,* meaning "health" and "to save," respectively. It means to be made whole and freed from sin and death.

Samaritans: They were the inhabitants of the territory of Samaria, the central region of Palestine lying west of the Jordan River. According to 2 Kings 17, they were descendants of foreigners who had intermarried with survivors of the Assyrian invasion of 721 B.C. They had become distinct and separate from the rest of Judaism around 400 B.C. inasmuch as by then they had canonized their own edition of the Pentateuch and had built their own temple on Mount Gerizim. This temple was destroyed around 128 B.C. by the Maccabean ruler John Hyrcanus.

Sanhedrin: The word is a Hebrew transcription of the Greek *synedrion,* meaning "a council." It was the highest Jewish tribunal during the Greek and Roman periods. According to Acts 9:2, its influence was recognized even in the diaspora. However, it is believed that during the time of the Roman procurators its authority was restricted to Judea. Its members were drawn from the chief priests, the elders, and the teachers of the law (Lk. 9:22). It did not have the power to use capital punishment. That is why Jesus had to be delivered over to the Roman procurator, Pontius Pilate.

Secular Humanism: It is a system of thought that denies the existence of an unseen supernatural order, what most religions call God. Secular humanists believe that they are left to their own initiatives in enhancing life in this "world" (from the Latin *saeculum*), because they can expect no divine guidance. Some secular humanists are virulently antireligious; others are not. The bishops at Vatican II praised the positive dimensions of secular humanism, calling it a "new humanism," because humanists want to cooperate with others in solving the outstanding problems of our times and to give human history a positive direction.

Septuagint: The Latin word *septuaginata* means "seventy." The term refers to the Greek translation of the Hebrew scriptures around 250 B.C. in Egypt. The abbreviation is LXX. The Greek translation received its name from the legend that the scriptures were translated in 70 days by 72 scholars.

Silas: This Christian prophet (Acts 15:32) is also known as Silvanus. He accompanied Barnabas and Paul to the Jerusalem assembly (Acts 15) and participated in Paul's second missionary journey.

Source criticism: It consists in an analysis of a biblical document to discover the written and oral sources used by an author. For example, the source of the sayings of Jesus in Matthew and Luke is called Q.

Symbol: It is any person, place, thing, or event that we perceive with our senses or grasp with our minds, but in which we see something other than itself. Symbols are signs which make something present and take its place. For many Christians any created reality can be a sign and instrument of God's presence, love, or judgment.

Synagogue: From the Greek *synagoge,* meaning "place of assembly." It is a Jewish institution for worship, the reading and explanation of the scriptures, and the administration of local Jewish affairs. It originated perhaps as early as the Babylonian exile (587 B.C.). To have a synagogue ten adult males had to be present. By the time of Jesus, synagogues were firmly established everywhere in the Mediterranean world where there were sufficient Jews to maintain one.

Synoptic gospels: From the Greek *synoptikos,* meaning "seeing the whole together." The gospels of Mark, Matthew, and Luke are given this name because they tell the same general story in the same kind of way of Jesus' ministry and death.

Textual Criticism: It is the comparison and analysis of ancient manuscripts to discover copyists' errors and, if possible, to reconstruct the true or original form of the document.

Theophany: This word is from Greek words that mean "to show God." It is a manifestation of God to people. In the scriptures these manifestations are described symbolically, e.g., the burning bush seen by Moses and the light that surrounds Paul on the road to Damascus. Theophanies are faith experiences that are impossible to describe except with symbols since they are eschatological events at the extreme limit of the imaginable. God is visible yet invisible, comprehensible yet incomprehensible, and within and yet beyond space and time.

Timothy: Paul called his friend and fellow missionary his "beloved son" (1 Cor. 4:17). Timothy was the son of a Greek father and devout Jewish mother (Acts 16:1). He was sent by Paul to deliver messages to the church at Macedonia and Corinth. The picture of him in the Epistle to Timothy is irreconcilable with what is known of him from Acts and Paul's genuine letters.

Titus: He was a Greek who was converted by Paul and who became one of his companions on his missionary journeys (2 Cor. 8:23; Gal. 2:1–3). Sent by Paul to Corinth, Titus was able to effect a reconciliation between the Corinthians and Paul (2 Cor. 7:5–7, 8:16–24, 12:18).

Tribes of Israel, Twelve: They are derived from the twelve sons of Jacob. His sons were named Reuben, Simeon, Levi, Judah, Issachar, Zebulum, Joseph, Benjamin, Gad, Asher, Dan, and Naphtali (Gen. 49:2–28). Although they had a common father, they had four mothers. The first six sons were children of Leah, Jacob's first wife. Benjamin and Joseph were the sons of Rachel, Jacob's favorite wife; Gad and Asher were the sons of Zilpah, Jacob's slave girl; and Dan and Naphtali were the sons of Bilhah, another of Jacob's concubines. The tribe of Joseph was later divided into the tribes of Ephraim and Manasseh, Joseph's grandsons.

Twelve, The: The twelve men, symbolizing the twelve tribes, called by Jesus to be his disciples (Mt. 10:2). After the resurrection they proclaimed the gospel and helped establish the church.

Bibliography

Abbott, Walter M., ed. 1966. *The Documents of Vatican II*. New York: Paulist Press.

Allegro, John. 1970. *The Sacred Mushroom and the Cross: A Study of the Nature and Origin of Christianity within the Fertility Cults of the Ancient Near East*. London: Hodder and Stoughton.

Anderson, Bernhard W. 1975. *Understanding the Old Testament*. 3rd ed. New Jersey: Prentice-Hall, Inc.

Armstrong, Karen. 1993. *A History of God*. New York: Ballantine Books.

Baum, Gregory. 1972. "Eucharistic Hospitality." *The Ecumenist* 11 (November): 11–16.

———. 1974. "Catholic Homosexuals." *Commonweal* 99 (15 February): 479–82.

———. 1975. *Religion and Alienation: A Theological Reading of Sociology*. New York: Paulist Press.

———. 1976. "Liberation Theology: First the Theory." *National Catholic Reporter* 12 (8 October): 8–9.

———. 1979. "Catholic Foundations of Human Rights." *The Ecumenist* 18 (November): 6–12.

———. 1983. "Gutiérrez and the Catholic Tradition." *The Ecumenist* 21 (September): 81–84.

———. 1984a. "Faith and Liberation: Development Since Vatican II." In *Vatican II: Open Questions and New Horizons,* edited by Gerald M. Fagin, 75–104. Wilmington, Del.: Michael Glazier.

———. 1984b. "Class Struggle and the Magisterium: A New Note." *Theological Studies* 45 (December): 690–701.

———. 1985. "After Liberal Optimism, What?" *Commonweal* 112 (21 June): 368–70.

———. 1986a. "The Theology of the American Pastoral." *The Ecumenist* 24 (January): 17–22.

———. 1986b. "Catholic Inconsistencies." *The Ecumenist* 24 (January): 23–30.

————. 1987. *Theology and Society.* New York: Paulist Press.

————. 1989. "Structures of Sin." In *The Logic of Solidarity,* edited by Gregory Baum and Robert Ellsberg, 110–126. New York: Orbis Books.

Block, Alfred E. 1982. "Beirut Attacks Break Sacred Link Between Israel and Jews." *National Catholic Reporter* 18 (27 August): 1, 24.

Boff, Leonardo. 1989. *Faith on the Edge: Religion and Marginalized Existence.* New York: Harper and Row.

Borowitz, Eugene. 1980. *Contemporary Christologies: A Jewish Response.* New York: Paulist Press.

Boucher, Madeleine, et. al. 1980. "Women and Priestly Ministry: The New Testament Evidence." *Council for the Study of Religion* 11 (April): 44–46.

Boyd, Malcolm. 1965. *Are You Running with Me, Jesus?* New York: Holt, Rinehart and Winston.

Brockman, James R. 1979. "Seventeen Days in Puebla." *America* 140 (10 March): 180–83.

Brouwer, Arie R. 1986. "The Steps of Ecumenical Formation." *Christian Century* 103 (24 September): 803–5.

Brown, Raymond E. 1973. *The Virginal Conception and the Bodily Resurrection of Jesus.* New York: Paulist Press.

————. 1977. *The Birth of the Messiah.* New York: Doubleday.

————. 1979. *The Community of the Beloved Disciple.* New York: Paulist Press.

————. 1981. "'And the Lord Said'? Biblical Reflections on Scripture as the Word of God." *Theological Studies* 42 (March): 3–19.

————. 1984. *The Churches the Apostles Left Behind.* New York: Paulist Press.

————. 1985. *Biblical Exegesis and Church Doctrine.* New York: Paulist Press.

————. 1994. *The Death of the Messiah.* 2 vols. New York: Doubleday.

Brown, Raymond, Karl P. Donfried, and John Reumann. 1973. *Peter in the New Testament.* New York: Paulist Press.

Brown, Robert McAfee. 1980. "Starting Over: New Beginning Points for Theology." *Christian Century* 97 (14 May): 545–49.

————. 1986. "Leonardo Boff: Theologian for All Christians." *Christian Century* 103 (2 July): 615–18.

Bultmann, Rudolf. 1951–1955. *Theology of the New Testament.* 2 vols. New York: Charles Scribner's Sons.

Cahill, Lisa Sowle. 1985. "Humanity as Male and Female: The Ethics of Sexuality." In *Called to Love: Towards a Contemporary Christian Ethic,* edited by Francis A. Eigo, 79–95. Pa.: Villanova University Press.

————. 1987. "Divorced from Experience: Rethinking the Theology of Marriage." *Commonweal* 114 (27 March): 171–76.

————. 1990. "Can We Get Real about Sex?" *America* 163 (14 September): 497–99, 502–3.

Callahan, Sidney. 1994. "Why I Changed My Mind: Thinking about Gay Marriage." *Commonweal* 121 (22 April): 6–8.

Camus, Albert. 1948. *The Plague.* New York: Modern Library.

Carmody, John, and Denise Lardner Carmody. 1987. *Interpreting the Religious Experience.* New Jersey: Prentice-Hall, Inc.

Coleman, Gerald D. 1987. "The Vatican Statement on Homosexuality." *Theological Studies* 48 (December): 727–34.

Collins, John. 1989. "The Origin of the Qumran Community: A Review of the Evidence." In *To Touch the Text,* edited by Maurya P. Horgan and Paul J. Kobelski, 159–178. New York: Crossroad.

Collins, Raymond F. 1986. *Christian Morality: Biblical Foundations.* Notre Dame, Ind.: Univeristy of Notre Dame Press.

———. 1993. *Divorce in the New Testament.* Collegeville, Minn.: Liturgical Press.

Cowell, Alan. 1994. "Vatican Rejects Compromise on Abortion at U.N. Meeting." *New York Times,* 7 September.

Cox, Harvey. 1980. "Theology: What Is It? Who Does It? How Is It Done?" *Christian Century* 97 (24 September): 874–879.

———. 1988. *The Silencing of Leonardo Boff: The Vatican and the Future of World Christianity.* Oak Park, Ill.: Meyer Stone.

Cragg, Kenneth. 1988. *Readings in the Qur'an.* London: Collins Liturgical Publications.

Crossette, Barbara. 1994. "Population Debate: The Premises Are Changed." *New York Times,* 14 September.

Curran, Charles E. 1970. *Contemporary Problems in Moral Theology.* Notre Dame, Ind.: Fides Publishers.

———. 1972. *Catholic Moral Theology in Dialogue.* Notre Dame, Ind.: University of Notre Dame Press.

———. 1974. "Divorce: Catholic Theory and Practice in the United States." *American Ecclesiastical Review* 1968 (January): 3–34; (February): 75–79.

Cwiekowski, Frederick J. 1988. *The Beginnings of the Church.* New York: Paulist Press.

Deschner, John. 1986. "What To Do with a 'Convergence.'" *Commonweal* 113 (31 January): 50–52.

Desseux, Jacques. 1983. *Twenty Centuries of Ecumenism.* New York: Paulist Press.

Diamond, James J. 1975. "Abortion, Animation and Biological Hominization." *Theological Studies* 36 (June): 305–24.

Dodd, C.H. 1961. *The Parables of the Kingdom.* New York: Charles Scribner's Sons.

Doerflinger, Richard. 1985. "Who Are Catholics For a Free Choice?" *America* 153 (16 November): 312–17.

Dominion, Jack, and Hugh Montefiore. 1989. *God, Sex and Love.* Philadelphia: Trinity Press International.

Donahue, John R. 1981. "Divorce: New Testament Perspectives." *The Month* 242 (April): 113–20.

———. 1988. *The Gospel in Parable*. Philadelphia: Fortress Press.

Dorr, Donal. 1983. *Option for the Poor: A Hundred Years of Vatican Social Teaching*. New York: Paulist Press.

———. 1984. *Spirituality and Justice*. New York: Orbis Books.

Drozdiak, William. 1994. "U.S. Nuns Challenge Vatican Over Role of Women in the Church." *San Francisco Chronicle,* 28 October.

Dulles, Avery. 1982. "Toward a Christian Consensus: The Lima Meeting." *America* 146 (20 February): 126–29.

———. 1986. "Paths to Doctrinal Agreement: Ten Theses." *Theological Studies* 47 (March): 32–47.

———. 1989. "A Half Century of Ecclesiology." *Theological Studies* 50 (September): 419–42.

Dwyer, John C. 1987. *Foundations of Christian Ethics*. New York: Paulist Press.

Edwards, Robin T. 1994. "'No' Again to the Divorced and Remarried." *National Catholic Reporter* 31 (28 October): 10–11.

Evans, Craig, A. 1993. "Life-of-Jesus Research and the Eclypse of Mythology." *Theological Studies* 54 (March): 3–36.

Ferm, Deane William. 1986. *Third World Liberation Theologies: An Introductory Survey*. New York: Orbis Books.

———. 1988. *Profiles in Liberation: 39 Portraits of Third World Theologians*. Mystic, Conn.: Twenty-Third Publications.

Finley, Mitch. 1991. "The Dark Side of Natural Family Planning." *America* 164 (23 February): 206–7.

Fitzmyer, Joseph A. 1981. *To Advance the Gospel: New Testament Studies*. New York: Crossroad.

———. 1982. *A Christological Catechism: New Testament Answers*. New York: Paulist Press.

———. 1986. *Scripture and Christology*. New York: Paulist Press.

———. 1993. "The Interpretation of the Bible in the Church." *America* 169 (27 November): 12–15.

———. 1994. *Scripture: The Soul of Theology*. New York: Paulist Press.

Flanagan, Neal. 1986. *Friend Paul: His Letters, Theology and Humanity*. Wilmington, Del.: Michael Glazier.

Fletcher, Joseph. 1966. *Situation Ethics: The New Morality*. Philadelphia: Westminster Press.

Fox, Thomas. 1994. "Vatican OKs Most of U.N. Document after Cairo Tactics Stir Bitterness." *National Catholic Reporter* 30 (23 September): 8–9.

French, Howard W. 1992. "Protests Follow the Pope on Santo Domingo Visit." *New York Times,* 14 October.

Frost, William. 1982. "Sagan's *Cosmos:* Secular or Religious?" *The Ecumenist* 20 (March): 43–46.

Fuller, Reginald H. 1971. *The Formation of the Resurrection Narratives.* New York: Macmillan.

Fuller, Reginald H., and Pheme Perkins. 1983. *Who Is This Christ?* Philadelphia: Fortress.

Gadamer, Hans-Georg. 1975. *Truth and Method.* New York: Seabury Press.

Gallagher, John. 1990. *Times Past, Time Future: An Historical Study of Catholic Moral Theology.* New York: Paulist Press.

Geertz, Clifford. 1968. "Religion as a Cultural System." In *The Religious Situation: 1968,* edited by Donald Cutler, 639–88. Boston: Beacon Press.

Gibeau, Dawn. 1976. "God Puts His Foot in History." *National Catholic Reporter* 12 (15 September): 7–9.

———. 1994. "Color Coding, By Vote, What Jesus Said." *National Catholic Reporter* 30 (26 August): 6–7.

Gore, Albert. 1994. "What We Really Want: Less Need for Abortion." *Los Angeles Times,* 2 September.

Grabowski, John. 1994. "Divorce, Remarriage and Reception of the Sacraments." *America* 171 (8 October): 20–24.

Greeley, Andrew M. 1981. *"Quadragesimo Anno* after Fifty Years." *America* 145 (8 August): 46–49.

———. 1992. "Sex and the Single Catholic: The Decline of an Ethic." *America* 167 (7 November): 342–47, 358–59.

Greeley, Andrew M., and Mary Greeley Durkin. 1984. *How To Save the Catholic Church.* New York: Viking Press.

Greenberg, Irving. 1988. *The Jewish Way: Living the Holidays.* New York: Summit Books.

Gustafson, James M. 1978. *Protestant and Catholic Ethics.* Chicago: University of Chicago Press.

Hamm, Dennis. 1994. "Rummaging for God: Praying Backward Through Your Day." *America* 170 (14 May): 22–23.

Hansen, Susan. 1986. "Vatican's Homosexual Letter Disputed." *National Catholic Reporter* 23 (26 December): 5.

Häring, Bernard. 1978–81. *Free and Faithful in Christ.* 3 vols. New York: Crossroad.

Hastings, Adrian, ed. 1991. *Modern Catholicism: Vatican II and After.* New York: Oxford University Press.

Haughey, John C. 1968. "Conscience and the Bishops." *America* 119 (12 October): 322, 324.

———, ed. 1977. *The Faith That Does Justice.* New York: Paulist Press.

Hauser, Richard J. 1995. "Where Is God in Suffering? A Lenten Reflection." *America* 172 (8 April): 17–20.

Hayes, John H. 1976. *Son of God to Superstar: Twentieth-Century Interpretations of Jesus.* Nashville, Tenn.: Abingdon Press.

Hebblethwaite, Peter. 1984. "Document Warns about Liberation Theology 'Abuses,' Does Not Condemn." *National Catholic Reporter* 20 (7 September): 1–2.

———. 1986. "Letter to Brazilian Bishops Termed Papal Turning Point." *National Catholic Reporter* 22 (4 May): 4.

———. 1989. "Hope, Anguish of the People of Our Time." *National Catholic Reporter* 25 (17 March): 15–17.

———. 1992. "Boff Leaves Priesthood and Order for 'Periphery.'" *National Catholic Reporter* 28 (17 July): 12–13.

———. 1993. "Ratzinger Comments on Changing Papacy." *National Catholic Reporter* 29 (26 February): 10.

———. 1994a. "Abraham As Father of Tumultuous Family." *National Catholic Reporter* 30 (1 April): 16–17.

———. 1994b. "New Scripture Document 'Thinking in Centuries.'" *National Catholic Reporter* 30 (25 March): 13–14.

Hengel, Martin. 1974. *Judaism and Hellenism: Studies in Their Encounter in Palestine During the Early Hellenistic Period.* 2 vols. Philadelphia: Fortress Press.

Hevesi, Dennis. 1992. "Gay Church Again Rejected by National Council Group." *New York Times,* 15 November.

Hewitt, W. E. 1986. "Basic Christian Communities in Brazil." *The Ecumenist* 24 (September): 81–86.

Hill, Brennan. 1991. *Jesus the Christ: Contemporary Perspectives.* Mystic, Conn.: Twenty-Third Publications.

Himes, Michael J., and Kenneth R. Himes. 1990. "The Sacrament of Creation: Toward an Environmental Theology." *Commonweal* 117 (26 January): 42–48.

Hollenbach, David. 1977. "Modern Catholic Teaching Concerning Justice." In *The Faith That Does Justice,* 207–32. See Haughey 1977.

———. 1979. *Claims in Conflict: Retrieving and Renewing the Catholic Human Rights Tradition.* New York: Paulist Press.

Horgan, Paul. 1954. *Great River: The Rio Grande in North American History.* 2 vols. New York: Rinehart.

Horgan, Thaddeus D. 1990. "The Second Vatican Council's Decree on Ecumenism." *America* 162 (2 June): 548–52.

Hyers, Conrad. 1982. "Biblical Liberalism: Constricting the Cosmic Dance." *Christian Century* 99 (4 April): 823–27.

———. 1985. "The Fall and Rise of Creationism." *Christian Century* 102 (24 April): 411–15.

Johann, Robert O. 1968. *Building the Human.* New York: Herder and Herder.

Johnson, Elizabeth A. 1992. *Consider Jesus: Waves of Renewal in Christology.* New York: Crossroad.

Johnson, Luke Timothy. 1994. "Debate and Discernment: Scripture and the Spirit." *Commonweal* 121 (28 January): 11–13.

Kamen, Al. 1987. "Top Court Deals Blow to Creationism." *Oakland Tribune,* 20 June.

Keane, Philip S. 1977. *Sexual Morality: A Catholic Perspective.* New York: Paulist Press.

———. 1982. "The Objective Moral Order: Reflections on Recent Research." *Theological Studies* 43 (June): 260–78.

Kee, Howard Clark. 1970. *Jesus in History: An Approach to the Study of the Gospels.* New York: Harcourt, Brace and World, Inc.

Kelleher, Stephen J. 1968. "The Problem of the Intolerable Marriage." *America* 119 (14 September): 178–82.

———. 1973. *Divorce and Remarriage for Catholics?* New York: Doubleday.

———. 1975. "The Laity, Divorce and Remarriage." *Commonweal* 102 (7 November): 521–24.

Kelly, J. N. D. 1958. *Early Christian Doctrines.* New York: Harper and Row.

———. 1986. *The Oxford Dictionary of the Popes.* New York: Oxford University Press.

Kilmartin, Edward. 1979. *Toward Reunion: The Orthodox and Roman Catholic Churches.* New York: Paulist Press.

Kinsey, Alfred Charles. 1948. *Sexual Behavior in the Human Male.* Philadelphia: W.B. Saunders Co.

Knauer, Peter. 1979. "The Hermeneutical Function of the Principle of Double Effect." In *Moral Norms and the Catholic Tradition,* 1–39. No. 1 of *Readings in Moral Theology,* edited by Charles Curran and Richard McCormick. New York: Paulist Press.

Kolden, Mark. 1984. "Marxism and Latin American Liberation Theology." In *Christians and the Many Faces of Marxism,* edited by Wayne Stumme, 123–31. Minneapolis, Minn.: Augsburg Press.

Kosnik, Anthony, William Carroll, Agnes Cunningham, Ronald Modras, and James Schulte. 1977. *Human Sexuality: New Directions in American Catholic Thought.* New York: Paulist Press.

Kübler-Ross, Elisabeth. 1970. *On Death and Dying.* New York: Macmillan Co.

Küng, Hans. 1976. *On Being a Christian.* New York: Doubleday.

———. 1986. *Christianity and the World Religions.* New York: Doubleday and Company, Inc.

———. 1992. *Judaism: Between Yesterday and Tomorrow.* New York: Crossroad.

Küng, Hans, and Karl-Joseph Kuschel, eds. 1994. *A Global Ethic: The Declaration of the Parliament of the World's Religions.* New York: Continuum Publishing Group.

Laumann, Edward O. 1994. *The Social Organization of Sexuality: Sexual Practices in the United States*. Chicago: University of Chicago Press.

Lernoux, Penny. 1985. "Act 'Shocks' Brazilians United With Theologians." *National Catholic Reporter* 21 (24 May): 1, 23.

———. 1989. *People of God: The Struggle for World Catholicism*. New York: Viking Press.

Lewis, Anthony. 1985. "Mr. Meese's Petard." *New York Times,* 4 November.

MacEoin, Gary. 1984. "Liberation Theology under Fire." *The Witness* 67 (December): 12–14.

———. 1991. "Struggle for Latin American Soul Quickens." *National Catholic Reporter* 27 (22 January): 15–19.

———. 1992a. "View of Rome Neocolonialism Issue Clearer." *National Catholic Reporter* 28 (28 August): 10.

———. 1992b. "Curia Faction Goes for Total Control over CELAM IV." *National Catholic Reporter* 29 (6 November): 14–15.

Maguire, Daniel C. 1983. "Abortion: A Question of Catholic Honesty." *Christian Century* 100 (14 September): 803–7.

———. 1984. "Visit to an Abortion Clinic." *National Catholic Reporter* 20 (5 October): 9, 14.

———. 1986. *The Moral Revolution*. New York: Harper and Row.

———. 1994. "Cairo Consensus." *Christian Century* 111 (12 October): 916–17.

Mahoney, John. 1990. *The Making of Moral Theology*. New York: Clarendon Press.

Martinez, Demetria. 1990. "Weakland on Abortion: Who's Confusing Whom?" *National Catholic Reporter* 27 (23 November): 7.

McBrien, Richard P. 1994. *Catholicism*. San Francisco: Harper San Francisco.

McClory, Robert. 1994. "Catholics' Sex Practices Follow U.S. Norm." *National Catholic Reporter* 31 (16 December): 6.

McCormick, Richard. 1966. "Modern Morals in a Muddle." *America* 115 (30 July): 116.

———. 1968. "The New Morality." *America* 119 (15 June): 769–72.

———. 1976. "Sexual Ethics: An Opinion." *National Catholic Reporter* 12 (30 January): 9.

———. 1981. *Notes on Moral Theology 1965 through 1980*. Lanham, Md.: University Press of America.

———. 1985. "Notes on Moral Theology." *Theological Studies* 46 (March): 50–64.

McDade, John. 1991. "Catholic Theology in the Postconciliar Period." In *Modern Catholicism,* 422–43. See Hastings 1991.

McGovern, Arthur F. 1989. "Liberation Theology Adapts and Endures." *America* 116 (3 November): 587–90.

McGovern, Arthur F., and Thomas L. Schubeck. 1988. "Updating Liberation Theology." *America* 159 (16 July): 32–35.

McKenzie, John L. 1980. "A Bill of Divorce." *Commonweal* 107 (30 May): 301–5.

————. 1985. *Source.* Chicago: Thomas More.

McLaughlin, Loretta. 1982. *The Pill, John Rock and the Church: A Biography of a Revolution.* New York: Little, Brown.

McNeill, John. 1976. *The Church and the Homosexual.* Kansas City, Mo.: Sheed Andrews and McMeel.

————. 1986. "No Time for Silence," *Commonweal* 113 (5 Dec.): 647.

Meier, John P. 1979. *The Vision of Matthew.* New York: Paulist Press.

Metz, Johann Baptist. 1969. *Theology of the World.* New York: Herder and Herder.

————. 1980. *Faith in History and Society.* New York: Crossroad.

Milhaven, John Giles. 1976. Review of *The Church and the Homosexual,* by John J. McNeill. *National Catholic Reporter* 14 (8 October): 12.

Molineaux, D. J. 1987. "Gustavo Gutiérrez: Historical Origins." *The Ecumenist* 25 (July): 65–69.

Mudge, Lewis S. 1995. "Gathering Around the Center: A Reply to Thomas Oden." *Christian Century* 112 (12 April): 392–96.

Myerson, Allen R. 1996. "For the First Time in 151 Years, Baylor Puts a Bounce in Its Step." *New York Times,* 30 January.

Nelson, James B. 1987. "Reuniting Sexuality and Spirituality." *Christian Century* 104 (25 February): 187–90.

Nelson, J. Robert. 1976. "The World Council's Second Generation Takes Over." *Christian Century* 93 (18 February): 144–47.

Neusner, Jacob. 1975. *First Century Judaism in Crisis.* Nashville, Tenn.: Abingdon Press.

Nickoloff, James B. 1993. "Church of the Poor: The Ecclesiology of Gustavo Gutiérrez." *Theological Studies* 54 (September): 512–35.

Niebuhr, Gustav. 1995a. "Abortion Clinic Violence Stirs Debate Among Church Leaders." *New York Times,* 9 January.

————. 1995b. "Stumping Gramm Invokes Second Coming of Christ." *New York Times,* 23 September.

Niebuhr, H. Richard. 1937. *The Kingdom of God in America.* New York: Harper and Brothers.

Norman, Edward. 1991. "An Outsider's Evaluation." In *Modern Catholicism,* 457–62. See Hastings 1991.

Nugent, Robert. 1981. "Homosexuality and the Hurting Family." *America* 144 (28 February): 154–57.

————. 1984. "Homosexuality and the Vatican." *Christian Century* 101 (9 May): 487–89.

O'Collins, Gerald. 1985. "The Resurrection of Jesus: Some Current Questions." *America* 153 (14 December): 422–425.

————. 1987. "The Appearance of the Risen Jesus." *America* 156 (18 April): 317–20.

Oden, Thomas C. 1995a. "Can We Talk about Heresy?" *Christian Century* 112 (12 April): 390–92.

———. 1995b. "Can There Be a Center Without a Circumference? A Response to Lewis Mudge." *Christian Century* 112 (12 April): 396–403.

Ogden, Schubert M. 1980. "Faith and Freedom." *Christian Century* 97 (17 December): 1241–44.

O'Malley, William J. 1981. "Carl Sagan's Gospel of Scientism." *America* 144 (7 February): 95–98.

———. 1994. "The Moral Practice of Jesus." *America* 170 (23 April): 8–11.

Ostling, Richard. 1992. "The Second Reformation." *Time,* 14 November.

Palmer, Paul F. 1975. "When a Marriage Dies." *America* 133 (22 February): 126–28.

Peerman, Dean. 1979. "Did the Pope Apply the Brakes at Puebla?" *Christian Century* 96 (28 February): 203–4.

———. 1993. "CELAM IV: Maneuvering and Marking Time in Santo Domingo." *Christian Century* 110 (17 February): 180–85.

Pelikan, Jaroslav. 1971–1989. *The Christian Tradition: A History of the Development of Doctrine.* 5 vols. Chicago: University of Chicago Press.

Perrin, Norman. 1969. *What Is Redaction Criticism?* Philadelphia: Fortress Press.

———. 1974. *The New Testament: An Introduction.* New York: Harcourt Brace.

Perrin, Norman, and Dennis C. Duling. 1982. *The New Testament: An Introduction.* 2nd ed. New York: Harcourt Brace Jovanovich.

Peters, E. Kirsten. 1995. "Upon This Rock: Fossils vs. Creationists." *America* 173 (18 November): 16–19.

Phipps, William E. 1983. "Darwin, The Scientific Creationist." *Christian Century* 100 (14 September): 809–11.

Pontifical Biblical Commission. 1994. "The Interpretation of the Bible in the Church." *Origins* 23 (6 January): 498–524.

Putney, Michael E. 1992. "Come, Holy Spirit, Renew the Whole Creation: Seventh Assembly of the World Council of Churches." *Theological Studies* 52 (December): 607–35.

Rahner, Karl. 1964. "On the Question of a Formal Existential Ethic." In vol. 2 of *Theological Investigations,* translated by Karl-H. Kruger, 217–34. Baltimore: Helicon Press.

———. 1967. "Reflections on the Experience of Grace." In vol. 3 of *Theological Investigations,* translated by Karl-H. and Boniface Kruger, 86–100. Baltimore: Helicon Press.

———. 1968. *Everyday Faith.* New York: Herder and Herder.

Rausch, Thomas P. 1984. "An Ecumenical Eucharist for a World Assembly. *America* 150 (21 January): 25–29.

———. 1985. "Rome and Geneva: The Experience of Ecumenism." *America* 152 (19 January): 41–45.

————. 1989. "Ethical Issues and Ecumenism." *America* 160 (21 January): 30–33.

Reimarus, Hermann Samuel. 1970. "The Intention of Jesus and His Teaching." In *Reimarus: Fragments,* edited by C.H.Talbert. Philadelphia: Fortress Press.

Renan, Ernest. 1867. *Life of Jesus.* New York: Carleton.

Ricoeur, Paul. 1976. *Interpretation Theory: Discourse and the Surplus of Meaning.* Fort Worth, Tex.: The Texas Christian University Press.

Rohter, Larry. 1990. "Pope, in Mexico, Faces Rising Protestant Tide." *New York Times,* 12 May.

Ruether, Rosemary Radford. 1978. "The Biblical Vision of the Ecological Crisis." *Christian Century* 95 (22 November): 1129–1132.

————. 1985. *Women-Church.* San Francisco: Harper and Row.

Rupp, E.G. and Benjamin Drewery. 1970. *Martin Luther.* London: Edward Arnold Publishers.

Rusch, William G. 1985. *Ecumenism.* Philadelphia: Fortress Press.

Ryan, Thomas. 1991. "Report on the World Council of Churches General Assembly." *America* 164 (25 May): 566–71.

Sagan, Carl. 1980. *Cosmos.* New York: Random House.

Sanders, E. P. 1985. *Jesus and Judaism.* Philadelphia: Fortress Press.

————. 1994. *The Historical Figure of Jesus.* New York: Viking.

Sartre, Jean-Paul. 1957. *Existentialism and the Human Emotions.* New York: Philosophical Library.

Scharper, Philip. 1978. "Toward a Politicized Christianity." *Commonweal* 105 (16 June): 392–99.

Schneiders, Sandra M. 1981. "From Exegesis to Hermeneutics: The Problem of the Contemporary Meaning of Scripture." *Horizons* 8/1: 23–39.

————. 1993. "Scripture as the Word of God." *The Princeton Seminary Bulletin* 14/1: 18–35.

Schweitzer, Albert. 1910. *The Quest of the Historical Jesus.* London: A and C Black.

Sloyan, Gerard S. 1973. *Jesus on Trial.* Philadelphia: Fortress Press.

Smart, Ninian. 1984. *The Religious Experience of Mankind.* Third edition. New York: Charles Scribner's Sons.

Spohn, Gustav. 1995. "Episcopal Diocese Votes to `Honor' Gay Unions." *National Catholic Reporter* 31 (17 February): 9.

Spong, John Shelby. 1988. *Living in Sin? A Bishop Rethinks Human Sexuality.* San Francisco: Harper and Row.

Stammer, Larry B. 1993. "Meeting of World Religions Leads to Ethics Rules." *Los Angeles Times,* 5 September.

Steinfels, Peter. 1976. "The Historian's Herod." *Commonweal* 103 (20 January): 50.

————. 1990. "Flexibility Urged on Abortion Issue." *New York Times,* 21 May.

Stransky, Thomas F. 1986. "Surprises and Fears of Ecumenism: Twenty Years after Vatican II." *America* 154 (25 January): 44–48.

Tavard, George H. 1960. *Two Centuries of Ecumenism*. Notre Dame, Ind.: Fides Publications.

Teilhard de Chardin, Pierre. 1960. *The Divine Milieu*. New York: Harper and Row.

Thompson, Betty. 1985a. "W. A. Visser't Hooft: Mover and Shaker." *Christian Century* 102 (17 July): 668–70.

———. 1985b. "Eugene Carson Blake: A Noble Prophet." *Christian Century* 102 (28 August): 756–57.

Toolan, David. 1982. "Is There Life after Ecumenism?" *Commonweal* 109 (29 January): 43–46.

Tracy, David. 1981. *The Analogical Imagination*. New York: Crossroad.

———. 1987. *Plurality and Ambiguity*. New York: Harper and Row.

———. 1990. "God, Dialogue and Solidarity: A Theological Refrain." *Christian Century* 107 (10 October): 900–904.

Tyson, Joseph B. 1984. *The New Testament and Early Christianity*. New York: Macmillan.

Van Beeck, Franz Josef. 1985. *Catholic Identity after Vatican II*. Chicago: Loyola University Press.

Von Harnack, Adolph. 1901. *What Is Christianity?* New York: G. P. Putnam's Sons.

Vawter, Bruce. 1973. *This Man Jesus*. New York: Doubleday.

Visser't Hooft, Willem A. 1982. *The Genesis and Formation of the World Council of Churches*. Geneva: World Council of Churches.

Welsh, John R. 1986. "Comunidades Eclesiais de Base: A New Way To Be Church." *America* 154 (8 February): 85–88.

Wilford, John Noble. 1996. "Suddenly, Universe Gains 40 Billion More Galaxies." *New York Times,* 16 January.

Whelan, Charles M. 1974. "Divorced Catholics: A Proposal." *America* 131 (7 December): 363–65.

Williamson, Peter. 1995. "Actualization: A New Emphasis in Catholic Scripture Study." *America* 172 (20 May): 17–19.

Wirpsa, Leslie. 1992a. "Rome Sails into Carribbean against the Wind." *National Catholic Reporter* 29 (23 October): 11–14.

———. 1992b. "Curia Ignites Angry Protest at CELAM IV." *National Catholic Reporter* 29 (6 November): 12–13.

———. 1993. "After 25 Years Medellin Spirit Lives, No Thanks to Vatican." *National Catholic Reporter* 29 (15 October): 11–13.

Woodward, Kenneth. 1982. "This Way to Armageddon." *Newsweek,* 5 July.

———. 1983. "Luther in Excelsis." *Notre Dame Magazine* 12 (October): 11–15.

World Council of Churches. 1982. *Baptism, Eucharist and Ministry*. Geneva, Switzerland: World Council of Churches Publishing.

Subject Index